WITHDRAWN

CRITICS OF THE ITALIAN WORLD
1530–1560

CRITICS OF THE ITALIAN WORLD

∘[*1530–1560*]∘

Anton Francesco Doni
Nicolò Franco
&
Ortensio Lando

BY PAUL F. GRENDLER

The University of Wisconsin Press
MADISON, MILWAUKEE, AND LONDON
1969

Published by
The University of Wisconsin Press
Box 1379, Madison, Wisconsin 53701

The University of Wisconsin Press, Ltd.
27–29 Whitfield Street, London, W.1

Printed in the United States of America by
Kingsport Press, Inc., Kingsport, Tennessee

Standard Book Number 299–05220–6
Library of Congress Catalog Card Number 69–16112

To Marcella

⦇ ACKNOWLEDGMENTS ⦈

I owe many debts of gratitude and would like to acknowledge the heaviest debts here. Giorgio Spini of the University of Florence introduced me to the world of the *poligrafi* and has continued to help me. Hans Baron of the Newberry Library criticized an early draft of Chapter V and has consistently supported my work. John Tedeschi of the Newberry gave me help at an early stage with Chapter IV. Conor Fahy of the University of London and Ruth Mortimer of the Houghton Library provided me with valuable references while Ruth P. Liebowitz of the University of Massachusetts in Boston generously checked references in Florence. I owe much to the enthusiastic interest of my colleague Natalie Zemon Davis of the University of Toronto. Luigi Firpo of the University of Turin made many useful suggestions. I wish to thank George L. Mosse of the University of Wisconsin for consistent support and a brilliant scholarly example in graduate school and after.

The Fulbright Commission, the Newberry Library, and the Canada Council enabled me to do research in Italy and elsewhere. The Institute for Research in the Humanities provided me the opportunity to write in a congenial setting. The staffs of many libraries aided my work but I would like to single out three for their unfailing cooperation and assistance: the Biblioteca Nazionale Centrale in Florence, the Newberry Library, and the Rare Book Room of the University of Toronto under Marian Brown.

All illustrations are reproduced through the courtesy of the Houghton Library, Harvard University.

My heaviest debt is to my wife, Marcella McCann Grendler, who aided in research and writing, and prepared the Index. All the above saved me from numerous errors; those that remain are my own.

PAUL F. GRENDLER

University of Toronto
June, 1968

⁍ CONTENTS ⁌

ix

⸰⟦ ILLUSTRATIONS ⟧⸰

xi

Note on the References

Full bibliographical details of the works of Lando, Franco, and Doni will be found in the bibliographical appendices. In the notes, shortened citations consisting of an abbreviated title and the year of the edition are used. Other references are cited in full on their first appearance.

Sixteenth-century Italian was not standardized, nor were the presses free from errors. In the quotations the original language with its inconsistencies and errors has been preferred to a corrected version.

ABBREVIATIONS

ASV   Archivio di Stato, Venice
GSLI   Giornale storico della letteratura italiana

CRITICS OF THE ITALIAN WORLD
1530–1560

Chapter I

VENETIAN PRESSES AND
POLIGRAFI

WITH the growth of the vernacular presses, a new group of authors developed in sixteenth-century Italy. Beside the conventional, court-patronized Latin and vernacular humanist writers grew the adventurers of the pen. In 1527 Pietro Aretino, a fugitive from the Roman court, settled in Venice. Plays, letters, tales, pornography, and devotional treatises flowed from his wonderfully prolific pen to the Venetian presses, and then to his European-wide audience. The proceeds from the sale of his books, augmented by judicious blackmail of fearful princes, enabled the "Scourge of Princes" to live extravagantly in his house near the Rialto bridge, where he freely entertained beggars, artists, and princes. Attracted by the example of Aretino, other authors flocked to Venice with the same desire to write freely away from the suffocating courts and to keep body and soul together from the sales of their books.

The new arrivals included Nicolò Franco of Benevento, Ortensio Lando of Milan, and Anton Francesco Doni of Florence. All three were born in modest circumstances between 1512 and 1515, attained some education, but rejected a conventional career in order to live by their pens. Between 1536 and 1544, they settled in Venice to write until circumstances caused them to disperse in the mid-1550's.

The role of the printers

The tremendous expansion of vernacular printing and its unfettered expression in Venice provided the milieu for literary adventurers. Venice

3

dominated Italian printing: perhaps one-half of all Cinquecento Italian books were printed there.[1] Political independence, prosperity, freedom from internal strife, and a position as an intellectual and commercial crossroad between northern Europe, Italy, and the East provided the commercial foundation for the publishers.

For many years the Venetian government ignored the printing industry, permitting it to grow with a minimum of regulation. The authorities established the principle of censorship before the end of the fifteenth century, but the practice was dormant. The first serious incident concerning an anticlerical book occurred in 1526 with the publication of a work that insulted the Franciscan order. The monks of San Francesco alla Vigna of Venice protested, and the Venetian government on January 29, 1527, issued an order establishing that all future works should carry its *privilegio,* to be granted only after the book had been examined by two censors. The appointed censors examined the book in question and permitted its republication without changing a comma. The frustrated Franciscans retaliated by buying and destroying as many copies as they could lay their hands on.[2]

This early example typified the policy of the Venetians. They established the principle of lay censorship in political, religious, and moral matters but did little to enforce it. Preambles of laws which attempted to curb blasphemous, scandalous, and obscene works in 1543, 1544, and 1547 lamented that previous laws were ignored. These laws had no more success than the law of 1527. A copyright law of 1545 protected the author's rights, but for several years the number of copyrights granted fell short of the number of books published. A group of semi-clandestine printers existed alongside the licensed printers, so that such licentious works as Aretino's *Ragionamenti,* which would probably have been refused a permit, could be printed without difficulty. The Venetian authorities simply looked the other way when books lacking notice of author, place, or printer, like *La Pazzia* and some of Ortensio Lando's works, or carrying fictitious imprints, like Aretino's *Ragionamenti,* were

---

[1] There were 493 different printers, editors, and booksellers (they often combined operations) in Venice in the sixteenth century, among 1100–1200 printers, editors, and booksellers in all of Italy. See Fernanda Ascarelli, *La tipografia cinquecentina italiana* (Florence, 1953).

[2] Horatio Brown, *The Venetian Printing Press* (London, 1891), 67–71, and Giovanni Sforza, "Riflessi della Controriforma nella Repubblica di Venezia," *Archivio Storico Italiano,* XCIII (1935), pt. 1, 5–8.

published. Works such as Scriptural commentaries by Antonio Brucioli, an early Italian Protestant, or Protestant materials printed by Brucioli and his brothers Francesco and Alessandro, were published and distributed without difficulty in the 1540's and early years of the following decade.[3]

Only rarely did they intervene to punish violators. For example, on August 2, 1544, the publisher of Lando's *Paradossi,* Andrea Arrivabene, was accused of having had the book printed without a license. The printer, Bernardino Bindoni, was fined 10 ducats. The officials then ordered the book burned because of its *mala qualità.* The name of the author was not mentioned.[4] Other than this Franco, Lando, and Doni, or their printers, had no difficulty in obtaining privilegi for most of their works from 1539 through 1553.[5] In April 1544, on the occasion of his first trip to Venice, Doni enthusiastically praised the Venetian signori for the freedom that they permitted writers. So long as one did not criticize the Venetian Republic or the faith, one could write what one pleased, Doni noted. No one would flagellate a free speaker, nor would whispered slander silence him.[6]

The Venetian printers reflected and reinforced changes in Italian literature. By the second quarter of the sixteenth century, Italian authors had turned overwhelmingly to the vernacular. In 1525 Pietro Bembo argued in his *Prose della volgar lingua* that Italian was preferable to Latin, and that the language of Petrarch and Boccaccio was the ideal model. Vernacular classics such as Baldassare Castiglione's *Courtier* (1528) and Ariosto's *Orlando Furioso* (1516) were influential models.

[3] Brown, *Venetian Press,* 96; Sforza, "Riflessi della Controriforma," pt. 1, 14; pt. 2, 203–6.

[4] ASV, Esecutori contro la bestemmia, Notatorio, Bu. 56, vol. 1 (1542–60), f. 41ᵛ (August 2, 1544), as reprinted in Giuliano Pesenti, "Libri censurati a Venezia nei secoli XVI–XVII," *La Bibliofilia,* XVIII (1956), 16–17.

[5] Privilegi were granted for Franco's *Pistole Vulgari* and *Dialogi Piacevoli;* for Doni's *Lettera* (1543), *Lettere* (1544), *Dialogo della Musica, Fortuna di Cesare, Disegno, Libraria, La Zucca, Seconda Libraria, L'Asinesca, Pistolotti Amorosi, Moral Filosophia, I Marmi,* and "Ragionamenti," which were probably *I Mondi* and/or *Inferni.* (The titles in the privilegi did not always correspond exactly to the printed titles.) Privilegi were granted for Lando's *Commentario, Miscellanae Quaestiones, Sermoni Funebri, Sferza, Vari Componimenti,* and *Cathaloghi.* The privilegi are copied from the original documents in the ASV in "Privilegi veneziani per la stampa concessi dal 1527 al 1597, copiati da Horatio Brown," Venice, Biblioteca Marciana, Mss. Italiani, Classe VII, Cod. 2500 (12077). Hereafter cited as "Privilegi veneziani."

[6] *Lettere,* 1552 ed., 226.

The popularity of these works and of poetry inspired by Petrarch led Italy to a literary culture with the vernacular rather than Latin as the medium of expression. In the new literature, printers like Gabriel Giolito de' Ferrari (d. 1578) played an important role.

Giolito's vision was broader and his resources greater than his rivals. Soon after his arrival in Venice in 1536 he adopted italic type and lengthened letter forms. Italic type had been introduced by Aldo Manuzio at the beginning of the sixteenth century, but the older printers clung to the larger block type until Giolito proved that italic cut costs. Although lacking formal education, he possessed excellent literary judgment and had a certain amount of capital. Other printers waited for clients and commissions, but Giolito led public taste by financing editions of lesser-known authors until their popularity reimbursed him with demands for reprinted editions. He actively encouraged and exploited the growing popularity of vernacular literature, while refusing works in Latin as well as large (and unprofitable) treatises in philosophy. From about 1540 to 1560 he published a large variety of dialogues, collections of letters, comedies, *novelle,* satires, and poetry, all in the vernacular, by contemporary authors. He buttressed his list with many editions of the most popular classics of his day—Ariosto's *Orlando Furioso*, Petrarch's *Rime*, and the *Decameron* of Boccaccio. On the other hand, he published the *Commedia* only twice in forty years because the Italian public was less interested in Dante.[7]

The shops of the vernacular printers were centers of intellectual activity. Authors from all over Italy, Venetian nobles, businessmen, and travelers from the rest of Europe met to examine new books, domestic and foreign, and to exchange ideas. The printers, booksellers, authors, and editors—one man often performed two or more of these functions—circulated in several levels of society. Francesco Marcolini of Forlì, another printer who specialized in vernacular literature, enjoyed the friendship of his authors, of the artistic elite, and the nobility of Venice. He set up and

[7] The number of editions of these writers presents an interesting picture of Italian literary preferences at mid-century. From 1542 to 1560 Giolito published 28 editions of *Orlando Furioso*, 22 editions of Petrarch's *Rime*, 9 of the *Decameron*, and 2 of the *Divine Comedy* (these were a reprint of Cristoforo Landino's annotated 1536 edition and the Dolce edition of 1555). In all of Italy from 1536 to 1560, 69 editions of *Orlando Furioso*, 61 of Petrarch's *Rime*, 26 of the *Decameron*, and 9 of the *Divine Comedy* were published. See Salvatore Bongi, *Annali di Gabriel Giolito de' Ferrari da Trino di Monferrato, stampatore in Venezia* (Rome, 1890), I, xxviii–xxix.

operated a vernacular press from 1535 to 1559, printing several first editions of Aretino and Doni. Excellent illustrations, with many of the incisions done by the engraver Enea Vico da Parma, adorned his books and aided his sales. Marcolini was an architect as well as a printer; his friends included Titian, Tintoretto, Jacopo Sansovino, and Sebastiano del Piombo, while he had access to the Venetian nobility as well. He provided his authors with introductions to wealthy patrons and they in turn praised him in their books.[8]

Venetian printers like Giolito and Marcolini made popular vernacular literature commercially successful, and provided Italian writers with a unique opportunity to live and write independently of courts and nobility. As long as the author's books sold well and he could continue to write and to revise, he was assured of an income. He could, within broad limits, write what he pleased. Aretino's blistering criticism of the papal court went uncensored. Insult, slander, even obscenity against friars and priests were so common that anticlericalism became a literary convention. Heretical works were permitted, and criticism of prelates, princes, and politics abounded. The vernacular authors avoided only criticism of things Venetian. Ortensio Lando's derogatory comments on the "swarms of sailors" in the streets stood alone amid praise of Venice as the city of peace, freedom, good government, and learned patrons.[9]

Pietro Aretino

In these years Italian literature enjoyed a period of great openness and freedom.[10] Writers, including some drawn from the lower classes, had more social and literary independence than for some time before or to come. Furthermore, women played a more prominent role in Italian literature than they have at any time since. Vittoria Colonna, Veronica Gambara, Gaspara Stampa, Tullia d'Aragona, and Laura Terracina were esteemed poetesses. Perhaps most indicative of the openness of the literary society was the praise awarded the sonnets of Veronica Franco, a Vene-

---

[8] Scipione Casali, *Annali della tipografia veneziana di Francesco Marcolini da Forlì* (Forlì, 1861), *iii–xvii;* Ascarelli, *Tipografia cinquecentina,* 188–90.

[9] *Paradossi,* 1545 ed., 18ᵛ.

[10] For this literary period, see the brilliant discussion of Carlo Dionisotti, "La letteratura italiana nell'età del Concilio," in *Il Concilio di Trento e la Riforma Tridentina* (Rome, Freiburg, 1965), I, 315–43. Also see Lea Nissim, *Gli "scapigliati" della letteratura italiana del Cinquecento* (Prato, 1921).

tian prostitute. Few literary rules and conventions bound authors. Probably the best known book to come from this period, Benvenuto Cellini's *Autobiography* (composed 1558), was written by an itinerant artist who ignored all literary conventions, including veracity.

The first author to shake himself loose from the courts to enjoy the free life of Venice was Pietro Aretino. Born of extremely humble origins in provincial Arezzo in 1492, he had pursued fame and good living at the court of Leo X and in the camp of the renowned condottiere, Giovanni delle Bande Nere of the Medici family, until his death in 1526. He had achieved notoriety, some fortune, and several enemies through his *Pasquinades* and *La cortegiana* (written in 1525, published by Marcolini in 1534). He arrived in Venice on March 27, 1527, and lived and wrote there until his death in 1556. The age was made to order for Aretino's facile pen, and his dialogues, letters, and plays were eagerly snapped up by Marcolini, Giolito, and other printers.

Not only did Aretino's example encourage other authors to come to Venice, but the style and spirit of his books set the tone for a generation of younger writers. Aretino boasted that nature had given him the privilege of speaking "fully and freely" and that he was doing his best to fulfill his nature, disregarding the bonds of convention. He reveled in besmirching paper as others "take pleasure in defacing the white walls of hostelries." In a letter to Franco, then his secretary, he urged authors to follow nature in writing and to take "models from life and truth." "Become a sculptor of the senses and not a miniaturist of vocabularies," he urged.[11] He transferred the concrete world of the senses to the printed page with great freshness and vivacity. His descriptions of a sunset, the joys of eating and drinking around a winter fireplace, and the bouquet of a wine were as alive and real as his description of the death of Giovanni delle Bande Nere was moving, and his love sonnets wittily lewd.

In conscious rebellion against Cinquecento literary norms Aretino ridiculed and mocked Petrarchan stylists for attempting to carve out poetry by established norms. "Poetry is a whim of Nature . . . which lives in her own madness." Ciceronian norms of rhetoric and rules of grammar earned the epithet "pedantic." In his dramas he boasted that he did not care how many times his characters entered or exited, nor how many scenes his comedies needed. He was conscious of the worth of his own

[11] Aretino, *Lettere,* ed. Fausto Nicolini (Bari, 1913) I, 126, 183, 188.

spontaneous style, and claimed to escape the "strangulation of the artifice of imitation," although he did not always succeed.[12]

There was more to Aretino's rebellion than a guerrilla action against literary conventions. He wrote both to entertain and shock in his *Ragionamenti* (first published in 1534). These ribald tales, told in a brothel by two prostitutes, combined vulgarity, humor, psychological observation and a perversion of established values. A story entitled "The Prisoner" described an incredibly sinful, ugly wretch, cancerous, syphilitic, with boils and lice, who was guilty of all manner of crimes. A respectable matron lusted for this ugly specimen of manhood, and committed sacrilege and blasphemy in order to be thrown into prison with the criminal. When this came to the attention of the townspeople, they made such an uproar that the mayor was forced to condemn the criminal to death by hanging. The story spread among the men and women of the town, causing much gossip and smutty jokes. One rich, "respectable country woman" self-righteously excelled the others in condemnation of the criminal and his paramour. On the day of the execution the respectable country woman was smitten by sudden compassion and the consuming desire to bed with the cancerous criminal. Overcome by the thought, she went back to her home, suffocated with a pillow her asthmatic wretch of a husband, and told her neighbors he had choked to death in a fit. Then she rushed to join a brothel in order to convince her neighbors that she was mad with grief. Meanwhile, the execution ceremonies for the loathsome criminal approached their grisly climax. The country woman forced her way through the crowd in the city square to the scaffold. Tearing her hair and beating her palms, she threw herself on the criminal and shrieked, "I am your wife!" By the laws of the land, this saved the criminal's life and he was led away by his "wife" to spend the rest of his days fulfilling her lust. The first woman remained in prison, tortured by the thought of another possessing her desired one.[13]

The conception and content of the stories in the *Ragionamenti* revealed a humorous rebellion against respectability. The prostitutes discussed in turn the life of women as nuns, wives, and as courtesans. Aretino portrayed convent life with the same perversion of values as appeared in his stories of married women. Only the courtesan's life was

---

[12] *Ibid.*, 187; *Lettere di M. Pietro Aretino* (Paris, 1609), I, 247, 210; IV, 291. *The Works of Aretino*, trans. Samuel Putnam (New York, 1933), I, 168.

[13] *Works of Aretino*, I, 88–93.

enjoyable and reasonable, and the prostitute was better than a nun or a wife because the latter two betrayed the vow, and destroyed the sanctity of marriage. The whore did neither; like a soldier, she was paid to do what was wrong, but should not be held to account for doing her job. Aretino seemed to summarize and justify his view of man with the comment that "war, plague, famine, and these times . . . have made a whore out of all Italy."[14]

Perhaps because he thoroughly enjoyed the sensual life, Aretino never became a complete rebel. His wholehearted pleasure in a banquet, a wine, a painting, or a woman, lulled the restless conscience of the rebel. There were few passages in Franco, Lando, or Doni which so innocently and beautifully described the joys of the table or the flesh as Aretino was wont to do. The themes of criticism common to the rebels existed in Aretino's writing, but they did not dominate. He was essentially a precursor, who by his life and works boisterously besmirched the white walls of respectability, while the younger generation of rebels watched, applauded, and scurried to find more mud.

The poligrafi

Aretino was a magnet drawing to Venice young literary adventurers, who provided non-scholarly vernacular literature for a broad segment of the population. They wrote tales, poetry, plays, moral fables, travel literature, satires, social and literary criticism, letters, and burlesques. Their books went into many editions, some being reprinted every three or four years for half a century. These small unpretentious octavos or duodecimos, inexpensively printed, and often profusely illustrated, fitted easily into pockets or saddle bags, and were avidly read in shops, courts, or on journeys. Their authors made no great claims for them. Doni avowed in his introduction that he had named the parts of *La Zucca* ("The Gourd") for what they were: "crickets, butterflies, and sparrows," or stories, witticisms, and commentary on the times.[15]

Franco, Lando, and Doni understood and defended their role in relation to the presses and the popularization of culture. In a dialogue on the merits of the press, Doni concluded by praising it because it made possible the diffusion of new and varied ideas. It supplied men with an

[14] *Ibid.,* I, 111, 203.
[15] *La Zucca,* 1565 ed., 103ᵛ.

infinity of "diverse foods," and was a "garden of many fruits" for the fortunate readers.[16] Defending his role as a popular writer, Doni argued that there were a variety of men, including the lowly; he as a writer should reach these different types of men. He noted that opinions on the worth of paintings were not uniform because men judged what pleased them to be good, and expressed a hope that his works, although not learned, would please. After all, he commented, not everyone could be a Sperone Speroni singing the praises of women in learned language; he himself would direct his writings to readers with other tastes, and hoped that his words would prove of some profit to them.[17]

These writers praised Aretino because he could do so well what they all had to do—produce quickly and effortlessly material from poetry to hackwork for a wide variety of readers. Doni noted that Aretino could address equally appropriately princes or peasants; he could distinguish between the proper language for writing about Christ and that for the *Ragionamenti*.[18] They agreed with Aretino that one should write naturally and from one's own inspiration and imagination.

The adventurers of the pen centered their publishing careers upon the presses. When they were not writing or supervising the publication of their works, they were often employed as editors and translators, and sometimes operated their own presses. At the peak of their publishing activity, Franco and Doni in Venice were closely connected with the presses for periods of five to eight years without other visible means of support, while Lando divided his time between nearby courts and Venice for a comparable period.

Yet it was a precarious existence. Although information on the financial arrangements between printer and author is lacking, it seems probable that the author's reward was not great. In an age of little copyright protection, the author was not paid when his works were reprinted by other publishers. Gifts from princes were welcome supplements to the printer's stipend. In practice, Lando, Franco, and Doni divided their lives between Venice and restless travel which often involved visiting courts. It was a fruitful division; travel provided the experience and information which was the raw material of their books, while the Venetian presses provided the opportunity to publish the result.

[16] Doni, *I Marmi,* 1928 ed., I, 173–92.

[17] *La Zucca,* 1565 ed., 112–12ᵛ, 107ᵛ–8. Sperone Speroni (1500–88), author, orator, and critic, was one of the acknowledged literary authorities of his time.

[18] Doni, *Libraria,* first 1550 ed., 39ᵛ–40ᵛ.

Historians of Italian literature commonly use the term "poligrafi" to designate the literary adventurers who wrote for the Venetian presses. "Poligrafo" connotes a versatile and prolific author in a pejorative sense—an author who wrote much but with little concern for accuracy, truth, or plagiarism. According to this view, the goal of the poligrafo was to earn a living, nothing more. These writers have been called "tradesmen of the pen," (*mestieranti della penna*), that is, authors who sold their words with the detachment of a merchant selling a bolt of cloth.[19] Literary historians have dismissed the notion that the poligrafi could be authors of content and originality, and while current histories of Italian literature discuss Aretino fully and thoughtfully, they then dismiss collectively Franco, Lando, Doni, and other poligrafi in a few pages.[20]

In their own time, the poligrafi were praised, condemned, and universally taken seriously, but since the eighteenth century modern scholars have scornfully dismissed their thought. Tiraboschi, whose judgments shaped much of Italian literary scholarship, thought Franco had not made use of his talent and justly was little honored. Doni was full of "sickening gossip" and only rarely contained some pleasing tale. Lando was a man of "much wit but little study," the author of booklets of slight value.[21] In the nineteenth and twentieth centuries, scholars have emphasized the pleasing tales and the colorful use of language of these authors while ignoring their thought. De Sanctis used Doni and Franco as examples of the mediocrities whose contemporary popularity symbolized the corruption of the Cinquecento. Benedetto Croce, surveying the sixteenth-century "de-

[19] Francesco Flora, *Storia della letteratura italiana*, II, pt. 1, *Il Cinquecento* (Verona, 1952), 486–87. Arturo Pompeati, *Storia della letteratura italiana*, II, *Dall'umanesimo al Tasso* (Turin, 1946), 492–93.

[20] For example, Flora, in *Il Cinquecento*, discusses Aretino on pp. 486–521, Franco, 521–22, and Doni, 522–30. He ignores Lando. Ludovico Dolce, Lodovico Domenichi, and Girolamo Ruscelli are noted briefly elsewhere. Pompeati, *Dall'umanesimo al Tasso,* discusses Aretino, on pp. 491–502, and devotes pp. 502–9 to Franco, Domenichi, Doni, Lando, and Dolce. Giuseppe Toffanin, *Il Cinquecento,* (Milan, 1960), gives a chapter to Aretino, pp. 284–310, and another chapter to the adventurers of the pen, pp. 539–57. For Toffanin, the latter are a mixed lot, including Niccolò Martelli, Dolce, Ruscelli, Domenichi, Francesco Sansovino, Lando, Doni, Tommaso Porcacchi, Orazio Toscanella, Tommaso Garzoni, and Giordano Bruno. In Emilio Cecchi and Natalino Sapegno, eds., *Storia della letteratura italiana,* IV, *Il Cinquecento* (Milan, 1966), Ettore Bonora devotes one chapter, pp. 411–31, to Aretino, and the following chapter to other poligrafi, mentioning Franco, Antonio Brucioli, Dolce, Domenichi, Ruscelli, Dionigi Atanagi, and Sansovino, pp. 432–36, and Doni, pp. 436–43.

[21] *Storia della letteratura italiana,* VII, pt. 3 (Florence, 1812), 1128, 1031, 800.

basement" of culture, concluded that Doni lacked any serious purpose and ignored Franco and Lando.[22]

The pejorative meaning of poligrafo also implies intellectual dishonesty. The poligrafi are accused of writing without self-commitment, and even contrary to their own beliefs. Their words, therefore, are not to be taken seriously. Toffanin dismisses the idea that the critics felt any concrete rebellion against the Renaissance; rather, in his judgment, the availability of the presses stimulated them to a meaningless orgasm of words.[23] Another scholar dismisses Franco as a scoundrel.[24] Linked with the charge of intellectual dishonesty is the tendency to dismiss the books of Lando, Franco, and Doni as facetious. At best, this view admits that there are passages which indicate a social conscience but dismisses their books as a whole as merely humorous.[25]

Doni, Franco, and Lando did not write without purpose and conscience. They returned in their books a broad challenge against Italian ideas, institutions, and leaders, and clearly recognized the provocative nature of their writing. In 1552 Doni avowed that he wrote in order to "chaff the world."[26] Their critical thought was too frequent and too consistent within itself to be ignored, and there is no mistaking the genuine anger and malaise in their works. The witty prose of Franco, the elaborate conceits of Doni, and the irony of Lando cloaked a rejection of the Cinquecento world. Contemporaries and readers of later generations recognized them as moralists who coated their bitter truths in colorful language and imaginative conceits, and in the later years of the century they were denounced as a group by those who did not share their views.

Given the opportunity to publish their views by the open literary society of the Venetian presses, Franco, Lando, and Doni rejected much of Italian civilization in their lifetime. Their criticism was based on their own experience and personal observation acquired through years of restless travel. They rejected Renaissance learning and values as pedantic,

[22] Francesco De Sanctis, *History of Italian Literature,* trans. Joan Redfern (New York, 1931), I, 432–33. Benedetto Croce, *Poeti e scrittori del pieno e del tardo Rinascimento* (Bari, 1945), I, 260–73, 85; II, 126.

[23] Toffanin, *Il Cinquecento,* 542.

[24] Pompeati, *Dall'umanesimo al Tasso,* 503.

[25] For example, see the judgments of Francesco Flamini, *Il Cinquecento* (Milan, 1901), on Doni, pp. 414–16, on Lando, 412–14, and on Franco, 402–4.

[26] ". . . egli c'è chi scrive per dar la baia al mondo, come il Doni." *I Marmi,* 1928 ed., I, 131. (All translations from sources are the author's.)

irrelevant, and useless. Two of them were ex-monks, but they could neither find religious peace in Catholicism nor commit themselves wholly to Protestantism. They bitterly criticized Italian princes for the political failures which had brought ruin upon Italy. The wars, in their opinion, had provoked widespread moral decay in the peninsula. A concern for social justice caused them to condemn the social and economic sins of the signori. But they had few alternatives to offer; they dreamed of primitive and just utopias far from the strain of contemporary life. They conveyed disorientation, disillusionment, and pessimism for their generation in the difficult years between 1530 and 1560.

Only anonymity limited their criticism: they normally avoided denouncing individuals by name. A writer lived a precarious existence, while a prince had means to rid himself of a critic. And since dedications to princes might supplement an author's income, Doni, Franco, and Lando prefaced their books with obsequious statements, which did not, however, inhibit their pens. Perhaps patrons did not often read beyond the dedication. Another common device was to praise a particular prince, for instance, a patron, while condemning the ruling class in general elsewhere in the book. The high clergy, though, did not always enjoy the protection of anonymity.

In expressing their personal views, the critics probably articulated ideas to which other Italians nodded assent. While major figures sometimes transcend the limitations of their own period, secondary authors, as Lando, Franco, and Doni surely were, are often more useful for understanding prevailing attitudes. Because their talent is limited, they are more likely to repeat commonplaces of the day when inspiration fails. Once having found a subject matter that wins readers and sells copies, they will continue in a similar vein. The poligrafi were the columnists and social commentators, and sometimes the gossip-mongers, of the day. Lando, Franco, and Doni do not represent the views of all the poligrafi nor the complete spectrum of Italian thought of this time. But they are a rich source for understanding the pessimism which existed in Italy in these years. The number of reprints and the reactions of readers indicated that their words were read and pondered.

Italian conditions

Lando, Franco, and Doni came to maturity and wrote their books in a period of profound political, social, and intellectual depression.

After 1530 there could be no doubt that Charles V dominated Italy and that his grip would become tighter. Although the wars in the peninsula were not over, they became less frequent and less important to the European balance of power. This meant less suffering and destruction for Italy, but at the same time, it caused Italian rulers to see clearly their own impotence. Since the beginning of the wars in 1494, the Italian states had dealt with the great powers of Europe on equal terms, and had had at least the illusion of determining their own fates. But after 1530 Milan and Naples were no longer autonomous political entities, Florence, though independent, was within the imperial orbit, Venice had withdrawn into frightened neutrality, and the Papacy was at the mercy of Spain. Italy's helplessness was apparent to all. The few Italian political initiatives from 1530 to 1559, e.g., those of Popes Paul III and Paul IV, and the revolts in Naples and Genoa, only demonstrated the futility of attempting to change the *status quo*. The major Italian states were forced to accommodate themselves to the Spanish political order while the smaller states tried to remain invisible.[27]

Perhaps more important to Italians below the ruling class than the loss of political independence was the aristocratic transformation taking place in the sixteenth century. The fluidity in the upper rank of society that had characterized the period of the communes and the fourteenth century had become in practice virtually a closed, and oppressive, directorate by the end of the fifteenth century. This produced a gulf between the ruling class and the rest; one of the reasons for the quick collapse of Italy in the face of the French invasion of 1494 was the lack of enthusiasm of Italians for their rulers. In the sixteenth century the ruling class formally and juridically turned itself into a caste. By the middle of the century, the nobility excluded admittance, by laws which forbade citizen status, i.e., the right to hold political office, to those who could not prove that their family had been free of the taint of manual or merchant activity for several generations. The professional groups of jurists, legal officials, and physicians aped the nobility with similar legal exclusions, and cooperated with the nobility to rule the *popolo*.

The spirit of caste of the aristocracy in the Cinquecento was accompanied by systematic oppression of the ruled. The political overlords, whether Spanish in Milan and Naples, or Venetian in the Terrafirma, left the local nobility alone to rule their subjects as they wished. Hence the

---

[27] Good surveys of this period are Gennaro Sasso, "L'Italia del Machiavelli e l'Italia del Guicciardini (1500–1559)," in Nino Valeri, ed., *Storia d'Italia* (Turin, 1959), II, 185–366; and Luigi Simeoni, *Le Signorie* (Milan, 1950), II, 711–946.

nobility in provincial cities and in the countryside systematically shifted the tax burden to the poor, shipped grain elsewhere for higher prices while their subjects starved, robbed the communal treasury and the financial organs of the lower classes, and dominated the courts of justice so that the popolo received no redress from the courts. Italian society assumed in the sixteenth century the rigid division between nobility and people which characterized it until the late eighteenth century.[28]

The period of the maturity of the critics coincided with religious unrest in Italy. Disapproval of clerical corruption had been widespread before, but Italians were not intensely involved in religious discussions until the decade of the 1530's. The sack of Rome in 1527 was seen as divine retribution for clerical sins, and Italians took up the issues of faith, predestination, and Scripture raised by thoughtful people, orthodox and Protestant. For many, the Catholic Church and its clergy had been decadent for some time, but the course to follow was unclear, and Protestantism not necessarily a preferable alternative. In the 1540's, the Inquisition and *Index* were established, and a revivified Catholicism appeared. After attempts at conciliation between old and new doctrines failed, religious strife added a new dimension to religious debate. The personal decision to cling to the old Catholicism, to continue efforts toward doctrinal and disciplinary change within the Church, or to follow Protestantism, became very serious and fraught with peril.

The destruction of the stable Italian world after 1494 forced men to reexamine their intellectual heritage. Many writers in the fifteenth century held the essentially optimistic faith that man could to a large extent control his destiny through commitment to the *vita civile,* the active life of participation in the affairs of the world. The disintegration of the Italian scene forced men to reassess the possibility of effectively controlling their own destinies. The *virtù* with which men had opposed *Fortuna* in the Quattrocento seemed inadequate to face the reality of the Cinquecento,[29] and the *studia humanitatis* which had prepared men for the vita civile irrelevant to the bitter experiences of the Cinquecento.

---

[28] For conditions in the Veneto, see Angelo Ventura, *Nobiltà e popolo nella società veneta del '400 e '500* (Bari, 1964), 275–471; for Lucca see Marino Berengo, *Nobili e mercanti nella Lucca del Cinquecento* (Turin, 1965); for Naples see Benedetto Croce, *Storia del Regno di Napoli* (Bari, 1925), 95–153; for Milan see the *Storia di Milano,* IX, *L'epoca di Carlo V* (Milan, 1961).

[29] Mario Santoro, *Fortuna, ragione e prudenza nella civiltà letteraria del Cinquecento* (Naples, 1966), 19–21.

Such thinkers as Machiavelli, Tristano Caracciolo, and Francesco Guicciardini reassessed man's relationship to the world, and tried to reconcile the Renaissance value of the vita civile with the new, darker reality, especially in the political context. The youngest of this group, Guicciardini, writing his *History of Italy* in the late 1530's, came to the most pessimistic conclusions. He recognized the political decay and moral corruption of his time, but still held out some hope that men could retain personal dignity. Lando, Franco, and Doni also had to face Italian conditions. Younger and less favorably located in the social scale, they were more pessimistic.

The end of the era of the poligrafi

Appropriate dates exist to mark the passing of the literary era of the poligrafi. Between the death of Aretino in 1556 and the Tridentine *Index* of 1564, Italian literature changed along with the political, social, and religious situation. New norms of literary criticism began to supplant the free, unfettered literature of the poligrafi. The first commentary on Aristotle's *Poetics* in 1548 by Francesco Robortello was followed by others.[30] Ludovico Castelvetro by 1560 had begun to develop an etymology of the Italian language, and in the second half of the Cinquecento the Accademia della Crusca attempted to formulate a standard, correct Italian. Definitions, classifications, and judgments of right and wrong overtook Italian writing at this time. Literature was not necessarily poorer for the change—the works of Torquato Tasso testify to its vitality and richness—but it was a different kind of literature.

The growth of literature which defended the concept of a closed aristocracy indicates that both the social and literary worlds changed after 1555–60. From the *Dialogo dell'onore* (1553) of Antonio Possevino, and Girolamo Muzio's *Duello* (1558) and *Il gentilhuomo* (1564), an increasing number of books laid down rules of conduct and the conditions of nobility, which was defined as a matter of blood; one inherited virtù at birth.[31] There was no room for the jibes and doubts of lower-class authors.

The Venetian printers published freely through the 1530's and 1540's

[30] See Giuseppe Toffanin, *La fine dell'umanesimo* (Milan, Turin, and Rome, 1920); and Bernard Weinberg, *A History of Literary Criticism in the Italian Renaissance* (Chicago, 1961).

[31] Berengo, *Nobili e mercanti,* 252–57; and Ventura, *Nobiltà e popolo,* 365–74.

and most of the decade of the 1550's. At mid-century, however, the first signs of effective state and religious censorship appeared, though for some fifteen years thereafter the state gave only grudging support to the *Index of Prohibited Books* and the Inquisition, and the printers fought a delaying action. Still, church and state slowly gained control over the press.[32]

Gradually Venetian censorship intruded upon Lando and Doni. In 1543 Lando mocked the censorship of senators and magistrates, commenting that they forbade the books of Luther, the sermons of Bernardino Ochino, and the works of Anabaptists, but ignored the moral evil done by the lascivious and immoral *Decameron* of Boccaccio. But in 1551 Doni complained sharply that "certain most learned secretaries" who knew nothing about books had to read everything before publication in Venice. He lamented that they permitted nothing to pass that would offend God, the Church, states, or any particular man. In December 1552 Lando also complained that the laws of Venice would not permit him to add to a list of ancient adulterers for his *Cathaloghi* modern adulterers among kings, dukes, counts, and marquises. Lando had to be content with initials.[33] Both comments indicated closer scrutiny, although a great deal still passed —for instance, Doni's thunderbolt against Aretino, the *Teremoto* of 1556.

The *Index* and the Inquisition were never completely successful in sixteenth-century Venice. In particular they continued to have difficulty with the unlicensed, semi-clandestine presses. Nevertheless, by 1560 the censors had seriously curtailed the publishing promiscuity of the previous three decades. Giolito mirrored the reaction of the printers. An excellent businessman who knew his public well, he altered the direction of his publications about 1560. He printed his last edition of Machiavelli in 1554 and of the *Decameron* in 1557, and thereafter concentrated less on contemporary literature and more on translations of Greek and Latin classics. He sponsored a series of popular histories based on the ancients, the *Collana istorica* edited by Tommaso Porcacchi. He had printed devotional works from the beginning, but many more vernacular works of piety, compendiums of prayers, and instructional books in religious practices for the family appeared after 1560. He still refused theological works. With a new group of authors, who focused on devotional and historical materials,

[32] See Sforza, "Riflessi della Controriforma," pt. 1, 5–34, 189–216; pt. 2, 25–52, 173–86; and Brown, *Venetian Press,* 109–34.

[33] Lando, *Paradossi,* 1545 ed., 73; Doni, *Seconda Libraria,* 1551 ed., 48ᵛ; Lando, letter to Lucrezia Gonzaga in *Cathaloghi,* 564–67.

Giolito reached the peak of his production in 1566 and 1567, and continued at a profitable pace until he stopped printing in 1578; he died shortly after.[34]

In addition to avoiding trouble with the censors, Giolito accurately perceived the heightened religious atmosphere of Italy. In the middle third of the sixteenth century, the Venetian presses printed a great amount of secular vernacular literature, especially the books of the poligrafi. After that, these same printing houses published sermons, meditations, saints' lives, guides to confessors, and the like. They printed the works of the famous preachers Cornelio Musso and Francesco Panigarola, Spanish devotional authors such as Luis de Granada, and contemplatives like Buonsignore Cacciaguerra and Vincenzo Bruno. Translators were as busy as before; now they translated Latin and Spanish religious works into Italian.[35]

For about thirty years after Aretino's arrival in 1527, the vernacular presses in free Venice provided a unique opportunity for authors to write what they pleased. In those years a generation of writers matured and came to Venice to write and publish. The literary adventurers wrote popular literature for a broad Italian audience and in their works commented on the troubled times. Three of these authors, Ortensio Lando, Nicolò Franco, and Anton Francesco Doni, were eloquent witnesses and a window through which we may view Cinquecento Italy.

---

[34] Bongi, *Annali di Giolito,* I, lxxiii.

[35] The overwhelming predominance of religious works in the last third of the century is clear from the privilegi issued from 1527 through 1597. "Privilegi veneziani," Cod. 2500-2 (12077-79). Before the 1560's, the number of privilegi granted for religious works was a small part of the total. After the Council of Trent, the religious works become more noticeable; in the 1580's and through 1597, most of the privilegi issued were for such works, as can also be confirmed from the catalogue of the Biblioteca Marciana. *The Short-Title Catalogue of Books Printed in Italy . . . now in the British Museum* is invaluable for an overall view of the publishing activity of the Venetian presses in the first sixty years of the sixteenth century, but is less useful for the later years, since it lacks the extensive and representative collection of religious works that it has of other kinds of literature.

Chapter II

THREE POPULAR WRITERS

Restless travel and intellectual discontent marked the lives of Lando, Franco, and Doni. In a partly autobiographical narration, Doni explained something of the unease that drove them on. His character, appropriately named Inquieto, "the restless one," related how he had entered into the world with his father's wealth and blessing. At first, he enjoyed his wealth among friends and pleasures, but this soon bored him, and he withdrew to his estate where he remained with his books, music, and thoughts. His friends, who thought that he had been possessed by a melancholy humor, forced him to re-enter society; the wretched Inquieto became a chameleon, laughing when others laughed, crying when the world was sad. To avoid insanity, he fled and wandered through far countries. Returning finally to his (and Doni's) native city of Florence, he sought in vain for a useful and pleasing way of life. Here at the age of 37 (Doni was 39 at the time this dialogue was published in 1553), he was rich, lettered, but very unstable. A servant did not content him for more than a day, he was bored with a woman in an hour. A hundred times a year he had to change the table at which he ate. No room pleased him more than three or four days. In his restlessness he tried many modes of life, including several monastic orders. (Both Doni and Lando had been monks.) In his torment Inquieto climbed the hillside of Fiesole and looked at Florence below. He mused that men were a cage of madmen who indulged in useless activities, while the world remained unchanged. The tiny people far below came and went, struggled and worked in their unhappy existence. They had a multitude of crafts, inventions, styles, and ways of living, but in a hundred years of effort would accomplish nothing. Inquieto concluded his discourse with a plea to Doni (personified as the other character of the dialogue) for help in understanding himself. Doni jeeringly told Inquieto that his dialogue had been so lengthy that he had lost the thread of the argument, and could offer no advice.[1]

Ortensio Lando

In an autobiographical passage similar in mood, Lando provided information on the beginning of his own restless life. He wrote in a dialogue printed in 1552 that he was "near the fortieth year of life"—born, then, about 1512.[2] Elsewhere he informed his readers that he was born in Milan,[3] the son of Dominico Lando of Piacenza and Catherina Castelletta of Milan, whom he called a noblewoman.[4] Nothing is known of his parents, and the assertion that his mother was a noblewoman, without mention of the social position of his father, implied that his father was not. There is no evidence that Lando was of the Piacenzan noble family of Landi. On the contrary, he never claimed nobility for himself, nor did he or his associates refer to him as Landi, but as Lando.[5]

---

[1] Doni, *I Marmi*, 1928 ed., II, 205–11.

[2] *Vari Componimenti*, 1555 ed., 100. By August 1529, Lando had left the monastery, was a physician, and had married. Although he could have accomplished all this at the age of 17, he may also have been slightly older.

[3] *Paradossi*, 1545 ed., 42ᵛ; *Confutazione*, n.d., 15.

[4] *Cathaloghi*, 300; *Vari Componimenti*, 1555 ed., 90.

[5] The eighteenth-century scholar Poggiali decided that Lando was of the Landi family of Piacenza on the evidence of a letter of February 2, 1551, from Ludovico Dolce, in Venice, to Count Costanzo Landi referring to "Messer Hortensio Landi." *Le Lettere volgari di diversi Uomini saggi . . .* (Cremona, Vincenzo Conti, 1561), p. 186, as cited in Cristoforo Poggiali, *Memorie per la storia letteraria di Piacenza* (Piacenza, 1789), I, 173. Hence the catalogues of the British Museum, Newberry Library, and Biblioteca Nazionale Centrale, Florence, as well as some scholars, refer to "Ortensio Landi."

Dolce was not an intimate of Lando, although he knew him. Lando called himself "Hortensio Lando" in the *Sferza*, 24ᵛ, and "messer Ortensio Lando" in *Ragionamenti Familiari*, 30ᵛ, *Commentario*, 1550 ed., 74ᵛ, and *Oracoli*, 1550 ed., 14. The *Lettere della Lucretia Gonzaga*, 1552 ed., contains 31 letters to "Hortensio Lando" (pp. 8, 13, 30, 64, 69, 73, 84, 92, etc.) and none to "Landi." A sonnet in Spanish by Alphonso Nuñez de Reynoso to "S. Hortensio Lando," is in the *Due*

Lando began his education in humanistic studies in Milan under Alessandro Minuziano, Bernardino Negro, Bernardino Donato of Verona, and Celio Rodigino, and later studied at the University of Bologna under Romolo Amaseo.[6] By his own admission, he studied theology and medicine in his youth (probably at Bologna) but discovered even then that he did not like theological study.[7]

Perhaps while still a child, he joined, or was placed in, a monastery of the Augustinian order, with the name Hieremias. Although scholars have long doubted that Hieremias Landus and Ortensio Lando were one and the same,[8] contemporary references do identify them. The scholar and papal secretary, Johann Albrecht von Widmanstetter (1506–57) wrote in his copy of Lando's first book, the *Cicero relegatus et Cicero revocatus* (published 1534), that the anonymous author was "Hieremias Augustiniani ordinis monachus" who then became "Hortensius Medicus." Widmanstetter added that Lando was a learned man whom he had known well in Naples in 1530, and, to make the identification certain, noted that

---

Panegirici, 1552 ed., in fine, no pag. Doni was well acquainted with most of the Landi family as well as with Lando, but referred to "Hortensio Lando" in his bibliographical *Libraria* and to "Giulio Landi" of the Piacenza family in another entry. *Libraria,* 1st 1550 ed., 26ᵛ, 25. The title pages of the few Lando works which carried his name credited authorship to "Hortensio Lando." See the *Sacra Scrittura* and *Vari Componimenti.*

[6] Salvatore Bongi, "Notizie sulla vita di messer Ortensio Lando," in *Novelle di M. Ortensio Lando* (Lucca, 1851), vi, n. 2; Giovanni Sforza, "Ortensio Lando e gli usi ed i costumi d'Italia nella prima metà del Cinquecento," *Memorie della R. Accademia delle Scienze di Torino,* ser. II, 64, no. 4 (1914), 2, n. 6.

[7] The *Sermoni Funebri* concluded with an *apologia* by Lando for the anonymous author (who was Lando, of course), which said of him " . . . s'egli havesse atteso a gli studi della giovevol medicina, overo havesse rivolto l'arte, l'ingegno suo alla santa Teologia, di cui tanto vago gia si dimostro fin da fanciullo." *Sermoni Funebri* in *Consigli de gli Animali,* 1622 ed., 60.

[8] Only Apostolo Zeno thought that Lando was a defector from the Augustinians. G. Fontanini, *Biblioteca dell'eloquenza italiana con le annotazioni del signor Apostolo Zeno* (Venice, 1753), II, 433. Tiraboschi, *Storia della letteratura italiana,* VII, pt. III, 802–4, and Poggiali, *Storia letteraria di Piacenza,* I, 179, doubted that Lando was an apostate monk. Cantù, Bongi, Sanesi, and Sforza echoed their judgment. Cesare Cantù, *Les hérétiques d'Italie,* French trans. Anicet Digard and Edmond Martin (Paris, 1870), III, 517; Bongi, in *Novelle di M. Ortensio Lando,* xxii–xxvi; Ireneo Sanesi, *Il cinquecentista Ortensio Lando* (Pistoia, 1893), 34; Sforza, "Ortensio Lando," 7–8.

he had written the *Forcianae Quaestiones*.[9] Since this appeared in 1535, Widmanstetter's notation came later, or several years after Lando had left the monastery and was living under the name of Ortensio. For his part, Lando ironically introduced "Hieremias Landus" into the dialogue as "a most distinguished brilliance and honor" of the Augustinian friars, and also mentioned Widmanstetter in the book.[10]

Other contemporary evidence confirms Lando's monastic career. On May 5, 1535, Sebastian Gryphius, printer of Lyons who issued a 1534 edition of the *Cicero relegatus et Cicero revocatus* and employed Lando as an editor[11] identified him as a monk. Gryphius was exasperated with Lando for his unreliability and restlessness, but still feared for his safety in Italy. According to Gryphius, the "empty-headed" Ortensio had left for Italy without concern for the possibility that "a monk of his order" might recognize him. "What do you think of his future?" Gryphius queried.[12] In 1560 a Dominican bibliographer wrote that Ortensio Lando was a

[9] According to A. G. von Oefele, a mid-eighteenth-century student of Widmanstetter, the following notation appeared in Widmanstetter's handwriting on the back of the title page of his copy of the *Cicero relegatus et Cicero revocatus* (Venice, 1534 ed.): "Author libri est Hieremias Augustiniani ordinis monachus, postea hortensius Medicus factus, qui et Fortianas quaestiones edidit, homo doctus et mihi Neapoli in aede J. Joannis Carbonariae familiaritate iunctissimus ao 1530." Munich, Staatabibliothek, Oefeleana 245, fol. 101, as quoted by Max Müller, *Johann Albrecht v. Widmanstetter, 1506–1557* (Bamberg, 1908), 15–16.

[10] "Hieremias Landus omnibus rebus ornatissimus suique Eremitani sodalitii splendor ac decus." *Cicero relegatus et Cicero revocatus*, Venice, 1534 ed., 2^v. *Eremitani* indicated the *Eremitanus Ordo Fratrum S. Augustini*, the Eremites of St. Augustine. Other references to Hieremias Landus in the book are on 14^v, 22^v, 24.

[11] H. L. Baudrier and J. Baudrier, *Bibliographie Lyonnaise: Recherches sur les imprimeurs, libraires, relieurs et fondeurs de lettres de Lyon au XVIe siècle* (Lyons, Paris, 1910), VIII, 32, n. 1.

[12] "Hortensius, vir levissimus, abiit hinc die mercurii ante pascha cum oratore regio in Italiam, nescio quod miser ille cogitet, quam non timeat se forte agnosci posse a quo quam suae factionis monacho: quod putat se futurum?" Autograph letter of Sebastian Gryphius to Joannes Angelus Odonus and Philaenus Lunardus at Strasbourg, dated Lyons, May 5, 1535, in the Basle Archive, Cod. Basiliensis, G^2, I, 18, n° 29, fol. 18, and also reprinted in Baudrier, *Bibliographie Lyonnaise*, VIII, 33. The "oratore" mentioned was probably Vincenzo Buonvisi of Lucca (c.1500–c.1576) who filled that office for the Luccan Republic to Duke Alessandro de' Medici of Florence in 1533, and the same office to Charles V in 1543. Sforza, "Ortensio Lando," 38. Lando wrote that Vincenzo Buonvisi brought him to Lucca. *Forcianae Quaestiones*, 1857 ed., 7.

deserter from the Augustinian order and attributed to him a heretical book.[13] Nor did the Tridentine *Index* hesitate to identify Ortensio as an alias for Hieremias.[14]

By August 1529, Lando had left the monastery, and had acquired a medical education and a wife. In a letter of that month to Joachim von Watt (Vadianus) at St. Gall, Lando related Italian political news and revealed that he was involved with Luther's writings. He began by noting that the "Christian cause" flourished in almost all of Italy. Although the "Antichrist" attacked here and there, Lando estimated that his efforts would be in vain. Lando went on to relate Italian political news, which centered upon the movements of Charles V and his relations with the pope, and lamented that these political affairs foretold more difficulties for his native Milan. He then identified himself, and discussed his activities and future plans. Moved by the gospel, he had translated "many writings" of Luther into Italian. Then, in order to avoid trouble from the pope, he had moved with his wife, who also "recognized and loved Christ," to Chur in the Grisons. However, he had found it impossible to earn a living there because of language difficulties. He had decided to leave, but did not mention his future destination.[15]

[13] "Hortensius quidam Landus, Augustinianae professionis desertor libellum . . . emisit *De persecutione barbarum* titulo satis impie jocoso praenotatum . . ." in Fra Sisto da Siena (1520–69), *Bibliotheca Sancta . . . ex praecipuis catholicae ecclesiae autoribus collecta* (Lyons, 1575), II, 93. The first edition appeared in 1560.

[14] Franz H. Reusch, ed., *Die Indices librorum prohibitorum des sechzehnten Jahrhunderts* (Stuttgart, 1886), 265.

[15] "Antonius Traversus et David, frater tuus, maximo me rogarunt opere, cum suo in me iure potuissent imperare, ut ad te aliquid scriberem. Scribo itaque, rem Christianam in tota ferme Italia maxime florere. Quamquam Antichristus hac atque illac circumcurset, hostem suum ut opprimat, ego frustra conaturum existimo. Papa est Bononie; illic Caesarem exspectat, qui adhuc est in Taraconensi Hispania, propediem Genuam navigaturus. Mediolanensium res non possent peiore in loco esse. . . .

.   .   .   .

Ego Mediolanensis, nomine Hortensius Landus, medicus, qui, cum multa Lutheri scripta promovendi evangelii gratia in Italicam linguam vertissem, ut vitarem infortunium, quod sanctissimus papa paraverat, solum vertere coactus sum, una cum uxorcula, que Christum agnoscit et colit. Itaque Rhaetorum Curiam veni; sed cum lingua sit difficilior multo, quam ego credideram, sitque annona carior nullumque accedat lucrum, statui alio commigrare. Deus optimus dirigat iter meum. Tu vale com tota ecclesia et me in Christo Iesu ama." *Die Vadianische Briefsammlung der Stadtbibliothek St. Gallen,* ed. Emil Arbenz and Hermann Wartmann, IV (St. Gall, 1902), letter no. 581, pp. 188–89. Although the letter lacks date and place, the editor

Vadianus (1484–1551) was a humanist scholar, follower of Erasmus, physician and *bürgermeister* of St. Gall who brought the Reformation to that town during the 1520's.[16] From the letter it is apparent that Vadianus was not acquainted with Lando at the time, and Lando used the names of David von Watt, Vadianus' brother, and Antonius Traversus, a pupil of Vadianus, as references.[17] This is the only letter of Lando and the only reference to him in the correspondence of Vadianus. The trouble that Lando anticipated from the pope could have been one of many attempts by the Papacy to suppress Protestant teaching and books in Italy at this time. From 1524 to 1542, the Papacy issued eighty briefs to Italian bishops and prelates directing them to take action against Lutheran heretics, but without great success.[18]

After Chur in 1529, Lando was in Naples in 1530 where Widmanstetter knew him. Lando next appeared in Lyons in 1534. Here he spent much of 1534 and 1535, earning the friendship of Etienne Dolet (1509–46) and the enmity of a fellow Italian, Joannes Angelus Odonus. Odonus, who was born in the Abruzzi, studied medicine, probably at Bologna, but then left Italy for Strasbourg where he studied Greek and Hebrew and lived with Martin Bucer. An enthusiast of Italian Renaissance learning, Erasmus, and the Reformation,[19] Odonus described Lando as avid for Cicero but lukewarm for Christ. Writing to Gilbert Cousin, secretary to Erasmus, on October 29, 1535, he described Lando as an exile from Italy.

---

dates it from the political news as the beginning of August 1529 and places it in Chur from Lando's mention of it. Lando's religious views will be discussed in Ch. IV.

[16] On Vadianus, see Werner Näf, *Vadian und seine Stadt St. Gallen* (St. Gall, 1944–57).

[17] David von Watt, who was not mentioned again by Lando, was in St. Gall with Vadianus in 1528, and probably shared his Protestantism. See Näf, *Vadian und seine Stadt St. Gallen*, II, 258. Antonius Traversus von Ortenstein from Rietberg in Domleschg in the Grisons was a pupil of Vadianus, a captain in the service of France, and an acquaintance of Johannes Comander, the Protestant pastor of Chur. See *Dictionnaire historique & biographique de la Suisse*, VI (Neuchâtel, 1932), 657; and other references to Traversus in *Die Vadianische Briefsammlung der Stadtbibliothek St. Gallen*, V (St. Gall, 1903), pp. 260, 375, 629.

[18] Delio Cantimori, "Italy and the Papacy," in *The New Cambridge Modern History*, II, *The Reformation 1520–1559* (Cambridge, 1958), 269.

[19] For information on Odonus, see *Opus epistolarum Des. Erasmi Roterodami*, ed. P. S. Allen et al. (Oxford, 1947), XI, 81–82, and the long letter that Odonus wrote to Erasmus (Ep. 3002, XI, 82–104). Odonus was, of course, also one of the recipients of the two Gryphius letters mentioned in nn. 12 and 25.

According to the hostile Odonus, Lando lived in Lyons by teaching the rudiments of grammar to small boys. Claiming that he based his judgment on "great intimacy" with Lando in Bologna as well as a recent visit to Lyons, Odonus judged him to be frivolous, effeminate, and irreligious.[20]

At the same time Odonus reported that Lando was a warm friend of Etienne Dolet, and that Dolet had begged Lando to write a preface to a book of orations that he was preparing, offering to dedicate them to whomever Lando wished.[21] Surely Lando found Dolet to be a kindred spirit. A Latin scholar and editor, Dolet shared his restlessness and iconoclasm, and was less circumspect. He hated authority, and with his quick temper made powerful and bitter enemies wherever he worked. Condemned *in absentia,* he was finally arrested on the dual charges of printing Calvinist books and denying the immortality of the soul, and executed in Paris in 1546.[22] Lando mentioned Dolet in 1535, 1540, and praised him as a modern poet in 1552.[23] However, he did not share Dolet's high regard for Cicero. Dolet defended Cicero and answered Erasmus in 1535, while Lando mocked the entire Ciceronian and anti-Ciceronian debate in his first work, the *Cicero relegatus et Cicero revocatus,* probably written between 1529 and 1531.[24]

Sebastian Gryphius used Lando in his printing shop at Lyons and as a messenger, but the unreliable Lando exasperated the hard-headed businessman. In February 1535 or 1536, Gryphius wished to send business letters to Strasbourg by Lando, but the "inconstant Ortensio" had left for Geneva instead and, according to Gryphius, intended to go on to Ger-

---

[20] This letter is translated by Izora Scott, *Controversies over the imitation of Cicero as a Model for Style and Some Phases of their Influence on the Schools of the Renaissance* (New York, 1910), 85–88.

[21] Dolet published his *Orationes Duae in Tholosam* in Lyons, Gryphius, between August 13 and October 15, 1534, but Lando did not write the preface. Baudrier, *Bibliographie Lyonnaise,* VIII, 38.

[22] See Richard Copley Christie, *Etienne Dolet: The Martyr of the Renaissance* (London, 1880).

[23] *Forcianae Quaestiones,* 1857 ed., 35; *Erasmus funus,* f. 16; *Cathaloghi,* 475.

[24] For a discussion of the *Cicero relegatus et Cicero revocatus,* see Ch. III. The date of composition can be inferred from a reference to Giovanni Morone as a bishop (he was consecrated on April 7, 1529), and a reference to a living Antonio Seripando, brother to Cardinal Girolamo Seripando. Antonio Seripando died on November 4, 1531. Hubert Jedin, *Papal Legate at the Council of Trent: Cardinal Seripando,* trans. F. C. Eckhoff (St. Louis, London, 1947), 65, 111.

many.[25] The details of Lando's visit to Geneva, and if he went on to Germany at this time, are unknown.

On May 24, 1535, Lando left with Vincenzo Buonvisi on the Italian trip deplored by Gryphius, whose fears that he would be recognized by his former order and would come to grief were unrealized. He spent eighteen days in Lucca and another twenty-eight at the nearby villa of the Buonvisi at Forci, visiting the Buonvisi family, leading Luccan silk merchants, and others. Lucca pleased Lando greatly: the city was well-governed, its architecture was splendid, the gentlemen liberal, and ladies gracious.[26] He often praised Lucca and the Luccans in his later writings;[27] perhaps the days at Forci seemed a happy idyl in the midst of wandering. In his next book, the *Forcianae Quaestiones* (1535), Lando recounted two days of conversations at the Forci villa. The topics ranged from philosophy to love, music, food, and military arts, often involving comparative observations on the customs and attitudes of the people of different Italian cities—the Florentines gave and received advice well but could never agree, the Venetians were the most sensual of lovers, and so on.

Information on Lando's movements between 1536 and 1540 is lacking. In works published in 1540 and 1544, he mentioned visits to Thuringia and "upper Germany," i.e., Germany south of the river Main. If Gryphius correctly understood Lando's intentions, he may have visited Germany after Geneva between 1536 and 1540. He may also have visited Venice before 1540. By this date he had established friendly relations with two sought-after Venetian patrons of *letterati,* Fortunato Martinengo and Benedetto Agnello, as he dedicated his next book (1540) to Martinengo and mentioned Agnello in it.[28] In May 1540, Lando possibly again visited

[25] "Accepi a vobis litterarum fascem XV Kal. decembr. cui inerant binae ad me, eodem tenore sed diverso tempore conscriptae, binae ad Hortensium qui tum non hic, sed Genevae agebat, profectus eo, ut in Germaniam iret. . . . Hortensius autem nunc rediit vir inconstantissimus, cui cum daret litteras vestras, ille autem traderet mihi interulam unam cum litteris suis, ego que expostularem de Euclide, respondit litteras suas vobis satisfacturas: id quod mihi vix fit verisimile." Autograph letter of Sebastian Gryphius to Joannes Angelus Odonus and Philaenus Lunardus at Strasbourg, dated Lyons, February 4, 1535, [or 1536 if the date was Lyons style] in the Basle Archive, Cod. Basiliensis, G², I, 18, n° 29, f. 17; also printed in Baudrier, *Bibliographie Lyonnaise,* VIII, 32–33.

[26] *Forcianae Quaestiones,* 1857 ed., 49, and the dedicatory letter to Francesco Turchi. On Lucca, see Sforza, "Ortensio Lando," 34–47.

[27] *Erasmus funus,* f. 12ᵛ; *Sermoni Funebri,* 1622 ed., 40; *Cathaloghi,* 281, 473, 475, 476.

[28] *Erasmus funus,* ff. 1ᵛ, 13.

Chur. At that time, Johannes Comander, the Protestant pastor of Chur, wrote to Heinrich Bullinger at Zurich informing him that a "doctor of medicine," who was a citizen of Milan, had expressed the wish to meet Bullinger at Zurich. Comander recommended the physician from Milan as a man of piety and erudition.[29] Lando made no mention of a visit to Bullinger in Zurich, but since his next book was published in Basel in August 1540, he may have journeyed north through Switzerland in that summer, halting to visit Comander and Bullinger.

Erasmus funus, Lando's next book, was published anonymously in Basel in August 1540. It was a dialogue in which two speakers described and commented on the manner in which some German monks desecrated the body and insulted the memory of Erasmus at the latter's funeral at Basel. Printed under the pseudonym, "Philalethis ex Utopia Civis," the book raised a storm. On August 5, 1541, Johannes (Basilius) Herold (1511–c.1580), German-born historian and Protestant polemicist,[30] delivered an angry oration at the gymnasium in Basel against the book and its author, who he mistakenly thought was Bassiano Lando (d. 1563), a Piacenza-born physician who taught at the University of Padua and had written several books on medicine.

Another report put Lando at Ferrara in 1540. Through his induction into the Accademia degli Elevati of Ferrara, founded by Alberto Lollio in 1540, he acquired the academic name of "Tranquillo."[31] The Accademia degli Elevati dissolved after a desultory six years,[32] but the name "Tranquillo," obviously the opposite of Lando's personality and restless life, clung to him, and he used it on several occasions, as did others.[33]

In the next five years, through 1545, Lando traveled constantly in France, Italy, and Germany, enjoying short periods of patronage from several sources. With Lodovico Orsini, the Count of Pitigliano, he made a

---

[29] "Presentium lator, doctor medicinarum, Mediolanensis civis pietatis studiosus et eruditorum virorum amantissimus, Tigurum invisere cupiens a me petiit literas ad aliquem praecipuum religionis antistitem, ut per hoc adeundi et colloquendi occasionem nactus in vestri notitiam perveniat." Ex Rhetiae Curia, 16 Maii, anno 40. *Bullingers Korrespondenz mit den Graubündnern,* ed. Traugott Schiess, I (Basel, 1904), letter no. 17, p. 21.

[30] *Grand Dictionnaire Universel du XIXᵉ Siècle* (Larousse), IX, 241.

[31] Fontanini, *Biblioteca dell'eloquenza italiana,* I, 125, quoting from a ms. source.

[32] Michele Maylender, *Storia delle accademie d'Italia,* V (Bologna, 1927), 260–61.

[33] *Cathaloghi,* 115; *Ragionamenti Familiari,* 31; *Commentario,* 1550 ed., 47ᵛ.

trip to France and visited the court of Francis I.[34] In 1542 he served Marco Vigerio della Rovere, Bishop of Sinigaglia, as Aretino mentioned him in a letter to the bishop in December of that year from Venice.[35] At this time Aretino knew Lando, either in person or by correspondence, for in August 1542 he exhorted Lando to keep his chin up; Fortune would eventually reward his merit.[36] Lando was also in the train of several Italian nobles, including Galeotto Pico, Count of Mirandola, and Cardinal Cristoforo Madruzzo, the bishop of Trent and host to the Council, whom he followed to Rimini, Ferrara, and Pesaro.[37]

In late December 1544 and early 1545, the restless Lando traveled to Germany, where in Augsburg he visited Johann Jacob Fugger (1516–75), a member of the famous banking family who was more interested in letters than loans, and the bishop of Augsburg, Cardinal Otto Truchsess von Waldburg (d. 1573).[38] In 1548 Lando dedicated to Fugger the *Sermoni Funebri,* and sent him a copy of his *Commentario.*[39] From Augsburg Lando went to Brescia, arriving for the pre-Lenten carnival in 1545, and remaining there for about four months. Here he was supported by the Venetian patrician, Marcantonio da Mula, newly created governor of Brescia, and published a short tract warning men of the dangers of women.[40] At some time in these years Lando met the bishop of Catania, Cola Maria Caracciolo, at Piacenza, and promised to write his coming *Paradossi* for him.[41]

Lando kept his promise with the publication in 1543 in Lyons of his first book in the vernacular, the *Paradossi.* His best-known work, the *Paradossi* defended thirty paradoxical theses, for instance, that it was better to be poor than rich, or more advantageous to be ignorant than

---

[34] *Confutazione,* n.d., 7ᵛ; *Paradossi,* 1545 ed., 42.

[35] *Lettere,* 1609 ed., III, 23.

[36] "A Messer Ortensio Tranquillo," August 12, 1542, Venice, in Aretino, *Lettere: il primo e il secondo libro,* ed. Francesco Flora (Verona, 1960), no. 426, p. 936.

[37] *Confutazione,* n.d., 7ᵛ; dedicatory letter to Madruzzo, *Paradossi,* 1545 ed., [2]. On Madruzzo, see Hubert Jedin, *A History of the Council of Trent,* trans. Dom Ernest Graf O.S.B., I (London, 1957), 568–74.

[38] On Cardinal Truchsess, see Jedin, *History of the Council of Trent,* I, 460.

[39] A copy of the 1548 *Commentario* in Munich contains the inscription: "Jo. Jacobo Pucckero domino mel colendissimo Hortensius Landi dictus Tranquillus dono mittit." See Conor Fahy, "Un trattato di Vincenzo Maggi sulle donne e un'opera sconosciuta di Ortensio Lando," *GSLI,* 138 (1961), 263, n. 1.

[40] Fahy, "Un'opera sconosciuta di Lando," 263–66. See Appendix II, no. 11.

[41] *Paradossi,* 1545 ed., 42.

learned. The genre of the paradox originated in antiquity, usually in the context of a philosophical problem. Cicero, for example, wrote essays in which he supported the uncommon viewpoint, arguing that only the wise man was truly rich and that virtue was the only good. As a Stoic, he could support such propositions, which he termed paradoxical because they were contrary to the opinion of ordinary men.[42] In the sixteenth century, Erasmus used paradox to convey a message with a humorous and ironic air. Much of the *Praise of Folly* was constructed on his paradoxical interpretation of what the world considered "wise" and "crazy" and his artful mixing of the two.

In his *Paradossi* Lando used humor, tongue-in-cheek remarks, and double-entendre, for the serious purpose of social and moral criticism. Man was unhappy when he saw all the evil around him; so it was better to be blind than to see; thus one would not see the evil conditions in Italy —the criminals in Naples, the prostitutes in Rome. In his sixth paradox, that it was not a bad thing if a prince lost his state, Lando criticized princes as avaricious, cruel, and monstrous and concluded that no one lamented the loss of a state by a prince. On the lighter side, in his eighteenth paradox, he argued that to be a bastard was neither shameful nor odious. On the contrary, since bastards were born of a more ardent love and as a result of more ingenious strategems than a legitimate heir, the bastard was more deserving of his father's estate.

Later in the sixteenth century, particularly in English literature, paradoxes represented nothing more than a display of intellectual adroitness. It has been suggested that Lando's *Paradossi* were of such levity,[43] in view of his next work, the *Confutazione del Libro de' Paradossi* (probably published in 1544). Again writing anonymously and pretending ignorance of the identity of the author of the *Paradossi*, Lando advertised that he would confute those "pestilential paradoxes" which even then, he admitted in a boastful aside, were being translated into French and Latin.[44] In the first paradox of the *Paradossi*, Lando had argued that it

---

[42] Elbert N. S. Thompson, *The Seventeenth-Century English Essay* (Iowa City, Iowa, 1926), 94–96; Warner G. Rice, "The *Paradossi* of Ortensio Lando," in *Essays and Studies in English and Comparative Literature . . .* (Ann Arbor, Michigan, 1932), 59–74; and Rosalie L. Colie, *Paradoxia Epidemica: The Renaissance Tradition of Paradox* (Princeton, N.J., 1966). Lando is discussed 461–63.

[43] Thompson, *Seventeenth-Century English Essay*, 96–102.

[44] *Confutazione*, n.d., 3–3ᵛ. French translations appeared in abundance (see Appendix II), but I have not located any Latin translation.

was better to be poor than to be rich. Citing a number of examples, he decried wealth because of its close relationship to evil, while in poverty, vice disappeared. He concluded that "riches were the mother of infinite evils," but poverty was blessed.[45] In the *Confutazione* Lando began his refutation with the knowing smirk that the author of the *Paradossi* was trying to induce others to abandon their wealth so that he could be rich. But this argument was nonsense. Money was a good thing; it was the instrument of all of man's actions, the sustenance of states, nerves of war, and the "true testimonial of nobility." It was an ugly thing to be poor. In poverty, one could not tell the ignoble from the noble, or the legitimate heir from the bastard. In order to flee poverty, beautiful women gave themselves to powerful lovers, and men lied, perjured themselves, and committed treason and murder. Great prelates abandoned their flocks and sought out princely courts where they became slaves of intemperate rulers. In conclusion Lando asked how one could possibly argue that it was better to be poor than to be rich.[46] Thus, in both the *Paradossi* and *Confutazione,* Lando used the poverty-wealth paradox to criticize the rich and highborn, and the desire for wealth which produced vice. In both books, although arguing seemingly opposed theses, Lando made critical social and moral comments.

The *Paradossi* produced the first contact between Lando and Doni. In a letter of April 19, 1544, from Venice, Doni, who was just beginning his literary career, enthusiastically praised the *Paradossi*. The book was ingenious and admirable; if he could learn the identity of the "clear intellect" who had written it, he would take him for a friend. The author had mocked Boccaccio and "checked the slynesses of Aristotle," and Doni opined that the many lampoons of the *Paradossi* had struck home. He especially approved of the third paradox, that it was better to be ignorant than learned. To summarize his approval, Doni coined two epigrams: "If today the tongue of ignorance buries a few scribbled pages, the mouth of truth could give birth to many printed volumes." Although one could not achieve good customs for many years, still one could "expose vices in a short time." The author of the *Paradossi* had accomplished this, in Doni's opinion.[47] Doni and Lando probably met shortly thereafter, for both were

---

[45] *Paradossi,* 1545 ed., 3–9ᵛ.

[46] *Confutazione,* n.d., 4–5ᵛ.

[47] "Quest'opera S. mio m'ha gustato tanto, & di tal maniera m'è piaciuta (o l'è ingeniosa, o l'è mirabile) che subito mi imaginai di mandarvene una copia. S'io conoscessi quel chiarissimo intelletto, io piglierei tanta letitia d'esserli amico, quanto

in Venice in May 1544 and in Piacenza in the summer of 1545. In September 1545, Doni wrote from Piacenza that he was preparing for the press an unnamed dialogue of "M. Hortensio."[48]

Gradually, but inexorably, Lando drifted to Venice. He left Piacenza when it became an ecclesiastical state in 1545,[49] and attached himself to the train of Cardinal Cristoforo Madruzzo of Trent. At the opening of the Council, Lando reported on the opening sermon, and the absence of the "Lutherans or Protestants as we call them lately," who, he said, had stayed away because they had been promised that the Council would meet somewhere else than at Trent.[50] In 1544 and 1545 the *Paradossi* were reprinted in Venice, without any softening of Lando's criticism except for the omission of a sentence which touched on the vainglory of the Venetian patriciate.[51] Lando probably spent some time in Venice in order to supervise these printings, and possibly spent 1546 and 1547 there. By 1548 he had lived in the house of Benedetto Agnello, the ambassador of the Duke of Mantua to Venice, and a generous patron of letterati. He had also visited Pietro Aretino several times.[52]

Lando wrote constantly in the years between 1544 and 1548, and in the latter year gave to the Venetian printers a translation, two original works, and an edition of letters. For the printer Aurelio Pincio, he produced, anonymously, the first Italian translation of More's *Utopia*, edited for the press by Doni. This, the only Italian translation until the

gli havranno invidia i suoi nemici. la S.V. la legga che ella troverà di molte belle inventioni; un'rabuffamento al Boccaccio, un'dar straverso alle soppiattonerie d'Aristotele, & molte altre acutezze d'ingegno con tanta gratia del mondo. Sonoci molti che non pigliano se non le parole, & vi si perdono sopra; col dire; la non è honesta; & non considerano che l'auttore s'ha messo la giornea della spensieraggine per dar da ridere alla brigata. . . . A me la mi par molto piacevole. O quel esser meglio trovarsi ignorante che letterato, mi quadra, & lo confermo per conoscer molti, che son da qual cosa, i quali strologano piu a sfamarsi, che non hanno lambiccato il cervello ne testi, nelle glose & fra dottori, & i manigoldi squazzano. E se hora la lingua de l'ignoranza sotterra pochi fogli scritti, la bocca della verità potrebbe partorire assai volumi stampati . . . Ma quel che non ha potuto fare la pace de buoni costumi in molti anni, disporrà la guerra de i vitii in poco tempo. . . ." Venice, April 19, 1544. Doni, *Lettere*, 1552 ed., 225–26.

[48] Letter of September 9, 1545, Piacenza, to Lodovico Domenichi. Doni, *Lettere*, 1545 ed., cxxxvi[v]–cxxxvii.

[49] *Vari Componimenti*, 1555 ed., 90.

[50] *Commentario*, 1550 ed., 33.

[51] Bongi, in *Novelle di M. Ortensio Lando*, xxxvii.

[52] *Commentario*, 1550 ed., 38–38[v].

nineteenth century, was the second vernacular rendering of the *Utopia,* preceded only by the German in 1524, and antedating the French by two and the English by three years. Lando's interest in More probably developed through his friendship with the Buonvisi of Lucca. Antonio Buonvisi (1484–1559), an elder brother of Lando's benefactor, Vincenzo, had been a good friend of More in England, even visiting him in prison. Antonio may have brought the *Utopia* with him upon his return to the continent, and Lando could have seen it in Lyons or Lucca. He may also have seen one of the early Latin editions, for example, that of Florence, 1519.[53] The *Utopia* made a lasting impression on Lando, who referred to More in his own books, and adopted pseudonyms derived from the idea of a citizen from Utopia. Lando signed four of his books as "Anonymo di Utopia," "Philalethis ex Utopia Civis," or "Philalethe Polytopiensi Cive."

Under the pseudonym "Messer Anonymo di Utopia," Lando published in September 1548 the work which is most typical of him, and as important as the *Paradossi*—a *Commentario* "on the most notable and monstrous things in Italy." More's *Utopia* had suggested to Lando the device of criticizing contemporary Italy through the impressions of a visitor from afar. In the *Commentario,* the narrator, a citizen of the island of Utopia, desired to see the "most beautiful, richest, and most civilized" land in the world, Italy. When a shipwreck threw on Utopia a Florentine who offered to act as a guide, Messer Anonymo undertook the journey. The book chronicled his extensive travels through Italy, as he landed in Sicily and traveled north, stopping at every city and mentioning the noble families of every region. The book was the ideal vehicle to exhibit the knowledge of people and places that Lando had acquired through fifteen years or more of incessant travel. Earlier, the *Forcianae Quaestiones* and *Paradossi* had contained comparative reflections on the people, customs, and cities of Italy, and the *Commentario* brought to fruition this tendency.

The second original work of 1548 was the *Sermoni Funebri,* or sermons on the deaths of animals, printed by Giolito, but without Lando's name. It was a collection of eleven sermons on the deaths of an ass, a horse, a louse, a dog, a monkey, an owl, a magpie, a cat, a fish, a chicken, and a cricket, done in mock oratorical style. With rhetorical flourish and

[53] R. W. Gibson, *St. Thomas More: A Preliminary Bibliography of His Works and of Moreana to the Year 1750* (New Haven and London, 1961), 3–4; Luigi Firpo, "Tommaso Moro e la sua fortuna in Italia," *Occidente, rivista di studi politici,* VIII, (1952), 233.

many classical references, Lando praised the good qualities of the dead animals. He compared them favorably to humans, and in the eulogy of the dead owl, he parodied Petrarchan *canzoniere* style and vocabulary as he sang the praises of the owl's eyes. "Oh my most beautiful owl, more dear than the light of my eyes; indeed he who did not love thee lacked love, he who did not willingly gaze fondly at you lacked eyes."[54]

Although these books were published anonymously, Lando left very clear signs that he was the author. The *Commentario* concluded with the letters SUISNETROH SUDNAL ROTUA TSE which, read backward, was "Hortensius Landus autor est." In addition, the printer announced that the author was "M.O.L.," that is, "Messer Ortensio Lando." And to aid the really dense readers who were still in the dark, Lando concluded both the *Commentario* and *Sermoni funebri* with a signed "brief apology" for the author.

The last book of 1548 was hack work for Giolito, a collection of letters of valorous women, edited (and probably partly written) by Lando.[55] At the end of the book Aretino, Ludovico Dolce, Girolamo Parabosco, and Francesco Sansovino added sonnets praising Lando. He was now an accepted member of the circle of vernacular authors around Giolito.

Settled in Venice between 1548 and 1552, Lando enjoyed his most prolific period. In 1550 he published six new books, four for Andrea Arrivabene and two for Giolito, again divided between original works and hack work. In *La Sferza de' Scrittori* (published by Arrivabene), Lando described the imperfections of all manner of authors and ideas from Aristotle to the present, concluding that they all had defects which rendered them worthless. But in a brief coda, he typically reversed himself and urged his readers to study letters, including many of the same authors whom he had before condemned. The *Ragionamenti Familiari* (Arrivabene) mined the same paradoxical vein as the *Cicero relegatus et Cicero revocatus,* the *Paradossi* and its *Confutazione,* and the *Sferza de' Scrittori.* The discourses of the *Ragionamenti* often argued first one side and then the other of miscellaneous issues. The first discussion spoke in contempt of music, the second argued in its favor, and so on through other topics.

---

[54] "O bellissima Civetta mia, o cara piu che la luce de gli occhi miei, ben era senza amore chi non t'amava, senza occhi chi volentieri non ti vagheggiava." *Sermoni Funebri,* 1622 ed., 40.

[55] This is the judgment of Salvatore Bongi, in *Novelle di M. Ortensio Lando,* liii. See Appendix II, no. 14.

As usual in Lando's paradoxical books, both sides did not receive equal space or eloquence, and he sometimes turned the argument around. In an exhortation to the reader to become a monk, he scathingly denounced friars. In the *Ragionamenti Familiari* Lando for the first time passed from anticlericalism to comments that strayed from religious orthodoxy as he spoke for justification by faith alone. The other four works of 1550 (listed in Appendix II as nos. 19, 20, 21, 26) fell into the category of hack work: a translation, two collections of sayings of others, and a collection of questions and answers on various subjects.

In 1552 Lando published another group of books, all in Venice. The *Vari Componimenti* (Giolito) were a collection of novelle, dialogues, fables, and jokes printed under his own name. Also for Giolito, Lando wrote a collection of questions and answers on natural science, moral philosophy, religion, and love, which he called *Quattro Libri de' Dubbi.* His religious interest was apparent both here and in his only work dealing entirely with religion, a dialogue on Holy Scripture—*Dialogo . . . di M. Hortensio Lando . . . leggendo la Sacra Scrittura*—printed by Comin da Trino for Arrivabene in April 1552. In this dialogue and in the *Dubbi,* Lando again strayed from orthodoxy.

In the years between 1548 and 1552, Lando enjoyed the patronage of Lucrezia Gonzaga (1522–76) as well as the profits from his books. Of the secondary Gonzaga family, the Gonzaga di Bozzolo e Sabbioneta, rather than the ruling Gonzaga of Mantua, Lucrezia, who had been tutored by the priest and author Matteo Bandello, patronized letterati at the family castle at Gazzuolo, about twenty kilometers southwest of Mantua above the banks of the Oglio, a tributary of the Po. Orphaned at eight, and widowed when her husband, the Venetian Giampaolo Manfrone, was captured and died in a Turkish prison, Lucrezia was praised by many authors for her generosity and beauty. In 1552 Lando published for Giolito a panegyric in honor of Lucrezia and Maria Cardona, the Marchesa di Palude. He also edited a collection of Lucrezia's letters for the printer Gualtiero Scotto, and again possibly wrote part of it.

In December 1552 Giolito printed for Lando his last original book, the *Sette Libri de Cathaloghi,* a 567-page collection of "catalogues," i.e., lists of every conceivable kind. The first book consisted of lists, often with comments, of handsome men, ugly men and women, prostitutes, chaste women, people with good memories, poor memories, adulterers, angry men, and on and on. Later in the work he classified men and women according to professions, deeds, moral qualities, what books they wrote, and in each case further divided them between ancients and moderns. The *Cathaloghi* displayed Lando's erudition and his knowledge of Italy's past and present.

In Venice Lando enjoyed access to the literary world around the presses and Aretino. He praised the poetesses Gaspara Stampa and Veronica Gambara, and was in turn praised by Girolamo Ruscelli.[56] Unlike Franco and Doni, Lando enjoyed continuous friendship with Aretino. They exchanged letters in November 1548, and the Scourge of Princes wrote a sonnet praising Lando as "a lamp of the most learned schools."[57] In August 1550 Aretino wrote to Lando again; in December 1552 he called Lando and Doni illustrious poets,[58] and in a letter of January 1553 described a joke that Lando played on him in his house.[59] In March 1553 he wrote to Ludovico Dolce thanking him for a sonnet delivered "by the mouth of the not less courteous than learned M. Hortensio."[60]

Lando was, furthermore, acquainted with men of religion. He received a warm letter in late 1550 from the dedicated Catholic apologist Girolamo Muzio (1496–1576).[61] In 1553 he described Cornelio Musso (1511–74), the bishop of Bitonto and the most famous Italian preacher since Ochino, as an old friend. Lando spent a few days in Padua where he persuaded Musso to let him edit for the press the sermon with which Musso had opened the Council of Trent on December 13, 1545. Giolito printed the sermon in 1553.[62]

But Venetian freedom was ending for Lando. The May 1554 *Index* contained an entry banning the books of "Hortensius Tranquillus" and "Philaletis civis Utopiensis,"[63] and on June 30 of either 1554 or 1555, Lando

[56] *Lettere della Lucretia Gonzaga*, 1552 ed., 325.

[57] Lando's letter to Aretino is in *Lettere scritte a Pietro Aretino*, ed. Teodorico Landoni, II (Bologna, 1875), pt. 1, pp. 244–45. Aretino's answer is in Aretino, *Lettere*, 1609 ed., V, 60ᵛ–61.

[58] Aretino, *Lettere*, 1609 ed., V, 307–7ᵛ; IV, 116ᵛ.

[59] *Ibid.*, VI, 152–52ᵛ.

[60] "Eccovi compar'magnifico duo Sonetti, in cambio d'uno che per bocca del non meno gentile, che dotto M. Hortensio mi havette imposto. . . ." Aretino, *Lettere*, 1609 ed., VI, 165. Lando was the sole "Hortensio" among Aretino's correspondents. The letter is undated but the previous and succeeding letters are dated March, 1533, Venice.

[61] *Lettere del Mutio Iustinopolitano . . .* (Venice, 1551), 135ᵛ–37.

[62] See Appendix II, no. 35. On Musso see Roger J. Bartman, "Cornelius Musso, Tridentine Theologian and Orator (1511–1574)," *Franciscan Studies*, New Series, 5 (1945), 247–76.

[63] Reusch, *Die Indices librorum prohibitorum*, 168.

wrote to Cardinal Madruzzo at Trent complaining that his books had been banned and that he was under suspicion. He protested that he was "a devoted servant of the Roman Church," and asked the cardinal to intercede for him with the Inquisitor. In conclusion, he confided that he did not have a *scudo* in his purse.[64] After this letter to Madruzzo, he dropped from sight, and may have died shortly thereafter.[65]

Lando's self-appraisal was unflattering but consistent with his critical writing. He termed himself a frenzied, melancholy spirit and disturber of tranquility, one who was "full of anger and scorn, ambitious, impatient, haughty, frenzied, and inconstant."[66] In the *Cathaloghi,* he listed himself under "angry, scornful, and raging men." By his own admission, he was quarrelsome, having broken friendships with one ill-chosen word. Half in boast, he admitted that he could not get along with patrons. When he quarreled with them, he returned gifts, and once had turned down the offer of a good farm. He could not serve a *gran signore* at court because he did not know how to adulate, lie, and perjure himself. When asked why he could not remain in one place, he passed off the question with a joke. To complete his self-portrait, he drew an unfavorable physical picture of himself. He was short, with black hair, donkey ears, pallid face, flat nose, and negroid lips. He had crooked hands, bad eyesight, was

[64] "Illustrissimo mio signore. Mando dui volumi alla vostra Illustrissima Riverenza dei quali piaceravvi darne l'uno al Signor Nicolò Madruccio persuadendogli con la vostra singolar eloquenza a mandarmi la Mancia accioche lo stampatore che alle mie spese gli ha stampati non mi faccia rattener per debito. Oltre questo, sendo da questo Tribunale dell'heresia stati banditi i miei libri quantunque riveduti fussero dagli Inquisitori prima che si stampassero et essendo io lor sospetto; desidero di appresentarmi; et mostrargli che sono devoto servidore della Romana Chiesa: supplico per tanto la cortesia vostra a scriver due parole al Reverendo Theologo Mastro Franceschino Visdomini da Ferrara perche prenda la protettione mia.

Tanto mi confido della vostra Cortesia che non havendo in borsa salvo che un scudo l'ho dato per mandar messo a posta: In casa del Carrettone alli 30 di Giugno,

Humil servo Hortensio Lando."

"all'Illustrissimo Principe di Trento Il Cardinal MADRUCCIO." Trent, Archivio di Stato, Archivio principesco vescovile, Corrispondenza madruzziana, fascicolo 1555, foll. 97–98. See Conor Fahy, "Per la vita di Ortensio Lando," *GSLI,* 142 (1965), 255. I am indebted to Dr. Fahy for furnishing me a prepublication copy of the letter.

[65] An uncomfirmed report states that an "Ortensio Landi" introduced the Reformation at Bellinzona at the end of the sixteenth century. *Dictionnaire historique & biographique de la Suisse,* IV (Neuchâtel, 1928), 442, referring to a work of E. Pometta on Bellinzona. I have been unable to date to locate the Pometta work.

[66] Sferza, 24–24ᵛ; *Confutazione,* n.d., 3ᵛ.

sickly, and spoke with a Lombard accent despite his efforts to speak Tuscan.[67] This was an unflattering but appropriate portrait for an author who dealt in paradoxical criticism.

Nicolò Franco

Despite Lando's inconstancy and professed scorn for nobles, he had more personal success in the Venetian circle of printers and poligrafi than did the second member of the trio, Nicolò Franco. Franco was born in the southern Italian hill town of Benevento on September 13, 1515.[68] Nothing is known of his parents, but they were undoubtedly humble people, possibly peasants, despite Franco's attempt to convince Aretino and others of his high origins.[69] His parents may have died when he was a child, because his older brother, Vincenzo, a schoolmaster of Benevento who enjoyed local fame as a Latin poet, raised and educated him. A precocious student, Franco acquired a thorough command of Latin and classical literature, wrote Latin poetry, and attempted to get a book of satires published at the age of fourteen.

The ambitious young man soon looked beyond Benevento's walls to Naples, the nearest courtly center, where he arrived in 1535. With the aid of Bartolomeo Camerario, a friendly native of Benevento who held official posts in Naples, Franco tried to make his way as a courtier. His first printed work, *Hisabella* (Naples, 1535), was a collection of Latin poems in praise of Isabella di Capua, wife of the imperial viceroy Ferrante Gonzaga. In the year at Naples, Franco made a lifelong friend of a

---

[67] *Cathaloghi,* 99–100, 115; *Oracoli,* 1550 ed., 14; *Confutazione,* n.d., 3ʳ.

[68] On Franco's birth, see Enrico Sicardi, "L'anno della nascita di Nicolò Franco," *GSLI,* 24 (1894), 399–404; and "Ancora dell'anno della nascita di N. Franco," *GSLI,* 25 (1895), 170–72. For Franco, though not for Lando and Doni, we have a reliable biography: Giuseppe De Michele, "Nicolò Franco. Biografia con documenti inediti," in *Studi di letteratura italiana,* XI (Rome, 1915), 61–154. Michele's account takes into consideration Biblioteca Apostolica Vaticana, Vaticanus Latinus 5642, "Nicolò Franco Lettere," 571 ms. folios of Franco's letters and letters addressed to him from June 15, 1540 to July 8, 1559, and is more accurate than Carlo Simiani, *La vita e le opere di Nicolò Franco* (Turin, Rome, 1894). Unless otherwise documented, the following account is based on De Michele.

[69] Alessandro Zilioli (d. 1650), literary historian, wrote that Franco was born of "humble condition." Venice, Biblioteca Marciana, Mss. Italiani, Classe X, Cod. I (6394), "Istoria delle vite de' poeti italiani di Alessandro Zilioli veneziano," p. 106.

Neapolitan writer, Luigi Tansillo (1510–68), composer of satiric and lascivious poetry, and also contributed a sonnet in honor of Giovanni Battista Pino in the latter's *Ragionamento sopra dell'asino* (published between 1535 and 1540), a satiric attack against the viceroy in Naples.[70] But the young Franco did not meet with great success; reduced to living by charity, he left for Venice. He arrived there in June 1536, carrying a letter of introduction to Titian, and found a temporary home with Benedetto Agnello, who had also aided Aretino and Lando. On his arrival in Venice, Franco published another work, the *Tempio d'Amore,* printed by Marcolini in 1536, a vernacular poem which praised thirty noble Venetian ladies, and which was largely a plagiarization of an obscure Neapolitan work praising thirty Neapolitan noblewomen.[71] The book did not achieve much success and Franco went to work as a corrector for Marcolini's press.

Then Fortune smiled on Franco. Through the aid of the poet Quinto Gherardo, he entered Aretino's employ. He helped Aretino collect and copy his voluminous correspondence for the first edition of his celebrated letters, and also translated the Church Fathers for him; Aretino then embellished the translations for his religious books. The Scourge of Princes who intrigued for a cardinal's hat a few years later could not read Latin.[72] In early August 1537, Franco left the house of Agnello to live with Aretino. The relationship between them was closer than master and secretary, for the expansive Aretino treated him like a son, publicly praising Franco's sonnets and immortalizing him by addressing to him the letter in which he set forth his literary credo.[73]

The friendship was as brief as it was warm. In December 1537 Aretino predicted that Franco would be another Aretino, the highest praise that he could bestow.[74] But by August 1538 they had broken, for reasons unknown. Aretino suppressed his previous praise of Franco in a new edition of his *Lettere,* and charged plagiarization; Franco sneered at his former mentor for displaying envy of his secretary's literary ability.

[70] The sonnet is reproduced in De Michele, "Nicolò Franco," 150.

[71] Franco's *Tempio d'Amore* was based on the *Opera nuova nomata vero Tempio de Amore* (in fine: Impressa in la Città di Allife per il Reverendo don Aloisio Acilio Primicerio . . . MDXXXVI), of Jacopo Campanile, called Campanio Napoletano. See Carlo Simiani, "Un plagio di Nicolò Franco," *Rassegna critica della letteratura italiana,* V (1900), 19–26.

[72] Letter to Francesco Alunno, 1541, in Vaticanus Latinus 5642, f. 12.

[73] See Ch. I, n. 11.

[74] Aretino, *Lettere,* 1960 ed., no. 337, p. 430.

These charges may or may not have been true; in any case the personalities of the two principals made a clash inevitable. Aretino blew hot and cold with the young writers whom he befriended, extravagantly praising them and then dropping them abruptly when a new person or interest appeared. The young Franco, on the other hand, had a high estimate of his own ability which was further inflated by Aretino's lavish praise. When Aretino inevitably lost interest in him, he reacted with the charge of envy. Aretino had taken him into his house as a penniless young man ready to defer to his mentor's wishes, and was now faced with a proud rebel. The swaggering confidant of Charles V and blackmailer of princes would hardly endure such an upstart in his own house.

Despite difficulties with Aretino, Franco matured as an author in Venice, and in 1539 the vernacular printers published three of his most important works. Inspired by Aretino's phenomenal success with his *Lettere,* which were reprinted as quickly as Marcolini could set the type, Franco gave his letters to Antonio Gardane, who printed them as *Pistole Vulgari* in April 1539. Franco was the second sixteenth-century Italian author to publish his letters, Doni, in 1544, the third, and by mid-century publishing one's letters was standard practice for authors. Some of Franco's letters were short and personal, others were long, pretentious orations, and still others may have carried fictitious dates. It was unlikely, for example, that he seriously presumed to address the king of France from Benevento at the age of sixteen (1531) as the dates on his letters claimed. Some similarities in ideas and conceits, particularly in letters to princes, showed that Franco had profited from his apprenticeship under Aretino.[75] His published letters on the whole lacked the intimacy and vibrant language of Aretino and Doni, but still contained originality and much effective writing.

In October 1539 Giolito printed Franco's *Petrarchista,* an elaborate satire on the slavish imitation of Petrarch and the innumerable Petrarchan commentaries. In the introductory letter Franco admitted that he was committing *lese majesty* against Petrarch, but went on to describe the misadventures of a poet who deeply revered Laura. This poet journeyed to Avignon and all the other places she had lived in order to learn

---

[75] See P. P. Parrella, "Le 'Pistole Vulgari' di Nicolò Franco e il I libro delle 'Lettere' dell'Aretino," *Rassegna critica della letteratura italiana,* V (1900), 97–122. On the other hand, there are significant differences in style and ideas between the two. For example, the letter of Lucerna has no counterpart in Aretino (see Ch. V).

FIG. I. Title page of the first edition of Franco's *Pistole Vulgari*

everything about her. At length he found the relics of Laura: a nail scissors and her nightcap. When the searching poet came upon the inkpot of Petrarch and a magic pen, he ecstatically believed that he could write sonnets as well as Petrarch and compose learned commentaries on the master. The rest of the book consisted of Franco's satirical glosses on authentic and feigned verses of Petrarch. Lando and Doni also satirized the Petrarchan cult, but Franco was most effective.

The last work of 1539, the *Dialogi Piacevoli* (Giolito) was more ambitious—ten long dialogues on a variety of subjects. In them, Franco combined his extensive classical knowledge with humor and shrewd commentary on sixteenth-century Italian life in a manner reminiscent of Erasmus' colloquies.

Despite his literary success, Venice was not safe for an enemy of Aretino. Sometime between the middle of 1539 and October of that year, G. Ambrogio Eusebi attacked and stabbed Franco, severely wounding him. Aretino's bitterness toward him undoubtedly emboldened Eusebi, one of Aretino's young protégés, but if Franco circulated in Venice at this time the sonnets against Eusebi that he later printed, Eusebi had ample provocation. In these sonnets Franco suggested that Eusebi was a minion of Aretino willing to ignore the intimacy between Aretino and his wife, who was one of the young women who shared Aretino's house. The Scourge of Princes had great influence in Venice; far from being punished, Eusebi danced under the window of the convalescent Franco threatening more violence. Under these circumstances, Franco was forced to leave Venice in late June 1540.[76]

Franco probably did not foresee that he would never return to Venice and that his career as a poligrafo for the vernacular presses of Venice was nearly ended. Many editions of his *Pistole Vulgari, Petrarchista,* and *Dialogi Piacevoli* were printed in the 1540's and 1550's by Giolito, but because of Aretino's enmity Franco could not live in Venice, and was forced to try the difficult life of a court letterato. He continued to write, but after 1547 his attempts to publish his new efforts were dogged by misfortune as, for example, when he lost a valise filled with manuscripts to the Inquisition in 1558. Franco was a poligrafo in exile, living apart from his natural habitat.

Franco left Venice with the purpose of going to France to win the

[76] Franco's last letter from Venice was dated June 18, 1540. Vaticanus Latinus 5642, f. 5.

patronage of Francis I. He had no offer of support but hoped that on the basis of his many previous adulatory letters he could be as favored by Francis I as Aretino was by Charles V. He was forced to call a halt at the small city of Casale Monferrato in Piedmont because the military campaigns made further travel difficult, and on the invitation of the local governor, remained there. His stay was dictated more by circumstances than by enthusiasm for the provincial town. Aretino continued to write insults and attempted through his connections with the Venetian government, the imperial ambassador, the Duchess of Mantua, and others to have Franco exiled from Italy.[77] But Franco could not leave for France because of the war. At the same time, Aretino tried to obstruct the publication of Franco's works in Venice. Franco complained that Aretino placed spies around Giolito's shop when the latter reprinted the *Dialogi Piacevoli,* and threatened the printers with injury.[78] The nobility of Casale Monferrato, happy to harbor the exile, refused to bow to pressure, and sheltered Franco as long as he wished to stay. In his haven Franco replied to Aretino with a collection of enraged sonnets against him and against society in general.[79] The sonnets were bitter and obscene, but the force of Franco's fury gave them life as he ignored sweet Petrarchan vocabulary and classical allusions to pour out his story.

In April 1542, Franco published a conventional dialogue on beauty, *Dialogo delle Bellezze,* which praised the Casale Monferrato aristocracy. Lodovico Domenichi, one of the few poligrafi who managed to win and hold the friendship of nearly all the authors around the presses of Giolito and Marcolini, wrote to Franco in Casale Monferrato from Venice, sympathizing with his plight, adding that the age of gold would return again to reward his valorous and "frank" (*franco*) heart.[80]

Although Franco was an honored poet in the provincial center, the president of the local Accademia, and had become enamoured of a local

[77] See Alessandro Luzio, "L'Aretino e il Franco, appunti e documenti," *GSLI,* 29 (1897), 265–66; and De Michele, "Nicolò Franco," 99.

[78] Vaticanus Latinus 5642, f. 11.

[79] The *Rime contro Aretino et la Priapea* were published in Basel, 1548, and may also have been printed in Casale Monferrato in 1541. Marina Bersano Begey, *Le Cinquecentine Piemontesi: Torino* (Turin, 1961), 270, cites *Sonetti (contra l'Aretino) con la Priapea* (Torino [ovvero Casale di Monferrato], Guidone, 1541). The citation is based on J. C. Brunet, *Manuel du libraire et de l'amateur de livres,* II (Paris, 1860), 1377, as Bersano Begey did not locate a copy. I have been unable to find a copy of this edition.

[80] Vaticanus Latinus 5642, f. 8–18ᵛ.

woman, he continued to write letters in his restless desire to leave. He succeeded, appearing in Mantua in January 1546, and in early 1547 Giacomo Ruffinelli, a Mantuan printer, published his most ambitious work, *La Philena*. Begun as early as 1536, *La Philena* was a prose epic designed to be Franco's masterpiece. The hero, Sannio, had a vision in which Amore showed him a most beautiful woman, Philena. The vision gone, Sannio sought to find her, and his peregrinations occupied the major part of the work. Boccaccio's *Fiammetta* inspired Franco, and he also followed closely a few passages of Mario Equicola's *Libro di natura d'amore*.[81] The 935-page work contained effective pages, but the fact that it was never reprinted indicated a harsh judgment by contemporaries. *La Philena* was his last new work to be published, although new editions of previous works continued to appear.

Franco dedicated *La Philena* to a new patron, Giuseppe Cantelmo, the count of the small Abruzzi city of Popoli. Franco had first written to Cantelmo from Casale in 1544,[82] and in 1547 he took Franco into his train for the next five years, happy years for Franco, because the two were more like companions in travel and revel than prince and courtier. With the Count of Popoli, Franco satisfied his wish to travel beyond Italy, visiting Germany in 1548 and arranging for a Basel printing of his *Rime contro Aretino*. Then they gradually returned south where the two made a circuit of Popoli, Naples, and small towns around Naples and Salerno. In 1551 Cantelmo was elected viceroy of Calabria and took Franco with him as secretary when he journeyed to visit his new lands. Franco visited Cosenza in 1551, where he was elected to an academy, and later in the year traveled to Sicily.

Franco continued to initiate literary projects, but either never finished them or they have been lost. As early as 1541 he wrote to a prospective patron that he had composed ten books of a vernacular history of the times; he continued to refer to a work of this kind, and spoke of enriching it with archival materials.[83] No such history has, however, appeared, and it is possible that Franco was exaggerating what he had accomplished. He also began, and then gave up as too difficult, the task of collecting the poetry of Francesco Maria Molza (1489–1544), and turned down an invitation in June 1554 from Girolamo Ruscelli to contribute

---

[81] Giuseppe De Michele, "La 'Filena' di N. Franco," *Rassegna critica della letteratura italiana*, 30 (1925), 8–28.

[82] Vaticanus Latinus 5642, f. 129ᵛ.

[83] *Ibid.*, ff. 7ᵛ, 9ᵛ, 457ᵛ.

sonnets to a literary tribute to Giovanna d'Aragona.[84] In his native southern Italy, Franco seemed to lose some of his literary ambition; he felt banished from the literary centers of north Italy, although he retained the friendship of individual authors. In October 1550 he went to Florence with the Count of Popoli, and lived anonymously in the house of Benedetto Varchi for several days. One evening he attended in disguise a session of the Accademia Fiorentina presided over by the illustrious Paolo Giovio. But Lodovico Domenichi recognized Franco outside the palace, and informed the members of his presence. Some of them, probably friends of Aretino, loosed a "courteous assault" (*cortese assalto*) on the discomfited, unhappy Franco at the meeting. Despite Varchi's friendship and a subsequent friendly letter from Domenichi, Franco was not unhappy to leave Florence. He threatened to note in his history that Domenichi had trifled with him.[85]

The happy arrangement with the Count of Popoli ended in 1552 when the count, probably short of money, dispensed with Franco's company. Franco went to Naples to find a new patron, as he had done when a young man of twenty, and had no more success. Abandoning the court in October 1553, he eked out an unhappy existence in Naples on the charity of friends. But in June 1555 occurred the kind of opportunity for which every courtier prayed. In that month Cardinal Gian Pietro Carafa was elected Pope Paul IV, and the Carafa entourage moved to Rome to enjoy the spoils. Franco believed that he too would share in the rich patronage because the Count of Popoli was a nephew of Paul IV, the son of the pope's sister. Moreover, Franco had been cultivating two favored nephews of the pope, Don Carlo and Giovanni Jacopo, the Duke of Palliano. They received important posts immediately, and generously promised Franco that they would do all that they could for him.[86]

Franco had wished to go to Rome for several years, but had been forbidden to do so by an interdict of Paul III. Nothing is known of the interdict, but the reason probably lay in some of Franco's previous sonnets in which he vulgarly attacked Paul III, suggested that Rome deserved the

[84] The work was subsequently published: *Del Tempio alla divina signora Donna Giovanna d'Aragona* . . . (Venice, 1555).

[85] See Franco's letter to Varchi, n.d., in Vaticanus Latinus 5642, f. 457–58 (reprinted in part in De Michele, "Nicolò Franco," 134–35), and Domenichi's letter of September 15, 1551, Florence, to Franco, Vaticanus Latinus 5642, f. 369ᵛ–70.

[86] See the exchange of letters between Franco and the Carafa princes reprinted in De Michele, "Nicolò Franco," 142–44.

sack of 1527, and exulted in the death of Pier Luigi Farnese. Moreover, perhaps Franco had forgotten another sonnet of the 1540's in which he attacked Paul IV (then a cardinal) as an evil, ambitious prelate.[87] Still, under the new pope he hoped to have the interdict lifted and to enjoy a place of honor and profit with one of the Carafa. He completely misjudged the new pope, who was absolutely determined to effect a thorough reform of Rome. Except for the appointment of his two worthless nephews, Paul IV stopped the lucrative patronage of the court, and not even his nephews could get the interdict lifted.

By September 1555 Franco had realized that nothing could be done for him in Rome at that time, and from then until 1558 he divided his time between Benevento, where his brother Vincenzo died in October 1556, and Naples, hoping for a break in the war between the pope and the Spanish, or a reprieve from the Roman court. In June 1558 Franco took the extremely risky step of going to Rome to plead his case in person; on July 15 he was discovered and imprisoned until February 1559. A valise containing many of his manuscripts, confiscated upon his arrest, was returned upon his release, empty. Franco was understandably bitter.[88]

In August 1559 the fearsome Paul IV died. The Romans joyously rioted as prisoners were freed and the enemies of the Carafa, or those persecuted by the dead pope, took their revenge. Franco's imprisonment won him the sympathy and friendship of those who were opponents of the Carafa. In this heady atmosphere, Franco moved in high circles. He was elected to the Accademia Romana, claimed Cardinal Morone as a friend, and became an associate of Cardinal Antonio Pallantieri, also a former prisoner of Paul IV. Pallantieri led the anti-Carafa group who instituted proceedings against the two Carafa nephews. Since these men had sowed the seeds of their own destruction by their malfeasance in office and the Duke of Palliano's grisly murder of his pregnant wife, the proceeding culminated in the execution of Giovanni and Carlo in March 1561. Franco contributed a harsh life of Paul IV and an obscene pasquinade against Cardinal Carlo Carafa.[89] In the years after the death of Paul

[87] *Priapea*, 1887 ed., lxxi, lxxiv–lxxviii; *Rime*, 1916 ed., nos. 84–85, pp. 40–41; nos. 297–98, pp. 145–46.

[88] These lost manuscripts may have included the Vaticanus Latinus 5642 letters, but from Franco's comments other works, for instance, his "Latin commentaries," disappeared as well and these have not been found.

[89] Vaticanus Latinus 2684, "Copia Pasquillorum et aliorum extractorum ex libro Nicolai Franchi." For an excerpt, see De Michele, "Nicolò Franco," 151–53.

IV, Franco achieved the highest position of his career. He had been a victim of injustice, and now was an honored poet with good connections with the dominant political faction in Rome. He spoke to princes and cardinals, perhaps waiting upon the pope. The son of a Benevento peasant had risen, like Aretino, to consort with princes.

But unlike the free poligrafi, a court letterato was always subject to the fortunes of his high patrons. In 1565 the easygoing Pius IV died, and his successor was the saintly, reform-minded monk, Michele Ghislieri, a friend of the Carafa. Pius V reopened the Carafa case, the tribunal restituted the confiscated goods of the Carafa, and then turned its attention to the anti-Carafa party. The pasquinades against the Carafa were examined, and it soon became apparent that Franco was their author. Indeed, he had not taken the trouble to hide his authorship.

The Inquisition arrested him and began a long interrogation on September 1, 1568. According to the testimony of one Girolamo Santacroce, a Neapolitan nobleman, Franco had written other works against prelates and princes in addition to the pasquinade against Paul IV, and had in July 1568 completed and hoped to publish a book named "Il duello" which contained many "very vituperative things against cardinals and signori." Moreover, he quoted Franco as saying that he wished to show the world the "vices and ribaldries of the Roman court," and the "knaveries of princes." According to Santacroce, Franco had also written sonnets against Paul IV, and in one of them Franco had supposedly demonstrated how "dogs had turned into friars because the friars had become dogs."[90]

At first Franco denied authorship of the pasquinade against Paul IV and the other works, and called Santacroce a lair. But he became entangled in a web of contradictions, and switched to an admission of authorship. On April 16, 1569, he admitted describing friars as dogs, but claimed that he referred to heretical friars like Bernardino Ochino and Giulio della Rovere. On May 7, he confessed to writing all the works which he had

[90] ". . . et che qua ha haveria lassato copia de detto libro, et che ne haveva fatto la tavola con la annotatione particularmente et oltra di questo esso ha composte infinite altre cose vittuperasissime contra cardinali et signori particulari . . . esso me ha detto che voleva chiarire al mondo li vitij et le ribaldarie della corte Romana . . . alla fine del sonetto è: pero li cani sono tornati frati perchè li frati sono tornati cani. . . ." Testimony of Santacroce, April 16, 1569, in Angelo Mercati, *I costituti di Niccolò Franco (1568-1570) dinanzi l'Inquisizione di Roma* (Vatican City, 1955), 117–18. On Santacroce, see p. 11. Mercati notes (p. 45) that one does not form a favorable impression of Santacroce from the transcript of the interrogation.

been accused of authoring, but maintained that he had not condemned the Papacy in general. He argued that there had been just cause for his anger; Paul IV had imprisoned him unjustly for eight months, and had stolen his manuscripts, thus reducing him to begging for a while.[91]

The tribunal did not accept all of Santacroce's accusations. He accused Franco of denying the existence of God, but the Inquisition was satisfied that Franco was neither an atheist nor a heretic. Toward the end of the interrogation, on September 5, 1569, and again on five occasions in February 1570, Franco was tortured for periods of thirty minutes to an hour. Torture revealed nothing new; by the end of February the inquisitors were satisfied that they had the truth.[92] Franco was condemned to death by hanging for his pasquinades against Paul IV. On March 10, 1570, after mass and communion, he was executed. His friends could do nothing for him; Pallantieri followed him to the gallows in June 1571.[93]

Franco thus met the fate predicted for him by Aretino years before—death on the gallows for his writings.[94] Scipione Ammirato (1531–1601), historian of Florence, reported sympathetically on the death of "the unhappy old man with the long beard," caustically remarking that in Rome "slight faults of language" were punished severely while "villanies of the hand" went unpunished.[95] Ironically, Franco who, unlike Lando

[91] *Ibid.*, 119, 127.

[92] *Ibid.*, 143–48, 198–226.

[93] Nicola Badaloni argues from an analysis of Franco's works and the interrogation of the Inquisition that he had a clearly articulated program for the social and religious reformation of society. He sees Franco at the center of a group of southern nobility who wished to create the conditions for a new social order through a revolution. According to Badaloni, Franco's decision to publish "Il duello" and a book against Paul IV meant that he had resolved to do public battle against Pius V. Badaloni reads too much into Franco's words. That Franco was acquainted with southern noblemen does not prove a revolutionary conspiracy, particularly when the noblemen did nothing revolutionary in deed or word. Moreover, Badaloni reads Franco's use of phrases of conventional Florentine platonic love philosophy in his *Bellezze* as evidence that Franco had a clearly formulated philosophy of nature which anticipated Giordano Bruno. The context of the *Bellezze* and the totality of Franco's writings do not support this view. Badaloni argues an extreme Marxist interpretation of Franco which is unsupported by the evidence. "Natura e società in Nicolò Franco," *Società*, XVI (1960), 735–77.

[94] "Ho visto, ho letto, & ho compreso il cioche il tuo calamo, & il tuo inchiostro mi notifica in carta. . . . Si sei destinato da i tuoi istessi peccati; alle forche. . . ." Letter of September 1550 in Aretino, *Lettere*, 1609 ed., V, 312.

[95] *Opuscoli del Sig. Scipione Ammirato . . .* (Florence, 1637), II, 249–50.

and Doni, never entertained heresy, was the only one to meet death at the hands of the Inquisition, and for a pasquinade.

The most attractive side of Franco's personality appeared in his loyalty to his brother and friends in Benevento. He kept himself informed on local events and wrote to them of his triumphs and disappointments. During his life Franco occasionally resembled a small-town boy who made mistakes in more sophisticated society. He achieved rapid success in Venice, and his early books enjoyed continued popularity, but the quarrel with Aretino cut short a publishing career which might have rivaled that of Lando or Doni. Away from Venice he was in the wrong environment. Reformed Rome in the 1560's could only be a setting of disaster for a critic accustomed to the free, abusive speech of the Venetian presses.

Anton Francesco Doni

Lando claimed nobility of his mother, and Franco tried to deny his humble origins, but Doni treated the question of his origins casually. A youthful admirer suggested that his poetic abilities might have come as an inheritance from Salvino Doni, a companion of Dante and founder of the Doni family of Florence. Anton Francesco Doni replied with a long disquisition upon the illustrious Salvino and the subsequent history of the Doni family. However, he added, there was another Doni family which was descended from a *fattore,* or retainer. This fattore had been employed by the Doni family for a long period of time and had taken the name of his noble employer. Consequently there were two Doni families in Florence, and Anton Francesco would not reveal to his correspondent whether he was descended from the nobility or a *plebeo.*[96]

The latter was the truth. Anton Francesco Doni was born on May 16, 1513, the son of Bernardo d'Antonio, scissors-maker of the district of San Lorenzo in Florence.[97] Little is known of Doni's childhood. He may have had youthful soldiering experience at the camp of Giovanni Bandini of

---

[96] *Medaglie del Doni,* 1550 Giolito ed., ff. 12–13.

[97] According to the custom for the lowly-born, the surname of the father was not listed in the baptismal record, although there was previous evidence that one Bernardo di Doni had married. Anton Francesco later confirmed that his father was Bernardo di Doni by a contract of 1546 in which he rented a house in Florence. The relevant documents from the Florence Archivio di Stato are summarized in Guido Biagi, intro. to *Doni Scritti* (Milano, [1916?]), 12.

the imperial forces in the siege of Florence in 1530, and the camp of Luigi Guicciardini, the vicar of Arezzo, in 1534 or 1535. At an undetermined age Doni entered the monastery of the Annunziata in Florence, taking the habit of the Servants of Mary. He was ordained under the name of Fra Valerio. In later life Doni wrote that he had enjoyed the patronage of Duke Alessandro de' Medici (1510–37) and Cardinal Ippolito de' Medici (1511–35). As the Annunziata was supported and patronized by the Medici, this would not be surprising.[98]

By 1538 Doni began to look beyond the monastery. In that year he wrote to Aretino from Rome a short laudatory letter, which, in its enthusiastic praise, indicated previous knowledge of Aretino's works.[99] In the early months of 1540 Doni and a fellow monk, sculptor Giovanni Angelo Montorsoli, left the monastery and Florence.[100] The pair journeyed to Genoa, and then split in October or November 1541. Montorsoli went to Naples, and Doni embraced with enthusiasm the life of the rootless letterato.

After short stays at Alessandria, Pavia, and Milan, Doni arrived in Piacenza by January 1543. At the request of his father, who wished that he enter a profession, he tried to read law, but soon gave it up because he found Baldus, Bartolus, and Justinian boring. He found letters more congenial, and became a member of the Accademia Ortolana of Piacenza, a typical sixteenth-century academy composed of letterati with ability and

---

[98] *La Zucca,* 1565 ed., 7, 19[v]; *Lettere,* 1544 ed., cxxix; *Lettere,* 1552 ed., 41–42, 45, 51, 56, 354–56; Luca Contile, *Il primo volume delle lettere . . .* (Venice, 1564), 97.

[99] Reprinted in Cesare Cantù, *La letteratura esposta alla gioventù per via d'esempj* (Milano, 1851), 230. It was first published in *Lettere scritte al signor Pietro Aretino . . .* (Venice, Marcolini, 1552).

[100] A persistent myth states that Doni left the monastery under a cloud. Alessandro Zilioli stated that Doni was forced to flee because he had "corrupted his brothers." "Vite de' poeti italiani," p. 119. This opinion has been echoed by Bongi, "Vita del Doni," in *I Marmi,* 1863 ed., I, xiii–xiv, the most careful study of Doni to date, and by many others. It cannot be sustained in the face of sixteenth-century evidence. Doni maintained good relations with Agostino Bonuccio, the General of the Servites, a leading churchman in the 1540's and a major figure in the first session of the Council of Trent, dedicating to him the 1547 edition of his *Lettere.* In the same year Doni wrote him a friendly letter offering two other works from his press. *Lettere,* 1547 ed., 2–2[v], 60. Michele Poccianti, Servite priest and bibliographer, indicated that Doni was a Servite and praised his writings, while omitting any reference to a scandal. *Catalogus scriptorum florentinorum omnis generis . . .* (Florence, 1589), 19–20.

NVNQVAM MELIVS TORQVEBIS IMPIOS,

QVAM VIRTVTI ET GLORIAE SERVIENDO.

Fig. 2. Anton Francesco Doni

noblemen with pretensions. None of the writers in the group produced masterpieces, but Bartolomeo Gottifredi, Lodovico Domenichi, Girolamo Parabosco, and Giuseppe Betussi were well-known in the sixteenth century. Ortensio Lando joined them in the summer of 1545. Several members of the noble families of Landi and Anguissola provided support and contributed literary efforts, including Ottavio, Giulio, and Agostino Landi, and Girolamo, Gabriello, and Teodosio Anguissola. Placing themselves under the protection of the god of the *orti* (gardens), they all took the names of various plants and vegetables. Doni became *il Semenza,* the seed.[101]

The Accademia preferred light literature and good times to dull erudition. In a letter of November 24, 1544, Doni described the contents of a shipment of books that had just arrived from Brescia. The titles included editions with new commentaries of Dante's *Commedia* and Pulci's *Morgante,* but the majority of the works were of a lighter nature, including Franco's *Petrarchista,* the Quattrocento satiric poet Burchiello and several works of light poetry or satire.[102] Wine, women, song, and anticlericalism supplemented literary activites at the enjoyable gatherings of the Accademia. Doni, a renegade priest, either brought to Piacenza or acquired there a mistress, Lena Gabbia, who lived with him for several years, bearing him at least two children. Father Vincenzo Dini, secretary to Cardinal Gasparo Gambara, Papal Legate to Lombardy then living in Piacenza, denounced the manner of life of the academicians. Doni, Betussi, and Domenichi subjected the luckless Dini to sharp invectives, but no steps were taken to halt the gay times of the Accademia.[103] While at Piacenza Doni first saw himself in print, with the publication of a small work under his name but containing sonnets of several other members of the Accademia Ortolana as well.[104]

Domenichi urged Doni to broaden his horizons and opportunities by going to Venice. Doni took this advice, and spent the first half of 1544 there, making initial contacts with the Venetian nobility and preparing his first two complete works for the printer. They were the first collection of his *Lettere* (1544) and a *Dialogo della Musica* (1544), both published by Girolamo Scotto, well known as a printer of music. The latter work

[101] *Lettere,* 1552 ed., 59–63, 5–6, 51–53.

[102] *Lettere,* 1545 ed., cxxxiii–cxxxiiii.

[103] *Lettere,* 1552 ed., 61–62, 167–69; *Lettere,* 1544 ed., iv; *Lettere,* 1545 ed., lxxii, xciii^v–xciiii.

[104] See Appendix III, Check-list of Doni Editions, no. 1.

reflected Doni's lifelong interest and activity in music.[105] He was a performing musician and was acquainted with several Venetian musicians, including Claudio Veggio and Jachus Buus, the organist of St. Mark's. The *Dialogo della Musica* contained a collection of madrigals for two to six voices, interspersed with witty dialogues and with music by such leading musicians as Adrian Willaert and Veggio. Doni claimed to have written part of the music, but in fact only composed the dialogues and some of the verse. On this visit to Venice, Doni attended a party with "wonderful music" at the home of Marchese Annibale Malvicino, and probably met Aretino for the first time.[106] In the following year he published an enlarged edition of his *Lettere* (Scotto, 1545).

He had achieved modest success in literature but still depended upon the temporary noble patronage of Piacenza and Venice, and anxiously sought a permanent position as a courtier to a northern Italian prelate or prince. In the years at Piacenza and Venice (1543-45) Doni offered his services to Duke Cosimo de' Medici, the young Cardinal Alessandro Farnese, Cardinal Uberto Gambara, Guido Ascanio Sforza, Cardinal of Santa Fiora, and Bishop Catelano Trivulzio of Piacenza, but without success. Then he turned his attention to lesser patrons, such as Giovanni Battista Asinelli of the noble Bolognese family, and the noted author, Bishop Paolo Giovio, but with the same lack of success. Giovio invited Doni to visit him at his famous home and museum on the shores of Lake Como but gave him no position.[107]

Despite the obsequious tone of his letters to prelates he found begging difficult. On the day following a letter to Duke Cosimo (March 28, 1543), Doni unburdened himself to Aretino. He conceded that he was the enemy of priests, friars, pedants, signori, and bastards (perhaps a reference to Cardinal Alessandro Farnese), and he realized that the prelates and princes hated him. But as one had to have money to be considered better than the beasts, he was trying to become a courtier. He dreamed nightly about getting his hands on the wealth of a rich prelate. In a parody of the

[105] On Doni as a musician, see Charles Burney, *A General History of Music from the Earliest Ages to the Present Period,* III (London, 1789), 158–59; Alfred Einstein, "Il 'Dialogo della musica' di Messer Anton Francesco Doni," *La Rassegna Musicale,* VII, no. 6 (nov.-dic. 1934), 405–14); Gianfrancesco Malipiero, *Antonfrancesco Doni musico* (Venice, 1946); *Antonfrancesco Doni Dialogo della Musica,* ed. G. Francesco Malipiero (Vienna, London, Milan, 1965).

[106] *Lettere,* 1552 ed., 219–20.

[107] Doni described Giovio's museum in minute detail in a letter of June 17, 1543, Como. *Lettere,* 1544 ed., xlv–xlviʳ.

obsequious letters in which he presented an "unworthy offering" to a prince, Doni was sending Aretino the first book of his *Lettere*. If the letters met with the approval of the Scourge of Princes, he was grateful—presumably for some tangible token of affection. But if the *Lettere* disappointed Aretino, he should present the book to the Venetian canals with other offal.[108]

The reason for Doni's lack of success in finding a patron stemmed from his irascible temper and his dislike for the signori, both of which were becoming known. In 1545 Doni, in reply to some now unknown slight, wrote a vindictive letter about Giulio Albicante, a minor literary figure. Albicante was inclined to reply in kind, but a mutual acquaintance, Luca Contile, dissuaded him, and the quarrel was patched up. In the course of his letters at the time, Contile evaluated Doni as a virtuoso of great ability, but with rabid and vengeful tendencies.[109]

Doni's need for a patron had become more acute because the good times of the Accademia Ortolana were at an end. Piacenza had been ceded to Pope Leo X and remained in the pope's domains, except for its occupation by Francis I from 1515 to 1521. In 1540 the cardinal legate, Giovanni Salviati, began to admit the lower classes into the government and to exclude the four great families, the Landi, Anguissola, Scotti, and Fontana. The political climate further deteriorated when Paul III created the dukedom of Parma and Piacenza for his son Pier Luigi Farnese (August 26, 1545). Pier Luigi reorganized the government and completed the exclusion of the nobility. The latter, led by Giovanni Anguissola and Agostino Landi (a member of the Accademia Ortolana) intrigued with Ferrante Gonzaga, imperial viceroy of Lombardy, to rid themselves of the Farnese.[110]

Politics split the Accademia Ortolana. Domenichi, Doni's closest confidant, inclined to the Farnese side and noticeably avoided Piacenza by remaining in Venice in 1545. Doni also was willing to sacrifice the friendship of the Landi and Anguissola if he could secure the patronage of such a prince as Pier Luigi Farnese. On May 8, 1544, Doni wrote a brilliant and vivacious letter, exhibiting wide literary knowledge, to Annibale Caro (1507–66), secretary to Pier Luigi. He enclosed an edition of his *Lettere*, with the obvious intention of reaping a reward, and when Pier

---

[108] *Lettere*, 1552 ed., 42–44. Other letters in which Doni discussed his desire to find a patron are in *Lettere*, 1552 ed., 68–70, 74–75, 172–74.

[109] Contile, *Il primo volume delle lettere*, 95–97^{v}.

[110] See Giovanni Drei, *I Farnese. Grandezza e decadenza di una dinastia italiana* (Rome, 1954), 26–80.

Luigi received his dukedom Doni eagerly expected preferment. On September 9, 1545, he wrote to Domenichi from Piacenza that he was on his way to Florence. But he would return in ten days to Piacenza, for Farnese had just arrived with Caro, his first secretary, and "I [will be], Christe Eleison, his second."[111]

Doni alienated the nobility of Piacenza without receiving Farnese patronage, and never returned there. In November 1545 Ottavio Landi addressed a sonnet to him which began "You, who betrayed every faithful service. . . ." Doni tried to pass off the whole matter by intimating that a love affair with a nun had caused an admittedly "necessary" and "sudden" departure. After a few hostile letters, he dropped all association with the Piacenza nobility.[112] The political dissension in Piacenza reached its climax in 1547 when the nobles, led by Agostino Landi and Giovanni Anguissola, assassinated Pier Luigi Farnese, and Spanish troops occupied the city.

Doni resolved to make his way in the world as a printer in Florence for Duke Cosimo, who had been searching for a politically reliable printer to break the monopoly of the Giunti. This old merchant family of republican sympathies was after 1537 the sole Florentine printing house, until Cosimo encouraged Doni to set up his press.[113] Doni, who had learned the mechanics of the printing trade in Piacenza and under Scotto in Venice, rented a house for himself and his equipment on March 26, 1546, and the first product of his press was a new edition of his own *Lettere*.[114] On February 24, 1546, he was elected secretary of the Medici-sponsored Accademia Fiorentina, which provided many of his clients. His printing shop prospered. He printed twelve books in 1546 and an additional eight in 1547, including works by Accademia members G. B. Gelli, Niccolò Martelli, Pierfrancesco Giambullari, and collections of Accademia lectures on Dante, Petrarch, and Boccaccio. He also printed the popular vernacular authors Luigi Pulci, Sperone Speroni, and Bartolomeo Gottifredi.[115]

[111] *Lettere*, 1552 ed., 233–39; *Lettere*, 1545 ed., cxxxvi^v–cxxxvii.

[112] *Lettere*, 1547 ed., 27^v–29.

[113] Ascarelli, *La tipografia cinquecentina italiana*, 133–37. Also see Doni's letter to Cosimo, "il dì S. Cosimo" [September 27], 1546, Florence, in Florence, Archivio di Stato, reprinted by Bongi, in *I Marmi*, 1863 ed., xxviii–xxx.

[114] His shop was located in the *popolo* of S. Pier Maggiore, "presso l'angolo di Via Nuova dicontro all'orto de' Caccini . . ." See Bongi, *Annali di Giolito*, I, 260, n. 2.

[115] For the complete list of books printed by Doni, see C. Ricottini Marsili-Libelli, *Anton Francesco Doni scrittore e stampatore* (Florence, 1960), 342–56.

Doni's prosperity enabled him to make a sightseeing trip to Rome, hire a manservant, and invite Domenichi to join him in Florence. During his trip to Rome in May and June 1547, he sent back long letters describing the palaces and paintings that he saw. He was particularly impressed by the paintings of Vasari.[116]

But modest financial success did not alter his explosive temper or vengeful nature. His letters showed the same blend of insult and satire against people whom he disliked. Moreover, in the course of living and working together, Domenichi and Doni quarreled. The reasons for the break in early 1548 are unknown, but possibly stemmed from a plagiarization by one of them, for they each included a nearly identical dialogue on the press in subsequent books.[117] Whatever the cause, Doni responded with extraordinary venom by denouncing Domenichi as a secret heretic to Cardinal Alessandro Farnese, the Imperial Viceroy Ferrante Gonzaga, and Duke Cosimo. He accused him of translating Calvin's *Nicomediana.* Domenichi was arrested, tried, and sentenced to ten years' imprisonment, although the sentence was commuted and he was completely exonerated, probably through the intervention of Renata of Ferrara.[118] Doni was not content with this revenge. For several years after 1548 his books contained thinly veiled insults against Domenichi, and in subsequent editions of his *Lettere* he included those to Domenichi but changed the addressee to "feigned friend."

In late 1547, Doni ceased to operate his printing shop. The last book from his press was dated September 9, 1547, and the last letter from Florence (March 3, 1548) was a bitter denunciation of Domenichi to the imperial viceroy. Cosimo called in a Flemish printer, Lorenzo Torrentino, to take over Doni's shop and to receive the ducal patronage. The manuscripts which Doni had in preparation were given to Torrentino, including one destined to become world-famous—Vasari's *Lives of the Artists,* printed in its first edition by Torrentino in 1550.[119]

[116] *Lettere,* 1547 ed., 64, 65–67.

[117] *I Marmi,* 1928 ed., I, 273–93; Lodovico Domenichi, *Dialoghi* (Venice, 1562), 367–99.

[118] See Bongi, in *I Marmi,* 1863 ed., xlii–liv, for the most complete account of the feud. See also Poggiali, *Storia letteraria di Piacenza,* I, 234–39, 246; and Goffredo Hoogewerff, "L'editore del Vasari: Lorenzo Torrentino," in *Studi Vasariani* (Florence, 1952), 96.

[119] In a letter of March 10, 1547, Florence, Doni listed the works he was preparing for the press. It included some, like the Vasari, that were eventually printed, as well as his own *Medaglie* and commentary on Burchiello, and some

With his printing materials and Lena Gabbia, Doni departed from his birthplace for the second and final time, and went to Venice. He cast his lot with the Venetian vernacular printers but started on a low rung, finding a job with the printer Aurelio Pincio as an editor in 1548. Doni's first task was the editing of Lando's translation of More's *Utopia,* to which he contributed an introductory letter. He then published as his own translation a slightly revised version of Seneca's *Epistole* published in 1494 by Sebastiano Manilio (see Appendix III, no. 10). From 1548 to 1550 Aretino also provided occasional work for Doni, procuring books and delivering messages outside Venice.[120] In 1550 he moved to Giolito's shop as an editor.

He advanced from editing and translating to composing original works for Giolito, probably at the latter's suggestion. These books were written in a sober, straightforward style, very different from his earlier satirical letters or his later major works. In 1549 Doni wrote a treatise on sculpture and painting, his *Disegno.* In it he added his voice to the Renaissance debate concerning the superiority of sculpture or painting, and the importance of nature and art. In the following year he wrote a historical work on the life of Caesar, *La Fortuna di Cesare.* With his *Libraria* (1550), Doni completed his literary apprenticeship under Giolito. The *Libraria* was a bibliography, the first in Italian and the second in European literature, of contemporary authors and past masters who wrote in Italian. In it, Doni offered tentative literary judgments.[121]

While Aretino entertained in an overflowing house on the Grand Canal near the Rialto bridge, Doni in 1550 was still a poor hack who could afford one tiny room, flea-ridden and stinking, above a fetid side canal. Yet Venice had its compensations. He could see Slavs, Greeks, Turks, Moors, Spaniards, Germans, and Italians of "diverse faces, various clothes, and strange customs" who floated or walked by. The endless variety of men and their ways fascinated him. He more than once expressed the wish to fly like an eagle from city to city to observe and

---

curious titles that were never published and are now unidentifiable. *Lettere,* 1547 ed., 61–62. On Torrentino, see Hoogewerff, "L'editore del Vasari: Lorenzo Torrentino," 93–104.

[120] Aretino, *Lettere,* 1609 ed., IV, 268ᵛ–69; V, 6.

[121] The first work of this type was the *Bibliotheca universalis* (1545) by Conrad Gesner, a German-Swiss writer and naturalist, who catalogued writers in Latin, Greek, and Hebrew. For the position of the *Libraria* in Italian literary histories, see Giovanni Getto, *Storia delle storie letterarie* (Milan, 1942), 19–23.

overhear the strange things that men were doing and saying. All the magnificent art of Venice was available to him in nearby churches. To a noble from Ferrara, Doni wrote that he preferred one room in Venice to a villa in Ferrara.[122]

In Venice Doni helped to found another literary group, the Accademia Pellegrina, or the "Wanderer Academy," in 1549.[123] According to Doni, it was founded with financial aid from the Venetian nobility in order to educate the sons of the nobility and to support virtuosi. Its first members included the letterati Doni, Francesco Coccio, Sansovino, Dolce, the philosopher Giason de Nores, and artist and writer Ercole Bentivoglio of Bologna. By 1552 the Accademia Pellegrina also included Jacopo Nardi, historian and republican exile from Florence; the painters Titian, Tintoretto, and Cecchino Salviati; Enea Vico da Parma, engraver and founder of modern numismatics; and other writers, including Bernardo Daniello, Giovanni Antonio Cibeschino called Domizio Gavardo, Ermolao Barbaro, and someone identified only as "Jacopo, author of the *Cosmografia*." The patrons included Domenico and Cipriano Morosini, and members of the Martinengo, Contarini, and Cornaro houses. The official printer of the group was Francesco Marcolini, and Doni was its secretary from 1553 to 1563.

Under the stimulation of the Accademia Pellegrina and with the aid of Marcolini's press, Doni embarked upon the most fruitful years of his literary life, from 1551 to 1553. Nine books, including his most important works, were written in these years. In June 1551 Marcolini printed Doni's *Seconda Libraria*. This work included lists of authors and books, but many of these were imaginary, and the comments were longer and seldom related to the work in question. Instead Doni offered the reader short stories and observations which mixed in glorious confusion mythology, witticisms, bits from ancient histories, novelle, and cynical comments on the contemporary world.

Doni's style differed from that of other poligrafi. Aretino's fame, for

[122] Letter of January 1, 1550, Venice, to Gieronimo Fava, in *Libraria*, 1st 1550 ed., 67–70.

[123] *Pellegrina* could also be translated "pilgrim," "vagrant," or "foreigner." Most of the information on the Accademia Pellegrina comes from Doni's writings. See *I Marmi*, 1928 ed., I, 68–69; Maylender, *Storia delle accademie d'Italia*, IV, 244–48.

Bernardo Macchietta in his introduction to the 1597 edition of *I Mondi* asserted that the Accademia Pellegrina was a figment of Doni's fertile imagination. This view cannot be sustained because of the number of letters written by Doni and others on behalf of the Accademia, and by the fact that it still existed in 1595, when it was suppressed by the civil authorities. Bongi, in *I Marmi*, 1863 ed., xxxv, n. 2.

example, deservedly rested on the vivacity and realism of his descriptions and the witty acuteness of his psychological observation. Doni was most effective when he wrote as if he were setting down without preconceived order ideas as they appeared in his mind. His books in the period 1551–53 gave the impression of ideas and stories overheard in the Piazza San Marco or in the gatherings of the Accademia Pellegrina, flowing in free association through his mind as he sat at a bench in Marcolini's shop, filling sheet after sheet to be set and printed immediately. This effect appealed to Doni; he advertised that he wrote what he heard, without plan or correction, and boasted of his speed and fecundity.

The next book in this period was *La Zucca*, printed by Marcolini in four parts in late 1551 and in 1552. Doni's "gourd" was a collection of moral tales, witticisms, aphorisms, and letters that totaled about 500 pages. The idea for the work was probably borrowed from the former friend Domenichi, who had compiled a collection of *facezie* in 1548, but the stories were typically Doni's.[124] His next venture was *La Moral Filosophia* (Marcolini, 1552), an Italian retelling of Oriental and Persian animal fables collected in Latin by John of Capua between 1263 and 1278.[125] After another large edition of his *Lettere* by Marcolini, he followed Franco and Lando in satirizing Petrarchism and love treatises of the sixteenth century in his *Pistolotti Amorosi* (Giolito, 1552). The genre of love philosophy had been initiated by Giovanni Pico della Mirandola, Marsilio Ficino, and Leone Ebreo; in the Cinquecento, Bembo's *Asolani*, Book IV of Castiglione's *Courtier*, Gottifredi's *Specchio d'amore*, and Betussi's *Raverta*, among others, maintained the tradition. The elaborate conceits and Petrarchan language of these love treatises were a natural target for satire, and one of Doni's acquaintances, Girolamo Parabosco, capitalized on the opportunity in 1545 for Giolito, with great success.[126] Doni attempted to emulate Parabosco, but with indifferent results. The *Pistolotti Amorosi*

---

[124] This was Domenichi's *Facetie, et Motti arguti di alcuni eccellentissimi ingegni* . . . (Florence, Torrentino, 1548). Other works in the tradition of the facezie were the *Liber facetiarum* of Poggio Bracciolini, Jacopo Pontano's *De sermone*, and the works attributed to Piovano Arlotto. On the history of the facezie, see Giovanni Fabris, preface to Lodovico Domenichi, *Facezie*, 1923 ed., vii–xxxii.

[125] On the history of these stories, see the introduction by Joseph Jacobs to *The earliest English version of the fables of Bidpai, "The morall philosophie of Doni" by Sir Thomas North* (London, 1888), a reprint of the 1570 English edition. Also see Biagi, *Doni Scritti*, 30–33.

[126] *Lettere Amorose di M. Girolamo Parabosco* . . . (Venice, 1545). They were reprinted with additional material perhaps a dozen times until the early seventeenth century. Bongi, *Annali di Giolito*, I, 102–3.

consisted of letters exchanged by various fictitious and ridiculous lovers. Doni avoided love philosophy for earthy situations in which the beloved spurned the suitor for money, or the lover compared his beloved's eyes to coals rather than heavenly stars. But the amusing letters were infrequent and the book as a whole was a bore.

In 1552 and 1553 Doni wrote his two best known and artistically most successful books—*I Marmi* and *I Mondi*, the latter with its accompanying *Inferni*, all printed by Marcolini. In the introduction to *I Marmi* Doni wrote that in order to jog his memory when he began to write, he imagined himself to be a "big, ugly bird" that could fly high in the air above all cities to see with a shrewd look everything that was done below. In the bat of an eye he could strip the covers from the deeds of men and see their diverse habits. From city to city he wandered, hearing and seeing various actions and discussions. In his imagination he settled in Florence on the top of the marble steps of the cathedral, where a fresh wind always blew and the Florentines came in the evening to chat and argue.[127] Hence the title of the collection of dialogues: *I Marmi*, or "things overheard on the marble steps." The occasional return to the theme of things overheard on the cathedral steps and Doni's consistent use of the Florentine idiom and characters unified the 500 pages of dialogues on a great variety of topics.

I Mondi purported to be a discussion of seven different worlds, described as the "little world," the "large world," the "greatest world," the "mixed world," the "imaginary world," the "laughable world," and the "world of the *pazzi*." The frontispiece of the book illustrated this theme, having seven circular spheres piled upon each other with three mythological characters grouped around the heaped worlds. The structure of the work was admirably suited for the sweep of Doni's imagination. As he progressed through the various worlds, the scene shifted wildly from earth to the skies, then to a utopian world, and back again to earth. Members of the Accademia Pellegrina under pseudonyms (for instance, "Svegliato" or "the awakened one," "Savio," "Pazzo,"), mythological characters, demons, angels, and ordinary men delivered improvisatory harangues, and engaged in ruminative dialogues, including the discussion of a utopian new world. Doni wrote *I Mondi* in twenty days.[128] It had dull and obscure passages, but the very haste with which it was written

<hr />

[127] *I Marmi*, 1928 ed., I, 5–6.

[128] See the introductory letter, "Il Bizzarro . . . a gli Ombrosi," in *I Mondi*, 1552 ed., sig. aiii⟨v⟩.

gave it a continuity of mood. Social and moral criticism and ridicule of man's learning and accomplishments dominated the work. Doni's free, seemingly formless imagination effectively conveyed the uncertainty of everything.

Its companion piece, the *Inferni,* was a Dantesque journey through hell. Doni's *Inferni* contained seven circles of hell, each filled with a group of sinners. Again various members of the Accademia Pellegrina traveled through hell, asking questions and receiving replies from a galaxy of figures, including Vergil, Matteo Palmieri, Momus, and the gods of the underworld. Doni meted out imaginative punishments worthy of his great model. Legists were condemned to eating their own dull writings. Theologians were skinned alive to strip them of their heresies, and soldiers were lacerated by fiery arrows. In the original edition the illustrations of the torments, repeated from a 1544 Marcolini printing of Dante's *Commedia,* contributed to its effectiveness.

Doni's last two works of 1553 were less important. *L'Asinesca Gloria,* published by Marcolini, was part of a genre of moral criticism which compared the strong, humble, patient, peaceable, long-suffering, useful, and even musical ass to sinful, weak, and warlike man. Giulio Camillo (1479–1550), the Spaniard Pedro Mexía (c.1500–52), Adriano Banchieri (1567–1634), and Cesare Rao (c.1532–c.1587) also write in this tradition. Doni's work differed from the others by the sharp social criticism which he added to the traditional moral criticism. Doni's commentary on the poetry of Burchiello (Marcolini, 1553) completed the burst of creativity between 1551 and 1553. Burchiello (1404–49), a Florentine barber banished by the Medici, lived in Siena in poverty and in prison where he wrote bizarre and obscure poetry, rich in allusions and difficult to fathom, but enjoying a measure of popularity in the Cinquecento. Doni's commentary added little to the understanding of this poetry. Occasionally he was helpful, as when he pointed out that certain poems were directed at dishonest signori or at the judges who sentenced Burchiello, but the major part of his commentary consisted of his own literary opinions.

With the success of his books, Doni enjoyed worldly prosperity. He had moved by 1552 from his single room into a villa of his own, with a collection of books and musical instruments. He possessed enough money to contemplate purchasing a farm, and moved in the artistic circles of Venice.[129] In the first edition of the *Rime del Burchiello,* dedicated to

---

[129] *I Marmi,* 1928 ed., I, 199; *Lettere,* 1552 ed., 313.

Tintoretto, Doni publicly thanked the artist for the portrait of himself
(now lost) which the artist had done.[130] Doni was a frequent guest of the
Morosini family at their estate in Noale where he enjoyed feasting and
music-making. Although he missed no opportunity to dedicate each part
of every book to a different patron, he no longer begged for a courtier's
position. With the birth in 1549 of a son, Silvio, upon whom he doted, and
a second son in May or June 1554, he enjoyed domestic happiness.[131]

From the height of his literary powers and worldly success in 1553,
Doni's fortunes plummeted in the following two years. In June 1554 he
was unable to write because he was ill with a fever,[132] and in 1555 he left
Venice in circumstances not completely understood. At an indefinite date
during 1555 he became involved in an altercation with an unidentified
Florentine priest who was conducting a school at Noale. He tried to
borrow money from the priest, was refused, and the notorious Doni
temper erupted. The priest threatened to provoke trouble for him. With
the advent of the reign of Paul IV, ecclesiastical discipline had tightened
and Doni, a renegade priest living in concubinage, probably felt himself
vulnerable. He decided to move to Urbino, and wrote to Aretino asking
for a letter of recommendation to the Duke of Urbino.[133] Aretino refused
the request, thus provoking one of the most colorful literary quarrels of
the century.

Doni's activities in 1556 are unknown, but his words were on the lips
of all Italy. On March 1, 1556, he published a denunciation of Aretino, the
Teremoto (lacking printer and place), subtitled "with the ruin of a great
colossus, bestial Anti-Christ of our age." The book was probably the finest
example of defamatory writing in the sixteenth century, for Doni hurled
every imaginable insult against Aretino in language worthy of the
Scourge of Princes himself. Aretino fought back, but Doni also could
effortlessly fill page after page with slanders. In the *Teremoto* he predicted that Aretino would die in the year 1556, and Aretino obligingly
expired in October of that year,[134] thus ceding the battle of the titans of
the insult to Doni.

[130] Letter of March 5, 1553, Venice, in *Rime del Burchiello,* 1553 ed., 3–6.

[131] *Lettere,* 1552 ed., 201; *Pistolotti Amorosi,* 1554 ed., 108; for Doni's letters
from Noale, see *Lettere,* 1552 ed., 319–20, 331–33, 310–13, 351.

[132] *Pistolotti Amorosi,* 1554 ed., 109–10.

[133] The information about Doni and his quarrel at Noale comes from a letter by
a printer, Giovanni de' Rossi, to Lodovico Domenichi at Florence, dated December
14, 1555, Venice, and reprinted in Bongi, *Annali di Giolito,* II, 40–41.

[134] "Là vedrai come io ho realmente detto, che in questo anno de LVI tu
morirai; perchè l'apparitione che fu della stella ai magi nella nascita del Signore, si

But Doni had to find a refuge. On his behalf, the president of the Accademia Pellegrina wrote two letters to the Este Duke of Ferrara in January 1557.[135] The letters must have borne fruit, for the only evidence of Doni's whereabouts in 1557 comes from a letter dated March 17, 1557, from Ferrara.[136] In the following year, he and a bookseller from Venice planned to open a printing press in Ancona. The General Council of Ancona approved the request on February 17, 1558, but the new venture never materialized, probably because of Paul IV's order of August 3, 1558, that all vagrant friars were to return to their monasteries.[137] Giovanni Montorsoli, the Servite sculptor with whom Doni had left the Annunziata in 1543, returned to the monastery, but Doni fled the papal territory of Ancona for an unknown destination. From the middle of 1558 until August 1562 he published nothing, and there is no trace of his activities.

He continued to write, although the literary efforts of his last years did not approach the level of the years 1551–53. In or about 1559 he wrote a comedy, Lo Stufaiolo, not printed until 1861.[138] It was fairly engaging and witty, but did not depart from the sixteenth-century stereotype, with the usual love triangles, an old man who was the butt of humor, irreverent servants, and an involved plot. In 1562 Giolito published three new works by Doni, two of them hack work, and the third a venture into cabalist numerology (an expansion of a section of I Marmi written ten years earlier) in order to prove that Luther was the great beast of the Apocalypse (see Appendix III, nos. 37, 38, 39). Something of the old critical and moralistic Doni spoke in Le Pitture (Padua, 1564), a series of allegorical word pictures representing love, fortune, time, chastity, and other subjects. Other literary efforts in these years were of little worth.[139]

---

tenne per gran segno, & hora per piccolo tengo io la cometa di questo anno, venuta per conto tuo per esser tu contrario a Christo. Ella è apparita innanzi alla tua morte, si come dopo la nascita appari quella divina." Il terremoto, 1861 ed., 15–16.

[135] See Luigi Suttina, "Anton Francesco Doni e il Duca di Ferrara," GSLI, 99 (1932), 276–78.

[136] Pistolotti Amorosi, 1558 ed., 2–3.

[137] Doni's letter of request to the Council is in Bongi, Annali di Giolito, II, 43.

[138] Lo Stufaiolo commedia in prosa di Antonfrancesco Doni (Lucca, 1861). The work was addressed to Jacopo Piccolomini at Montemarciano in 1559. An autograph copy with Doni's own decorative artwork exists in Florence, Biblioteca Riccardiana, Ms. 1184.

[139] See Appendix III, no. 45. The "Discorsi del Doni" (undated) is in Florence, Biblioteca Nazionale Centrale, Fondo Landau Finaly, no. 257. As its subtitle ("I Piacevoli Humori del Doni") indicates, it is a collection of jokes. A similar collection of jokes based on a ms. dated 1550 in the Museo Correr, Venice, has been published as Humori di Messer Anton Francesco Doni Fiorentino, 1550 (Venice, 1860). An

By 1567 Doni had retired to Monselice, a small town about thirty miles southwest of Venice, where he lived in a semi-seclusion interrupted only by trips to Venice to oversee new editions of his books and to visit friends. With his son Silvio, he lived in a house or castle at the summit of the high hill which overlooks the town. Doni, who was interested in agriculture, worked with his hands by day and pursued his studies at night, although he did not indicate the nature of his study. He continued to receive visitors and correspondence.[140]

Some sixteenth- and seventeenth-century sources report that Doni acted strangely in his last years at Monselice, playing the lute and dancing "like a little boy" by day, and wandering about in his nightshirt singing verses by night.[141] However, his last writings showed no signs of mental deterioration nor change of attitude. In 1567 he wrote a long poem, *La Lumiera,* which lamented man's miserable fate and his failings. Doni castigated the rich and identified wealth with moral evils. The wheel of fortune determined man's destiny and his unhappiness; all of man's goods and efforts were unavailing. The poem recommended that man throw himself solely upon God's mercy, but he echoed a solution of form rather than belief. The last two lines summarized Doni's view of his life:

> And cry: "At the end life is a sorrow,
> A fatal use, a living loss."[142]

---

undated autograph ms. entitled "Ornamento della Lingua Toscana" is in Florence, Biblioteca Nazionale Centrale, Fondo Nuovi Acquisti, no. 268. This is a collection of political and moral sayings. It was published in 1606 as *La Sibilla del Doni,* in Recanati by Antonio Braida, and again in 1880. Doni also wrote "Una nuova opinione del Doni circa all'imprese amorose militari," in Florence, Biblioteca Nazionale Centrale, Fondo Nuovi Acquisti, no. 267. This was published in Venice, 1858, from another ms. copy in the Museo Correr.

An autograph ms. of Doni, "Florentinorum scriptorum nomina," from Fiesole, Biblioteca del Seminario Vescovile, was lost during World War II. See Paul Oskar Kristeller, *Iter Italicum,* II, *Italy, Orvieto to Volterra, Vatican City* (London, Leiden), 503. The lost ms. may have been a book on Florence that Doni announced that he was going to write. See Mario Pepe, "Di alcune lettere di Anton Francesco Doni e di una sua opera perduta," *Accademie e biblioteche d'Italia,* XXXIV (1966), 136–40.

[140] *I Mondi & Inferni,* 1575 ed., 430; *La Moral Filosophia,* 1567 ed., ff. 2–3.

[141] Zilioli, "Vite de' poeti italiani," 119; Ieronimo Gioannini, "Annatomia della Zucca," in *La Zucca,* 1st 1607 ed., ff. 2–3.

[142] "Et grida: – Alfin la vita è un' affanno, un utile mortale, un vivo danno." Fredi Chiappelli, "Un poema inedito e sconosciuto di Anton Francesco Doni," *La Rassegna della letteratura italiana,* 58, ser. VII, no. 4 (oct.–dic. 1954), 567.

Nothing is known of what Doni did or wrote from August 1568 until late July 1574, when Henry III of France arrived in Venice. Doni journeyed there to present to him his poem on the battle of Lepanto, but whether the king rewarded him mattered little, for in September of that year he died, probably in Venice.[143]

Although Tintoretto's portrait of Doni has disappeared, Enea Vico da Parma cut an engraving of him which was often reprinted in Doni's later works. He is drawn with a large head, dark hair, and a long, unruly beard. His eyes are opened wide and stare fixedly at the viewer. The forehead is high, the nose large but straight. The expression on the portrait is brooding but hints at his mercurial temper and vengeful personality. Contemporaries knew him as lively and bizarre, although irascible and unhappy.

Other Poligrafi

Into the large category of poligrafi, scholars have placed a number of Cinquecento authors including Franco, Doni, Lando, Lodovico Domenichi, Ludovico Dolce, and Francesco Sansovino. Less often Girolamo Ruscelli, Tommaso Porcacchi, Orazio Toscanella, and Dionigi Atanagi are included. The word "poligrafo" is useful as a general designation for authors who wrote vernacular literature in close association with the Venetian presses.[144] But the term as normally understood fails to account for the significant differences among the poligrafi, and in particular, the differences between Lando, Franco, and Doni, and other poligrafi.

In the first place, Doni, Franco, and Lando produced more original works, as opposed to editions, translations, and compilations, than did

---

[143] "Dal Canto Quarto Della Guerra di Cipro Poemetto di A. F. Doni," in *Nozze Vianello-Maluta* (Padua, 1889). Gioannini, in *La Zucca,* 1st 1607 ed., f. 5, and Guilio Negri, *Istoria degli scrittori fiorentini* . . . (Ferrara, 1722), 57, state that Doni died in Monselice. Zilioli, "Vita de' poeti italiani," 119; Poccianti, *Catalogus scriptorum florentinorum,* 19, and Girolamo Ghilini, *Teatro d'huomini letterati* (Venice, 1647), 19–20, who are more accurate with regard to the facts of Doni's life, state that he died in Venice.

[144] In this study, poligrafi will be used in this sense (but without pejorative connotations) to include Aretino, Franco, Doni, Lando, Domenichi, Dolce, Sansovino, and Ruscelli.

Domenichi, Dolce, and Sansovino.[145] Using the criterion of original works to differentiate between poligrafi may, at first glance, seem implausible, for on examination one soon discovers books presented as original to be unacknowledged translations and compilations. Yet despite widespread plagiarization and the accepted practice of pillaging the ancients for materials,[146] Cinquecento authors had high regard for originality. Doni made the point that there were four kinds of authors of descending worth. In the highest place were those who wrote original works, second were the translators, third were the commentators who clarified the works of the learned, and finally there were the compilers and editors—those who, in Doni's words, put together mosaics of quotations, patchworks of this and that.[147] Doni reserved his highest praise for the first group; he moderated his approval through the next two categories, while recognizing their limited usefulness, and heaped scorn on those in the last category.

Nearly every poligrafo, under pressure of economic necessity, produced books in all four categories. But Franco, Lando, and Doni could justly claim that a higher percentage of their literary output was original than could other poligrafi. Moreover, a poligrafo tended to specialize in one of the four categories named by Doni, or in one subject. Doni, Franco, and Lando specialized in imaginative prose literature directed to

[145] Since Dolce, Domenichi, and Sansovino are most often mentioned as poligrafi of exactly the same kind as Franco, Doni, and Lando, it is useful to make a comparison with them.

[146] The poligrafi treated the classics of ancient Greece, Rome, and the Middle Ages as a common storehouse from which to borrow concepts, sentences, and sometimes long passages. These sources were used as building materials, and Cinquecento authors seldom felt it necessary to cite their sources. Their originality consisted in the selection of materials and the way in which they trimmed, altered, or otherwise used this material for their own purposes. One can at times identify the borrowed elements in the discourses of Franco, Lando, and Doni, but this did not necessarily detract from their originality. Bonora, in *Storia della letteratura italiana,* ed. Cecchi and Sapegno, IV 443, states that a study of Doni's sources is the proper way to understand his mind. While such a study would be interesting, it would not, I think, fulfill Bonora's expectations, but would mainly establish Doni's great eclecticism in his use of sources, and that he tended to mix his borrowings in such an individualistic fashion as to make the result wholly original. A study of the sources of Franco and Lando would yield a similar result.

[147] ". . . cioè, de' rappezzatori, de' maestri di tarsie, che mettono i pezzi insieme di questo e di quello, e fanno i libri." *Nuova Opinione sopra le Imprese Amorose e Militari* (Venice, 1858), 46–47.

a broad audience. Doni wrote seventeen books and published a large collection of letters which were not translations, commentaries on the works of others, or compilations of any sort. Lando published fourteen original works. Franco, whose publishing career was prematurely shortened, left eight original works, and over a thousand manuscript pages of letters; moreover, he lost an undetermined number of manuscripts to the Holy Office.

By contrast, Domenichi's bibliography includes five original works and one disputed, thirty-five translations, and sixteen editions of the works of others.[148] Ludovico Dolce produced forty-five translations, twenty-eight editions and commentaries on the works of others, and five original prose works exclusive of drama. He also wrote a number of comedies and tragedies in prose and verse but, as Toffanin exclaims, "where does the original author begin and the translator end? Not even he [Dolce] knew!" For his dramas Dolce translated, paraphrased, or borrowed the argument from his Latin and Greek sources.[149] A contemporary correctly remarked that the art of translation in the Cinquecento was focused in Domenichi and Dolce.[150] Sansovino made fifteen translations, forty-five collections and editions, and wrote eleven original works. However, his special interest was history, not imaginative literature, and

---

[148] The original works of Domenichi were the *Nobiltà delle donne, Dialoghi, La Donna di corte, Le rime,* and the unpublished ms. of the "Storia della guerra di Siena." For Domenichi's bibliography, see Poggiali, *Memorie per la Storia letteraria di Piacenza,* I, 253–90. Poggiali also lists as original works the *Historia varia, Facezie, Le due cortigiane,* and *La Progne.* The *Historia varia* is a collection of historical sketches and anecdotes culled from many ancient and modern historians. The *Facezie,* Domenichi's best known and most reprinted work, is also a collection from many sources. See Giovanni Fabris, preface to the *Facezie,* 1923 ed., vii–xxxii. *Le due cortigiane* is, in Poggiali's words, almost a translation of the *Bacchides* of Plautus. The originality of *La Progne: Tragedia* (in verse) is disputed. See Poggiali, 256.

[149] The original works of Dolce were the *Dialogo della pittura, Osservazioni nella volgar lingua, Vita di Carlo V, Vita di Ferdinando I,* and *Imprese.* His *Giornale delle historie del mondo* is an historical compilation much like the *Historia varia* of Domenichi. For the bibliography of Dolce, see Emmanuele A. Cicogna, "Memoria intorno la vita e gli scritti di Messer Lodovico Dolce letterato veneziano del secolo xvi," in *Memorie dell'I. R. Istituto Veneto di scienze, lettere e arti,* X (1862), 114–72, although Cicogna does not note all the plagiarisms and translations. Also see A. Salza, *Delle commedie di Lodovico Dolce* (Melfi, 1899). Toffanin's remark is in *Il Cinquecento,* 546.

[150] Luigi Groto writing c. 1564 as cited in Cicogna, "Dolce," 95.

his expressed reason for writing was to be of use to men. Hence, of his original works, six are historical works and the remaining five are practical guides, e.g., on how to be a secretary or a lawyer.[151]

This analysis could be extended to other poligrafi with similar results. Girolamo Ruscelli's *corpus* consisted of annotations and commentaries on vernacular classics, handbooks of orthography, vocabularies, and much editing. Authors such as Tommaso Porcacchi, Pietro Lauro, and Orazio Toscanella were primarily translators and editors.[152]

There are important social differences between Doni, Franco, and Lando, and poligrafi such as Domenichi, Dolce, and Sansovino. The former group shared humble origins, while Dolce, Sansovino, and Domenichi were born higher in the social scale and enjoyed the advantages of wealthier parents. Dolce was a member of a Venetian family which had been of patrician status before 1248, and regained this status in 1657. His father held high civic office in Venice, and although he died when Ludovico was two, the Loredano family, including Doge Leonardo Loredano who had appointed Dolce's father to office, and the Cornaro family supported Ludovico and paid for his studies at Padua. Later his daughter married into the patrician Martinengo family of Venice.[153]

Francesco Sansovino was not of high birth, but his father, Jacopo, was the most honored sculptor of Venice, a man who received extensive state patronage. Although Jacopo harbored some doubts concerning his paternity, he paid for Francesco's study of law in Padua, and was instrumental in arranging his appointment to the court of Julius III in 1550. Francesco inherited his father's estate in 1570, and later successfully brought suit to collect unpaid commissions owed to his father by the Venetian govern-

---

[151] Sansovino's original historical works included his *Cronologia del mondo, Ritratto delle più nobili et famose città di Italia, Origine et fatti delle famiglie illustri d'Italia, Istoria della Casa Orsina, Simolacro di Carlo Quinto,* and *Origine de Cavalieri. Gl'annali turcheschi* is for the most part a compilation of the works of others. The practical guides included *Venetia città nobilissima, Delle cose notabili in Venetia, Il segretario, L'avvocato,* and an unpublished ms. "Dialogo della pratica della ragione" which discussed law. On Sansovino's works, see Emmanuele A. Cicogna, *Delle iscrizioni veneziane,* IV (Venice, 1834), 40–87; Giovanni Sforza, "Francesco Sansovino e le sue opere storiche," *Memorie della R. Accademia delle Scienze di Torino,* ser. II, 47 (1897), 27–66; and Grendler, "Francesco Sansovino and Italian Popular History," *Studies in the Renaissance,* XVI (1969).

[152] Other prolific vernacular authors, like Claudio Tolomei, Annibale Caro, and Girolamo Muzio, to name three, were in the employ of princes and were not poligrafi.

[153] Cicogna, "Dolce," 93–111, 142.

ment. These enabled him to live more comfortably in later years, although he continued to write, translate, and edit.[154]

Lodovico Domenichi was the son of a *notaio* of Piacenza,[155] whose family also held the title and privileges of nobility as well as the tangible assets of some farms. Lodovico studied at Pavia and at Padua, where he received his degree in law, and was later inscribed in the Collegio de' Dottori e Giudici in Piacenza in 1539.[156]

A different way of life also set these two groups of writers apart from one another. Because they were unable to win consistent, long-term patronage from the nobility, Lando, Franco, and Doni were forced to become restless travellers, while Dolce, Sansovino, and Domenichi lived more sedentary existences and enjoyed more patronage from the great. Dolce spent most of his life in Venice, with only brief trips to other cities. He earned his living by teaching children, editing for the press of Giolito, and writing. Sansovino loved Venice and seldom left it after his youth and the failure of his career at the Papal court. He wrote, edited, and operated his own press in Venice, journeying away occasionally to gather historical materials and to collect his reward from the Orsini family, who commissioned him to write their history. Domenichi returned to Piacenza after his studies, but quarreled with his father over his intended legal career. He moved to Venice in 1543 and by March 1546 was in Florence, where he spent the rest of his life, with brief visits elsewhere, as a translator at the press of Lorenzo Torrentino, and in the employ of Cosimo I. In 1559 Cosimo I appointed him court historian at the salary of 200 scudi per year.[157] Domenichi repaid his employer with a history of the war with Siena, in which he justified Medici aggression.[158]

Thus the poligrafi were not all alike in their writing, origins, or lives. Franco, Lando, and Doni were more similar to each other than to other poligrafi. More original in mind, they were eager to publish their critical and pessimistic views. Their humble origins, uncertain financial situation, and impermanence made them quick to anger at the flaws in Italian society.

[154] Cicogna, *Delle iscrizioni veneziane*, IV, 31–40, 89–91; and Guido Pusinich, "Un poligrafo veneziano del Cinquecento," *Pagine istriane*, VIII (1910), 121–30, 145–51.

[155] On the growing social and legal status of the notai in north Italy who took on the coloration of the nobility, see Ventura, *Nobiltà e popolo*, 317–21.

[156] Poggiali, *Memorie per la storia letteraria di Piacenza*, I, 221–23.

[157] *Ibid.*, I, 242.

[158] This is the judgment of Roberto Cantagalli, *La guerra di Siena (1552–1559)* (Siena, 1962), xi, xiv.

◦ᴵ❘ *Chapter III* ❘❘◦ᴼ

LA MISERA ITALIA

THE political situation of Italy dur-
ing the lifetimes of Franco, Lando, and Doni was depressing. After the
brutal sack of Rome and the gradual extension of the power of the Emperor Charles V in the 1530's, Italian princes and the leaders of republican city-states had few choices. On those occasions when they permitted
themselves to believe in some political program or leader their hopes
proved vain. The Florentine republicans of 1527 could not withstand the
combined forces of the Medici and the emperor, and their dream came
to an end, as did Sienese independence about thirty years later. The
initiative of Paul III in the establishment of the duchy of Parma and
Piacenza failed, like Paul IV's daring but ill-advised campaign against
the Spanish in 1555. Venice, the most powerful state, stood on the side-
lines, fearful that any move might lead to a repetition of the disasters
of the war of the league of Cambrai. Brave uprisings against the political order had no success. Francesco Burlamacchi, either patriot or madman, organized a conspiracy to establish a free Tuscan republic but
lost his head in 1548.[1]

The only possibility for political leaders was accommodation to the
new order. At best, Italians could identify with the cause of the emperor.
A Christian war against the Turks could recover military self-respect,
while the emperor's cause was also that of Catholicism against the Protestants of the north.[2] Italian captains and soldiers fought bravely and well in

[1] See Francesco Ercole, *Da Carlo VIII a Carlo V: La crisi della libertà italiana*
(Florence, 1932), and Alessandro Visconti, *L'Italia nell'epoca della Controriforma
dal 1516 al 1713* (Milan, 1958), 37–54.

[2] For an example of this view, see the letters of Paolo Giovio. Giuseppe Guido
Ferrero, "Politica e vita morale del '500 nelle Lettere di Paolo Giovio," *Memorie
della R. Accademia delle Scienze di Torino,* ser. II, 70–71 (1940), pt. 2, 57–102.

the armies of Charles V and his rival, France. But accommodation also meant that the princes and signori of the city-states maneuvered, switched sides, sold and resold their loyalties in efforts to retain, at the pleasure of Charles or the French, their tiny states or few square miles of territory. It was this aspect of the political reality that provoked Aretino's remark that the times had made Italy into a whore.

From the early years of the foreign wars, thoughtful men had tried to understand what was happening to the peninsula and to discover some moral stance in the face of the disasters. The unparalleled disasters of the earlier sixteenth century forced men to re-examine their world, and the darkening political scene colored the discussion.[3] Doni, Franco, and Lando were latecomers to this discussion. They wrote when the Italian situation seemed most dismal, and this was reflected in their writing. But they also brought a fresh perspective to the discussion. They were not men from a secure social position or of normal political allegiance to a city or prince, and they did not evaluate the world in traditional terms, but described the Italian scene and assigned blame in their own way.

These unhappy times

In their animadversions upon *la misera Italia* or *questi infelici tempi,* the critics made use of several different literary devices to describe Italy.

In 1548 Lando employed the device of a non-European traveler reporting a visit to Italy to lament its decline from a happier time, blaming the bad conditions, for the most part, on the Spanish. One Messer Anonymo of the island of Utopia wished to see the fabled land of Italy, the "most beautiful, richest, and most civilized" part of the world. An old Utopian hermit, with an unexplained knowledge of Italy, warned him that the peninsula had changed: it once had been a "celestial paradise," but the "divided wishes of the unhappy Italians"[4] had caused them to change their customs and the face of Italy. Messer Anonymo decided to see for himself.[5]

---

[3] See the works of Mario Santoro, *Fortuna, ragione e prudenza,* and *Il concetto dell'uomo nella letteratura del Cinquecento* (Naples, 1967).

[4] This is probably an allusion to the political divisiveness which defeated any attempt to unite in a common military alliance against the foreign powers.

[5] *Commentario,* 1550 ed., 2–3ᵛ. An early, brief treatment of the story of the visit to Italy is in *Paradossi,* 1545 ed., 18ᵛ–19.

Indeed Messer Anonymo found Italy much changed. Landing in Sicily, he traveled the island for seventy-five days. He saw men and women sold into slavery like horses and oxen, and vividly described the tears and lamentations of women on the auction block. He noted the extreme poverty of the Sicilians. Journeying to the mainland, he marveled at beautiful Naples, but its people were slothful and pleasure-loving. Naples was an "ambitious city," where everyone insisted upon being greeted with the Spanish form of noble address, "Don" or "Doña." Whip in hand, haughty cavaliers galloped through the streets spreading havoc among the helpless pedestrians, while swarms of panderers plied their trade on street corners. Although warned by the old hermit not to be scandalized by what he would see in the Eternal City, Messer Anonymo still deemed Rome "monstrous." Prostitutes pervaded every social level of the city. Queenly concubines became rich while the infirm poor languished in misery. The condition of Rome was an insult against God.[6]

The tragic fate of Lando's native Milan further depressed Messer Anonymo. It had been a great city, rich and populous, before France, Spain, and Germany had sucked its blood. In earlier times Milan had armed a hundred thousand knights and called herself a second Rome. Now, no city in Europe was so flagellated, persecuted, and crushed. As a sign of Milan's degradation, Messer Anonymo gave a long list of atrocities and unnatural events that had occurred there.[7] But Milan was only a little worse than everywhere else. Messer Anonymo saw beggars in Apulia, Calabria, Lombardy, and Piedmont, and courtesans in all the major cities. All over Italy, but especially in the states of Naples, Lombardy, and the Papacy, an infinite number of petty tyrants devastated their subjects more severely than a plague. At the conclusion of his trip, Messer Anonymo decided that there were so many things in Italy that displeased him that he did not wish to live there.[8]

Although Messer Anonymo noted bad conditions all over Italy, he focused on areas under Spanish control: Sicily, Naples, and Milan. He did not exaggerate; conditions in Spanish-occupied Italy were as bad as or worse than Lando's description. In Milan contemporary sources relate that the people were starving in 1536 because they could not afford to buy bread. Even when the harvest was good, famine existed because much of the grain was sold outside Lombardy where prices were higher. In 1545

[6] *Commentario,* 1550 ed., 3ᵛ, 10ᵛ–11, 15; *Paradossi,* 1545 ed., 18ᵛ, 60ᵛ.

[7] *Commentario,* 1550 ed., 3, 25–27.

[8] *Cathaloghi,* 136; *Commentario,* 1550 ed., 4, 38ᵛ.

the viceroy protested to Charles V that the state bureaucrats and noble landowners took the grain and left the poor with little or nothing. With constant wars and the financial needs of the Spanish administration, taxes rose higher, but only the poor and the weak paid them. In 1543 the viceroy reported that in order to avoid paying taxes, peasants were leaving the land for the forests where they lived like beasts. Forced loans were extorted from the merchants and small shopkeepers. While the poor were squeezed beyond endurance, wealthy and influential nobles easily and inexpensively acquired large tracts of land through court influence, while Charles V himself was in the habit of granting large pensions to his favorites. The Spanish rule of Milan under Charles V was a sustained period of heavy taxation and insolent soldiery, misery and war, seldom relieved by peace and plenty.[9] In the kingdom of Naples and Sicily, the Italian barons after 1528 proved to be loyal soldiers in the armies of Charles V. In return the Spanish permitted the barons to rule their subjects as they willed, and supported them against peasant uprisings. The result was a general reduction of the lower classes to serfdom.[10]

The critics had no love for Charles V and the Spanish. France, though it had also contributed to the destruction of Italy, escaped condemnation, for it was Spain that dominated the peninsula and was, in their opinion, the oppressor. In 1548 Franco addressed a blunt, angry sonnet to Charles V. Does it please you, he wrote to Charles, that the Romans have been sacked, Florence unhorsed,[11] Naples stripped and put into the claws of the Catalans? Are you happy to see the Venetians broken by the league of Cambrai? He then mocked the emperor for his failure to halt Protestantism in Germany, calling the emperor's brother Ferdinand, "King of

[9] Federico Chabod, "L'epoca di Carlo V," in *Storia di Milano*, IX, 298, 366–67, 341, 343, 348–50.

[10] Benedetto Croce, *Storia del Regno di Napoli* (Bari, 1925), 95–133. Recently scholars have pointed out that the Spanish were not exclusively responsible for the improverishment of Naples and Milan. In Naples, it is possible that the indigenous financial and administrative disorder was worse than Spanish management. In Milan, although taxes were high, they did not always meet imperial expenses, and the Spanish were obliged to pour in money to meet military expenses and to keep the government afloat. This, of course, did not alleviate the lot of the people; whatever the division of responsibility between the Spanish and the Italian nobility, the situation of the people was bleak. For a review of the problem, see Lino Marini, *La Spagna in Italia nell'età di Carlo V* (Bologna, 1961).

[11] Franco probably referred to the overthrow of the Florentine Republic and the restoration of the Medici in 1530, accomplished with the aid of the imperial army.

the Lutherans." He concluded that Charles V was a common thief who put his hands on the purses of others and his snout into foreign mangers. Unfortunately, Franco lamented, those who tried to halt him came to unhappy ends.[12]

Lando also objected to Spanish domination of the hearts and minds of Italians. At one point he chided Lucrezia Gonzaga for being "too imperial," calling her half-seriously, a "great Caesarienne" (*la gran Cesariana*). The charge was accurate; the imperial sympathies of the Gonzaga were strong enough to induce some of Lucrezia's relatives to serve in Charles' armies. She rebuked Lando in a long letter and tried unsuccessfully to change his position. On another occasion Lando objected to the growing number of Spanish humanistic books available in Italy, and advised Italians to buy in their place the Greek and Latin originals upon which they were based.[13]

The anti-Spanish sentiments of Lando and Franco were normal and somewhat conventional although delivered colorfully and with feeling. Both had personal knowledge of areas under Spanish control; Lando lived in both Milan and Naples while Franco was a native of the south. Their objection to Spanish political domination, to the impoverishment of the territories under Spanish control, and to the cultural Hispanization of Italy was a healthy contrast to the obsequious praises of Charles V to be found elsewhere in Italy, in the letters of Aretino, among others.

> [12] "Non ti piace, Ser Carlo, che i Romani
> aggi posti in un sacco? e scavallata
> Fiorenza, e tutta Napoli spogliata
> e postala ne l'unghie a' Catalani?
>
> Non ti piace egli che a'Viniziani
> aggi la Lega rotta e mariuolata?
> e che ne l'Alemagna scristianata
> sia Ferdinando Re dei Luterani?"

Rime, 1916 ed., nos. 114 (quote), 117, 118; pp. 53–57.

[13] *Lettere della Lucretia Gonzaga,* 1552 ed., 193–95; *Sferza,* 30. A Spanish humanist work which was popular and widely available in Italy was Antonio de Guevara's *Relox de principes.* Luigi Firpo informs me that there were 54 editions of Guevara's works in Italy between 1542 and 1598. See also Hugues Vaganay, "Antonio de Guevara et son oeuvre dans la littérature italienne. Essai de bibliographie," *La Bibliofilia,* XVII (1916), 335–58. Another example is the dialogues of Pedro Mexía (c. 1500–52) which had at least five Italian editions between 1547 and 1564. On the cultural Hispanization of Italy in the Renaissance, see Benedetto Croce, *La Spagna nella vita italiana durante la rinascenza* (Bari, 1922), especially 151–74.

One might expect more anti-Spanish material in their books, but prudence dictated that men so given to travel as these should not give free rein to their pens. In addition, they were convinced that Italian princes were more culpable than the Spanish for Italian evils. Lando's Messer Anonymo described the misery in Spanish-controlled Italy but he also noted the "infinite number of petty tyrants" all over Italy who despoiled their subjects.

Tyranny of the petty princes

The critics laid the major blame for Italy's political woes on these "petty tyrants"; Italian princes and signori, and their system of government. By their tyranny, rapacity, and exploitation of their subjects before 1494, they had brought Italy to a point where Spanish domination was scarcely a worse alternative.

Franco wrote in 1539 that the independent city-states of the Quattrocento had created a climate of tyranny which prepared the way for Spanish domination. In Franco's metaphor, where the soul of tyranny was, so also lived the body of servitude. Under the guise of seigneurial liberty (la Libertà Signorile) violence, pillage, and discord immediately appeared and flourished, a clear augury of the future. The princes governed through the use of imprisonment, executions, and theft, means which produced servitude rather than liberty. Spain completed the dismal story by reducing Italy to submission with sack and sword.[14]

In ancient times, citizens had fought to liberate their *patria*, the critics noted. But contemporary princes and city-states were unworthy of such support. The honor and joy of serving his patria were urged upon Sannio, the protagonist of Franco's *Philena,* but Sannio rejected his (unnamed) patria. If "good disciplines" and "holy customs" reigned in them, today's

---

[14] "Certo, di qua si puo credere senza fallo, che dove è l'animo de la Tirannide, sia il corpo de la Servitu, perche nel domicilio de i pristini tiranni tuoi, sotto la spetie de la Liberta Signorile, tutta via apparivano segni di violenze, di rapine, di stupri, d'homicidi, di zizanie, e d'ogni altro appetito, nel qual lhuomo si puo far servo del libero e sciolto arbitrio de la monarchia del desidero. Onde fu chiaro augurio, che mentre essi tutto il giorno incatenavano l'universo, i gioghi, i ceppi, le prigioni, & i lacci adoprati in triomphare di questa natione, e di quella, non ferono tanto acquisto di Liberta breve, quanto di servitu eterna." *Pistole Vulgari,* 1539 ed., xciii.

cities would be the homes of "civil spirits" (*civili spiriti*). Sannio sorrow-fully concluded, however, that a herd of menial rabble ruled in his patria.[15] Modern princes were "new monsters born only to torment their miserable subjects." They studiously attended to their private pleasure rather than the public good.[16] There was no reason to rally behind Italian political leaders.

Franco's judgment that tyrannical princes of the Quattrocento pre-pared the way for foreign domination did not coincide with Guicciardini's idealized picture of Italy before 1494, but it was based on popular senti-ment and reality. To a certain extent, social and economic pressures drove the princes to tyranny. Rising prices necessitated higher taxes. Then, higher food prices, restrictions on commerce, and the protection of the privileges of the nobility made the subjects of the princes more aware of their lack of *libertà* in the political systems of the signorie. Alert to growing dissatisfaction and their shrinking popular base, princes reacted with stronger governmental centralization and police measures. Even Venice and Florence, the champions of republican libertà, used despotic methods to exploit their subject cities and lands.[17] In Milan, Ludovico Sforza had alienated his subjects through trade restrictions and higher taxes. In the south, the Aragonese rulers were hated for their growing absolutism and their expropriation of the land of their subjects. All these measures fanned the hatred of the popolo and justified their accusations of tyranny. When the French entered Italy, they were often hailed as liberators. The anonymous *Diario ferrarese dall'anno 1490 fino al 1502* reported that all Italy cried with one voice: "France, France!"[18] The *Diario ferrarese* may have overstated the non-aristocratic point of view but certainly many Italians had little love for their native rulers.

The critics could not follow or praise contemporary rulers because they believed that the practice of government by the signori had become a naked quest for personal gain through the consistent exploitation of the ruled, unrelieved by any concern for their rights and welfare. With this

---

[15] *Philena*, 424-30.

[16] *Ibid.*, 437-37ᵛ.

[17] See D. M. Bueno de Mesquita, "The Place of Despotism in Italian Politics," in *Europe in the Late Middle Ages*, J. R. Hale, J. R. L. Highfield, B. Smalley, eds. (London, 1965), 301-31.

[18] As quoted in Franco Catalano, "La crisi italiana alla fine del secolo xv," *Belfagor*, XI (1956), 409. See also his recent discussion, "Il problema dell'equilibrio e la crisi della libertà italiana," in *Nuove questioni di storia medioevale* (Milan, 1964), I, 366-73.

LA PHILENA
DI M. NICOLO
❧ FRANCO. ❧

HISTORIA AMOROSA VLTI,
MAMENTE COMPOSTA,

❧

AL SVO NOBIL SIGNORE
IL CONTE DI POPOLI,

❧

N.  F.

Difficile est Satyram non scribere.

Fig. 3. Title page of the first edition of Franco's *La Philena*

firm conviction, Lando, Franco, and Doni vented their anger against the signori with the wealth of colorful literary resources at their command.

Lando composed a paradox that it was not a bad thing if a prince should lose his state, for the consuming desire to rule caused princes to shame themselves by committing evil to prevent the loss of their princedoms. Elsewhere he opined that princes thought only of violating the purses and daughters of their subjects. Lando cited the example of an unnamed Lombard baron who had laughingly related to him how he had stolen the grain of a subject through a ruse. Lando knew princes in Naples who had the souls of wolves. Modern princes were instruments of Satan, he wrote in 1552. Why should princes expect to be above the human condition of other men? Why should we suffer these cruel and implacable monsters who were born only to devour the goods of the humblest peasant, he asked.[19] Instead, he lauded those groups and the isolated men of courage who fought to overthrow the political order. He praised the Neapolitans who had risen in 1547 in spontaneous opposition to the introduction of the Spanish Inquisition, and he approved the ill-fated Francesco Burlamacchi, the Luccan who attempted to revive a Tuscan republic free of the Medici, as one who loved his patria. Further, he praised Francesco Ferrucci, the condottiere who led the unsuccessful Florentine resistance to the imperial armies in 1530.[20]

Franco used two types of sonnets to condemn princes. In the first, he obscenely insulted dukes, counts, princes, and Charles V; in the second, he begged Christ to free the world of the vices of infamous princes. Lando, and especially Doni, in *L'Asinesca,* used the device of comparing signori unfavorably to the humble ass. Doni opined that "Messer," the customary title for signori, ought to be reserved for the more deserving beast. The ass was patient, humble, faithful, and virtuous—just the opposite of men in high places. Lando composed a mock funeral oration at the death of an ass in which he lauded the ass for keeping in mind the public good instead of private gain. He commended the ass for using his strong teeth on *sindaci,* the heads of city governmental administration. Switching to a pejorative meaning of ass, Lando preferred the four-legged beast to "two-legged asses," the signori.[21]

[19] *Paradossi,* 1545 ed., 24ᵛ–25ᵛ; *Sacra Scrittura,* 30.
[20] Lando, *Cathaloghi,* 281, 272.
[21] For an example of Franco's obscene sonnets, see *La Priapea,* 1887 ed., lxxviiᵛ; for an example of the lamentation to Christ sonnet, see *Rime,* 1916 ed., no. 65, p. 32. Lando, *Sermoni Funebri,* 1622 ed., 9–11.

The rulers that Lando, Franco, and Doni described obviously did not measure up to the traditional picture of the perfect prince. According to medieval and Renaissance theory, the prince should be a mirror to his people, the example of justice, charity, and paternal concern, a man educated according to Christian and classical precepts of duty and virtue. In the seat of government the prince should protect his people but also govern them with just laws, provide for them in times of want, punish the wicked and reward the good, and rule for the benefit of all, not for himself and thieving courtiers.[22]

In a brilliant vignette Doni contrasted the theory of the perfect prince with the current practice of the signori. In his story, Jove in the heavens embarked upon a scheme to reform the world. Little by little, as men died, he formed new bodies for every sort of person. Then he called all the souls in heaven and informed them that he wished to return them to earth in these new bodies in order to make over the world according to his instructions. To his chagrin, Jove discovered that the souls did not wish to return to earth under his conditions. Philosophers, physicians, scholars, historians, poets, and others turned down the opportunity. Finally the soul of a signore stepped forward and informed Jove that he would happily return to earth in his profession as prince.

Overjoyed, Jove began to instruct the signore. First he questioned him about his past life. Had he ever assassinated anyone on the word of an evil favorite? Had he ever caused famine in his princedom in such a way that others were blamed? Had he cheated the poor, or taken the money of his subjects by mixing leaves and branches into the grain that he sold them? Did he put people to death unjustly? To all these questions the prince silently admitted his guilt, and promised to do his duty in the future, as Jove should direct him, if his past would be forgiven. Jove began an instruction of Renaissance admonitions to the prince. He should turn a deaf ear to adulators, restrain his appetites, be concerned for the common good, reward those of talent and ability, refrain from injuring those who lived by their own sweat, and give to the poor. If he wished to be better fed, dressed, and mounted, more comfortable than the rest of mankind, and wished to sit on the highest tribunals, he should be accountable to his people. Hearing these instructions, at first the prince turned his head, silently demurring. Then he smiled, and finally broke

[22] See Lester K. Born, "Erasmus on Political Ethics: The 'Institutio Principis Christiani,'" *Political Science Quarterly*, 43 (1928), 520–43; and Alan H. Gilbert, *Machiavelli's Prince and Its Forerunners* (Durham, N.C., 1938).

into raucous laughter. Jove asked why he laughed, and the signore answered that he laughed because he would not be a prince if he did not do what he pleased. He could not do half of what Jove asked. Appalled, Jove ordered him away, and gave up his plan for reform.[23]

Doni's point was that precepts of good government did not alter the conduct of princes. To the signori, government was personal license unchecked by any concern for the ruled. Doni believed that there was a psychological incompatibility between absolute power and the restraints of justice and charity urged, but not forced, upon the ruler. If the prince was not amenable to good advice, or at least educable, there was no point to composing treatises on the education of princes or books of edifying maxims on how a good prince should rule.

Doni's attitude contrasted sharply with the common Renaissance idea that politics was susceptible to reason and the signori to education in good government. This can be seen by comparing his story with a treatise on government in a similar setting by Leon Battista Alberti.

In Alberti's *Momus* or *De principe proemium* (written between 1443 and 1450, printed in 1520), Momus was a god sent to earth to learn how men lived. He was particularly charged to investigate the government of men. He found much to criticize in the practices of princes—militarism, tyranny, deceit, and susceptibility to flattery. His report to Jove initiated a great debate in the heavens; should mankind be destroyed or could men be saved through reform? Finally the gods opted for reform. Upon commission by Jove, Momus prepared a treatise on government which expressed Alberti's ideas on political reform. Alberti's reforms were in the tradition of Quattrocento Florentine thought. Men who ruled should follow "reason and method," that is, they should eschew passion and govern in a balanced, just, and sensible way to ensure a prosperous state for all. The preferable form of government was an enlightened oligarchy.[24]

The differences between Alberti and Doni on the possibility of political reform resulted from the chasm separating the optimism about

---

[23] *I Mondi,* 1552 ed., 42–45.

[24] Leon Battista Alberti, *Momus o del principe,* ed. Giuseppe Martini (Bologna, 1942). On Alberti's political thought, see Valeria Benetti Brunelli, *Il rinnovamento della politica nel pensiero del secolo xv in Italia* (Turin, Milan, 1927). Although the works of Alberti and Doni were similar in conception, they were different in substance and detail. Possibly both found common inspiration and the figure of Momus in Lucian.

human nature of the Quattrocento Florentine humanists, and the pessimism of the critics. Moreover, Alberti reflected independent Italy of the Quattrocento, and Doni subjugated Italy of the Cinquecento; Alberti was from the upper strata of society, Doni was not. With their pessimistic view of political power and government, Doni, Franco, and Lando had no use for Renaissance political theory. If the process of rule was simply exploitation of the ruled, discussions of the form and conduct of government were valueless.

Other sixteenth-century Italians who mistrusted the personal government of princes argued that the rule of law within an impersonal structure of government would ensure the supremacy of justice in the Italian city-states. Mid-century political authors, especially Venetians, put their trust in abstract laws and their fair administration rather than in men. Posing the question whether good laws or good princes were more important, Girolamo Garimberto, relying on Aristotle, concluded that since laws were devoid of passion but princes were not, laws were more important. Gaspare Contarini exalted Venetian legal procedure because it was far more just than the justice of passionate men. For Giovanni Francesco Lottini law, made by universal consent, embodied broad ethical and political values. Hence law would punish by the will of all rather than the caprice of one. In the eyes of Garimberto, Contarini, and Lottini, law strengthened man's rationalism and his peaceful tendencies while avoiding man's passions and sins. Through the works of these theorists ran a faith that law and its impersonal administration according to abstract norms of justice could correct the abuses of men. They did not squarely face the problem of human participation in the formulation and implementation of law.[25]

The critics lacked this confidence in law and its impersonal administration through the organs of government. They noted that laws spoke sharply to the poor plebeian but were mute in the face of wealth. Lando rebuked councilors, judges, governors, and presidents who governed poor, miserable republics. They ruined cities and destroyed rival families in order to enrich their own relatives. The common people hated them

---

[25] The treatises are Girolamo Garimberto, *De regimenti publici de la città* (first ed., Venice, 1544); Gaspare Contarini, *De magistratibus et republica Venetorum libri quinque* (first ed., Paris, 1543); Giovanni Francesco Lottini, *Avvedimenti civili* (first ed., Florence, 1574). See Carlo Curcio, *Dal Rinascimento alla Controriforma: contributo alla storia del pensiero politico italiano da Guicciardini a Botero* (Rome, 1934), 61–68.

because they levied heavy exactions. Many sat in the "great chairs" (*gran cathedre*), but few ruled well or governed with just laws. The "highest councils" and the "government of republics" did not examine a case before them in terms of the rule of law, Franco charged. Rather they measured every law or ordinance according to their own profit. Governmental investigators were only too eager to punish with blind severity on false proof. To show his hatred for law and its so-called impersonal servants, Doni placed legal scholars, procurators, lawyers, notaries, and solicitors in hell, condemned to the appropriate torture of eating their own dull writings and police ordinances throughout eternity. In short, law and the organs of government were still in the hands of the signori who were uninterested in justice.[26]

There was a factual basis for the charges of the critics. In the cities of the Veneto, an area which Doni and Lando knew well, local government and criminal courts were in the hands of the local nobility. The merchant or artisan who sought redress for an injury sustained from a nobleman ran the risk of seeing his antagonist, or someone closely allied, presiding over the court. The aristocrat could commit even murder and after paying a small fine walk the streets again. The notai at the courts tended to be in league with the aristocrats.[27] Other authors demonstrated awareness of the inability of law to check the rich and powerful. Giovanni Della Casa, nobleman and papal diplomat, wrote, between 1544 and 1549, a *Trattato degli uffici comuni tra gli amici superiori e inferiori* that advised inferiors how to survive and get ahead in the world of the powerful, and exhorted the high to behave with moderation toward those below. At one point he

---

[26] "Sono i Giudici per la maggior parte precipitosi nell'essaminare, et strabocchevoli nel proferire la conceputa sententia. . . . Molti sagliono sopra de i Tribunali. Molti seggono sopra le gran cathedre, ma pochi, pochi sono quelli, che con giuste & sante leggi i popoli governano, & santamente reggono. . . .

. . . .

Sono cotai huomini in estremo odio a i popoli piu che certi essendo, che essi gli divorano con dure, & importune essattioni. . . . Questi sono quelli che ruinano le città, & distruggono le altrui case per rizzar le proprie. . . . Questi sono quelli che tengono in quiete, & tumultuose le misere republiche. Vi ho sommariamente toccato & Giudici, & Rettori: et Presidenti, non debbo dirvi anche si come da principio vi accennai degli Avvocati, et de i Giurisperiti?" Lando, *Vari Componimenti*, 1555 ed., 114–15. Doni, *Inferni*, 1553 ed., 78–80, 151, 156. Franco, *Philena*, 453–53ᵛ. Since the critics hated laws and their administrators, there are many references like the above throughout their books and letters.

[27] Ventura, *Nobiltà e popolo*, 440–54

urged the ruler to deal with the rich as if they too were subject to laws. Unlike the critics, Della Casa accepted without comment the fact that the law had little to say to the rich and powerful, but he hoped that rulers would exercise self-restraint.[28]

Law was also one of the chief devices by which the nobility of the Cinquecento consolidated their hold on government and excluded the popolo. A tangle of ordinances blocked the path to public office of the aspiring merchant or artisan. He could be legally excluded on the grounds of occupation, residence, ancestors, or taxation. The legal bureaucracy which administered these laws was the visible obstacle and the natural object of abuse.[29] Then, to the indigenous web of laws and restrictions, the legalistically inclined Spanish added a new layer of laws and ordinances in the areas that they ruled.[30] For the critics, laws and the organization of government were the means by which unjust men, especially the signori, used power for their own profit and the exploitation of the weak.

Yet another aspect of Renaissance political theory came in for criticism. Renaissance treatises on politics stressed the importance of honest and trustworthy courtiers while advising the prince to avoid avaricious men who pandered to his weaker nature. Manuals of advice to princes ascribed great influence to the courtier; a bad prince was often one who had followed the bad advice of his wicked courtiers whereas honest advisors could lead the prince to do good. At best the duty of rendering good advice to the prince ennobled the role of the courtier; Castiglione's idealized courtier took service with a prince in order to lead him to justice.[31]

The critics did not see the role of courtier in this way, because they believed no reform could be accomplished through princes. Since princes only favored courtiers as dissolute as themselves, advisors had degenerated into lying sycophants. Lando claimed that he had seen such lying cour-

[28] Santoro, *Il concetto dell'uomo nella letteratura del Cinquecento*, 222–23.

[29] Ventura, *Nobiltà e popolo*, 275–87.

[30] On one occasion Lando linked his criticism of law with anti-Spanish sentiments. He opined that states were better governed without imperial laws. Those nations who had not adopted Bartolus and Baldus (fourteenth-century jurists who symbolized for the critics the hated laws) were governed with better order and justice. His examples were Venice, England, and the Grisons of Switzerland, all lands free of Spanish or imperial control. *Paradossi*, 1545 ed., 13; *Sferza*, 23ᵛ. For the spread of Spanish laws in Italy, see Visconti, *L'Italia nell'epoca della Controriforma*, 72–73.

[31] *Book of the Courtier*, bk. IV.

tiers in Naples, Rome, France, and Germany; Franco called them prosti-tutes.[32] There was no justification for serving a prince except occasionally that of economic necessity.

Thus these men saw politics in Italy as the naked quest for personal aggrandisement unrelieved by any concern for the welfare and rights of the ruled. The signori of Italy had been tyrants before the invasions, and subsequently did not deserve loyalty. The bad prince was no exception, the product of wicked courtiers or a bad education, as some argued; rather, the whole process of government, not merely the individual, was unjust. The critics did not offer any alternative system of rule or programs of governmental reform, although Lando hinted at belief in popular participation. On one occasion he endorsed the practice of the island of Taprobane (Ceylon) where, he claimed, the most valorous and studious person was elected prince "by the will of the people," and could be deposed by the people as well.[33]

Franco, Lando, and Doni were not political or historical analysts like Machiavelli, Guicciardini, Donato Giannotti, Giovanni Botero, and oth-ers. The characteristic Renaissance response was to apply *ragione* to the conditions of politics. At best the theorist could bring the unruly world of politics under the control of reason and could suggest alternatives. At worst, he could understand what had happened and why, if only to attribute the disasters to a malignant Fortune. Lando, Franco, and Doni did not analyze; they denounced. Their political comments were basically protests against the practice of politics in their day.

The unjust social structure

In addition to describing Italian misery and the failure of the signori to provide political leadership, the critics condemned the social structure based upon the division between the rich signori and the poor popolo. They looked beyond the condemnation of individual princes and Italy's political collapse to question a society which permitted idle men to exploit

---

[32] Franco, *Pistole Vulgari*, 1539 ed., xxiv^v–xxv; Lando, *Vari Componimenti*, 1555 ed., 108–9; *Sferza*, 23^v; *Ragionamenti Familiari*, 64.

[33] "Ho io spesse volte detto, disiderare grandimenti si servasse una vecchia usanza dell'isola di Taprobane, ove il piu valoroso & piu studioso di commodi di soggetti Principe si eleggeva & il medemo per arbitrio del populo (se per aventura piegato havesse dal diritto camino) si deponeva." *Paradossi*, 1545 ed., 25.

those who toiled. The concentration of wealth in the hands of a few was a fundamental cause for the misery of the low and the depravity of the high. At the base of Cinquecento decadence, they believed, lay a maldistribution of wealth.

Doni vigorously protested the division of wealth in a dialogue in *I Mondi*. One speaker, Sbandito ("the banished one"), upheld a conventional position of satisfied acceptance of the *status quo,* while the second, Dubbioso ("the doubter"), vehemently challenged him. Sbandito placidly began with the comment that the world was justly divided; both rich and poor had difficulties and triumphs. Dubbioso reacted with an outburst:

> Not having anything and others possessing much does not seem a good division to me. Many go on horseback and I walk; this again is not right in my opinion. There is a great amount of money in the purses of others, and in my pocket not a sign of cash. How that fellow is decked out! He dresses richly and is nobly draped, and I cover my life with a shift. I want you to make up your mind, to want to make the scale balance.[34]

The debate became heated as Sbandito restated a moderate position that attempted to console the less affluent by placing wealth within a perspective of worries and responsibilities. All men were substantially equal. They were born equal in strength and size, and shared equivalent worries. A poor man who rented a house worried about his payments, but the landowner of several houses anxiously tried to defend his property. In any case he lost them at death. Heaven ordained that life was divided evenly. Sometimes a man consumed and at other times of his life he earned. If he acquired too many material goods, he would have to give them up at some point.

Dubbioso's answer was withering: "Many consume and do not earn." Reality did not coincide with Sbandito's balanced picture of life. With this, Sbandito began to retreat. He admitted that consumption and labor were not balanced. "And many earn more than they consume. . . . I wish

---

[34] "Non havendo cosa alcuna, & gli altri havendone molte non mi par diviso già ben questa, molti vanno a Cavallo, & io a piedi; questa non istà anchora a mio modo: i danari sono in gran quantità nelle borse d'altri & nella mia scarsella, non apparisce segno alcun di moneta: come s'acconcerà quest'altra? Colui veste atillato, riccamente & di nobil drappo, & io con una gabbanella mi cuopro la vita, alla risolutione ti voglio: a voler por la bilancia pari. . . ." *I Mondi,* 1552 ed., 19ᵛ. The entire dialogue is on 19ᵛ–23ᵛ.

I MONDI
DEL DONI,
LIBRO PRIMO.

ΗΟΡΙΑΤΑΡ ΕΣΤΙ ΤΩ ΘΕ

Η ΓΑΡ ΣΟΦΙΑ ΤΟΥ ΚΟΣΜΟΥ ΤΟΥΤΟ

IN VINEGIA
PER FRANCESCO MARCOLINI,
CON PRIVILEGIO MDLII.

Fig. 4. Title page of the first edition of Doni's *I Mondi*

that every person would eat the bread of his own sweat, and would be as useful to another man as the other is to him."[35]

After a little more resistance, Sbandito came around completely to the view of Dubbioso, and together they expostulated on the unwarranted privileges which the rich expected. The wealthy sought too much; they distorted life's natural balance. The rich indulged in gross desires and simultaneously expected exemption from taxes and immunity from theft. Fortunately their money could be pried from them by trickery and murder; otherwise they would be insufferable. The ideal alternative would be man's recognition that he could live with a little, just as nature was content with little. "If we would live according to nature we would never be poor."[36] But as the world now stood, many men worked in order to feed a single person, while the signori ate in mortal fear for their lives from those with less.

This protest against the maldistribution of wealth was one of the most original elements in the thought of the critics, and was most vividly expressed by Doni. At the bottom of his condemnation of the social division between the rich and the poor was the vision of a natural balance between men. If this balance were maintained, the poor would not be miserable, and the rich would render to the poor the respect due to every man. Rich and poor could then live in mutual peace and trust.

At the conclusion of the story in *I Mondi* in which Jove discovered that only a prince was willing to return to earth, Doni made the point of the necessity of a natural balance. Jove, dismayed at the unwillingness of the souls to return to earth, turned to Momus for an explanation. Momus pointed out to Jove that the unhappy souls had refused to return to earth because some suffered pain and poverty, while others enjoyed pleasure and wealth. Momus insisted that human life should be a natural balance. If Jove were really the ruler of the world, he ought to "keep the scales even" rather than give some men everything and others nothing.[37]

Doni continued his thought in *I Marmi* (also written in 1552). The division between rich and poor was a perversion of Nature's order. Men

---

[35] "Et molti guadagnano piu che non consumano, onde ci sono d'ogni sorte genti, s'egli stessi a me gli otiosi per la fede mia non istarebbono al mondo, perche vorrei che ogni persona mangiassi il pane del suo sudore: et facessi utile all'altro huomo, come quell'altro fa utile a lui." *I Mondi*, 1552 ed., 21.

[36] "Se noi vivessimo secondo la natura, non saremmo mai poveri." *I Mondi*, 1552 ed., 22.

[37] Doni, *I Mondi*, 1552 ed., 51–51ᵛ.

entered the world as workers, not as signori. The signori deserved to beg their bread by their own sweat like everyone else, but Fortune had placed gold in their hands. If the highborn would remember that, they would respect, not despise, the poor, because each had a role to play. The signori needed the lowly to cultivate their crops and to work in the trades. The rich man protested that he did not exploit his servants; he paid them for their labors. Doni rejected this explanation. Do you pay them from your own labor, he queried the signori? Of course not, but from the work of others, he replied to his own question. The earth produced gold which the poor mined and refined. But then by Fate, Fortune, and Destiny rather than by industry, intelligence, or virtue, it fell into the hands of the signori. In the end, Doni warned, gold would return to earth, its natural place.[38]

The maldistribution of wealth which gave to a few men a great deal of money was a major cause for the decadence and lack of leadership among Italy's signori. Doni contrasted the ancients, who performed feats of arms, wrote books, and built theatres, with the wealthy ones of the present, who lived only for the flesh. Again invoking the theme of "Italy is a whore," he termed contemporary signori pimps running from one prostitute to another. Because they possessed too much wealth, gross-bellied signori, bejeweled, oiled, and perfumed, performed womanly tasks instead of governing republics. Doni added a mocking disavowal, that his criticism was directed against those who led dissolute lives, and not against those who attended to public affairs. His disavowal served to underline his criticism.[39]

With their attacks on the social structure, the critics tore down part of the framework of ideas which supported the notion of an aristocracy. In the Quattrocento authors spoke of the importance of striving for honor, glory, and virtue in the world. At best these ideas spurred the leaders of society to moral rectitude and unselfish service to the city. Following Aristotle, fifteenth-century Florentines led by Leonardo Bruni stressed that wealth could have a positive moral value, and that it was a prerequisite to the morally good and active life. The citizen needed riches in order to play his full active role in the affairs of the city, to care for his family, to beautify his city, and to do virtuous deeds in honor of God. This attitude

---

[38] *I Marmi*, 1928 ed., II, 12, 63; *La Zucca*, 1565 ed., 122^v–23. Franco exhibited the same outrage against the undeserving rich and the desire that every man ought to live by his own skills. *Dialogi Piacevoli*, 1554 ed., 75–82, 9, 183, 201.

[39] *I Marmi*, 1928 ed., II, 29–35.

corresponded to their own positions, as the Quattrocento Florentine humanists were comfortably wealthy and enjoyed high social status. Although the view that wealth could be morally beneficial was challenged
by Savonarola and ameliorated by the contemplative ideal of Renaissance
Platonism, the belief in its indispensability for the morally good, active
life remained in the sixteenth century. For example, Alessandro Piccolomini's widely reprinted treatise of education, *De la institutione di tutta la
vita de l'uomo nobile e in città libera* (1542) educated the sons of wealthy
noblemen in the ideals formulated in the Quattrocento. Aristotle's *Politics*
and *Ethics,* and the pseudo-Aristotelian *Economics,* continued to emphasize the ideal of the rich citizen who would lead his city and attain
virtue.[40]

For the critics, wealth was acquired through Fortune or deceit and
was morally corrupting. It rendered the possessers incapable of leadership
and created conditions of misery for the rest of society. A society divided
between wealthy leaders and poor followers was contrary to the balance of
nature and led to corruption and misery. The reality of the Cinquecento
as they saw it, obliterated the possibility of wealth contributing to any
positive moral values.

Another theoretical justification for the social division of society was
the idea that noble birth conveyed virtue. The two had not always been
identified: in the Quattrocento authors tended to affirm that true nobility
was the result of personal virtue.[41] This position was gradually eroded in
the sixteenth century. Castiglione in the *Courtier* discussed at length
whether nobility was a matter of virtue and ability, and if high birth
conferred any intrinsic benefits. He insisted upon honor, virtue, and
ability for complete nobility, but was convinced that these qualities were
most often possessed by those of noble birth. Indeed, the challenge of
noble ancestors spurred a young man to greater heights. After Castiglione,
Cinquecento theorists assigned more tangible benefits to high birth. Eminent ancestors, wealth, and magnificence, all indispensable components of
nobility, were acquired by birth. Prudence, justice, and worthy deeds
became secondary considerations. Even the words "honor" and "nobility"
took on extrinsic meaning. Personal honor, earlier essential to true nobil-

---

[40] See Hans Baron, "Franciscan Poverty and Civic Wealth as Factors in the Rise
of Humanistic Thought," *Speculum*, XIII (1938), 1–37; Eugenio Garin, *Italian
Humanism: Philosophy and Civic Life in the Renaissance,* trans. Peter Munz
(Oxford, 1965), 43–46; Curcio, *Dal Rinascimento alla Controriforma,* 116–18.

[41] Ventura, *Nobiltà e popolo,* 294.

ity, came to mean externals, i.e., the "honors" showered upon those born into the higher ranks of society. An "honorable" style of life meant a life of magnificence untainted by mercantile or manual labor. This became the test of nobility rather than deeds. Castiglione's portrait of nobility as a subtle balance between ancestors and personal worth changed.[42]

The critics rejected the claims of nobility. With their eyes firmly on social reality, they asserted that money was the "true testimony of nobility;" in poverty one could not distinguish the noble from the lowborn. According to Franco, the only difference between higher and lower nobility was more or less money. No man was inherently better through noble birth. Doni related an encounter with a barber, beginning with the remark that barbering seemed a vile occupation because one had to wash, cut, and comb the hair of all sorts of men. On the contrary, the barber answered, barbering was a useful education. When he washed the heads of kings and signori, rich and poor, he discovered that each head was alike. Lando punned that in Apulia and Calabria, the nobles committed so many homicides, treacheries, and robberies that nobility (nobiltà) was the prize for notable (*notabil*) iniquity.[43]

The critics summarized their catalogue of the social ills afflicting Italy by petitioning Jove in heaven to reform the world. In a dialogue by Franco, men asked Jove to aid the poor against the rich, the infirm against the malpractice of doctors, and poets against princes. They begged him to hear the protest of the good who were constrained to do evil for survival, and asked him to take up arms against the frauds of the legists, the injustice of tribunals, and the looting of heretic soldiers. Unfortunately, there was no relief from above. Weighing their requests, Jove wanted the consent of all the gods before deciding to ruin and reform the world, so he called for a council. But his aides could not find a trumpet with which to summon the gods, and the scene dissolved into comic confusion.[44]

A more eloquent petition to Jove by Doni yielded no more results. Oh Jove, he cried, do you not perceive the cries of the good, the laments of the just, the afflictions of the poor, the miseries of the unsheltered, and the anguish of those who have been robbed of the fruits of their labor? He

---

[42] Berengo, *Nobili e mercanti,* 252–57, discussing the *Discorsi* (1585) of Annibale Romei and the *Discorsi* (1586) of Alessandro Sardo. See also Ventura, *Nobiltà e popolo,* 365–74.

[43] Lando, *Confutazione,* n.d., 5–5ᵛ; *Paradossi,* 1545 ed., 61ᵛ; *Commentario,* 1550 ed., 26. Franco, *Pistole Vulgari,* 1539 ed., xviiᵛ; Doni, *I Mondi,* 1552 ed., 63ᵛ.

[44] *Dialogi Piacevoli,* 1554 ed., 207–14.

begged him to listen to the tyrannized, the overtaxed, and the plundered. "Jove, oh Jove, wake up to the fact that justice falls to force . . ." he cried. Conditions were so lamentable that starving fathers sold the honesty of their children, and mothers entered into adultery. Hopelessly, he concluded, "Alas Jove, everything is despicable, everything is mixed up, confused, and turned upside down."[45]

As the fruitless response to Franco's petition to Jove indicated, the critics did not believe that any social reform was possible. Legislation would not reform society because of the unchanging and unimprovable nature of man. This Doni explained in a discourse on reform in his *Pitture* in 1564. He began the discussion by laughing at those who sought to reform the world with glorious enterprises and notable deeds. The nature of man made fundamental reforms impossible. It was useless to make changes to eliminate human disorders; a government might forbid public concubines but private prostitutes would take their place. Remove the dice and cards, and men would somehow manage to begin gambling again. Doni doubted the effectiveness of the Counter-Reformation. One could extinguish heretics that molested the Church and burn their books, he noted, but in time other heretics and worse books would appear. In a jibe probably directed against the reforming Pope Paul IV, Doni mocked old men of eighty years who expected in eighty days to restrain prostitutes, eliminate heretics, give laws to the Church, and rearrange kingdoms.[46] These were all matters that required a thousand years or more. Doni concluded his discourse on reform with a nihilistic passage on the cyclical affairs of men. Men initiated many enterprises, but after a number of years they failed. Landlords lost their houses, signori lost their lands and contracts, while account books and taxes vanished. Step by step everything returned to its original rusticity: land returned to the peasants, houses to the poor, and noble rank to those who could hold it. Men were stupid to labor so hard to change the world; rather they should enjoy life. In the end, the shapeless earth absorbed all.[47]

[45] "Oime Giove, tutto si sprezza, tutto è mescolato, confuso & voltato sotto sopra." Doni, *I Mondi*, 1552 ed., 71ᵛ–72ᵛ.

[46] Doni may have had in mind Paul IV, who was almost 79 when he began his turbulent reign.

[47] This discourse was printed as part of *Le Pitture* (1564) and reprinted in the 1565 ed. of *La Zucca*, 275ᵛ–80ᵛ. It was expurgated from all the subsequent editions of *La Zucca* (1589, 1591, 1592, 1595, and the two published in 1607), probably because of the reference to the impossibility of eliminating heresies and reforming

Franco, Lando, and Doni drew a social portrait of their times and condemned the upper classes. Some of what they wrote could have been inspired by the grumbling of the popolo, i.e., complaints by merchants, artisans, or anyone not of the wealthy and privileged classes, that the latter were thieves and villains. The critics put these into colorful literary form. They did not propose any concrete program of reform because they doubted that men could be reformed or could improve themselves. Only a new social plan such as Doni proposed in his utopia could provide the necessary environment for social equality and moral regeneration.

Moral decay

Accompanying the political failures and social injustice was a general moral decay in Italy. The critics described a habit of viciousness and sin; they thought that every group of people, every profession, from the highest to the lowest, practiced vice in order to acquire wealth and get ahead. This was a peninsula-wide disease caused by the wars and social injustice.

Franco summarized the feelings of the critics: he noted in 1541 that he was living in "the most vicious century ever," and in 1552 he lamented that there never was a century more evil than his.[48] Franco used Aretino's metaphor of the whore to make the same point. He wrote that prostitutes were honored because they were the teachers of the contemporary world. They used their blond hair and snow-white bosoms to overhear secrets and penetrate walls. Who did not imitate their crafts, deceits, and stratagems in order to win treasure and reputation?[49] It is not difficult to interpret Franco's prostitutes as Italian princes and signori who sold their services to the highest bidder even if it meant destruction for Italy, or to interpret the "craft, deceits, and stratagems" of Franco's prostitutes as the practice of politics and diplomacy.

Vice pervaded every part of society. All the professions practiced

---

men. "Il Tempo ancor egli, è Riformatore & Formatore, perche fa Modelli, & gli guasta. La sua potenza spegne gli eretici, che molestano la Santa Chiesa, & arde i libri loro; poi ne fa rinascere de gli altri, & scrivere se non quelle cose, delle peggiori." *La Zucca,* 1565 ed., 277ᵛ.

[48] Letters to Christofero Picco and to Capitan Gioan Battista Franco in Vaticanus Latinus 5642, ff. 7, 390ᵛ.

[49] Franco, *Pistole Vulgari,* 1539 ed., xxivᵛ–xxv.

criminal dishonesty in order to make money, and none of them was concerned for the consequences. Men of every profession employed the appropriate dishonest stratagem, or the knowledge peculiar to their profession to defraud. In a long poem Franco described these deceits. Scholars used learned tricks to take money from the purses of the ignorant, tailors robbed drapers of the fruits of their labor, and cobblers used dishonest means to stretch their leather. Lando used the device of a cavalier who tried many occupations but rejected them all because of the evils practiced in them. He tried shipbuilding in Genoa, but discovered that shipbuilders used rotten timbers in order to save money—at the cost of lives and ships lost at sea. Sailors and fishermen were no better: the former consorted with infidels while the latter blasphemed heaven when their luck was bad. Peasants lived like beasts, and were rapacious, perfidious, and deadly enemies of landlords.[50]

Physicians and merchants were just as evil. The charges against physicians were avarice, ignorance, and lack of concern for the poor. Too many refused to teach their science to others or to treat the poor, while eagerly responding to the call of a rich miser who feared death. After bilking the patient for a fat fee, they often killed him through ignorance. Doni condemned deceitful medical men who pretended knowledge by examining chamber pots to eating the contents of the pots for eternity in hell. Merchants with their monopolies nourished themselves on the blood of the poor. In order to become rich they merchandized their souls, putting their faith on the sale bill, as they cheated their customers.[51]

As might be expected, the critics condemned soldiering and war. Soldiers were a cancer of Italy in league with Charles V, thieves who deserved to be dispatched with mace and fire like beasts. Doni reserved the seventh and last of his *Inferni* for their punishment. Captains and soldiers floated in a pool of boiling blood, while from cliffs overhanging the pool, beings, half-horse and half-man, shot redhot arrows into them. The soldiers sought relief from this pain under the surface of the pool, but as they sank into its depths, the boiling blood consumed the flesh from

---

[50] Franco, *Rime*, 1916 ed., no. 190, pp. 92–94; Lando, *Vari Componimenti*, 1555 ed., 97–98, 92.

[51] Against physicians, see Franco, *Pistole Vulgari*, 1539 ed., lxi–lxiii^v; Dorothy M. Schullion, "Nicolò Franco, Vilifier of Medicine," *Bulletin of the History of Medicine*, 24 (1950), 26–37; Lando, *Vari Componimenti*, 1555 ed., 103–4; Doni, *Inferni*, 1553 ed., 123, 156; *I Marmi*, 1928 ed., II, 143. Against merchants, Franco, *Rime*, 1916 ed., no. 190, p. 93; Lando, *Vari Componimenti*, 1555 ed., 100–101.

their bones. Reaching bottom, they were fleshed anew, and rose to the surface to be again lacerated, and to repeat the cycle eternally.[52]

In short, the critics described moral anarchy. Italy was a land where justice and right hardly existed, as men universally practiced evil.

Other writers in the fifteenth and sixteenth centuries had described vice. Poggio Bracciolini's witty *Liber facetiarum* often revolved around moral turpitude, Aretino's *Ragionamenti* focused on adultery and fraud, as did many of the comedies of the Cinquecento. Beginning with Boccaccio, the ever-popular novelle were filled with stories of debased morals and corrupt manners. The best of the Cinquecento *novellieri*, Matteo Bandello, claimed that his novelle were true stories, not fables,[53] and filled them with violence, avarice, jealousy, revenge, and ambition, to convey what one scholar calls a disordered reality.[54]

The criticism of morals and customs that Franco, Lando, and Doni voiced was of a different kind.[55] They condemned whole professions, indeed most of the occupations of the day. The facezia or novella often revolved around an individual, a particular situation, or a witty sentence; the authors did not generalize about people or professions. The critics believed that there was a widespread moral decay, resulting from the political failure and unjust social system. If men were not oppressed by wars, by the signori, or by extreme poverty, they would have less need to practice deceit. If the various kinds of exploitation mentioned in the petitions to Jove were remedied, a great deal of the vice would be eliminated.

Miserable Italy, beset by political ills, social injustice, and moral decadence, produced a mood of restless disorientation in the critics. Man and the universe were united in their common instability and purposelessness, man's hopes and values were of little worth. Doni's discourse of Inquieto, who could find no person, place, or profession to allay his

---

[52] Against soldiers, Franco, *Priapea*, 1887 ed., lxxx'-lxxxi; Lando, *Vari Componimenti*, 1555 ed., 104–5; Doni, *La Zucca*, 1565 ed., 293'-94; *Inferni*, 1553 ed., 217.

[53] *Tutte le opere*, ed. Francesco Flora (Verona, 1952), I, 778. On the historicity of Bandello's novelle, see T. Gwynfor Griffith, *Bandello's Fiction: An Examination of the Novelle* (Oxford, 1955).

[54] Santoro, *Il concetto dell'uomo nella letteratura del Cinquecento*, 136.

[55] When they wrote novelle and facezie, Doni, Franco, and Lando conformed to tradition, which demanded an individual story with much human interest. The moral criticism discussed in these pages is not to be found in their novelle and facezie.

restlessness, portrayed this disorientation.[56] A tortured weariness of the spirit dominated man's life. Doni at times used the term *noia* to convey this. "Noia" was a spiritual discontent, an inescapable and insatiable weariness with everything and everybody.[57] This, man tried to escape by running about in circles, i.e., by constant, restless activity. Doni imaginatively adapted the medieval-Renaissance idea of the wheel of Fortune to convey the instability of the 1550's. In Doni's words, everything whirled, a concept he expressed three times between 1551 and 1553. After describing man's instability and unhappiness, Doni asked rhetorically, are we not just turning a wheel in our continual efforts to give, have, take, rend, build and destroy? Everything in man's life could be explained in terms of ceaseless revolving activity; men pursued different objects fruitlessly. ". . . if one considers, then, his life, he will find at the final end that the whole world turns. States turn this one, buildings this one, possessions another, clothing this one, books and learning this other, this other writings, accounts, shops, business deals, armies, soldiers, banners, guns. . . ."[58] In the same way, all of man's deeds and words were a repetition of the past. ". . . our deeds and words are a wheel; [they] turn and go, come and go back; that which happens today, happened other times, that which one says, was said. . . ."[59] Man corresponded to the ceaselessly turning heavenly bodies. "So all the elements turn, the heaven turns, the brain turns, in writing the pen turns as the hand makes it turn, as the head causes the hand to turn, which the circles inside [the head] in turning, make [the head] turn. And so everything whirls; the sun, the moon, the stars, and he who believes that he does not whirl, whirls more than the others. . . ."[60] And to emphasize his point, Doni ended one of his whirling discourses by piling words, mostly pejorative, upon one another

[56] *I Marmi*, 1928 ed., II, 205-11. See Ch. II.

[57] ". . . la noia ti tormenta," *I Marmi*, 1928 ed., I, 269.

[58] ". . . se considera poi il suo vivere, troverrá alla fine alla fine che tutto il mondo s'aggira: quel gira stati, quel fabriche, quel possessioni, quel vestimenti, quell'altro libri, dottrina, quell'altro scritture, conti, botteghe, traffichi, eserciti, soldati, bandiere, falconi. . . ." *I Marmi*, 1928 ed., II, 179.

[59] ". . . i nostri fatti e detti, sono una ruota; che tornano & vanno, vengono & ritornano; Quel che accade hoggi è accaduto dell'altre volte, quel che si dice è detto. . . ." *Seconda Libraria*, 1551 ed., 5.

[60] "Così tutti gil elementi girano: il ciel gira; il cervel gira; nello scriver si gira sempre la penna che la gira la mano, che la fa girare il capo, che le girelle che vi son dentro girando fanno girare; e così ogni cosa gira, il sole, la luna, le stelle; e chi crede di non girare, gira più di tutti. . . ." *I Marmi*, 1928 ed., II, 178.

without sense or sentence. "Arrogante, arido, astuto, audace, assassino, adulatore, arrabbiato, adultero. . . ."[61]

With his image of the constantly revolving world and the instability of all things, Doni imaginatively voiced a common idea of the 1530's and 1540's, that the stability of Italian life was gone. Italians realized that not only governments and states, but also fixed ideas and customs had been destroyed in their lifetime. Guicciardini in the early pages of the *History of Italy* wrote "The King [Charles VIII] entered Asti on September 9, 1494, bringing with him into Italy the seeds of innumerable disasters, terrible events and change in almost everything. His invasion was not only the origin of changes of government, subversion of kingdoms, devastation of the countryside . . . but also of new habits, new customs. . . ."[62] Claudio Tolomei noted in 1529 that the wars had "mixed up everything." Cities, kingdoms, and provinces had been turned "upside down." Laws were no longer obeyed, and, most disturbing to Tolomei, the social hierarchy had been destroyed.[63] Matteo Bandello wrote that very few ages had seen such sudden changes as people of his day saw every day, and he feared that the changes were not beneficial.[64] In 1547 Paolo Giovio believed that the calamities of war had caused a "sad change of almost everything" not only in Italy but in all the world.[65] Doni in his discourse poignantly conveyed the impact of these unsettling changes on man's spirit.

Other pessimists

Franco, Lando, and Doni were not the only men of the first half of the Cinquecento to discuss the disasters and problems of Italy. In one way or another this was a preoccupation of many authors. The writing of the critics shared characteristics with others but still was unique.

[61] *I Mondi*, 1552 ed., 78–79.

[62] *History of Italy*, trans. Cecil Grayson (New York, 1964), bk. I, ch. 9, p. 148.

[63] "Oratione per la Pace," in *Delle orationi volgarmente scritte da diversi huomini illustri de tempi nostri*, I (Venice, 1584), 6, 3, 7. On Tolomei, see Luigi Sbaragli, *Claudio Tolomei: umanista senese del Cinquecento* (Siena, 1939).

[64] *Tutte le opere*, II, 569.

[65] "Perciocchè, se noi vorremo riandare le grandi calamità di guerre le quali non pure all'Italia ma a tutto ancora l'incognito mondo hanno apportato dolorosa mutazione quasi di tutte le cose." Paolo Giovio, *Le Vite del Gran Capitano e del Marchese di Pescara*, ed. Costantino Panigada (Bari, 1931), 10.

A pessimistic view of man and the world existed in Italian humanist thought of the fifteenth century. Coexisting with the enthusiastic affirmations typified by Giovanni Pico's "Oration on the Dignity of Man" was the view that man could not achieve happiness in the world because he was too fragile to cope with the evil conditions of the world without external aid. Poggio Bracciolini in *De miseria humanae conditionis* (c.1455) lamented that constant frustration was the lot of man. Any attempt to achieve security, wellbeing, or position was destined to fail because nature and Fortune opposed man. The only way that some measure of happiness could be achieved was through internal adjustment whereby the rare individual triumphed over his own passions and external conditions. The nature of individual adjustment was dependent upon whether the humanist followed Christian ascetic, detached Stoic, or Neoplatonic contemplative views.[66] This pessimism of life among some Quattrocento humanists often directly contradicted their own relatively comfortable and affluent position in Italian society.[67]

In the early decades of the sixteenth century, Italians were forced to look beyond personal unhappiness to examine the problem of the individual in the midst of calamity. Gianfrancesco Pico, Prince of Mirandola (1475–1533) described, about 1515, the disasters of Italy—wars, disease, sedition, the deaths of great men of letters—and concluded that these were a punishment of God. If men would return to virtuous living and cease quarreling among themselves, they could resist invasion with new moral vigor.[68] Tristano Caracciolo, Neapolitan historian (c. 1439–c. 1520) saw the political calamities of his time as evidence that man could not oppose the evil power of Fortune. In his *De varietate fortunae* (1510) he described the political misfortunes of the house of Aragon in Naples, the calamities of the Sforzas in Milan, the disasters of the Venetians, and the tribulations of many Neapolitan nobles. His conclusion was joyless: because of the evil power of Fortune it was foolish for man to anticipate any worldly success, riches, or honors. The only alternative to the caprices of Fortune was the stability of God's commandments. Caracciolo came close to suggesting that men should cease striving to live the civic life of

---

[66] Charles E. Trinkaus, Jr., *Adversity's Noblemen: The Italian Humanists on Happiness* (New York, 1940), 80–120.

[67] See Lauro Martines, *The Social World of the Florentine Humanists, 1390–1460* (Princeton, N.J., 1963), which shows that the Florentine humanists came from the top layer of society and enjoyed considerable wealth.

[68] Trinkaus, *Adversity's Noblemen,* 130–31.

political activity and the pursuit of riches and honors. But he did not advocate complete withdrawal; men should continue to strive for just and honest affairs, but without real hope for the future.[69]

Franco, Doni, and Lando continued the discussion of man's unhappiness and the disasters of Italy, but they differed from Bracciolini, Gianfrancesco Pico, and Caracciolo in that they were more concerned with the general decadence of Italian life than the fate of individual men. They saw more extensive political, social, and moral decadence within Italian society, and assigned most of the blame for this collapse to Italian leaders and their system of government and society; they did not blame disaster exclusively on foreigners or Fortune. There was furthermore a social gap between Pico and Caracciolo and the critics. The treatises of the former were concerned with the leaders of society. For Caracciolo the "vulgar multitude" was one of Fortune's obstacles to success. The critics, whose sympathies were with the lower part of the social structure, tended to blame the signori for Italian ills, while charging that the moral decadence affected high and low.

Authors like Bracciolini, Pico, and Caracciolo continued to hold to Renaissance values. They did not lose confidence in the value of liberal studies and the importance of attempting to understand and direct politics. They still thought that the civic life of virtue and accomplishment was essential to both personal well-being and that of society, and were willing to continue their efforts to improve the world through service with signori. But they lamented that the world was in such an evil state that their values were no longer honored. Writing after another generation of disasters, the critics doubted Renaissance ideals of government, the usefulness of learning, and the active life.[70]

Finally, Gianfrancesco Pico and Caracciolo suggested a religious alternative. Men could achieve personal peace in the midst of disaster only through holding to God. While concerned with Scripture and faith, the critics did not offer religion as an alternative to worldly catastrophe. Although they doubted that there could be any practical result, they preferred to consider utopias which would change the world rather than religious consolation.

There were other writers closer in age and background to Franco, Lando, and Doni who criticized Italian life and who felt some of the

---

[69] *De varietate fortunae Tristani Caraccioli* (Bologna, 1934–35), 73–105.
[70] See Ch. V.

disorientation the latter noted. The restless macaronic poet Teofilo Folengo (1491–1544) predated Lando, Franco, and Doni by a generation. His masterpiece, *Baldus* (first edition 1517), burlesqued the chivalric romance in a free form of Latin which incorporated newly coined onomatopoeic words, Italian words with Latin endings, and dialect forms. The plot was a grotesque parody of the epic whose larger-than-life hero was Baldus. Guido, a paladin, seduced Charlemagne's daughter, Baldovina, and fled with her to Italy. Here Baldovina gave birth to Baldus who, endowed with tremendous strength but not a great deal of sense, embarked on his life's goal of becoming a new Roland. Surrounded by unsavory characters, he brawled and drank his way through a series of gross adventures on land, sea, in and out of prison, and through the depths of hell.

Part of Folengo's appeal consisted in his use of Italy as the setting and his mocking criticism of things Italian. In one episode, Baldus, made ruler of a mythical city by popular acclaim, ran afoul of the deposed prince, who used the devices typical of Renaissance tyrants—poison, fraudulent stratagems, and false charges, including a speech against Baldus closely modeled on Cicero's first oration against Catiline—to turn the people against him.[71] In his earlier Italian attempt to burlesque the epic, the *Orlandino* (written before *Baldus* but not published until 1526), Folengo compared the invasions of the Goths and Lombards to the despoilation of Italy by the modern "swine" (*porci*)—the German, Spanish, French, and Swiss soldiers. Italy had become a brothel for strange peoples. In a burlesque of the Last Judgment, Folengo described how at the last trumpet the mutilated Swiss, French, Germans, and Spaniards would rise from their graves in Italy and fight one another again for their decapitated limbs lost in the wars.[72]

Folengo also noted a moral decline, specially in the upper classes of Italy. On one occasion, Baldus approached the gates of heaven, and found an old man who ran an inn to house travelers on their way to Paradise. While on earth, living in Rome, the old man had discovered that only three arts were necessary to win the praise of kings and popes: "buffoonery, knavery, and pandering." At death, thanks to the intercession of his patrons, especially courtiers and courtesans, he had been granted this sinecure. But very rarely did he house popes, kings, dukes, signori,

---

[71] "Merlin Cocai," *Il Baldo* (Milan, 1958), bk. IV, lines 419–552; V, 154–371.

[72] Teofilo Folengo, *Opere italiane,* ed. Umberto Renda, I (Bari, 1911), *Orlandino,* bk. II, stanzas 52, 59; I, 14, 43; VI, 56–57.

marquises, and barons. If a judge or a lawyer came, he counted it a miracle![73]

By his free, mocking spirit, criticism of Italian affairs, and restless life as he entered, left, and then returned to the monastery, Folengo anticipated the disorientation of the critics of the next generation. But he expressed more optimism about man than Franco, Doni, and Lando. The heroes of *Baldus* and *Orlandino* were larger-than-life men who possessed human powers and possibilities, including appetites, to exaggeration. They dominated the world into which Folengo placed them, mastering situations, getting into and out of difficulties, and triumphing in burlesque fashion over the whims of Fortune. Folengo had a healthy, mocking lack of concern for fate, and affirmed man's potentialities. This humorous optimism departed with Franco, Doni, and Lando, much of whose writing reflected helplessness in the face of political and social disaster. They were angry at the Italian situation and rulers, and petitioned heaven for relief from their grievances, but the situation to them was hopeless: they excluded the possibility of doing anything positive about it and dreamed of utopias.

Another author of an earlier generation who shared some of the criticism of Doni, Franco, and Lando was the Florentine hosier, Giambattista Gelli (1498–1563). Of humble birth, Gelli developed a passion for learning, and spent the earnings from his shop in the Piazza della Signoria on books. He attended sessions of the Orti Oricellari and in 1540 appeared as one of the first members of the Accademia Fiorentina. He wrote comedies, translated philosophical works, and lectured on Dante, but is remembered chiefly for two vernacular prose works, *I capricci del bottaio,* the first edition of which was printed by Doni in 1546, and *La Circe* (1549).

La Circe was a discussion of man's condition. It had its roots in the tenth *Odyssey* in which Ulysses and his men fell into the hands of the enchantress, Circe, who turned the sailors into beasts. In Gelli's work, Circe agreed to turn the animals back into their human state, if the animals so desired. Ulysses spoke to eleven different animals in an attempt to persuade them to return to their human form. To his surprise, they much preferred the happy animal state to the troubles of man, and in the course of the debates described the evils of human existence in terms similar to those of Doni, Franco, and Lando.

Although Gelli shared with the critics moral and social criticism, and

---

[73] *Il Baldo,* bk. VIII, lines 606–7; XXII, 151–96; XXIII, 260–335.

also evoked a primitive utopian age, he, like Folengo, held a more optimistic view of man. In *La Circe,* Ulysses was at first badly discomfited by the arguments of the animals, but in the latter half of the book he argued more effectively in favor of the state of man. In the last encounter, with an elephant, Ulysses argued that man was far superior to the animals because man had intellect and free will. With the former man could reason and learn, and reach a knowledge of the Supreme Cause; with the latter he had the power to raise himself to a celestial nature (to reach God), or sink to the level of a brute. Gelli enthusiastically praised man in terms used by Ficino, Hermes Trismegistus, and Pico della Mirandola in his *Oration on the Dignity of Man.* Because of his intellect, man was a terrestrial god, and a miracle of nature; he could do what he pleased. Ulysses convinced the elephant of the superiority of the state of man, and the elephant eagerly consented to be turned back into a human being.[74]

More aware of man's difficulties and moral decline than Pico and Ficino, Gelli did not exhibit the degree of rebellion and disillusionment that marked Lando, Franco, and Doni. The intellectual and social differences that separated him from these three writers may explain his greater optimism. He did not share their rejection of learning, as he held to an Aristotelian psychology and translated works of philosophy. He was born, lived, and died in Florence; he did not wander. A tradesman who lived comfortably, Gelli came into an inheritance which provided him a substantial library and leisure to study.[75] He did not have to depend on the favors of princes, nor did he have to write constantly for the vernacular presses to support himself. Gelli can perhaps be seen as a transitional figure, neither as optimistic as Giovanni Pico and Ficino, nor as gloomy about man's fate as the generation that followed him.

The author whose views on man and society most closely approached those of Franco, Lando, and Doni was not an Italian, but Heinrich Cornelius Agrippa of Germany, whose *De incertitudine et vanitate scientiarium* (published in 1526) contained both an attack on learning and much political, social, and moral criticism. Agrippa saw society as anarchy; to quote a recent scholar, for Agrippa "every rank of society . . . depends on cruelty and deceit for its being."[76]

---

[74] Giambattista Gelli, *La Circe e I Capricci del Bottaio,* ed. G. G. Ferrero (Florence, 1957), dialogue 10, pp. 123–42.

[75] Armand L. De Gaetano, "Giambattista Gelli: A Moralist of the Renaissance," unpubl. Ph.D. diss., Columbia University, 1954, 5–6.

[76] Charles G. Nauert, Jr., *Agrippa and the Crisis of Renaissance Thought* (Urbana, Ill., 1965), 309.

Agrippa criticized all forms of government, especially that of princes and the nobility. Princes and kings defended only their own grandeur and prerogatives while abusing their subjects at their pleasure. Where the nobility ruled, factions, seditions, slaughters, civil war, and ultimately total ruin resulted. Agrippa, who had lived in Italy, briefly cited the peninsula to prove his point. "And to this day in most of the Cities of Italy, the Effects of these miscarriages are to be seen."[77]

In chapter 80, Agrippa turned his attention to the nobility in general. The first noble had been Cain, a parricide; the long historical sketch of the nobility which followed made it obvious that Agrippa felt that they had not improved since Cain. The nobility, he claimed, had risen to power by warfare, lust, and selling their wives and daughters. Their identifying characteristics were oppression of the lower classes, rapaciousness, love of pleasure, and contempt for the law.[78]

Like Doni, Franco, and Lando, Agrippa criticized many professional groups in society. Merchants were usurers and cheats. "For no men grow Rich without deceit."[79] Courtiers, by fawning and flattery, became secretaries and ministers of state, and then gave themselves to vice.[80] Agrippa was also harsh on laws and the legal profession. He believed that "there is no law so carefully written that lawyers cannot overturn it. And legal remedies are weak and ineffective unless the plaintiff is strong enough to assert his rights."[81]

None of these four writers could find anything to praise in princes, the nobility, or the professions; all saw a general moral decay in society. None of them believed that the Renaissance solution, the application of man's reason, would solve the problems of the world. There were some differences in emphasis. The critics, and Doni in particular, were more concerned with the social structure and the maldistribution of wealth than Agrippa. The criticism of Franco, Lando, and Doni was based specifically on the Italian situation while Agrippa generalized more.[82] Overall, there were significant differences in their general intellectual positions. Occult

[77] *The Vanity of Arts and Sciences* (London, 1676), 157.

[78] *Ibid.,* 257–76.

[79] *Ibid.,* 238.

[80] *Ibid.,* 224–34.

[81] Nauert, *Agrippa and the Crisis of Renaissance Thought,* 312.

[82] Doni certainly and Lando probably knew *De vanitate* (see Ch. V) but it is difficult to pinpoint any borrowing of social and political criticism. If they did borrow ideas, they could easily clothe them in new metaphors or examples.

learning played an important part in Agrippa's intellectual development, and attracted him throughout his life, while the criticis never took it seriously, and often mocked magic and demonology.

The most important difference between Agrippa and the Italian writers was that Agrippa provided a religious alternative to the disordered, cruel world. If men would humbly follow the teachings of Christ, they could reform themselves and the world. This is the positive message of the last two chapters of *De vanitate:* "Men should stop relying on depraved human nature and should rely instead on the Word of God as expressed in the illuminated soul and the Bible."[83] The critics lacked Agrippa's spiritual assurance that derived from a mystical reliance on God. They did not suggest religious remedies for the social and political disorder of the world; their utopias included only a rudimentary naturalistic religion.

All of the sixteenth-century Italians mentioned in this chapter had to come to terms with the Italian situation. The intellectual history of the first half of the Cinquecento was in large measure the varied responses of men to that situation. Franco, Doni, and Lando contributed one response, a description and analysis of the situation which indicted political leaders and the social system. Enough knowledge of the Italian scene exists to confirm the general outline of their bleak description and condemnation. Their objections to the rulers of society may well have reflected the verbal discontent of the popolo. In their discussion of the political, social, and moral evils, Doni, Franco, and Lando began to express doubts about ideas that had long been part of the Renaissance political framework. Reality, as they saw it, did not conform to the theories. The mental restlessness that Doni evoked reflected intellectual uncertainty in the face of change.

If the political and social situation was beyond control, perhaps men could find spiritual stability. A number of authors argued that men should seek God when evil Fortune ruled the world. Although Franco, Doni, and Lando did not offer spiritual escape from worldly evils, they were caught up in the religious concerns of their century.

---

[83] Nauert, *Agrippa and the Crisis of Renaissance Thought,* 313.

᳀⟦ *Chapter IV* ⟧᳀

RELIGIOUS RESTLESSNESS

THE disturbed condition of Italy
helped to nourish a spiritual ferment and the desire for religious reform.
Perhaps the clergy of sixteenth-century Italy exhibited the same mixture
of virtue and vice as in earlier centuries, and certainly anticlerical literature existed previously. But when the Italian world was upset by wars,
foreign troops, and the overturn of governments, a reaction against the
immediate past appeared in religion as well as in politics. A concern
with religious matters affected all classes.[1] The political and social
problems stimulated an awareness of man's fragility and impermanence,
and turned attention to God. Popular preachers favored apocalyptic
themes, linking them to the sack of Rome and the invasions.[2] Moreover,
new ideas, first Erasmian and later Protestant, offered alternatives to
spiritually disturbed Italians.

Italian Evangelism

The years of the critics' maturity coincided with the sixteenth-century
religious revival. In the early years of the century, Italians in secular
unconcern had ignored the religious revival while northern Europe
sought to understand the central paradox of grace and sin, and pored over
SS. Paul and Augustine, studying redemption in Christ and justification

[1] Federico Chabod, *Per la storia religiosa dello stato di Milano durante il
dominio di Carlo V* (Rome, 1962), 96–100, 140–41.

[2] See Giampaolo Tognetti, "Sul 'romito' e profeta Brandano da Petroio," *Rivista
Storica Italiana,* 72 (1960), 20–44.

by faith. Only after the penetration of the new ideas from the north and the disasters of war, climaxed by the shock of the sack of Rome, did latent Italian religious unrest find a focus. Then the reform-minded saw the sack of Rome as a warning from God to correct abuses, and they looked to Luther's emphasis on Scripture although they did not always perceive that his ideas differed from their native faith.[3]

Either through Luther's ideas or from the renewed study of Scripture and St. Augustine, Italian clergy and laymen became involved in the great sixteenth-century discussion of faith and justification. In the 1530's and 1540's Italian prelates such as Thomas de Vio Cajetan, Jacopo Sadoleto, Marino Grimani, and Girolamo Seripando wrote Scriptural commentaries, while Venetian Dominicans published translations of the Bible in 1536 and 1538. Antonio Brucioli, later suspected of being a Protestant, published his translations and commentaries on Scripture in Venice in the same period. Preachers, including the greatest at this time, Bernardino Ochino, devoted their Lenten exhortations toward inspiring an inner renewal along the lines of faith and Scripture. Interest in these was allied with a mounting desire to correct ecclesiastical abuses. When the Papacy seemed unresponsive, laymen sought new means. In November 1545, for example, an anonymous writer addressed an appeal to the new doge of Venice, begging him to use his power to effect reform in the Church.[4] New religious orders stressing worldly engagement rather than monastic isolation sought to meet the spiritual needs of the people through charitable activity in cities and towns. After their earlier lethargy, Italians took up religious concerns amid the European-wide desire for reform and reunion in the expectancy of the coming general council.

The first phase of the religious revival, from the early years of the century to 1542, has been called "Evangelism," an imprecise term for a phenomenon which was more an attitude than a movement.[5] Evangelism included a desire to reform abuses, emphasis on Scripture, and a belief in the primacy of justification through faith, without, however, a denial of the value of good works. Erasmus' concern for individual moral reform,

---

[3] Delio Cantimori, *Eretici italiani del Cinquecento: ricerche storiche* (Florence, 1967), 10–23.

[4] Aldo Stella, "Utopie e velleità insurrezionali dei filo-protestanti italiani (1545–1547)," *Bibliothèque d'Humanisme et Renaissance*, XXVII (1965), 133–82.

[5] See the discussion of the phases of the Reformation in Italy in Delio Cantimori, *Prospettive di storia ereticale italiana del Cinquecento* (Bari, 1960), 27–35.

for the understanding of Scripture rather than commentaries, and his hope for Christian unity influenced it. Such diverse persons as the aristocratic ladies Vittoria Colonna and Giulia Gonzaga, the Spaniard Juan Valdés, Cardinals Gaspare Contarini, Pietro Bembo, Reginald Pole, Giovanni Morone, Sadoleto, and Seripando were influenced by Evangelism. Some who fled Italy for Protestant Europe as Bernardino Ochino, Pier Martire Vermigli, and Piero Paolo Vergerio, and others like Pietro Carnesecchi and Aonio Paleario, who remained and were executed in the 1560's as heretics, could be termed Italian evangelicals.[6]

In the period of Evangelism it is difficult to distinguish between movements of Catholic reform and "philo-Lutheranism," "philo-Zwinglianism," or general sentiments in favor of Protestantism. Only later were some men and books from the period of Evangelism judged heretical or close to heresy, and even after the decrees of Trent, distinctions were often difficult to make. To cite an example, the small but extremely influential *Beneficio di Cristo* was published anonymously in Venice in 1543. Giovanni Della Casa's *Index* of 1549 condemned it, although cardinals Mo-

---

[6] See Cantimori, *Prospettive di storia ereticale,* 28, 33–34; Jedin, *Cardinal Seripando,* 104–7; *History of the Council of Trent,* I, 363–67; and Eva-Maria Jung, "On the Nature of Evangelism in 16th-Century Italy," *Journal of the History of Ideas,* XIV (1953), 511–27, who limits it to aristocratic circles. Jedin makes a distinction between the "Erasmian programme of reunion" and "Evangelism" but states that "both were due to a tendency to seek an understanding with the Protestants on the basis of what both parties retained of the substance of Christianity." *History of the Council of Trent,* I, 370. Also see the excellent discussion of Evangelism in Philip McNair, *Peter Martyr in Italy* (Oxford, 1967), 1–50. McNair criticizes Jung, Jedin, and Cantimori, arguing that Evangelism was a more Protestant phenomenon, i.e., it represented the response of some Italian Catholics to "the challenge of Protestantism and in particular to the crucial doctrine of Justification by Faith. (p. 8). He sees the key figures to be Valdés, Ochino, and Vermigli. Moreover, he separates Evangelism from Erasmianism and sees the former as more precise theologically (e.g., focusing on justification by faith understood in a quite Protestant sense) than Cantimori, Jung, and Jedin.

In my judgment, whether the inspiration to read Scripture to understand justification by faith came from Protestant, Biblical, or patristic sources, the Italian religious figures of the period of 1517 to 1542 sought to follow Scripture and to understand the paradox of faith with little concern about whether these ideas and those who inspired them were Protestant or Catholic. Deciding on the relative Catholicity or Protestantism of Evangelism seems to me to be less important than understanding the fluidity, openness, and excitement of the search for salvation that characterized this period.

rone, Pole, Cristoforo Madruzzo, Tommaso Badia, and Gregorio Cortese praised the work. Despite the fact that entire heretical passages were copied or paraphrased from Luther, Calvin, and Melanchthon, modern scholars have found it difficult to detect open heresy in the work.[7] Beginning in the pontificate of Leo X (1513–21), the first phrase of Italian religious unrest, unrestricted Evangelism, ended in 1541 and 1542 with the failure of the Ratisbon colloquy, the death of Contarini, the apostasy of Ochino and Vermigli, and the institution of the Roman Inquisition.

The years from that time until about 1560 were years of crisis for Evangelism, with the introduction of religious repression into Italy. The Inquisition sought to extirpate heresy but the process was slow. Drawing the line between Catholic and heretic involved definition and investigation, but only after the Council of Trent and general acceptance of its decrees could this be done with consistency. The authorities were often satisfied with a simple abjuration of ideas identified as Protestant and the promise of obedience.

In this period some Italians began to feel obliged to make a decision, to conform to Catholicism or to flee to Protestant Europe. Others took a "Nicodemite" position. In Italy the term "Nicodemism" was applied to those of Protestant leaning who continued to live as Catholics while treating Catholic dogmas and sacraments as matters indifferent to salvation.[8] Calvin condemned Nicodemism: the believer should bear witness under persecution or, in some circumstances, might flee. The Italian Nicodemites, however, argued that they could continue to persuade others to the Protestant way by accepting the affirmative side of their faith and avoiding any condemnation of Catholic practices, which might bring down on their heads persecution that would destroy the movement. They argued that it did not matter if they kneeled at mass while they continued to believe as they pleased in their hearts. Less convinced than Calvin that

---

[7] See Ruth Prelowski's introduction and edition of the *Beneficio di Cristo* in John Tedeschi, ed., *Italian Reformation Studies in Honor of Laelius Socinus* (Florence, 1965), 21–102; and Valdo Vinay, "Die Schrift 'Il Beneficio di Giesu Christo' und ihre Verbreitung in Europa nach der neuren Forschung," *Archiv für Reformationsgeschichte,* 58 (1967), 29–72.

[8] Nicodemus, it will be recalled, was the man who came to Christ by night, fearing to profess Him openly (John, xix, 39). Delio Cantimori, "Italy and the Papacy," in *The New Cambridge Modern History*, II, *The Reformation 1520–1559* (Cambridge, 1958), 267–68; and "Nicodemismo e speranze conciliari nel Cinquecento italiano," *Contributi alla Storia del Concilio di Trento e della Controriforma,* I (Florence, 1948), 12–23.

only one Protestant sect was the true Church, they perhaps were willing to undergo martyrdom for Christ but not for another Christian cult. Neither did they believe that the painful, uncertain path of flight and exile from family, friends, native land, and possessions was necessarily Christian and humane. Rather than fleeing, many dissenters placed their hopes in the Council of Trent and stayed under the often effective protection of prelates and princes.

The Inquisition gradually intensified its activity and the number of those who fled increased. By the 1560's most Italian dissenters had to decide whether their religious consciences were fundamentally Catholic or whether they should make the long journey into Protestant Europe. For avowed Protestants who remained in Italy, like Pietro Carnesecchi, it was a period of imprisonment and death. The years from about 1560 to about 1580 marked the practical end of Protestantism in Italy with the exception of a small residue of clandestine, tacit groups.

The Italian religious situation during the adulthood of the critics was complex and fluid, particularly for those who to some degree criticized, and dissented from, the old Church. Lando, Franco, and Doni reflected the religious turbulence and uncertainty of their generation. They criticized corrupt prelates and friars, and evoked a simple religion of piety and morality. They emphasized Scripture and justification by faith under the influence of Erasmianism and northern Protestantism. But militating against spiritual peace either within Catholicism or Protestantism was the restlessness characteristic of their lives and thought.

A simple religion without abuses

Like many other Italians in the Cinquecento and earlier, Franco, Lando, and Doni energetically condemned clerical abuses.

Fifteenth-century humanists, such as Coluccio Salutati, Leonardo Bruni, Poggio Bracciolini, Masuccio Salernitano, and Antonio de Ferrariis (il Galateo) had condemned the worldliness and ignorance of the clergy, and the temporal pretensions of the Papacy. But the criticism was rhetorical; it was not related to any precise program of effective reform. With the advent of Florentine Platonism, censure of the Church and the impulse toward religious reform became a thrust toward inward perfection and individual salvation. The dialogue between God and the individual of the Florentine Platonists left little room for the practical reform of the Church and society.[9]

At the end of the fifteenth century, however, Savonarola brought a new depth and scope to the criticism of clerical abuses. Sixteenth-century Italy abounded with anticlericalism, and Franco, Lando, and Doni shared these sentiments. The critics condemned prelates who were more concerned with garnering ecclesiastical honors than teaching the Gospel. They flayed them for the abuses for which Cinquecento prelates were notorious: nepotism, nonresidence, neglect of their dioceses, avarice, and meddling in politics. Even for anticlerical literature, Franco's sonnets against Paul III were particularly abusive. The charges were familiar, but the language partook of gutter obscenity. In 1542 he termed all prelates frauds. The Papacy should be happy that the emperor bowed at its feet, but ambition and simony would bring it down, he predicted, and its wealth would turn to poison.[10] On the other hand, the critics were willing to grant credit where credit was due. Lando praised the reforming bishop of Verona, Gian Matteo Giberti, as "the glory and honor of the episcopate," a true image of Ambrose and Augustine.[11]

It is unnecessary to detail at length or to document this criticism of the clergy. The report of the official reform commission of Paul III, the *Consilium . . . de emendanda ecclesia,* in 1538 confirmed the existence of extensive abuses. The critics simply joined many of their contemporaries in condemning these scandals.

On the positive side, the critics expressed longings for a simple religion of belief and good customs, lacking rational theology or elaborate ceremony. Just as they preferred a primitive, pastoral life to the decadent and oppressive social structure, so they preferred a simple, nonrational, even fideistic religion to a complex and corrupt church, and held up the ideal of primitive and original Christianity. Sixteenth-century Italian communities, in particular, were notorious for their worldly concern for

[9] Eugenio Garin, "Desideri di riforma nell'oratoria del Quattrocento," in *La cultura filosofica del Rinascimento. Ricerche e documenti* (Florence, 1961), 166–82. See also Charles Trinkaus, "Humanist Treatises on the Status of the Religious: Petrarch, Salutati, Valla," *Studies in the Renaissance,* XI (1964), 7–45.

[10] For some of the sharper criticisms of prelates, see Lando, *Vari Componimenti,* 1555 ed., 118–23; Franco, *Rime,* 1916 ed., 41, n. 85; *Priapea,* 1887 ed., lxxiv^v–lxviiv^v, xcviii^v; *Bellezze,* 1542 ed. (Monferrato), ff. 73^v–74.

[11] *Paradossi,* 1545 ed., 24.

ceremonies, precedents, rights, and privileges, in contrast to the simple, monastic life envisaged by the founders.[12] As might be expected from two ex-monks, Doni and Lando sharply criticized monasticism and contrasted its present state to the purity of the original institution. Monastic orders, they claimed, had degenerated since their inception. In the early Church, monks had lived holy lives in the wilderness but, as the world had slowly declined, so also had monks become mundane. They had moved to the cities where they dressed well, made female friends, and mixed in worldly affairs. The critics urged monks to return to the holier and simpler ways of the past. As an example of how monks had betrayed their origins, Doni criticized Savonarola, whose profession, in his opinion, was to preach the salvation of souls and not to ruin states. Good people had abhorred Savonarola, while the pope had destroyed him because he had strayed from his proper sphere. Doni would curtail the responsibilities of monks to carrying out devotional ceremonies and giving good examples, while leaving to bishops and canons the more complex tasks of preaching and caring for men's souls.[13]

The desire for a simple religion of belief was not limited to the critics. Aretino, in his devotional and non-pornographic secular writings, spoke of religion as a matter of infused belief in the chief tenets of Catholicism, for example, the Virgin birth. When he went to church, Aretino expected to hear a straightforward sermon on virtue and vice, not a "strident dispute." Such brazen arguments were "a reproach to the silence of Christ, who simply gave man a sign, in order not to take away the premium which He places on faith." These disputes had "nothing whatever to do with our gospels or with our sins."[14] Religion should be a personal benefit to man as well as a bond to a remote time of a better life. The characters in his stories looked back to a life of simple virtue and purity in the past. The simple devotion that Aretino described in his saints' lives typified his religious ideas.[15]

---

[12] For some examples, see Chabod, *Per la storia religiosa dello stato di Milano,* 27–32; and Berengo, *Nobili e mercanti,* 369–70.

[13] Doni, *Lettere,* 1552 ed., 124–33 (letter of 1543); *Lettere,* 1547 ed., 22ᵛ–25; Lando, *Commentario,* 1550 ed., 33–34ᵛ; *Ragionamenti Familiari,* 18–23ᵛ; *Erasmus funus,* ff. 19–20ᵛ.

[14] Aretino, *Lettere,* ed. Nicolini, I, 268; letter to Antonio Brucioli, November 7, 1537, Venice.

[15] See Giorgio Petrocchi, *Pietro Aretino tra Rinascimento e Controriforma* (Milan, 1948), 72–81.

The critics' stress on a simple religion of belief brought them to fideism. Agrippa's *De vanitate* expressed similar sentiments. In contrast to the uncertain, doubtful, and ambiguous sciences, the Word of God was clear and simple, he argued at the conclusion of his work. Divine truth depended solely on the authority of God who revealed it to man, who found it without difficulty in the Bible. As an illustrative example, Agrippa pointed out that Christ had chosen simple men for His apostles. Things divine could not be comprehended by human reason or sense; man should put his trust in Christ.[16]

Lando, Franco, and Doni were uninterested in fideism as a philosophical and religious position, but expressed fideist sentiments. Central to their religious thought was a dislike of theology because it represented the attempt to apply reason to religion. The attempts of theologians to know secrets of the Trinity were against the honor of God. Christ had told men to forget the wisdom of this world and to know Him by ignorance. Scripture taught the Word of God, which was incomprehensible to reason. Reason should content itself with what it could see and comprehend by itself. Theologians used "probable reasons", allusion, allegory, anagogy, tropology—all the trappings of reason—and ended accusing one another of heresy. In his longest discussion of man's attempt to reach God, Doni emphasized the importance of love above all other aspects of religion. Do not search to know divine secrets with "subtle human interpretations" nor with acute *ragionamenti,* but rather love God. The divine light was infused in man; one did not need the vain intellect.[17] God came to men who lived simple, good lives.

Erasmianism of Franco and Lando

The critics' concern for clerical abuses and their desire for a simple religion linked to the primitive perfection of Christianity were fertile grounds for the call to follow the "philosophy of Christ." Erasmianism attracted Franco and Lando, as it did many other Europeans in the sixteenth century. Doni remained aloof; there is no evidence that he was influenced toward personal Christian renewal by Erasmus.

[16] *L'Agrippa Arrigo, Cornelio Agrippa, della vanita delle scienze tradotto per M. Lodovico Domenichi* (Venice, 1547) 193–203^v.

[17] Lando, *Paradossi,* 1545 ed., 12^v, 14–14^v; *Sferza,* 19–19^v; *Dubbi,* 1552 ed., 309; Franco, *Philena,* 462; Doni, *I Mondi,* 1567 ed., 207–9, 219–20.

Erasmianism had complementary negative and positive aspects.[18] *The Praise of Folly* and More's *Utopia* subjected clerical and lay vices to the attack of clear reason—intolerant of hypocrisy, pretense, or sham—as Lucian had attacked the hypocrites of the ancient world. Erasmianism exposed political clergymen, superstitious peasants, corrupt laymen, and Scholastic commentators who obscured the message of Christ. The purpose of the attack was to stimulate men to return to the simple, virtuous life of the philosophy of Christ, the positive side of Erasmianism. The philosophy of Christ meant following the ethical example of Christ through the clear comprehension of Scripture, especially the New Testament. In the *Enchiridion militis christiani* Erasmus provided a blueprint of the philosophy of Christ, and he dedicated much of his life to immense editorial labor designed to make the message of Scripture available in accurate, unadulterated texts.

The critics differed on at least two points from Erasmianism, which held that the Christian man must first be a learned man. The classics, the basis of secular humanist learning, were worthwhile in themselves for their moral teaching and necessary to approach Scripture and the Church Fathers in the right spirit and with the proper knowledge. Franco, Lando, and Doni, on the other hand, lacked faith in learning in general, and humanist learning in particular, considering it irrelevant and pedantic. Erasmianism also placed faith in the leaders to reform society. As Erasmus explained in the *Education of a Christian Prince,* the prince was an example to his people, and the means through which ordinary men were morally and physically cared for. The critics had no such optimistic beliefs. With these two exceptions, however, Erasmianism attracted Franco and especially Lando.[19]

Franco was a lifelong admirer of Erasmus and believer in his program. Just as Cicero had been the wonder of his century so "the divine Erasmus" was the marvel of ours, he wrote in 1539.[20] The philosophy of

[18] See the discussion of Erasmianism in James K. McConica, *English Humanists and Reformation Politics under Henry VIII and Edward VI* (Oxford, 1965), 13–43.

[19] Erasmus's books were readily available in Italy. The *Praise of Folly* was printed in Venice in 1515, the *Colloquies* were available in a Latin edition of Venice, 1521, and in a vernacular translation by Pietro Lauro in 1545. Other works were also available in Venetian printings or in the easily obtainable Basel editions.

[20] *Dialogi Piacevoli,* 1554 ed., 142. The influence of Erasmus on Franco was noted by Delio Cantimori, "Note su Erasmo e la vita morale e religiosa italiana nel secolo XVI," in Armando Saitta, ed., *Antologia di critica storica,* II, *Problemi della civiltà moderna* (Bari, 1958), 478–79.

Christ was the path to follow. "Who does not know that one can truly call Christians those who live as simply as possible under the laws and teachings of Christ?"[21] If men did this and were inspired by the example of the Cross, they would attain salvation. Not where superstition reigns, but "where there is pure and simple belief, there is true religion."[22] In a typically Erasmian gibe, while discussing the abundance of gods in ancient Rome, Franco mockingly alluded to the abundance of saints in the Church calendar. How many of these "32,000 gods" in the calendar had been canonized, he asked? How many of them had performed miracles or had died as martyrs and confessors? Elsewhere Franco denounced Clement VII and the college of cardinals for prohibiting the sale of Erasmus's books (presumably in Rome), and denied the accusation of heresy levelled against Erasmus. The real reason for the prohibition and accusation, he said, was that the Dutch humanist had exposed the corruption of Rome. The "good Erasmus" was as Catholic as he was eloquent.[23] Even in peril of his life, Franco objected to the Church's prohibition of Erasmus's writings. During his interrogation in 1569, the Inquisitors quoted a passage from the pasquinade against Paul IV in which Franco condemned the *Index* prohibition of Erasmus. Confronted with this, Franco defended his words. He asserted that he had never observed anything heretical in Erasmus.[24]

In the dialogue *Erasmus funus* (1540) Lando discussed the impact of the life and message of Erasmus on the religious conscience of Europe. The book was, first, a satire which chastised the Swiss reformers for their lack of fidelity to the message of the great humanist, and the hostile reaction to it of the Basel Reformed Church showed that Lando's comments struck a sensitive nerve. Then, Lando expressed his approval of the Erasmian program of calling men back to Christ through reading Scripture, and indicated that he had been influenced to turn to Christ by Erasmianism. Finally, Lando criticized Luther and Bucer by name—a contrast to his earlier enthusiasm for German and Swiss Protestantism.

[21] "Chi non sa, che Christiani veramente si possono chiarmare coloro che vivono quanto piu semplicemente è possibile, sotto le leggi e gli instituti di Christo?" *Dialogi Piacevoli,* 1554 ed., 129-30.

[22] "E perciò dove è la pura e semplice credulità, è la vera religione, e non dove è la superstitione di voi huomini . . ." *Ibid.,* 267.

[23] *Ibid.,* 263, 245. All references to Erasmus were suppressed in the expurgated editions.

[24] Interrogation of May 7, 1569 in Mercati, *I costituti di Niccolò Franco,* 129-30.

The central incident in the dialogue is an account of the desecration of Erasmus's tomb by some unidentified monks. As the title of the work indicates, the starting point of the dialogue is Erasmus's funeral. There are two speakers: Arnoldus, a German, and Arianus, an Italian. Arnoldus has just returned from a trip to upper Germany, and in response to questions, narrates what has happened. He sorrowfully explains that a heavy blow has fallen upon Germany: Erasmus has died. Sacred letters and the arts mourned his death, but not impious German monks. When Erasmus died, they drank and celebrated as if at a great triumph. Gathering at his catafalque, they wrote, "May he be denied eternal peace." After the funeral oration, the monks returned at night, opened the casket, and tore the cadaver to pieces. They danced around the mutilated body, mocking the dead Erasmus, saying, "Play with us now, if you can, Erasmus; cut us if you can, oh deserter!" Later, better, youthful men came and built a small shrine to Erasmus, but the monks returned at night to demolish it, and defiled the stones to warn others.[25]

The funeral of Erasmus had occurred in Basel, where he had long lived and worked. Later in the dialogue Lando identified and praised a list of Swiss Protestants including leaders of the Reformed Church in Basel, some of whom Erasmus had known.[26] Who, then, were the monks who defiled the corpse of Erasmus in Lando's humorous description?

The Basel Reformed Church interpreted the dialogue to mean that the monks who desecrated the grave of Erasmus signified the Basel Protestants who had betrayed the Erasmian program. Joannes Herold delivered an impassioned oration against the dialogue before the Basel gymnasium on August 5, 1541, with Boniface Amerbach and Simon Grynaeus, the rector of the gymnasium, in attendance. Six times as long as the original dialogue, Herold's condemnation included line-by-line

---

[25] *Erasmus funus.* ff. 6ᵛ–10ᵛ.

[26] Lando praised the "very wise and very holy" Fabricius Capito (1478–1541), a Strasbourg Protestant; the "most learned" Kaspar Megander (1495–1545), Zwinglian theologian; Oswald Myconius (1488–1552), who led the Basel Reformed Church from 1532 until his death; Konrad Pellikan (1478–1556), Hebrew scholar at Zurich who was close to Zwingli; Theodor Bibliander (c. 1504–64), theologian who succeeded to Zwingli's chair and was second to Bullinger in the leadership of the Church at Zurich; Simon Grynaeus (1493–1541), Protestant scholar and theologian at Basel; Johannes Comander; and "Amerbach," presumably Boniface Amerbach (1495–1562), Erasmus's executor. Of the above, Capito, Myconius, Grynaeus, and Megander were among the seven reformers who composed the First Helvetian Confession at Basel in 1536. *Erasmus funus,* f. 18.

refutation and abuse of Lando's work. The title of the oration indicated that its purpose was to defend Erasmus against the calumny of the author of the dialogue, but Herold was just as concerned to defend Basel as he was to praise Erasmus. He concluded that Lando charged the city with a lack of respect for the great humanist. How could this infamous book have appeared in the Basel which so loved Erasmus, he cried, and indignantly avowed that all the monks in Basel lived good lives. Lando had written that a youth gave the funeral oration for Erasmus; Herold angrily asserted that the "most pious" Oswald Myconius, the highest churchman in Basel, had delivered the oration. Lando had described how the monks mutilated a monument to Erasmus; Herold retorted that Boniface Amerbach had built a column of marble in the Basel cathedral to Erasmus with an honorable epitaph composed by "worthy men" of Basel. When he came to the passage in which Lando praised the Swiss Reformers, Herold wrathfully accused him of "lying adulation." You really hate them, you dog of an adulator, he bawled.[27]

Lando's charges that monks had defiled the dead Erasmus and that official Basel had slighted his funeral were, in fact, untrue. Upon his death on July 12, 1536, he was given a large public funeral in the cathedral with the city's leading citizens in attendance. After Myconius' funeral oration, Erasmus was interred in a magnificent sepulchre and a laudatory inscription was placed in the cathedral, where it still remains.[28] But Herold's oration bared the sensitivity of Reformed Basel to the spiritual estrangement of Erasmus from the Reformation at Basel. When Erasmus established himself in the city in 1521, it was Catholic, led by a moderate bishop. But gradually after Oecolampadius became a professor of theology there in 1522, the city left the Catholic fold. In February 1529, at the insistence of Oecolampadius, the city council threw in its lot with the Reformation: the mass was prohibited and images removed. Although earlier a friend of Oecolampadius, Erasmus would not remain in the city, and left for Freiburg in April 1529. Estranged from the reformers, he

[27] "Philopseudes, sive pro Desiderio Erasmo Roterodamo V. C. contra Dialogum famosum Anonymi cujusdam Declamatio, Joanne Herold Acropolita Auctore: In Gymnasio Basiliensi. . . ." (August 5, 1541), in *Desiderii Erasmi Roterodami Opera Omnia* . . . (Leiden, 1706), VIII, cols. 591–652. See cols. 600, 603, 615, 617, 621, 629–630.

[28] Letters of Henry Stromer, c. July 1536, Basel, and John Herwagen, July 17, 1536, Basel, in *Opus epistolarum Erasmi,* XI, 343–44, Ep. 3134, lines 25–30, and Ep. 3135, ll. 14–17. The epitaph is reprinted in vol. XI, 356.

called them "Pseudevangelici," and mockingly suggested that although Zwingli and Bucer might be inspired by the spirit, Erasmus as a mere man could not comprehend the spirit. At length, convinced that his advanced age and feebleness would safeguard him from the religious conflict, he returned to Basel in June 1535 to supervise the printing of his works at Froben's shop. He died there the following year, but whether or not he died an orthodox Catholic with the last rites is a subject of controversy.[29]

The rest of the book discussed the meaning and results of Erasmus's life. Lando praised Erasmus for inspiring a love of Scripture in all men. Erasmus had struggled to bring people and nations to Christ through Scripture; he had brought men into light from the dark cloud which overshadowed them. His words on divine letters had dragged men forcibly back to Christ. Men were astonished and provoked, but they turned aside from prolix tomes (i.e., Scholastic commentaries) to examine the forgotten books of Scripture. Joyful letters spread the message of Erasmus to Italy, and many men opened the Gospel and moved forward to the glory of Christ. The Luccans not only read all of Erasmus but learned his words by heart. Anianus explained that he himself had been persuaded to believe by Erasmus's message.[30] That Anianus may have been an autobiographical figure is indicated by two subsequent passages. While making a general condemnation of monks, Anianus cautioned Arnoldus that "many among us are monks," but were still pious; later, he lamented that when eloquence was not permitted (presumably in the monastery) great vices most dangerous to "our souls" appeared.[31] Lando may have implied that he, as a monk, had been inspired by Erasmus to study Scripture, and in his new piety had left behind monastic life with its prohibition against Erasmian learning and its resultant vice.

The dialogue showed no enthusiasm for the German Reformation and implied that Luther was to blame for the German neglect of Erasmus. Early in the discussion Arnoldus lamented that although one could find a few modest theologians in Germany, the majority were madmen

---

[29] Johan Huizinga, *Erasmus and the Age of Reformation* (New York, 1957), 173–87; and Vittorio De Caprariis, "Qualche precisazione sulla morte di Erasmo," *Rivista Storica Italiana*, XLIII (1951), 100–108.

[30] *Erasmus funus*, ff. 12ᵛ, 14–15ᵛ.

[31] "Itaque intelligis Arnolde, que multi sint apud nos monachi, quorum pietas efficere potest, ut multorum indignitatem aequiore feramus animo." *Erasmus funus*, ff. 20–20ᵛ.

and bawling advocates. Once emitting light—the light of Erasmian humanism—Germany, now sordid and dark, ignored Erasmus. One man had thrown all into misery—the implication being that this was Luther.[32]

In the dialogue Lando posed the question of whether Erasmus had been a heretic, and the two speakers agreed that he had not. Anianius suggested that Erasmus could be condemned by his association with evil men, i.e., Protestants. Arnoldus stoutly denied this charge; Erasmus had overcome heretics with his books. Lando conceded that Erasmus had had a sharp pen, and had provoked the ill-tempered Luther and Bucer to furious outburst. But he had no sympathy for Erasmus's targets. Luther was irascible and ignorant, and nothing Christian had come from Bucer's many volumes.[33]

Faith and Scripture in Lando

Lando, as is clear from the above discussion, was more involved in the sixteenth-century debate about Scripture and faith than were Franco and Doni. At various times in his life he associated with religious dissenters, and in 1552 he published a tract on Scripture. Both his associations and his ideas merit detailed examination.

Lando may have first come into contact with unorthodox ideas in the monastery. The Milan province of the Eremites of St. Augustine included some of the most heterodox monastic communities in Italy. Prominent Lombard Augustinians when Lando was a monk were Agostino Mainardi and Giulio della Rovere. Lando left the Augustinians in or before 1529; in the next decade the other two came under suspicion. In 1541 they fled to Switzerland, where Mainardi became Protestant pastor of Chiavenna and Giulio della Rovere a Calvinist.[34] In that same year, the Augustinians were so widely suspected of heresy that the secular authority, the Spanish viceroy, Alfonso D'Avalos, Marchese del Vasto, moved to expel those of heretical opinions. Cardinal Girolamo Seripando, elected General in 1539, devoted much of his tenure of office to safeguarding orthodoxy, especially in the Lombard province. Since Lando was from Milan, it is possible that he was a member there of the congregation of San Marco, the center for Augustinian studies in Lombardy, and a congregation

[32] *Ibid.,* ff. 1ʳ, 2ᵛ.
[33] *Ibid.,* ff. 4–6, 16–16ᵛ.
[34] Chabod, *Per la storia religiosa dello stato di Milano,* 124–29.

which Seripando believed to be so infected by heresy that he almost completely suppressed and dispersed it in 1547 and 1548.[35]

During the years of travel outside Italy through 1540, Lando knew both Protestants and Catholics. By 1529 he had "for the sake of the Gospel" translated some of Luther's writings and had gone to Chur, perhaps with the intention of remaining. In 1540 he may have known Comander and have met Bullinger, if the letter of May 1540 which introduced "Hortensius medicus" to Bullinger referred to Lando. This, with the mention of the Swiss reformers in *Erasmus funus* indicated an interest in the Swiss Reformation. In Germany, on the other hand, his known acquaintances were German Catholic prelates.

In Italy nearly all of the religious figures whom Lando knew had in common their interest in reform, whether they remained Catholic or became Protestant exiles after 1542. Lando's only known contact with an Italian community of dissenters was in Lucca, whose large merchant community, with its connections across Europe, brought Lutheran books to the Tuscan city as early as 1525.[36] Prohibitions against the heretical books were not enforced, and the new ideas flourished in the homes of the ruling class and penetrated the monasteries of Lucca. The absenteeism of the bishop and the evident corruption of the clergy stimulated the growth of ideas of reform.

The new ideas demonstrated an inconsistent, generalized Protestant impulse rather than a coherent, identifiable creed. Belief in predestination and the priesthood of all believers, doubts about confession and about many Catholic devotional practices appeared. Some Luccans denied purgatory and the Divine Presence in the Eucharist while others affirmed them. Some contested Papal authority but others were unconcerned with it. In the mixture were ideas that could be labeled Lutheran and Calvinist, and, among the lower classes, traces of Anabaptism and anti-Trinitarianism. Belief in salvation through a steadfast, unadorned faith in Christ, and desire to purify the church, both typical of Evangelism, were widespread among the Luccan dissenters.

For some time the government of Lucca, composed of members of the leading families, some of whom were influenced by the new religious ideas, ignored the conventicles. Only in 1542, under threat of the Inquisi-

[35] *Ibid.*, 162–65. On Seripando's reform activities as General, see Jedin, *Cardinal Seripando*, 200–39.

[36] For the history of heresy in Lucca, see Berengo, *Nobili e mercanti*, 357–454; Cantù, *Les hérétiques d'Italie*, III, 307–43; and Augusto Mancini, *Storia di Lucca* (Florence, 1950), 228–42.

tion, did the city government force Pier Martire Vermigli and Celio Secondo Curione, two leaders of dissent in the Luccan monasteries, to leave. With their flight, Luccan heresy became silent. Other dissenters lived tacitly in the city until 1555, when they began to leave for Geneva. The exodus continued for a decade until members of all the leading families of the city had emigrated.

On his visit in 1535 and throughout his life, the religion of the Luccans favorably impressed Lando. He praised their evangelical studies; they concentrated with fixed purpose on sacred Scripture in order to know God. In 1543 he praised them for being "religious without any superstition," and again approved of their concern for Scripture. In 1552 he credited Curione with opening the "highest mysteries of Divine Providence" by means of a book which praised a spider (doubtless Curione's heretical *Aranei encomion* [Venice, 1540]).[37] In December 1551, Lando's Luccan patron, Vincenzo Buonvisi, and another Luccan merchant, Francesco de Micheli, were denounced by a lower-class Luccan for holding Calvinist opinions. Later the accuser retracted his denunciation and admitted that he had perjured himself for reasons of personal rancor and avarice, but Micheli was in fact a Protestant and fled to Geneva in 1555. If Buonvisi also entertained heretical beliefs, they were not detected.[38] Lando obviously approved of Luccan unorthodoxy, but it is difficult to know how Protestant were the beliefs which he applauded. In 1535 Luccan religious dissent was confused; it lacked the Protestant leadership it received from Curione and Vermigli in 1541 and 1542, and its subsequent Calvinist orientation.

In the *Erasmus funus* Lando commented favorably on several Italian religious figures, all at that time Catholic. He praised Agostino Mainardi, who had already been harassed by Church authorities but had not yet left for Protestant lands, and the liberal and reforming cardinals Seripando and Gregorio Cortese.[39] Elsewhere he approved of Gian Matteo Giberti.

[37] *Forcianae Quaestiones*, 1857 ed., 9, 12, 51–52; *Paradossi*, 1545 ed., 39^v; *Cathaloghi*, 479.

[38] Berengo, *Nobili e mercanti*, 436–38.

[39] *Erasmus funus*, ff. 19^v–20. Other contacts with heretics are conjectural. In the *Cathaloghi* Lando mentioned several Italian Protestants including Francesco (Buonamente) Negri of Bassano (1500–63), Francesco Stancaro of Mantua (d. 1574), Aonio Paleario (Antonio della Paglia, b. 1503 and executed for heresy in 1570), whom Lando correctly placed in Lucca in 1552, and Curione. But only the reference to Curione had a religious context. The *Cathaloghi* contained the names of hundreds of contemporaries, many of whom Lando could not have known. *Cathaloghi*, 287, 450, 272, 460, 474, 479.

Other orthodox Catholics whom Lando knew were Girolamo Muzio, whose beliefs were of the Counter-Reformation, Cardinal Madruzzo, a generous patron, and Cornelio Musso, Bishop of Bitonto, known for his eloquence, and later in life a reformer of his diocese. The references in Lando's books and correspondence indicated knowledge of a range of religious figures from Swiss Protestants to Catholic prelates, from Italian religious exiles to a heretic hunter.

However varied may have been the eventual religious beliefs of the religious figures whom Lando knew, his own religious thought was steadfast and consistent. Throughout his life, Lando emphasized Scripture as the foundation of religion, and his few religious comments in the 1540's stressed it. In 1543 he commented that the monks had affirmed that one could not understand Holy Scripture without Scotus and Aristotle. As a result, they had abandoned the Bible in their discussion of "predestination conjoined with free will." Then Luther appeared. Lacking the favor of Aristotle or the "formality" of Scotus, but "armed only with Holy Scripture understood in his own way," he routed the "reverend Aristotelian theologians" of Leipzig, Louvain, and Cologne.[40]

In 1550 Lando linked justification by faith to belief in Scripture as an antidote for the ills of the Church. At the conclusion of a violent anticlerical tract, he tendered advice to bishops. Above all, they should implant the Bible in the hearts of the faithful. To do this, they had first to teach the force and true use of faith. Faith was a pure gift from God given to men to mortify the flesh, and for man's justification in Jesus Christ. Faith made good works spring up (*fa pullular le buone opere*); good works were evident signs of true and lively faith. By faith one came to works, and through works man was affirmed in faith. Teach the people, Lando admonished bishops, that works were signs of faith, faith a sign of grace, grace a sign of justification, salvation, and divine good will.[41] This imprecise and untheological combination of justification by faith and good works approximated the Italian Evangelism of Gaspare Contarini and Reginald Pole.[42]

Lando amplified his belief in Scripture and faith in his *Dialogo della Sacra Scrittura* of April 1552, and repeated it in condensed form in the religious questions of the *Quattro Libri de Dubbi,* also 1552. Published under his own name, the *Sacra Scrittura* instructed Lucrezia Gonzaga of

---

[40] *Paradossi,* 1545 ed., 79ᵛ.

[41] *Ragionamenti Familiari,* 47ᵛ.

[42] Jung, "On the Nature of Evangelism in 16th-century Italy," 517, 521.

Gazzuolo on the consolation and usefulness of Scripture by discussing its message book by book. In these writings Lando repeated his position of 1550 on justification by faith rather than by works. Citing St. Paul's epistles to the Romans and the Galatians, he stated that men were born subject to sin, and only by the grace of Christ, and not through works or man's merits, were the believers justified. The justified lived a full life of penitence guarding themselves from the world. The epistle of St. James showed that true religion consisted not in words, nor in "easy boasts of faith," but only in piety, the soil of good works.[43]

Those who could hear the Word of God and who recognized the true voice of their pastor, Christ, were the elect. From the beginning of the world they had been "elected and predestined." Created to know and serve God with perfect hearts, they were taught by God Himself because they had been given the power to hear the Gospel. In answer to the objection that God wanted all men to be saved, Lando answered, citing St. Augustine, that God meant some men of all states and conditions, but not that all men would be saved. Lando assured Lucrezia that her ability to listen avidly to him speaking on the glory of God was a sign that she was of the number of the elect.[44]

Lando spoke of the Church in two senses: a completely spiritual, invisible congregation of the good, and a visible, external union with a ministry and outward signs. Posing the question of what constituted the true Church, he answered that it was the "congregation of the good." It could not err, was without stain, and "completely spiritual." The Church was Christian, holy, and anointed, with Christ as bishop, pope, and mediator, at its head.[45] But the Church also was an external body with clear signs. In response to a question on the signs of the true Church of

[43] "Quivi [in Paul to the Romans] sopra ogni altra cosa egli disputa del peccato, & convince esser tutti gli huomini nati al peccato soggetti. Poscia egli disputa della giustitia; et dimostra che solo per la gratis di Christo, & non per l'opre, o per li meriti sono giustificati i credenti: non indugia molto, ch'egli esplica l'effetto della Gratia, & della fede, insegnando, che i Giustificati vivono una vita piena di penitenza guardandosi dalle mondane malvagità." *Sacra Scrittura,* 51 (quote), 23, 53ᵛ.

[44] "Hor poi che si avidamente m'udite favellare della gloria d'Iddio; ben è segno, che siete del numero de predestinati. . . ." *Sacra Scrittura,* 9ᵛ (quote); *Dubbi,* 1552 ed., 236, 273, 248, 259.

[45] Lando used the same words to describe the Church: "La congregatione de tutti i buoni" in *Dubbi,* 1552 ed., 292; and "la congregatione dei buoni" in *Sacra Scrittura,* 7ᵛ; "tutta spirituale" was used in *Sacra Scrittura,* 7ᵛ, and *Dubbi,* 1552 ed., 292. Also see *Sacra Scrittura,* 65ᵛ, and *Dubbi,* 1552 ed., 241, 292.

Christ, Lando answered: the preaching of the Word of God, confession of faith, baptism of water, correction of the errant, the Lord's Supper, and excommunication of the obstinate. He approved of infant baptism, and thought that the Church should include the "infirm" in faith. The Church had a ministry with priests who were to study, teach, and preach the Word of God, dispense the sacraments, and minister to the poor. Lando affirmed that all the faithful were priests of an internal priesthood, but added that they were not the ministers of the sacraments.[46] Christ was the head of the spiritual Church, but Lando implied a hierarchy for the visible Church when he advised that correction of the vices of the heads of the Church was sometimes necessary. Excommunication was justified from St. Paul; those who were persuaded by another belief, or a salvation outside of Christ's were to be excommunicated.[47]

Lando strayed from orthodoxy in his discussion of sacraments, which he viewed as "signs and testimonies" (*segnacoli & testimoni*) of divine benevolence and man's redemption, designed to restore and aid man's infirmity.[48] In his discussion, Lando recurrently used the verb "signify." In the *Dubbi* he posed the question, "What does the Lord's Supper signify? It signifies that all those who eat and drink together take part in the body and blood of Christ; in such a way they are united together with Christ through faith and charity like a body to the head in the same spirit." He went on to explain that whoever was not united to Christ in faith and to his neighbor in love, and yet participated in the Eucharist, was a hypocrite and simulator "showing himself to be what he was not."[49]

Lando strengthened this interpretation in his explanation of the "true

[46] "Tutti i fideli sono sacerdoti? Cosi è . . . ma non propriamente ministri di sacramenti." *Dubbi*, 1552 ed., 293; "Che tutti i fedeli sono sacerdoti del sacerdotio interno: & non dell'esterno." *Sacra Scrittura*, 7ᵛ.

[47] *Dubbi*, 1552 ed., 276; *Sacra Scrittura*, 22, 15ᵛ, 41ᵛ, 66.

[48] "furono ordinati gli sacramenti, segnacoli, & testimoni della divina benivoglienza, & della nostra redentione. . . ." *Sacra Scrittura*, 66; also *Dubbi*, 1552 ed., 298.

[49] "Che cosa significa la cena? Significa, che tutti coloro, che mangiono, & beveno [sic] insieme, hanno parte nel corpo & sangue di Christo, di maniera, che sono insieme uniti a Christo per fede, & charità come un corpo al capo in un medesimo spirito, & sono insieme uniti l'uno all'altro per carità, come un membro all'altro membro in un medesimo corpo. Talmente, che chiunque non è unito a Christo per fede, & carità, & al compagno per carità non puo degnamente convenire alla partecipatione della cena, anzi è hippocrita & simulatore mostrando essere quello ch'egli non è." *Dubbi*, 1552 ed., 277.

use" of the Lord's Supper. It proved to the communicant himself that he had true faith and contrition for his sins, had charity toward his neighbor, and was not contaminated by vice.[50] God used corporeal means, the bread and wine, to represent the spiritual, and to confirm and stimulate in man His infallible promises.[51] In a strict sense, Lando implied that the sacraments were not necessary for salvation. But he added a strong plea for participation in the sacraments on the ground that no one was perfect in faith. Man would have no need for the Eucharist if there were not in him "imperfections of faith and charity" which the Eucharist remedied.[52] To refuse the sacraments would be an "insupportable temerity" and would weaken the Holy Spirit.[53]

In his discussion of the Eucharist, Lando strayed furthest from Catholic orthodoxy. His view was very close to that of Zwingli, who argued that the sacraments were signs and seals, not originating or conferring grace, but presupposing the grace of the elect, and that they were public testimonies of faith in God. For Zwingli, and in the First Helvetian Confession, the Eucharist was a commemoration signifying and demonstrating the spiritual union of man and God, and the fact that Christ had died for men. There was no miracle of Transubstantiation, nor were sacraments channels of sanctifying grace; Zwingli acknowledged, however, that they were necessary to strengthen man's faith.[54] Lando came close to the Zwinglian position, but he did not deny Transubstantiation or that the sacraments were channels of grace; he made no mention of these points.

Passing to other sacraments, Lando spoke of two kinds of confession, private and public. Private confession he defined by the example of David

---

[50] "Quale è il vero uso di cotesto sagramento [the Lord's Supper]? Che l'huomo provi se stesso s'egli ha la vera fede & il vero pentimento de suoi peccati, et habbia verso il prossimo carità, non sia punto macchiato di odio, & contaminato di rancore." *Ibid.,* 301.

[51] "Disio di ricreare et di aiutare la nostra infirmità. perciochè sendo ali animi nostri aviluppati in questi corpi, habbiamo bisogno ch'anchora con le cose corporali ci sieno rappresentate le spirituali, accioche tutti i nostri sensi sieno essercitati nelle sue infallibili promesse, per confermarci in quelle." *Ibid.,* 298.

[52] "Anzi noi non havremo bisogno di tal cena se non fosse in noi imperfettione di fede & di carità sendo ordinata per aumento di l'una & dell'altra." *Ibid.,* 301.

[53] "il riffiutar adunque i sagramenti sarebbe una insupportabile temerità & un'ammorzare lo spirito Santo." *Ibid.,* 298.

[54] Philip Schaff, *Creeds of Christendom* (New York and London, 1905), I, 372–75; III, 223.

who had confessed his injustice directly to God, who then loosed him from the impiety of his sins. Thus, Lando concluded, if we will confess our sins, God will faithfully remit them. Then he asked Lucrezia if she wanted to hear of public confession, but she did not, and they went on to another topic. Similarly, Lando spoke of two kinds of penitence, legal and evangelical. The first came from divine laws, detestation of sin, and great sorrow. It was common to the pious and impious alike. The second kind of penitence was perpetual effort to mortify the flesh and reform one's life according to the will of God because one had received a pardon through a living faith in Christ.[55]

Ceremonies and religious practices were of little importance to Lando, but he did not eliminate them. He posed the question: If God wished to be adored only in spirit and truth, why did the Old Testament mention ceremonies? The Fathers of the Old Testament, who saw that the Jewish people were childlike, instituted ceremonies to manifest God's glory and to provoke the Jews to remember the benefits received from God. Hence they remained to rouse the love of God and virtue in the hearts of men. Again Lando asked why so many devotional cults were instituted in the Church, and answered that human reason always sought to justify itself through its own works. He did not attack any specific Catholic practices or ceremonies, but minimized the importance of fasts and abstinence from meat.[56]

But Lando spent little time discussing sacraments and ceremonies. The primary purpose of the *Sacra Scrittura* dialogue was to guide the reader to a better life through the reading of Scripture. The major part of the book was an explanation of the spiritual message of the Bible couched in terms of moral exhortation derived from biblical examples. In a corollary to his rejection of Renaissance learning, Lando argued that the Bible was superior to all other models of conduct and learning. Scripture was better than Cicero, Seneca, Plutarch, and the early Renaissance educator, Pier Paolo Vergerio (1370–1444), for teaching virtue, including "civil faith" (*civil fede*). The Bible was superior to any of the perfect types that inspired men: Cicero, the perfect orator; Plato's perfect republic; Thomas More's perfect reign of Utopia; Castiglione's perfect courtier; and Erasmus' perfect Christian knight of the *Enchiridion militis christiani*.[57] Anticlericalism was omitted from the *Sacra Scrittura* and

---

[55] *Dubbi*, 1552 ed., 298–99, 252; *Sacra Scrittura*, 14ᵛ–15.

[56] *Dubbi*, 1552 ed., 244, 315, 288, 259–60.

[57] *Sacra Scrittura*, 26, 28, 31ᵛ–32.

Dubbi, since Lando proposed a positive religious program, although in 1552 he again bitterly rebuked monks in the *Vari Componimenti.*

With the definitions, by the first session of the Council of Trent (1545–47), of faith and works, Scripture, tradition, and the objective nature of the sacraments, Lando's views on the sacraments, Eucharist, justification by faith, and predestination became heretical—more by omission than by assertion. But the Council was not completed, and the decrees were far from official promulgation, implementation, or widespread acceptance. A great deal of Lando's religious thought would have been acceptable to Catholic, Lutheran, Calvinist, and Zwinglian. The only group whose doctrines he rejected by name was the Anabaptists. He invoked Scripture against them to argue that princes and magistrates did have legitimate authority, criticizing the Anabaptist rejection of civil government.[58] Lando did not attack such Catholic beliefs and practices as purgatory, veneration of saints, the Virgin birth, the role of tradition as a supplement to Scripture, the mass, indulgences, sacramentals, or holy orders. In most instances he made no mention of them.

Lando, on the whole, was uninterested in theology, and did not develop a consistently heretical position. Indeed, the circumstances of the publication of his religious ideas in 1552 argue that he did not anticipate that his *Sacra Scrittura* would be considered heretical at all; for if he had foreseen difficulties with the Inquisition, he could have published it anonymously or outside of Italy. Lando's affirmation to Madruzzo that he was "a devoted servant of the Roman Church" indicates that he was not prepared to leave Italy.

From Lando's religious thought and the known facts of his life, one can tentatively reconstruct his religious life as follows. He was attracted to the study of Scripture alone while young, and probably while still in the monastery, under the inspiration of Erasmus and possibly of Luther. He left the monastery and translated Luther's works into Italian; he was perhaps more interested in Luther's emphasis on and interpretation of Scripture than his doctrines. Fearing papal reprisal, Lando went to Chur but left because of the difficulty of supporting himself and his wife. In 1540 he again went to the Grisons and on to Basel, but either at this time or earlier he had become disillusioned with organized Swiss Protestantism. In the decade of the 1540's he had little to say about religion, though he did attack the clergy, and attend the opening of the Council of Trent.

[58] "Imparasi nelle sacre lettere contra degli Anabattisti havere i Principi, & i Magistrati la debita possanza, & convenevole in autorità." *Ibid.,* 16–17ᵛ.

Then between 1550 and 1553 Lando published his beliefs and edited Musso's sermon. Why after long silence he decided to do this is not known; perhaps he underwent a spiritual crisis of some kind. The ideas expressed in 1550 and 1552 indicated that he continued to emphasize Scripture but held ceremonies and theological definitions as unimportant. Lando's religious thought fitted within Italian Evangelism. Beyond this one can only speculate. It is possible that from about 1544 until 1553 or 1554, during which time he lived in Italy, he was a Protestant Nicodemite. On the other hand, his religious thought of 1550–52 could have been an attempt to stress the fundamentals of Scripture and faith while maintaining allegiance to the Catholic Church.[59]

The consistent elements in Lando's religious life and thought were his adherence to Scripture, the necessity of moral reform especially of church abuses, and lack of concern for ceremony and practices. In his loyalty to these principles Lando may have wavered between Protestant and Catholic orthodoxies, and have travelled between the lands of the two faiths. Other Milanese dissenters weary of Italian corruption also looked to Switzerland as a paradise but did not always find that the reality matched their expectations. In the 1540's, Pietro Bresciani, a physician

[59] From the sixteenth to the early twentieth century scholars have been uncertain about Lando's religious affiliation. Conrad Gesner's bibliography credited Lando with a series of heretical works which have never been located, but made no mention of the *Sacra Scrittura* or *Dubbi*. These works were *Oratio adversus coelibatum; Conciones duae; De Baptismo unam & alteram de Precibus; Disquisitiones in selectiora loca scripturae; Explicationem Symboli Apostolorum, orationis Dominicae & Decalogi*. Sixteenth-century *Indices* do not include these books. *Bibliotheca [universalis]* (Zurich, 1583), 361.

Fra Sisto da Siena credited Lando with a book called *De persecutione barbarum* which he called contrary to sacred Scripture and Catholic teaching, but made no reference to *Sacra Scrittura* or *Dubbi. Bibliotheca Sancta*, II, 93. Apostolo Zeno vehemently judged Lando to be a heretic, basing his judgment on the unseen heretical works that Gesner and Sisto da Siena credited to him. Fontanini, *Biblioteca dell'eloquenza italiana*, II, 433–34. Tiraboschi wrote that the *Sacra Scrittura* had "not a few perilous and erroneous propositions" but did not judge Lando to be a heretic. *Storia della letteratura italiana*, VII, pt. 3, 809. Cantù noted that the *Dubbi* contained heresies and the *Sacra Scrittura* "erroneous propositions" but did not think that Lando professed Protestantism. *Les hérétiques d'Italie*, III, 516–17. Bongi could find nothing to justify the charge of heresy in the *Sacra Scrittura* or *Dubbi. Novelle di M. Ortensio Lando*, xxii, lxi. Sanesi entertained doubts about Lando's orthodoxy but thought that he was probably neither Catholic nor Protestant. He noted the *Dubbi* in this regard but found nothing heterodox in the *Sacra Scrittura. Lando*, 34–38. Sforza doubted that Lando was a heretic. "Ortensio Lando," 15.

from Casalmaggiore in Lombardy, was involved in a heretical conventicle and had an extensive heretical library. Under the threat of the Inquisition, he fled in 1546 to Chiavenna, thinking that he would find, in his words, "a paradise of habits and of faith." Upon arrival he was scandalized by the lives of the Protestants and doubted their beliefs. He returned to Italy and abjured his heresy in 1552. But he still was restless with Catholic orthodoxy, and was again tried by the Inquisition between 1565 and 1570.[60] The case of Bresciani indicated a disturbed, unsatisfied religious conscience. Lando, who was restless in other aspects of his life and thought, might have wavered in the same way for many years, between the attempt to live by Scripture and faith in the old Church and the appeal of Swiss Protestantism. Had he settled permanently in Switzerland, one wonders if the Swiss Reformed Church would have found him sufficiently Protestant. If Lando fled to the Grisons after 1554–55, one suspects that he was a dissenter there as he was in Italy, and as were many other Italian Protestant exiles who could not endure Protestant orthodoxy in Switzerland.[61]

Doni's religion

Doni also felt the tug of justification by faith. In a letter of November 28, 1546, at Florence (printed in the 1547 *Lettere*) he recounted the confession of faith of a dying man, an anonymous unlearned weaver, who, despite his lack of worldly learning (*senza lettere mondane*), was aflame with the spirit of God. Hence, he understood Scripture better than many who called themselves theologians. The weaver had lived an innocent life that was an inspiration to all. On his deathbed he spoke for two hours, and, wrote Doni, I have summarized the confession of faith that he made.[62] What followed was a concise, although not strictly logical, confession of faith of twenty-one articles, each beginning with "Io confesso. . . ."

In the first article, the weaver confessed God in terms that all orthodox Catholics and Protestants could accept, but added that one should not call on anyone except God for aid, perhaps implying a rejection of the intercession of saints. In the second article, he confessed

---

[60] Chabod, *Per la storia religiosa dello stato di Milano*, 145–50, 240–47.

[61] Frederic C. Church, *The Italian Reformers, 1534–1564* (New York, 1932); Cantimori, *Eretici italiani del Cinquecento.*

[62] For the text of the wearer's confession, see Appendix IV.

his belief in Christ, the Divine Son of God, who was man's sole "intermediary and advocate." The weaver then confessed in the fourth article that one must adore one God "in spirit and in truth, and not under a figure or visible thing." This could be interpreted as a simple prohibition of idolatry or, taken literally, as a denial of Transubstantiation, in which God appeared as bread and wine.

From this foundation, the weaver explored salvation, at first linking it to the Holy Spirit. Man had to have the grace of the Holy Spirit because he was subject to sin, and could not do good by his own efforts or free will. Then, after an interval of two articles, the dying man made salvation a byproduct of predestination and faith, stating his belief in predestination of the elect *ab eterno* and without qualification. In the sixth article, he stated that the Word of God was in itself enough for salvation. Doni amplified these bare declarations in the tenth article. Faith was a gift of God through which man had "certain experience" of the promise of God. Man was saved by God's grace through faith, not through his own effort, because faith was not granted through man's efforts. In short, God saved the elect through His gift of faith.

Although he made no distinction between visible and invisible church, the weaver implied one in his comments on the church. He confessed a church which was the gathering of all the elect "through divine predestination" and whose head was Christ. Then he described a simplified external church. Without making it clear whether he referred to infant or adult baptism, the weaver stated that baptism renewed man's life in Christ and admitted the believer into the "people of God." The ministers of the church, "such as bishops and priests," had to be irreproachable in conduct and doctrine; if not, they should be replaced by others. This vague structure of hierarchy and authority was completed by affirming obedience to God's representatives in secular authority—kings, princes, and magistrates—who carried the sword to protect the good and punish evildoers.

After baptism, Doni, through the weaver, discussed the sacraments without specifically calling them such. He affirmed a Zwinglian definition of the Lord's Supper, terming it "a holy memory and thanksgiving of the death and passion of Jesus Christ, which we do together in faith and in charity." The "unfaithful ones" should be sent away at the Lord's Supper, a practice reminiscent of the Anabaptists—compare, for example, the Schleitheim Anabaptist confession. Doni went on to affirm that matrimony was a good, holy state ordained by God, from which no one

TRE LIBRI

DI LETTERE DEL DONI,

E *i termini della lingua Toscana.*

CON PRIVILEGIO.

Fig. 5. Title page of Doni's *Lettere*, 1552

should be removed, whatever his condition, if he was not impeded from preaching the word of God. That is, the weaver preferred clerical marriage to clerical celibacy. On the subject of confession, Doni stated the hopeless sinfulness of man in terms close to Luther and Calvin. But Christ had pardoned the sins of the elect and satisfied divine justice by His death. If one sought any other satisfaction than Christ's death, one denied the efficacy of His passion and death. Hence, the only "necessary confession" was to God, trusting in His forgiveness.

The remaining articles expressed a general distaste for Catholic devotional practices. The true purpose of fasting was not to tame the rebellious flesh, but to stimulate prayer. Prayer itself ought to be spiritual, to God in faith. It should come from the heart, rather than the mouth, without regard to time or place. Christians were permitted to eat any food that they pleased. The Sabbath and "certain other days" (obviously holy days) should be equal to all other days, rather than celebrated. Finally, in the twenty-first and last article, the weaver affirmed excommunication of public and obstinate sinners.

After the confession, the dying man read from the gospel of St. John and the Psalms before expiring. Doni finished the letter with the statement that the deceased had been a great consolation to "us who were present there," and that he was happy to pass on the news as the "fruit of our new friendship, and you will be happy to communicate it to the other brothers (*fratelli*)."

The total result was a confession of faith centered on justification by faith, predestination, and reduction of the role of Catholic practices. From the post-Tridentine viewpoint, Doni's anonymous weaver proposed a confession embodying the core of sixteenth-century orthodox Protestantism, although it lacked a polemical attack on Catholic practices and doctrines. The confession cannot be characterized as predominantly Lutheran, Calvinist, or Zwinglian. The description of the Lord's Supper was not Zwinglian, and the weaver's confession lacked the emphasis on discipline that characterized Zwingli and Calvin. The confession mentioned bishops; this would not be countenanced by Zwinglian or Calvinist. Some of the confession could be considered Lutheran, for instance, the short description of the sinfulness of man, but the exhortation to obey civil authority lacked Luther's use of the distinction between the city of men and the City of God to explain secular authority. Nor could Luther have been the source for the weaver's position on the Lord's Supper. Doni's brief, sketchy confession did not develop a consistent Protestant position.

Rather, it read like the thought of a layman attempting to understand for himself the mysteries of faith and salvation, exactly as Doni described the anonymous weaver.

From the eclectic nature of the confession, and if Doni's statement about communicating the message to the fratelli can be taken at face value, Doni may at this time have been a member of a conventicle, i.e., a group of laymen who met to discuss religious issues, to read from Scripture, or to listen to reports from Protestant Europe. Doni's Florentine working-class background would have given him access to a group that could include an unlearned weaver. However, Doni did not identify the addressee of the letter, Basilio Guerrieri, who is not mentioned elsewhere in his works or letters and who remains unknown. There is no mention in Doni's other letters at this time of any conventicle, and, beyond the usual anticlericalism, no unorthodoxy.

But religious ideas later condemned as heretical did exist in Florence in these years, despite Duke Cosimo's hostility toward religious deviation. In 1546, Doni printed the first edition of Gelli's *I capricci del bottaio,* which contained ideas that ecclesiastical authorities later interpreted as heretical. Paradise came to men through the death of Christ, Gelli wrote. Men had to do good works anyway, but only for the honor and glory of God. Thus, without quite expressing the Lutheran position on faith and works, Gelli reduced the importance of works in salvation. He also came close to Luther's position on the unavoidability of sin. God had made man so weak that he could not avoid it, but he only rejected men when they persevered in evil and turned away from him. Man will sin because of his infirmity, but he should return to Christ, admitting that he was conceived in sin. Gelli praised Lutherans for emphasizing that men should read Scripture and forget Scholastic disputations.[63]

Neither Gelli nor Doni suffered any hardship for their published religious views of 1546 and 1547. But in December 1551, three years after Doni's departure from Florence, two autos-da-fé, one of them involving twenty-two persons, were held in Florence. After making their abjuration, the Florentines were absolved, but their books and writings were thrown into the fire. Bartolomeo Panciatichi, who led one of the 1551 autos-da-fé, and Piero Gelido da San Miniato, who fled to Geneva about 1560, were

[63] Gelli, *I Capricci,* ed. Ferrero, 251–52, 239, 218. On Gelli's unorthodoxy, see Armand L. De Gaetano, "Tre lettere inedite di G. B. Gelli e la purgazione de I capricci del bottaio," *GSLI,* CXXXIV (1957), 297–313; and "G. B. Gelli and the Rebellion Against Latin," *Studies in the Renaissance,* XIV (1967), 146–54.

members of the Accademia Fiorentina, which also included Gelli and, while he was in Florence, Doni.[64]

During his Florentine period, Doni had contacts with three heretics, but his association with them seems to have been nonreligious. On February 14, 1547, he wrote to Christoforo Trenta of Lucca, a friend of Pier Martire Vermigli and a Protestant who fled to Geneva in 1555. Doni merely thanked Trenta for the favors shown him in Trenta's home, presumably in Lucca, and described at length the music and merrymaking at a pre-Lenten carnival in Pistoia.[65] No trace of other contacts with Lucca or the Luccan dissenters can be found.

Another letter of this period indicated that Doni may have known the anti-Trinitarian, Lelio Sozzini (Laelius Socinus, 1525–62), and a Bolognese bookseller, Francesco Linguardo, later accused of heresy. On April 1, 1547, Doni wrote to Sozzini from Florence that through letters of Linguardo he had learned that Sozzini wanted certain (unnamed) books, and that he had forwarded some of these to him. He wrote that he had never met Sozzini but looked forward to doing business with him in a few days in Bologna. True to his word, Doni arrived in Bologna by April 12, returning to Florence by May 1; but he failed to mention in his letters any meeting with the youthful Sozzini. The latter had by April 1547 arrived at heretical views, and in that summer he left Italy for Protestant Switzerland.[66] In 1548 Linguardo was arrested in Bologna for holding Lutheran opinions and selling heretical books. He took flight, but then returned to confess the Lutheran opinions. A search failed to uncover the heretical books, and upon confession, Linguardo was absolved and permitted to return to his bookshop.[67] Doni's letter to Sozzini reveals no more than an ordinary business transaction, with Doni acting as intermediary.

The letter recounting the confession of the dying weaver may not have indicated any religious concern at all on Doni's part. His books and letters were at times reportorial, reproducing conversations, gossip, and stories making the rounds of the city. His ready ear missed little of topical

---

[64] Cantù, *Les hérétiques d'Italie*, III, 215, 222–30.

[65] "Al Signor Christophoro Trenta da Lucca," February 14, 1547, Pistoia, in *Lettere*, 1547 ed., 58–60, and reprinted in *La Zucca*, 1565 ed., 93ᵛ–98ᵛ; Cantù, *Les hérétiques d'Italie*, III, 317, 337; McNair, *Peter Martyr in Italy*, 236, 270.

[66] *Lettere*, 1547 ed., 62ᵛ, 63ᵛ–65.

[67] Luigi Carcereri, "Cristoforo Dossena, Francesco Linguardo e un Giordano, librai processati per eresia a Bologna (1548)," *L'Archiginnasio*, V, no. 5, (1910), 177–92.

interest, and he eagerly related new ideas. In 1552, for example, he defended the Copernican hypothesis, but he did not espouse Copernicus' ideas, nor ever again mention the heliocentric system.[68] In the same manner, he may have heard or read Evangelical or Protestant materials and have reproduced them without giving his allegiance to them. One cannot rule out the possibility that the ill-tempered Doni may have written the letter maliciously in order to provoke difficulty for Basilio Guerrieri, just as in 1548 he denounced the innocent Domenichi as a heretic after a personal quarrel.

Despite the uncertainty of its motivation, Doni's confession of the anonymous weaver pointed to a concern with justification by faith and a de-emphasis of Catholic religious practices that characterized Italian Evangelism, although Scripture was not stressed. But this concern was probably transitory. There is no evidence after 1547 that he entertained heretical ideas or that he was part of a heretical group; indeed, he ridiculed Lutherans and Anabaptists,[69] and his comments on the Catholic Church were perfectly orthodox, if lacking in great sincerity.

After 1547 Doni's attitude veered between utopian attempts to reform the Church and materialism; in his New World utopia, he offered a combination of the two. With the example of the new, reformed religious orders before his eyes, Doni in 1564 constructed a utopian religious order to reform the Church in Italy. He named his new order "The Order of the Knife" (*La Religione del Coltello*), deriving the title from a saying attributed to Plato that man's life was similar to a knife, keen and lustrous when used, but rusty when unused. The Order of the Knife would be resplendent through the use of doctrine, good will, and true observance of religion.

In each of thirteen Italian cities—Milan, Pavia, Piacenza, Bologna, Ferrara, Venice, Verona, Genoa, Mantua, Florence, Naples, Salerno, and Rome, but nowhere else—a large circular temple worthy to be a cathedral should be built. All should be constructed on the same design, with a high altar in the center with a depiction of the Calvary scene, and twelve side chapels, one for each apostle, placed around the circumference of the church. The church in Rome, named San Salvatore della Chiesa, was the most important of the thirteen. To each temple were attached a bishop, twelve canons (one for each chapel), and thirteen priests to assist bishop and canons in reading daily mass and the office at the high altar and

[68] *I Marmi*, 1928 ed., I, 16–19.
[69] *La Zucca*, 1565 ed., 233, 204.

chapels. In Rome a cardinal protector assisted by twelve bishops presided. By Doni's count, the Order of the Knife consisted of a cardinal, 24 bishops, and 313 canons and priests, "all learned and admirable."

Doni decreed strict rules of conduct and dress for the members of the order. Before admission, every character stain had to be eliminated. After entry, upon the commission of a notable crime or sin, a member was placed in penance and, at the second offense, expelled. The canons were to dress in a clear purple habit, and the priests in "honorable" black. But the members of the order were not to be restricted by monastic rules or forced to live in poverty. All were free to come and go as they pleased, to study, to ride, and to do anything characteristic of a signore. For maintenance each bishop received 500 scudi (presumably for one year), each canon 200 scudi plus as many servants as he pleased, and each priest 100 scudi. They lived alone except for the principal liturgical feasts, when all met together to celebrate. Doni provided a path of advancement which he believed would reward learning. When death depleted the ranks, the vacant places were to be filled by the most learned friars and priests to be found. The applicants would pray, and then read and dispute before the Holy See, after which the pope and bishops would select the new members. The path of advancement within the order was from priest to canon to bishop, and then at the death of the cardinal, the eldest bishop would become the new cardinal protector. The entire order would be at the disposal of the Church, prepared to defend the Church and the Papacy in disputes or in any other way. Doni also alluded to a personal tie to the Papacy, but did not explain.[70]

One must approach Doni's plan for a reformed religious order with caution. Only four pages beyond the conclusion of the discourse on the Order of the Knife, he wrote a cynical disclaimer of the possibility of reform.[71] Such contradictions within a few pages were characteristic of Doni, who swung from the extremes of complete cynicism to wild hopes of reform throughout his writing. The Order of the Knife was part of a series of allegorical word pictures, analogous in conception to Vasari's allegorical paintings, which Doni admired. He may have provided for his readers such a word picture of a reformed religious order with the Jesuits in mind as a model, while More's *Utopia* suggested the setting of the thirteen temples and uniform clothing. Although one can question the sincerity of Doni's belief in reform, the utopian approach to solving such complex social and moral problems as monastic decline by the use of

[70] *Ibid.*, 270–73ᵛ.
[71] *Ibid.*, 275ᵛ–80ᵛ.

simplistic, rigidly ordered external devices was also characteristic of his New World dialogue. The Order of the Knife was an extension of his belief that monastic institutions should return to their original, purified state within the primitive Church.

Doni entertained doubts about an afterlife as well. In 1564, at the end of a bitterly pessimistic diatribe in which he derided man's attempts to achieve anything enduring, Doni concluded that the oblivion that existed before man would return, implying a denial of an afterlife. In this way, man who came from nothing would return to nothing, lacking name, fame, or any sign that he was remembered. Doni parenthetically asserted that he was speaking of "mortal man," presumably not denying the immortality of his soul, but a few lines later, he concluded, "and this for now is the end . . . because everything ends with Death."[72] The passage did not literally deny immortality, but the entire discussion lacked any mention of heaven or hell, and its mood denied hope of immortality. In 1567 the conventional words of religious comfort failed to console the aging Doni, and in his New World utopia he developed a materialist view of man.

The religious ideas of the critics were consistent with the general tenor of their lives and thought. Franco, Lando, and Doni sharply condemned the abuses of Italian churchmen. The Erasmian way attracted Lando and Franco, and all three advocated a simple, non-theological Christianity of Scripture and faith, lacking concern for ceremonies. Lando and Doni fitted within the broad spectrum of Evangelism. Both wrote heretical passages but their heretical ideas did not comprise a fully developed Protestant position. Lando was in contact with Protestants and their ideas, and went farthest toward Protestantism. Doni possibly entertained Protestant ideas for a limited time before giving way to utopianism and materialism. Franco, despite the fury of his anticlericalism, remained completely orthodox. For all three, dissatisfaction with the Catholic Church found expression in a spiritual restlessness that complemented their political and social criticism.

---

[72] "Cosi va camminando il mondo, per le mani de gli huomini mortali, che mortale cose producono insin a tanto che l'oblie di prima, inanzi che fosse l'huomo abbraccia l'oblio dipoi, che egli è stato. Cosi torna nulla quel nulla, che era prima nulla, inanzi che fosse (questo che io dico, dell'huomo mortale dico) senza nome, senza fama, senza ricordo, senza memoria, et senza segno alcuno di ricordanza. . .

.   .   .   .

et questo per hora sia il fine delle pitture, perche ogni cosa si chiude con la Morte."
Ibid., 296ᵛ.

Chapter V

THE REJECTION OF LEARNING FOR
THE VITA CIVILE

⎯⎯⎯⎯⎯⎯⎯⎯⎯⎯

THE core of sixteenth-century learning was the studia humanitatis, defined by Paul O. Kristeller as grammar, rhetoric, history, poetry, and moral philosophy based upon the reading and interpretation of its standard ancient writers in Latin and, to a lesser extent, in Greek.[1] Learning in the Cinquecento also included vernacular literature based on the study of modern authors, as well as philosophy, logic, mathematics, and geometry. Its purpose was the training of the young patrician to serve his family, city, or prince in the affairs of the world.

Education for the vita civile

In the fifteenth century, Italian—especially Florentine—humanists had developed a system of education for the active life. The education favored by Leonardo Bruni, Matteo Palmieri, L. B. Alberti, and others has been termed "civic humanism" by Hans Baron and education for the vita civile by Eugenio Garin. It sought to form critical judgment and moral obligation in the young student by study and reading in the Latin classics and a reliance upon the past experience of man in history.[2] If one wished to

[1] Paul O. Kristeller, *Renaissance Thought: The Classic, Scholastic, and Humanistic Strains* (New York, 1961), 10, 120–23.

[2] Hans Baron, *The Crisis of the Early Italian Renaissance* (Princeton, N.J., 1955), and numerous articles; Eugenio Garin, *L'umanesimo italiano: filosofia e vita civile nel Rinascimento* (Bari, 1952). English tr. by Peter Munz (Oxford, 1965).

avoid the reputation of a rustic, one should be educated in letters above all, but also arithmetic, geometry, grammar, philosophy, oratory, and poetry. Alberti recommended such authors as Cicero, Livy, Sallust, Homer, Vergil, Demosthenes, and Xenophon. This scheme of education would make a child *lecterato, costumato, savio e civile,* and, joined with physical exercise and military training, would enable him to live the vita civile.[3]

Reacting against what they felt was sterile, solitary monkish virtue, Bruni, Palmieri, and Alberti stressed the bonds of community. The purpose of learning was to prepare men for community life. For Matteo Palmieri in his *Della vita civile* (written in the 1430's), a well-ordered republic in which men lived together harmoniously was the highest human goal. Man's task was to work for this harmony as head of his family, as businessman, and as a member of the government.[4] The virtuous and happy life was the life of participation for the common good, while he who withdrew into solitary idleness or contemplation did not fulfill his humanity. Alberti warned that solitude and idleness quickly made one "pertinacious, depraved, and bizarre."[5]

In the sixteenth century vernacular literature grew in importance, and the urban patriciate became a courtly society. With the exception of treatises inspired by the example of Venice, like Paolo Paruta's *Della perfettione della vita politica* (1572–79), most sixteenth-century champions of education for the vita civile laid less emphasis on dedication to a city and were less concerned with history than their Quattrocento predecessors.[6] The purpose of learning often became service to a prince at court rather than to one's native city in local government. Nevertheless, the basic program of studies whose purpose was to prepare the young man for life in society remained, as did the aversion to a solitary life. The ideal courtier, for Castiglione, should be well educated in letters, poetry, oratory, and history.[7] Giovanni Della Casa affirmed in his *Galateo* (published in 1558) that those who wished to live in fellowship with other men in

[3] L. B. Alberti, *La Famiglia,* in *L'educazione umanistica in Italia,* ed. E. Garin (Bari, 1959), 133, 160–62, 145, 164.

[4] *Della Vita Civile,* ed. Felice Battaglia (Bologna, 1944), bk. IV, pp. 176, 127–32.

[5] L. B. Alberti, *La Famiglia,* in *L'educazione umanistica in Italia,* ed. Garin, 137.

[6] Hans Baron, "Secularization of Wisdom and Political Humanism in the Renaissance," *Journal of the History of Ideas,* XXI, no. 1 (1960), 143–45.

[7] *The Book of the Courtier,* tr. Charles S. Singleton (Garden City, New York, 1959), 70.

populous cities, rather than "in solitary and deserted places" like hermits, needed learning and skill in manners.[8] In *La civil conversatione* (1574) Stefano Guazzo argued that no sensible man would live in solitude, and provided a book which discussed relations between men. For him "civil conversation" signified an honest and commendable kind of living in the world as citizen, neighbor, and spouse.[9] Annibale Romei, Flaminio Nobili, Girolamo Garimberto, and G. B. Giraldi Cinthio discussed the education of man to fit him for an honored place within civil society.[10]

An example of the program of sixteenth-century learning at its best was Alessandro Piccolomini's *De la institutione di tutta la vita de l'uomo nato nobile e in città libera* (1542) which went into fourteen Italian, three French and one Spanish editions between 1542 and 1594.[11] Piccolomini, Sienese nobleman, archbishop, philosopher, and member of the influential Accademia degli Intronati of Siena, eptiomized the Cinquecento learning to which Franco, Lando, and Doni objected. In the "Prohemio" Piccolomini announced the purpose of the work. Since God had given man free will and the privilege of living and governing himself as he willed, Piccolomini would offer a guide to "finding the happiness that is appropriate to man as man."[12] To accomplish this purpose, he would not speculate on the causes of things but would discuss the manner of educating children through knowledge and "moral disciplines" to virtue and good habits.

As for the Quattrocento Florentine humanists, the center of life for Piccolomini was the active life in the city. His book would educate children in their actions and duties to God, parents, spouse, children, friends, servants, "and in what manner they must live among citizens, in the forum, in the senate, and in whatever high place they should converse; and according to such duties, they came to act so that they could

---

[8] *A Renaissance Courtesy-Book, Galateo of Manners and Behaviours by Giovanni della Casa*, introd. J. E. Spingarn (Boston, 1914), 15.

[9] John L. Lievsay, *Stefano Guazzo and the English Renaissance 1575-1675* (Chapel Hill, N.C., 1960), 19-44.

[10] Garin, *Italian Humanism*, 159, 179-85.

[11] *De la institutione di tutta la vita de l'huomo nato nobile e in città libera* . . . (Venice, 1542). Piccolomini revised the work in 1560, adding new material and changing the title to *Institutione morale*. For bibliography, see Florindo Ceretta, *Alessandro Piccolomini: letterato e filosofo senese del Cinquecento* (Siena, 1960), 184-86. On *De la institutione*, see Garin, *Italian Humanism*, 172-75.

[12] ". . . di trovar la felicità che si conviene al'huomo come huomo . . ." (p. 2).

make their city similar to a celestial republic."[13] Piccolomini even suggested that the young nobleman should not build a villa so far outside the city that he could not go and return in one day.[14]

The *humane lettere* were of central importance to Piccolomini's educational program. Early in the book he affirmed that the boy should begin his study of Latin and Greek letters before any other discipline for the purpose of acquiring style, the comprehension of history, and the understanding of allegorical fables. The recommended authors were quite similar to Alberti's list for Greek history—Plutarch, Polybius, Xenophon, and Thucydides—while for Roman history, Piccolomini recommended Plutarch again, Livy, Caesar, Sallust, and Suetonius. Important poets were Homer, Horace, Pindar, Menander, Hesiod, Euripides, Sophocles, Vergil, and Terence. For Latin prose style Cicero was the most important model.[15]

Of equal importance to Latin was Tuscan literature. Piccolomini approved the rules of "the most learned Bembo" and *La poetica* (1536) of Bernardino Daniello, which showed Aristotle's influence, as guides for writing vernacular verse. As models he offered Petrarch, Bembo again, Francesco Molza, Giovanni Della Casa, and Benedetto Varchi. He also recommended Boccaccio as a prose example, the dialogues of Sperone Speroni for their conceits, and the "most ingenious" Claudio Tolomei. In short, Piccolomini's list of recommended models was practically a roll-call of approved authors in the sixteenth century.[16]

After the boy had established the foundation of humane letters, he studied other disciplines. Piccolomini approved the same curriculum as Alberti—rhetoric or oratory, dialectic and logic with Aristotle the recommended guide, mathematics, geometry, and natural and moral philosophy based on Aristotle and Plato.[17]

While Cinquecento learning for the vita civile continued the educational program of the Quattrocento, there were differences of spirit and

---

[13] ". . . e in che maniera si debbi vivere tra i cittadini, nel foro, nel senato, o in qual si sia altro luogo, dove uopo faccia di conversare: e secondo tali officij operando; venivano a far si che la città loro ad una celeste republica assomigliavano" (p. 3ᵛ).

[14] *De la institutione di tutta la vita,* 237ᵛ–38.

[15] Bk. II, ch. 8, *la grammatica e humane lettere.*

[16] *Ibid.*

[17] Bk. III, chs. 7–8, 14–15, 4.

emphasis. The contact between the ancients and fifteenth-century men through the studia humanitatis was a dialogue, as the humanists used or adapted what was relevant to them.[18] Quattrocento men went to the classics for advice on how to meet situations in their lives, whether it was to the political writers of Rome when drafting an oration, or to the Stoics for consolation when disaster struck. The humanists were conscious of the historical distance between the ancient world and Quattrocento Italy; they did not accept blindly the authority of the ancients, whom they regarded as guides and examples but not unquestioned authorities. Scholasticism, they believed, had become a set of rules, formulas, or attitudes. Fifteenth-century educators, on the other hand, argued that they were training a person rather than passing on a body of learning. Thus they used the ancients eclectically and reminded the reader that experience should temper learning.

Beginning in the 1540's, learning took more authoritarian directions, and became less of an exchange between text and reader. There grew up a new concern for laws, definitions, and classifications, and a subsequent constriction of outlook. The literary academies, which were originally established in order to escape the narrowness and lack of concern for humanistic learning of the universities and monastic schools, became as authoritarian and specialized as the institutions which they were designed to supplant. Under the leadership of Sperone Speroni the Accademia degli Infiammati of Padua after 1542 turned from earlier wide-ranging study of various fields and languages to concentrate on philosophy and, to a lesser extent, vernacular literature.[19] Similarly, the Accademia della Crusca codified the vernacular and became an arbiter of the language. By the 1560's authorities were established in several fields of Italian intellectual endeavor.

The texts of Aristotle dominated more than one area of learning. A science of literature based on the *Poetics* developed between the late 1540's and 1560. Involved and minute arguments of literary criticism waxed hot for the rest of the century as Italians sought to arrive at standards of

[18] Eugenio Garin, *Medioevo e Rinascimento, studi e ricerche* (Bari, 1954), 204–5.

[19] Count Fortunato Martinengo, one of the earliest members and perhaps a founder, stressed the eclectic nature of the early months of the Infiammati in contrast to the more specialized program under Speroni. See *Quattro libri della lingua Thoscana di M. Bernardino Tomitano* . . . (Padua, 1570), I, 6–10.

correctness.[20] A similar development occurred in guides for the vita civile. The bases for these were Aristotle's *Politics, Ethics,* and the pseudo-Aristotelian *Economics,* as they had been in the fifteenth century. Again beginning in the late 1540's, many translations and commentaries on the above works, and a number of political treatises heavily based on Aristotle, appeared. In the middle ages and the fifteenth century, men had tended to adapt Aristotle to their own experience of government. In contrast, men in the sixteenth century attempted to make a science out of his teachings. For them, Aristotle gave laws to govern facts, and reduced variable political and ethical reality to a system. He became an authority who inspired abstract models of the best form of government.[21]

Thus education in the second half of the sixteenth century became more authoritarian and abstract, whether the authority was a text, the teacher, or the Church.[22] The tendency to rely on external authority produced learning which emphasized "words" rather than "things," according to its critics, and which was based on the application of abstract principles and rules to the problem at hand, rather than on the interaction between principles and experience. The Church did not instigate the change, but the Counter-Reformation reinforced it. By the end of the sixteenth century a "new Scholasticism" based on Aristotle, which reduced the studia humanitatis to a grammatical function, dominated Italian education,[23] although the basic pattern and goals of the Quattrocento education for the vita civile continued. This was the education that Franco, Lando, and Doni knew and rejected.

In their opinion learning was part of the decadent, corrupt, and oppressive world which they opposed. Just as they railed against political authorities and religious leaders, so also were they intolerant of the inadequacies of learning. Lando's Messer Anonymo, who was shocked at the misery of Italy and her swarm of petty tyrants, also found fault with

---

[20] Dionisotti, "La letteratura italiana nell'età del Concilio," 336–37; Toffanin, *La fine dell'umanesimo,* 1–14; Weinberg, *A History of Literary Criticism in the Italian Renaissance.*

[21] Curcio, *Dal Rinascimento alla Controriforma,* 49–53, with an extensive list of translations and commentaries on the *Politics.*

[22] The pedagogical texts from the period 1545–1645 in *Il pensiero pedagogico della Controriforma,* ed. Luigi Volpicelli (Florence, 1960), illustrate the emphasis on authority and rules.

[23] Eugenio Garin, *L'educazione in Europa (1400–1600). Problemi e programmi* (Bari, 1957), 188–94.

the curricula and teaching at Italian universities. Franco in his letter from Lucerna (see below) interspersed a condemnation of signori amidst criticism of learning.

The fundamental criticism of Lando, Doni, and Franco was that contemporary learning was not relevant to the spoiled reality. Implicitly the critics agreed that learning should be preparation for the vita civile, but they doubted that, in its contemporary state, it did or could accomplish this. They put greater emphasis on practical experience as an alternative. Second, the critics doubted the motivating ideal of the studia humanitatis, the active life. The world, they believed, was beyond reform; it was not amenable to reason as Quattrocento humanists had thought. Rather than trying fruitlessly to change the world, and becoming corrupted in the process, man should spurn the active life and withdraw into himself for a small measure of peace.

In addition to their fundamental criticisms, the critics devoted much space to a general mockery of contemporary learning. They laughed at the authorities, and looked upon the growing abstraction and specialization of learning as irrelevant pedantry, while the debates over the interpretation of authoritative texts seemed to them trivial, unrelated to life. Lando, Franco, and Doni found many deficiencies in sixteenth-century learning.

Divorce between learning and reality

In a passage perhaps inspired by Lucian's *Sale of Creeds,* Franco argued with wit and humour that learning was irrelevant in a declining world. In the eighth dialogue of the *Dialogi Piacevoli,* one of the characters read an advertisement that offered to teach men all manner of learning and virtue in a few days. First, Latin letters could be poured into the fortunate recipient, and on the second day, Greek. Hebrew could be learned in two more days, Chaldean in three, grammar in four, and logic in five, followed by philosophy, poetry, arithmetic, astrology, medicine, and "all the rest" by the time that ten days had elapsed. For only ten scudi man could learn "the true method of understanding every mystery."[24] But the

---

[24] "Inventione, bella, nuova, utile, et admirabile al parangone, ritrovata da Sannio, ne la quale, con l'aiuto di quel dio che nascendo gli diede tanta vertu, puote infondere in ogni intelletto ogni dottrina. Primieramente lettere latine, e greche in un giorno al piu. Hebree in due. Caldee in tre. Grammatica in quattro. **Logica** in

other character rejected the offer for the reasons that summarized Franco's fundamental opposition to learning; he was sated with the triviality
of the *scienze;* letters had fallen so low that only a rogue tried to be
learned. Moreover, the world had gone to ruin. Ignorant workers and
tradesmen triumphed in the world, so that one would be well advised to
learn a trade rather than acquire learning.[25] The dialogue continued to a
comic end. One of the characters tried to sell books on various subjects,
but found that no one wished to buy them. Even at the lowest price (one
scudo) no one would purchase anything on philosophy, law, astrology,
and medicine. Poetry was not worth the price of a salad. They concluded
that all learning was valueless.[26]

The critics explored the divorce between learning and reality in
several ways. In another dialogue Franco argued that contemporary
learning would not stand the scrutiny of sound judgment, and at worst
attempted to teach the contrary to what every man knew to be true. An
example of this kind of questioning was Franco's letter from Lucerna
(the Lantern). Lucerna corresponded to "wise judgment acquired by long
study."[27] She wandered through the world at night in order to compare
man's self-description from his books with reality, and found that the
reality was different from the ideal. Lucerna noted that men wrote
sonnets and *canzoni* in praise of the beauty and goodness of women, but
discovered from peering into bedrooms that their beauty was artifice, and
the supposed honesty, chastity, and virtue were in reality lasciviousness,
pride, and instability.[28]

Lucerna spent much of her time investigating the practitioners of

---

cinque. Philosophia in sei. Poesia in sette. Aritmetica in otto. Strologia in nove.
Medicina, e tutto il resto in diece. Promette doppo questo, il vero modo d'apprendere
ogni mistiero, e la strada d'ascendere ad ogni grado. E tutto s'insegna per diece
scudi." *Dialogi Piacevoli,* 1541 ed., cvii[v].

[25] "Io ti dico il vero, o Sannio, de la pidocchieria de le scienze son tanto satio;
che vorrei vomitarle quando potessi. Le lettere hoggi (mercè del cielo) sono ite
tanto al basso, che tristo chi pensa haverne. Quanto l'huomo e piu dotto e piu carico
di dottrina, piu dolente, e misero va piangendo. Hoggi i meccanici, e gli artigiani,
per quanto veggo, trionphano di questo mondo. E percio havrei a caro d'apprendere
qualche buon'arte." *Dialogi Piacevoli,* 1541 ed., cviii.

[26] *Ibid.,* cxi[v]–cxii.

[27] "Dovereste pur' avertire, che la lucerna allegoricamente ne significa lo
studiare . . . e saggio giuditio acquistato con lungo studio." *Pistole Vulgari,* 1539
ed., xc.

[28] Franco, *ibid.,* lxxxii[v]–lxxxiii.

various branches of learning, subjecting their work to the test of sound judgment. She discovered that contemporary learning was embroiled in irrelevant pedantry. Gammarians, she noted, wasted their time investigating matters of little consequence in the lives and works of classical authors. Of what importance was the question of the true fatherland of Homer? What did it matter if Pliny came from Verona or Brescia, or whether Ovid had composed six or twelve books of *Fasti?* Other branches of learning bewildered men or tried to prove as true what men knew to be false. Philosophers were greatly confused because of their own work, involved as it was with principles, ends, prime matters, and distinctions (Aristotle), atoms (Democritus), and Ideas (Plato).[29] Logicians tried to prove that *si* denied and that *non* affirmed.

Lando contrasted learning and reality in order to make the point that books could not prepare men for the world. Quattrocento humanists had stressed that learning prepared men for careers in the marketplace and in council chambers, but Lando argued that they had to rely on experience, not treatises. He could see no value in educational treatises based on Aristotle's *Politics,* and *Ethics,* or on the *Economics.* How could the confused Aristotle advise moderns about governing family, household, and servants, he asked? Lando held up for his readers' emulation Francesco Sforza, who had learned about warfare from experience rather than from books.[30]

Similarly, Doni opposed the studia humanitatis because he was convinced that the studi liberali could not teach virtue, and, further, that it was pedagogically impossible to implant virtue by means of books; in so far as man had virtue, he possessed it innately. In a dialogue in *I Marmi* he discussed how to foster virtue, which he defined in traditional terms as the love of native land, wife, and children.[31] Grammar, he thought, could

---

[29] "Veggo primi i PHILOSOPHI, e con essi la gran confusione de i lor scritti, i cui ciarlamenti, tutti sono impecciati di Principi, e di fini; di corporeo, e d'incorporeo; di generabile, e di sensibile, e d'incorruttibile; di mortale, e d'immortale; di finito, e d'infinito; di materie prime, d'atomi, e d'Idee." *Ibid.,* lxxxiiii^v–lxxxv^v.

[30] *Paradossi,* 1545 ed., 12–17.

[31] "Si può ancóra dir questo, che senza gli studi liberali si può pervenire alla sapienza, imperochè, benché sia necessario imparare la virtù, non di meno non s'impara per gli studi liberali." *I Marmi,* 1928 ed., II, 67. Doni's words here are a translation of Seneca, *Ad Lucilium Epistulae Morales,* Ep. LXXXVIII, 32, and the entire discussion of the studi liberali in this discourse shows the influence of Ep. LXXXVIII.

DIALOGI

PIACEVOLI DI

M. Nicolo Franco, no-
uamente con somma di/
ligenza stampati.

CON VNA TAVOLA DI
nouo aggiunta di tutto quello,
che ne l'opera si contiene.

CON GRATIA ET PRIVILECIO.

IN VENETIA PER GABRIEL
IOLITO DI FERRARII.
M. D. XLII.

Fig. 6. Title page of Franco's *Dialogi Piacevoli*, 1542

teach style, and poetry was important. Knowledge of the lives and activities of the ancients acquired from history had only a negative value, a warning to men to avoid their faults. With arithmetic and geometry one could count one's possessions, but it was of no avail if one did not divide them for charity. The study of Stoic or Aristotelian philosophy was useless for moral instruction. Men had to learn from their own experience, not from books. In Doni's example, one could read "fire burns," but if one did not touch the fire, one would never know the sensation of burning. Further, after a man had learned through experience, he could not teach another unless he also touched the flame.[32] Virtue was an innate knowledge of good and evil which man possessed through being a man.[33]

For Renaissance educational authorities, the world had been susceptible to the analysis and control of trained reason. The learner practiced and perfected by experience in the world the knowledge and virtue acquired through study. The trained mind was effective because there was a continuity between the classroom and the world. The wisdom of the ancients could penetrate the world; the studia humanitatis had relevance. For Lando, Doni, and Franco, there was no continuity between study and reality. They did not, for example, believe that the moral precepts, learnt from the ancients, that taught men to rule with justice had any effect on the signori. Force might change their ways, but not liberal studies. Man learned from experience, if at all.

One possible conclusion from these propositions would be to disregard book learning and to embrace the world, as Montaigne argued, later in the century. The critics did not follow this conclusion; they urged instead withdrawal.

Doni advised men to withdraw from the vita civile into ignorant self-concern—to stop striving to change and improve the world and to attend to their own affairs. He lauded the life of "good ignorance" (*ignoranza da bene*), a non-intellectual approach to life which meant

---

[32] " 'Il fuoco cuoce,' trovo scritto: s'io non lo tócco, mai vi saprò dire che cosa sia fuoco; ma quando mi sentirò quell'incendio, allora non lo saprò insegnare ancóra, perché colui non saprà mai, a chi l'insegnerò, che cosa è fuoco, se non è tocco alquanto da esso." *I Marmi,* 1928 ed., II, 61.

[33] "La umanità ti vieta che tu sia superbo alli tuoi compagni; viètati che tu sai avaro di parole, di cose, di affetti; ella è commune e facile a tutti, nessun male stima essere alieno, e il suo bene però grandemente ama, perchè sa che deve esser bene per qualche uno altro. I liberali studi t'amaestrano in questi costumi? Non più ti amaestrano in questo che nella semplicità, nella modestia, nella temperanza la quale così perdona all'altrui sangue come al suo e sa che l'uomo non debbe usar l'uomo più che non si conviene." *Ibid.,* 1928 ed., II, 66–67.

living without thought or care, and attending only to one's own affairs.[34] Explaining, he affirmed that learning was not necessary. Reverence for Cicero and an intense study of Priscian's grammar were superfluous. The learned racked their brains over whether the soul was mortal or immortal, they protested that the streets of the city were laid out incorrectly, and that the architecture of the cathedral ought to be improved. They were never satisfied to leave things as they were and, in their learned arrogance, assumed that the unlettered lived dissolute lives. But the man of good ignorance lived by a different credo. He was uninterested in knowledge and had no concern for the activities of others while attending to his own affairs. Doni preferred him to striving busybodies who sought to improve the world.[35]

Quattrocento humanists had condemned solitude as conducive to vice; Franco lauded it because it stripped men of vain appetites.[36] He concluded his attack on learning in the letter from Lucerna with an appeal to withdraw into the peace and solitude of rustic life. Lucerna praised the life of shepherds and farmers who were content with a few slices of bread over a little fire. In similar vein, Lando advised men to flee not only cities and palaces but also peasant villages and country villas. Only in complete solitude could man obtain peace. This advice came, not in the context of an attack on learning, but at the conclusion of a discussion of the professions of man, where, in a dialogue between a cavalier and a hermit, Lando criticized nearly every human profession as dishonest or vicious. He rejected signori, councilors and rulers of cities, members of the legal profession, physicians, ambassadors, soldiers, merchants, clergymen, shipbuilders and sailors, down to lowly fishermen and peasants.[37]

It might seem inconsistent to criticize learning on the grounds that it

[34] "Ultimamente Ignoranza da bene, è quando l'huomo se ne va alla carlona, & non si da impaccio de fatti d'altri, come dire." *La Zucca*, 1565 ed., 66.

[35] "E sarà uno ignorantaccio che sparlerà in questa forma, Il tale non ha lettere; (e mentirà per la gola) il quale fa la tal vita dissoluta, (e non serà vero) & quell'altro capiterà male. Colui che ha abbracciato l'ignoranza da bene, subito se ne va in la dicendo; io non vo sapere se egli sà, o se non sà, che vita sia la sua capiti dove e vuole la non m'importa nulla; assai ho io da fare ad attendere a casi mia." *Ibid.*, 66 (quote), 67ᵛ.

[36] *Pistole Vulgari*, 1539 ed., lxxxvii.

[37] "Ragionamento fatto tra un Cavalliero errante, et un' huomo soletario, nel'quale si tratta delle fallacie, & malvagità mondane: mostrando non potersi in verun stato ritrovar alcuna bontà: con una lode nel fine della vita Soletaria," in *Vari Componimenti*, 1555 ed., 89-128.

was divorced from reality, and then to reject participation in reality. However, in the Renaissance view, preparation for the vita civile and belief in the value of the vita civile were linked. The critics rejected both. Basic to this rejection was their pessimistic view of the world; when the traditional intellectual training proved inadequate to cope with the corrupt reality, it was condemned as inadequate and withdrawal advocated.

Thus Franco, Lando, and Doni rejected a fundamental component of the intellectual Renaissance. One should not, however, overemphasize the practical consequences of their protest. The critics were not educational philosophers; they offered only hints of an alternative based on experience and on a preference for a rustic or solitary life. Neither did the rejection of the vita civile have great personal consequences for them. By choice and because of their social position, the critics did not play an active role in affairs.

Mockery of ancient and modern authorities

More frequent in the writings of the critics than fundamental considerations of the inadequacies of Renaissance learning was a general mockery of learning. This took two forms: the statement that learning as it was practiced was irrelevant, trivial, and pedantic; and the condemnation of the ideas, texts, and institutions which were the authorities of learning. There was much overlapping, and sometimes just simple ridicule. Although the mockery of ancient and modern learning was neither analytical nor profound, it was extensive, as the critics detailed the authors, institutions, and features of learning which they disliked.

Lando treated important issues and esteemed authorities with a studied mockery which left with the reader the idea that the matter under discussion was of no consequence. At times he employed the devices of Renaissance learning in order to ridicule it. He enjoyed using the rhetorical device of arguing both sides of an issue. His purpose was not to prove that the skilled orator could defend both sides but to cast doubt on the importance of the question.

In *Cicero relegatus et Cicero revocatus* Lando treated the sixteenth-century debate over Ciceronian imitation with rhetorical satire. The question was, how closely ought Cicero's canons be followed in Latin composition? The corollary was, did a strict adherence to Ciceronian norms mask a pagan spirit? Erasmus had criticized strict Ciceronian imitation and was answered by Girolamo Seripando, Gaudenzio Merula, and others.[38] Lando mocked both sides of the Ciceronian polemic. In the first dialogue of his work, a council of eminent Italians met to judge Cicero. After lengthy discussion with many references to his works, they decided that Cicero was inconsistent, boring, ignorant, and seditious, and should be banished from Italy. Since the whole world was filled with Ciceronians, they banished him to the distant land of Scythia. In the second dialogue, a great lamentation began when the decree was announced at Rome. Knights, citizens, and scholars protested. At length the Senate looked into the matter. This time, he was defended so eloquently by such eminent Ciceronians as Jacopo Sadoleto, Pietro Bembo, and Giulio Camillo that he was recalled to Italy in triumph on January 1, 1534.

Lando's defence of the two sides was sufficiently balanced for contemporaries to entertain contradictory evaluations of his real opinion. Erasmus commented that the book attacked Cicero harshly and defended him indifferently. But Joannes Angelus Odonus, not referring specifically to the book, described Lando as an avid Ciceronian.[39] In reality, Lando was unsympathetic toward Cicero as an authority and model. Elsewhere in his books, he attacked him as ignorant in philosophy, mistaken in his history, and valueless as a teacher of rhetoric.[40] In this his attitude contrasted with that of Alberti, Piccolomini, and many others who praised Cicero for style and content. The purpose and effect of the *Cicero relegatus et Cicero revocatus* was to ridicule the importance of a learned issue of the time.

All the critics indulged in wholesale ridicule of classical learning, with the implied judgment that it did not accomplish any significant purpose. Lando's *Sferza* was an account of a dream in which he accumulated so many books that they filled his house. They should have made him learned, but instead they "confounded the wit and weakened the memory." All the esteemed authors of the classical world contained some imperfections. Of the ancient historians, Diodorus Siculus told fables, and Xenophon's history was fictitious and prolix. Herodotus was not the

[38] See D. Gagliardo, "Il ciceronismo nel Cinquecento e Ortensio Lando," *Le parole e le idee,* III, nos. 1–2 (1961), 15–21; and Scott, *Controversies over the Imitation of Cicero.*

[39] "In eo Cicero odiosissime laceratur, frigide defenditur." *Opus epistolarum Erasmi,* Ep. 3019, May 21, 1535, XI, 134. For Odonus, see Scott, *Controversies over the Imitation of Cicero,* 85–88.

[40] *Paradossi,* 1545 ed., 80ʳ–85ᵛ.

father of Greek history as Petrarch had deemed him, but the progenitor of Greek falsehoods, while Thucydides exaggerated. Tacitus told too many lies, and Plutarch tried to be philosopher, grammarian, and historian but succeeded in none of them. Other classical authors, including Menander, Lucian, and Quintilian were dismissed—the last-named because of his corrupt style. Lando mocked the study of philosophy, from Plato, who did not reason well and employed "monstrous Ideas," through the ignorant Aristotle, Averroes, and Alexander of Aphrodisias.[41]

Franco and Doni attacked the classical heritage in the same spirit. In the seventh dialogue of the *Dialogi Piacevoli,* Franco placed a large number of ancient authorities, including Hesiod, Pindar, Euripides, Homer, Vergil, Horace, and Seneca, in hell. Jove had condemned them for a variety of reasons, ranging from their crazy ideas to fondness for young boys.[42] Doni claimed that ancient history was in practice a pack of lies written to conceal crimes and to please readers, not a mirror before men's eyes, the "teacher of life," and a means of acquiring immortality, as Cicero claimed. In particular, Doni criticized Herodotus, Diodorus Siculus, and Roman historians for including patriotic lies in their histories. As an example, Doni cited the story of Mucius Scaevola, considered "a great father of his country" for saving Rome by impressing the Etruscan chieftain, Porsenna, with his courage in burning his hand in the fire. Doni commented that Mucius Scaevola's deed had had nothing to do with Porsenna's actions or Rome's salvation.[43]

Obviously much of the criticism of the ancients was lighthearted. Poking fun at ancient learning was a game practiced by others, not least by Lucian. The critics were natural inconoclasts who lived in an age saturated with the authority of the ancients. They could hardly resist the temptation to deny the worth of these texts or to attribute personal faults to such revered figures. The age of rediscovery of the ancients and the passionate quest to interpret them had passed. Now they were a familiar part of the intellectual furniture and familiarity bred contempt. But there was a serious element in this light-hearted criticism. Even in the humorous passages, it was evident that the classical heritage had lost much of its meaning for these men.

Lando, Franco, and Doni also criticized modern authorities of learning—humanists and writers of the fifteenth and sixteenth centuries. In the

---

[41] *Sferza,* 3ᵛ–4, 5, 7ᵛ–8ᵛ, 9ᵛ, 19–19ᵛ, 25.

[42] *Dialogi Piacevoli,* 1541 ed., xcix–cvᵛ, cxiiiᵛ–cxxviiiᵛ.

[43] *I Mondi,* 1552 ed., 83–84, 45ᵛ–46ᵛ; *Lettere,* 1547 ed., 44ᵛ–45.

Sferza, Lando, after disposing of the ancients, went on to comment on the moderns. Petrarch's *Triumphs* demonstrated ignorance of history and a languid style. The historian Flavio Biondo wrote too many lies. Lando did not think highly of Guillaume Budé or the Ciceronians Ermolao Barbaro and Cristoforo Longolio. Valla's precepts were for the most part evil although Erasmus, who escaped criticism from Lando and Franco, had followed them. Cristoforo Landino had "bizarre chimeras and fantastic visions." In his ignorance Landino quoted Vergil and Terence as authorities in agreement while ignoring the way the two classical authors contradicted each other. Among modern poets, Lando rejected Pulci, Boiardo, Ariosto, and Sannazzaro, recommending that his readers try "fresher" authors.[44]

In the conclusion of his *Sferza,* Lando stated that he had flagellated historians, philosophers, medical scholars, mathematicians, ancient poets, and modern authors of prose and poetry. They were of no value. He advised his readers to abandon "studies of letters" because they were valueless. Then, typically, Lando reversed himself in a brief *coda.* He announced that he had been writing "in jest rather than seriously" and exhorted his readers to study ancient and modern letters.[45] Lando's brief exhortation did not carry the weight and conviction of the body of the book. Moreover, he repeated his criticism of the same authors, in abbreviated form, two years later without any concluding aboutface.[46]

In a more general way, without listing particular sins, Doni punished contemporary men of learning in his *Inferni.* In the first inferno doomed scholars of unspecified disciplines ran around and around in a huge wheel with as many serpents pursuing them as they had written books. In Doni's words, the serpents bit the authors as their books had bitten readers. Grammarians were condemned to carrying their moaning heads in their hands as they trudged around and around in the ghastly wheel.[47]

A favorite target among Cinquecento authorities of literature was Pietro Bembo. Franco attacked him for establishing rules of writing as if he were a prince threatening "the prison of infamy" for those who disregarded his decrees. When Bembo died, on January 18, 1547, Franco composed abusive sonnets condemning him as one who had led others

[44] *Sferza,* 16ᵛ–17ᵛ, 19ᵛ–21.

[45] *Ibid.,* 25, 28ᵛ–36.

[46] *Sacra Scrittura,* 4ᵛ, 22ᵛ, 26, 27–28, 31ᵛ–32ᵛ, 59ᵛ–61.

[47] *Inferni,* 1553 ed., 34–38, 156. Doni was particularly hostile to grammarians. See also *La Zucca,* 1565 ed., 124–25; *Lettere,* 1552 ed.. 13–16.

LA SFERZA DE

SCRITTORI ANTICHI ET
MODERNI DI M. ANO-
NIMO DI VTOPIA

ALLA QVALE, E' DAL ME-
desimo aggiunta una essortatione
allo studio delle lettere.

CON PRIVILEGIO.

PRIA CHE LE LABBRA BAGNERAI A FRONTE

IN VINEGIA M. D. L.

FIG. 7. Title page of the sole edition of Lando's *Sferza de' Scrittori*

into pedantry. Among those who followed Bembo into pedantry, according to Franco, were Molza, Speroni, Bernardo Tasso, Luigi Alamanni, Benedetto Varchi, and Luigi Tansillo. Alessandro Piccolomini upheld several of these authors as models of style; Franco thought that they had become lost in the "shadows and clouds" of their own forms and were worthless. Lando sneered at Bembo as an irreligious "wiseacre" (*baccalare*) who declined to pray in Lent.[48]

The critics were also impatient with the universities and academies of the sixteenth century. Lando's traveler from Utopia, Messer Anonymo, was very disappointed by his visit to the University of Padua. He found the legists shouting contradictions, fighting with one another, obscuring the truth, and charging sixty scudi for such "lessons." He hoped to hear moral philosophers lecturing on justice, prudence, modesty, fortitude, and chastity, but discovered that they debated Aristotelian matter. The lectures on being and oneness (*ente et uno*) in the school of metaphysicians wearied him. He went to hear a lecture on *De anima* and found it to be satanic. Lando's objection to the universities was that they were devoted to Aristotelian quarrels rather than to imparting knowledge and virtue. Similarly, Franco criticized the academies for their ignorance, malice, and greed for fame.[49]

The critics were well aware that they were flouting the established educational institutions and authorities of Italy. In paradox twenty-seven of the *Paradossi,* an attack on Boccaccio's works as worthless, Lando commented that he expected to provoke a tumult in the many academies of Italy. The Infiammati of Padua led by the "authoritative Speroni" would sharpen their pens against him, and the Intronati of Siena war against him as if he had sinned against God. However, he professed unconcern.[50]

As with their treatment of ancient learning, part of the dismissal of modern authors was facetious. One should not, for example, take too seriously Lando's attack on Ariosto, whose genius was recognized by all.

[48] Franco, *Rime,* 1916 ed., nos. 193-99, pp. 97-100; *Pistole Vulgari,* 1539 ed., lxxxvi[v]. Franco's evaluation of these authors was not consistent. Elsewhere he praised Tansillo and in the 1550's he considered editing Molza's poetry. Lando, *Paradossi,* 1545 ed., 79-79[v].

[49] "Vado alle scuole de legisti, sto ad udir ciò che dicono di bello, appartenente al viver civile, & alle unione de cittadini, & non odo salvo che contradittioni, l'uno impugnar l'altro. . . ." Lando, *Commentario,* 1550 ed., 36-36[v]. Franco, *Pistole Vulgari,* 1539 ed., xxxiv[v].

[50] Lando, *Paradossi,* 1545 ed., 70[v]-71.

Despite this, however, the mockery of modern authors and institutions of learning was consistent. The fifteenth- and sixteenth-century authors whom Franco, Lando, and Doni ridiculed were the teachers and authorities of the irrelevant studia humanitatis. The basic point was the same; as Lando put it, the study of letters was of no value. By the lifetimes of Lando, Franco, and Doni, the battle against thirteenth-century Scholasticism had been won, and the Renaissance humanists had in turn become irrelevant and pedantic to them. Just as they argued that men should write spontaneously and for a broad audience, so they were opposed to authors or institutions who laid down programs and rules for learning. The mockery of learning was an extension of the rejection of the studia humanitatis and the vita civile.

The low reputation of humanists

Others in Italy at this time demonstrated impatience with what they believed was the irrelevance and pedantry of Cinquecento learning.

An anonymous work of c. 1541, *La Pazzia,* echoed in abbreviated form the charge of pedantry against modern learning, especially grammar. The author noted that Latin grammarians claimed their discipline to be the "foundation of all disciplines and the science of the sciences," the position accorded to grammar in the studia humanitatis. But in his opinion, Latin grammarians in his day had descended into inconsequential pedantry. They worried about accents, vocabulary, sentence construction, and parts of speech instead of more important matters—which he failed to name. However, vernacular grammarians were no better. They also gave themselves to foolish attempts to compose rules and laws. They attempted to establish a word-by-word anatomy of Tuscan in the sixteenth-century *questione della lingua.* The author went on to criticize the Renaissance attempt to revive classical eloquence. Those who composed orations and histories in order to renew Roman eloquence in "our centuries" showed stupid judgment, in his opinion. He termed pedants the modern poets who argued about Vergil, elegies, epigrams, sonnets, and madrigals.[51] The author did not elaborate his cryptic comments, nor did he suggest the paths that modern learning ought to follow instead of the

---

[51] *La Pazzia,* n. pl., MDXLVI, ff. 5ᵛ–6, 18, 21ᵛ–22ᵛ. For a discussion of the authorship of *La Pazzia* and editions of the work, see Appendix V.

pedantic grammar, archaic eloquence, and disputatious literary criticism that he disliked.

Domenichi joined the critics and the author of *La Pazzia* in their ridicule of humanists. In *La nobiltà delle donne* (1549), he advised humanists not to marry and elaborated his reasons with a page of amusing abuse to the effect that while humanists successfully pursued their studies in schools, at home they were failures as husbands and fathers. "Men draw a nice fruit from studies and letters," Domenichi wrote; humanists criticized in school the deeds of Venus and Mars but later in bed verified in act the fables of the gods. In school they preached Homer and Vergil, and contemplated the Ideas of Plato, but when they returned to their wives at home, they were poor husbands, and fathered monstrous children.[52] Domenichi's ridicule was not profound; it was a variation on the perennial idea that scholars and teachers were ineffectual outside the study or classroom. His comments, show, however, that sixteenth-century humanists had fallen into low repute.

Authors outside the circle of the poligrafi also criticized humanists. Benedetto Varchi, one of the esteemed authorities for whom the critics had little respect, noted the low reputation of men of learning in his time, and, in a letter written in 1545 or 1546, he rebuked humanists of the preceding century for quarrelling over matters of "very little importance or of no doubt." Leonardo Bruni, Giovanni Pontano, Lorenzo Valla, Poggio Bracciolini, Giorgio Merula, and Domizio Calderini, by senseless vituperation and cries of "villainy" over trivial matters, had contributed to the very low opinion held at present of humanists, philosophers, and men of letters and science in general.[53]

---

[52] *La nobiltà delle donne di M. Lodovico Domenichi* . . . (Venice, 1549), 89ᵛ-90. The references of Domenichi, Varchi, and Gilio to *umanisti* are discussed in my article, "Five Italian Occurrences of *Umanista*, 1540–1574," in *Renaissance Quarterly*, XX (1967), 317–25.

[53] "La qual cosa quanto stia bene e sia richiesta, e massimamente a quegli che fanno professione d'umanità, lasciarò giudicare agli altri, e dirò solamente che queste ed altre così fatte non so se sciocchezze o malvagità, hanno e meritamente in buona parte cagionato quella poca riputazione, per non dire dispregio, nella quale sono oggi non solamente gli umanisti, ma i filosofi, e generalmente tutti coloro i quali o si dilettano delle lettere o attendono alle scienze." *Lezioni sul Dante e prose varie di Benedetto Varchi*, ed. Giuseppe Aiazzi e Lelio Arbib (Florence, 1841), II, 81. However, Varchi went directly from these reflections into a long philological discussion of the very sort that Franco, Lando, and Doni labelled pedantic and irrelevant. Obviously he did not include himself among pedantic humanists.

In 1564 another figure outside the circle of the poligrafi took a disdainful attitude toward humanists. Giovanni Andrea Gilio da Fabriano (fl. 1550–80), an ecclesiastic and author, implied that humanists were inclined to carry their scholarly disputes beyond the point that a sensible man would go. In the middle of an effort to trace the etymological development from *civium unitas* to *civitas* to *città,* Gilio broke off his discussion with the comment that he had gone as far as he wished to go in the question and would leave such a quarrel to the humanists, implying as he did so that humanists were quarrelsome pedants.[54]

All these criticisms of learning suggest that the mockery of humanists and grammarians existed beyond the books of Doni, Franco, and Lando in the sixteenth century. For more than a century, charges of triviality and irrelevance had been levelled against Scholasticism; now they were directed against the studia humanitatis and its representatives.

European reaction against Renaissance learning

The attack on learning described above can be understood in the context of other reactions against Renaissance learning.

In contrast to the optimistic belief in the unlimited potentiality of man's mind held by his uncle, Giovanni Pico, Gianfrancesco Pico taught the inadequacy of all learning compared to the certainty and efficacy of Christian faith. In his *Examen vanitatis doctrinae gentium, et veritatis christianae disciplinae* (begun before 1510, published in 1520), he explicitly adopted a Pyrrhonist attitude based on that of the ancient skeptic, Sextus Empiricus, in order to destroy all philosophic systems, especially that of Aristotle. The only useful purpose of philosophy was to destroy arguments against Christianity. In the end, only divine revelation could lead men to God.

To prove this was Pico's prime concern, but in Book III he turned his attention to the liberal arts, subjecting them, as a group and individually, to the same Pyrrhonist doubt. Instead of leading to truth, certitude, and wisdom, the liberal arts produced falsity, ambiguity, and controversy,

---

[54] *Due Dialogi di M. Giovanni Andrea Gilio da Fabriano* . . . (Camerino, 1564), 126. On Gilio see Filippo Vecchietti, *Biblioteca Picena o sia notizie istoriche delle opere e degli scrittori Piceni* (Osimo, 1796), V, 91–93.

from the variety of opinions held concerning them, and their uselessness in aiding men to approach God.[55]

The critics demonstrated no knowledge of Gianfrancesco Pico's work[56] and their criticism of learning differed. They did not subject it to philosophical skepticism in works intended for learned readers, but ridiculed it and argued that it was irrelevant to life in books designed for a more popular audience. While faith and Scripture attracted the critics, they did not make their rejection of learning in a religious context, as Pico did.[57] Rather, they found it inadequate for the secular world. Pico's work shows that a philosophic attack on the liberal arts, while differing in purpose and execution from that of Lando, Franco, and Doni, existed previously in sixteenth-century Italy.

From a viewpoint similar to that of Pico, but closer in mood to the critics, Agrippa's *De vanitate* attacked learning along four lines: (1) that a given science was uncertain because the authorities were at odds with one another; (2) that various sciences were usually sources of evil; (3) that human learning did not lead to happiness or salvation; (4) that human life was too short to master even one branch of learning well.[58] Agrippa made his ferocious attack against learning in tones of moral

[55] *Examen vanitatis doctrinae gentium et veritatis Christianae disciplinae* (Mirandola, 1520), ff. lxxvi–cx. On Gianfrancesco Pico see Charles B. Schmitt, *Gianfrancesco Pico della Mirandola (1469-1533) and His Critique of Aristotle* (The Hague, 1967); Nauert, *Agrippa and the Crisis of Renaissance Thought*, 148–52; Giuseppe Saitta, *Il pensiero italiano nell'umanesimo e nel Rinascimento* (Florence, 1961), I, 635–43.

[56] The only mention of Gianfrancesco Pico was Lando's notice of Pico as a man of learning who had come to an unfortunate end (he was murdered by his relatives). *Paradossi*, 1545 ed., 15ᵛ. The *Examen vanitatis* appeared only in the 1520 Mirandola edition until Pico's *opera omnia* were published in 1573, Basel. Schmitt's study of Pico's influence uncovers no references to Pico among literary sources. Charles B. Schmitt, "Who Read Gianfrancesco Pico della Mirandola?" *Studies in the Renaissance*, XI (1964), 105–32.

[57] There is one exception. In the *Sacra Scrittura*, Lando argued that Scripture was more effective than the studia humanitatis in teaching men virtue and knowledge. He objected that secular learning did not achieve its purpose, and that Scripture, while primarily concerned to guide men to salvation, could do a better job. But he did not argue that men should reject secular learning in order to follow God. *Sacra Scrittura*, 26–28.

[58] For an analysis of *De vanitate*, see Nauert, *Agrippa and the Crisis of Renaissance Thought*, 292–321.

outrage rather than dispassionate skeptical analysis. He was convinced that learning was nearly always morally harmful to men. For example, Chapter 64, "On Pandarism or Procuring," was a sustained attack against various liberal studies as devices which led men to sin. Grammar and poetry were written in order to corrupt women. No man was strong enough to withstand the evil influence of a "wanton history." Boccaccio's *Decameron* led men and women to moral ruin. Agrippa's list of "panderers" included some of Italy's greatest authors and humanists: Dante, Petrarch, Boccaccio, Aeneas Silvius Piccolomini, Giovanni Pontano, L. B. Alberti, and Pietro Bembo.[59] In the last three chapters and the conclusion, Agrippa offered his alternative, a fideist call to adore God as simple, ignorant men.

Agrippa's ideas were available and known in Italy while Doni, Lando, and Franco were writing. In addition to the numerous Latin editions printed outside of Italy,[60] Domenichi translated *De vanitate* into Italian in an edition published by Andrea Arrivabene of Venice in 1547, and reprinted in 1549 and 1552. The translation was completed while Domenichi and Doni were still friends in Florence.[61]

A member of the Accademia Ortolana of Piacenza published a work similar in theme to *De vanitate* a few years after the group had dispersed. In 1551 Count Giulio Landi (1500–79), of the noble Landi family of Piacenza, published his *Lode dell'ignoranza* (Venice, Giolito, with Doni the editor.) Landi, who earned a degree in jurisprudence and served in government posts and diplomatic missions, was a member of the Accademia Ortolana between 1543 and 1545 when Doni was a member and Lando a visitor to the city.[62] He devoted the major part of his short tract

---

[59] *The Vanity of Arts and Sciences* (London, 1676), 197–211.

[60] There were no Latin editions of *De vanitate* printed in Italy in the sixteenth century.

[61] The dedicatory letter by Domenichi was dated June 6, 1546, Florence. These three editions of the translation carry the place of publication, Venice, but not the printer. The British Museum catalogue attributes the 1547 edition to "G. de Farri & Bros.," and the 1549 printing to Doni, while the *Primo catalogo collettivo delle biblioteche italiane* (Rome, 1963), II, 118, attributes all three editions to Farri. However, on August 29, 1547, the Venetian Senate issued a privilegio for 10 years for "Cornelio Agrippa de vanitate scientiarum" to "Andrea dal pozo libraro," i.e., Andrea Arrivabene. Presumably all three editions were printed by or for Arrivabene. See "Privilegi veneziani," Cod. 2500 (12077), f. 74.

[62] For biographical information on Giulio Landi, see Poggiali, *Memorie per la storia letteraria di Piacenza*, II, 195–207.

to a description in general terms of the inadequacies and moral dangers of current learning. Logic made men insolent and tanglers of the truth, algebra was the tool of lying merchants, geometry made men abstract. He noted approvingly that the Romans had banished lying poets and orators from the city. Landi criticized theologians for attempting to know the highest mysteries of God, and praised ignorance as morally beneficial. Man was better and happier in ignorance, and God could be known only through ignorance. Ignorance rather than knowledge led to virtue.[63] Landi's *Lode dell'ignoranza* thus expressed in abbreviated form Agrippa's thesis that learning was a hindrance, and ignorance a prerequisite, to holiness.

Doni knew *De vanitate* and Lando may have been familiar with it. In 1551 Doni began his discussion of ignoranza da bene by listing other types of ignorance including an "ignorance in order not to have knowledge; which Agrippa called the happiest life."[64] The ignorance which he attributed to Agrippa was the rejection of learning in order to love God, found in the last three chapters and conclusion of *De vanitate*. Doni's own ignoranza da bene differed; it was an ignorant withdrawal from the active life but not into union with God. Lando, in the introduction to his *Sferza de' Scrittori,* remarked "I will not speak of the instability and uncertainty of the sciences; I will discuss only the imperfections in these same authors"—perhaps an indication that he knew *De vanitate*.[65] Lando followed his announced intention; the *Sferza* was quite different from Agrippa's work.

Agrippa may have helped stimulate in the critics a re-examination of Renaissance learning, but there were major differences between them. The critics, despite their attack, did not see learning as corrupting. For example, Doni noted that the liberal studies could not teach virtue, but he did not argue that the liberal studies were in themselves evil, or that they taught vice. Thus, they did not condemn learning on moral grounds. Gianfrancesco Pico, Agrippa, and Giulio Landi offered a religious alternative: that man should turn in ignorance to Christ. The critics did not link their rejection of learning with religious salvation. Finally, Agrippa

[63] *La Vita di Cleopatra Reina d'Egitto* . . . (Venice, 1551), 53–62. The *Lode dell'ignoranza* was reprinted in 1575 and 1601.

[64] "Ignoranza per non haver cognitione; quella che chiamò l'Agrippa vita felicissima." *La Zucca,* 1565 ed., 65ᵛ.

[65] "taccio l'instabilità et incertezza della scientie; & ragionovi sol delle imperfettioni che sono ne gli istessi authori." *Sferza,* 3ᵛ.

differed from the critics in that he groped for a solution to the skeptic's dilemma, how to attain knowledge. While rejecting theories in general, he held to the sense perception of singulars. He believed that "one might in practice follow any abstract system as long as it met the pragmatic test of experience and utility."[66] Although they emphasized the importance of experience, the critics did not see it as an answer to an epistemological problem, but simply as a guide to life. However, despite differences in outlook and emphasis, the writings of all these men offer evidence of a widespread criticism of learning.

To a limited extent the critics anticipated a revolt against Renaissance learning in the late sixteenth and early seventeenth centuries. Garin points out that the revolt was expressed in terms of a polemic between learning based on *parole* or *cose*. A learning based on "things," i.e., on reality and the fostering of virtue and judgment, was opposed to literary pedantry, which filled the mind with abstract and disconnected words. For example, in 1572 Girolamo Muzio (1496–1576), discussing the education of a young prince, wished him to be taught things rather than words—meaning that he should learn heroic examples and moral doctrines rather than grammatical details.[67] Montaigne, Campanella, and Francis Bacon argued against a learning of letters in favor of learning based on experience, reality, and the book of nature. Campanella argued that one could learn more from the anatomy of an herb than from all the books written from the beginning of time. From this viewpoint, the Greek and Roman classics which had been the foundation of the Renaissance studia humanitatis had been superseded. They were no longer seen as the indispensable foundation, the introductory manuals, for all learning. They were still read and treasured, but their great task of teaching Renaissance men to think critically and historically in order to provide the foundation of the active life had been accomplished. The new learning would be guided by experimentation, the book of nature, and Descartes' *Method*.[68]

Montaigne's *Essays* offer a good example of the view that learning should be based on "things" and not "words." Montaigne complained that book learning filled man's head with knowledge but did not teach judgment and virtue. He offered the Italians of the late Quattrocento as an example of the decadence produced by useless learning. Charles VIII had mastered Tuscany and Naples without drawing his sword because

[66] Nauert, *Agrippa and the Crisis of Renaissance Thought*, 221 (quote), 315–16.
[67] *Avvertimenti Morali Del Mutio Iustinopolitano* . . . (Venice, 1572), 18.
[68] Garin, *L'educazione in Europa (1400–1600)*, 219–52.

"the princes and nobles of Italy spent more time in making themselves learned and clever than vigorous and warlike."[69] Montaigne contrasted unfavorably the knowledge of the "letterstruck" scholar with the practical knowledge of a peasant or a shoemaker. He wished that learning be integrated into the personality of the learner. In the *Apology of Raimond Sebond* he attacked liberal studies as being of no use to men, and, with a variety of examples and authorities, argued the impotence of philosophy. He noted that the savage but tranquil inhabitants of Brazil spent their lives in an admirable simplicity and ignorance without letters, law, king, or religion.[70]

Montaigne's position represented the culmination of the criticism of Franco, Doni, and Lando, as well as of other sixteenth-century critics of learning. Before Montaigne these writers perceived that current learning was irrelevant to reality, and doubted the value of the fundamental Renaissance ideal of education for the vita civile. Their position was a minority one; the existence and popularity of educational treatises such as that of Alessandro Piccolomini showed the perseverance of the traditional view. And as usual Franco, Lando, and Doni offered no positive alternative beyond the tentative suggestion that learning should be based on experience. Withdrawal from the vita civile in fact precluded the necessity for educational reform. Their rejection of learning reflected their rejection of the Italian world of the sixteenth century as a whole, and they turned to the construction of utopian societies which would remedy this world at its foundation.

[69] *The Essays of Montaigne,* trans. E. J. Trechmann, introd. J. M. Robertson (London, 1927), I, 25, pp. 133, 135–37, 142 (quote).
[70] *Ibid.,* I, pp. 504–5, 481–83, 486.

Chapter VI

UTOPIAN ALTERNATIVES

HAVING rejected the learning, religion, politics, and social structure of contemporary Italy, our authors turned to myths and utopias as alternatives. They dreamed of a perfect society where in primitive simplicity all men had enough to live without depriving their neighbors. In such a life, men would exist without corrupting knowledge and without involvement in the evil affairs of the world. In contrast to the challenge to men to master themselves and their environment formulated in the earlier Renaissance, they wished to abandon the world for a small measure of personal peace.

The Renaissance utopia

A well-developed utopian genre existed in the Renaissance. Although Plato's suggestions in the *Republic* and the *Laws* for a well-governed city, social regulation, and educational reform were the ultimate roots of all utopias, the practical starting point for the Renaissance was the abstract city models of the Quattrocento architects. These exhibited two fundamental characteristics of the Renaissance utopia: a city plan of geometrical regularity, and regimentation of the lives of the inhabitants for the sake of the city as a whole. Leon Battista Alberti's *De re aedificatoria* (written in 1452, published in Latin in 1485 and in Italian in 1546) listed plans and ideas for an organic city in which the inhabitants could live in peace. His plans went beyond architecture to encompass social considerations: he planned asylums for the poor, and separated different social classes from each other. More complete was the utopia of Antonio Averlino, called

Filarete (c. 1400–66), the architect of the Sforza castle at Milan. Filarete's plan for a perfect city, named Sforzinda for his patrons, was in the shape of a regular eight-pointed star with streets leading from the eight city gates located between the points of the star to the center of the city. Filarete placed the various shops and crafts in specified areas of the city, and regulated the color of dress and value of jewelry permitted to the nobility of Sforzinda. He devised social regulations for the schools and prisons with a communal utilitarian aim in view. However, Filarete's plans for Sforzinda, the earliest complete Italian utopia, remained in manuscript until the twentieth century, and probably had no influence on other utopias.[1]

With *The Best State of a Commonwealth and the New Island of Utopia* (1516) of Thomas More, the Renaissance utopia acquired moral purpose. More's *Utopia* was part of his program as a Christian humanist for the renewal of contemporary society. It was based on the idea that men were not hopelessly corrupt; given the proper external conditions, they could attain the good society. More investigated the social evils of the day, and determined that sin, especially the sin of pride, was at the root of human evils. His *Utopia* was an elaborate social structure for the purpose of subjugating sin, written as an example and model for the education of European rulers.[2]

Lando and Doni brought the *Utopia* to vernacular readers in Italy. In 1548 an Italian translation of More's work by Lando was published in Venice without the name of publisher or translator. Doni wrote the dedicatory letter, praising the courageous, God-fearing More, and his book, which contained, in Doni's opinion, ". . . excellent customs, good arrangements, wise rules, holy admonishments, sincere government and royal men. . . ."[3]

---

[1] Luigi Firpo, "La città ideale del Filarete," in *Studi in memoria di Gioele Solari* (Torino, 1954), 11–59. See also the collection, *Les Utopies à la Renaissance* (Brussels, Paris, 1963), especially the articles of Eugenio Garin and Robert Klein; and Alberto Tenenti, "L'utopia nel Rinascimento (1450–1550)," *Studi Storici*, VII (1966), 689–707.

[2] St. Thomas More, *Utopia*, ed. Edward Surtz (New Haven and London, 1964). See J. H. Hexter, *More's Utopia: The Biography of an Idea* (Princeton, N. J., 1952), 58, 73–83, 93.

[3] "Voi troverete in questa repubblica, ch'io vi mando, ottimi costumi, ordini buoni, reggimenti savj, ammaestramenti santi, governo sincero e uomini reali; poi ben composte le città, gli officj, la giustizia e la misericordia. . . ." Doni's dedicatory letter to Gerolamo Fava, n. d., n. pl., *La republica nuovamente ritrovata, del*

As often reproduced as More's *Utopia* was the utopian land of the Garamanti in the *Relox de principes* (written about 1518 and printed in 1529) of the Spanish humanist Antonio de Guevara (c. 1480–1544). Guevara, a Franciscan bishop at the court of Charles V, intended this work as a Christian humanist handbook for princes. Early in the book, he interpolated the story of the "barbarous people called Garamanti" as an example to princes. As Guevara narrated the story, Alexander the Great, in the midst of conquering the world, heard of the Garamanti and commissioned his ambassadors to threaten them with destruction if they did not submit to his power. But the Garamanti neither fled nor offered resistance. Alexander came to see for himself, and an old man was commissioned by the Garamanti to explain themselves and to create an example for future princes.

After rebuking Alexander as a tyrant, the old man explained how the Garamanti lived short, happy lives with few goods and laws, without enemies, and in continual peace and love. They lived under seven laws which contained "all virtue and resistance to vice." The first law established that there should be no more than seven laws because new ones caused people to forget the good old customs. The second law decreed that they should adore no more than two gods, one for life and the other for death, because one god served dutifully was worth more than a thousand served "jokingly." All had to dress alike because variety of dress generated madness and scandal, according to the third law. The fourth law ruled that no woman could bear her husband more than three children, because a large number of children made the father desirous of goods, and this anxiety gave birth to every vice. If women bore more than three children, the excess were sacrificed to the gods. The fifth law forbade lying. Liars were decapitated because one liar was "enough to ruin a people." The sixth law ordered that all had to inherit equally, because the desire for goods gave rise to great jealousies and scandals. The seventh and final law decreed that no woman could live more than forty years and no man more than fifty years. At these ages they were sacrificed to the gods. The reason was again moral; human beings became vicious if they knew that they could live indefinitely. With the aid of these laws, the

---

governo dell'isola Eutopia . . . (Venice, 1548), [3–5]. In 1561 Francesco Sansovino wrote that More's *Utopia* was ". . . tradotta della latina del Moro da Hortensio Lando." *Del governo de i regni et delle repubbliche . . . di Francesco Sansovino* (Venice, 1561), sig. *3ᵛ. Doni corroborated this evidence by the fact that he never claimed the 1548 translation as his.

Garamanti possessed all things equally, ate and drank temperately, avoided struggles among themselves, and carried no arms because they had no enemies.[4]

Like More's *Utopia*, Guevara's land of the Garamanti influenced Doni directly. In Part I of *I Marmi*, written within six months of *I Mondi*, Doni included a dialogue in which the characters mentioned a book containing "holy laws" (*legge sante*), and began reading from the imaginary work. These healthy laws were six of the seven laws of the Garamanti. Following Guevara's order, Doni closely paraphrased the laws, omitting only the law concerning inheritance, and commented briefly, approving them.[5] He probably learned of the Garamanti through the Italian translation of Guevara's work by Mambrino Roseo, *Institutione del prencipe christiano,* which went through fifteen editions from 1543 to 1608.[6]

Two other Italian utopias followed in the second half of the sixteenth century. Nearest in time if not in spirit to Doni's New World was *La città felice* (1553), by the Platonic philosopher Francesco Patrizi da Cherso (1529-97). *La città felice* was an aristocratic utopia modeled on Plato, Aristotle, and the Venetian state. Rejecting egalitarianism, Patrizi organized the city into a rigid caste system which separated irrevocably the warriors, magistrates, and priests from the peasants, artisans, and merchants who served them. The upper caste lived in peace, virtue, and wisdom, as they progressed toward the "supercelestial waters," a vaguely defined Platonic perfection. In short, *La città felice* was a utopia for philosopher-kings.[7]

---

[4] *Comiença el primero libro del famosissimo emperador Marco Aurelio con el Relox de principes nuevamente annadido* . . . (Barcelona, 1532), chs. 32-34, pp. 55ᵛ-59ᵛ. Writers of antiquity knew the Garamanti as a powerful tribe in the interior of Africa, but with one exception did not mention utopian characteristics. Pomponius Mela attributed to them the holding of women in common. *De chorographia,* I, 8.

[5] *I Marmi,* 1928 ed., I, 26-27. *I Mondi* was printed in April 1552. The dialogue which utilized material from Guevara was in part I of *I Marmi,* the dedicatory letter for which was dated October 25, 1552.

[6] The pages describing the Garamanti in Roseo's edition were a faithful translation without omissions, although placed in a different section of the book. *Institutione del prencipe christiano, tradotta di Spagnuolo* . . . (Venice, 1545), 8-13ᵛ.

[7] *Utopisti e riformatori sociali del Cinquecento: A. F. Doni—U. Foglietta—F. Patrizi da Cherso—L. Agostini,* ed. Carlo Curcio (Bologna, 1941), xv-xvi, 122-42.

Later in the Cinquecento the utopia assimilated the heightened religious emphasis of the Catholic Reformation. In *La repubblica immaginaria* (written between 1585 and 1590, unpublished until the twentieth century) of Ludovico Agostini (1536–1612), parallel civil and religious governments closely supervised the physical and spiritual welfare of the people. Agostini, a lawyer and administrator of the city of Pesaro, dictated a highly regulated life for the citizens of the imaginary republic, including a specified daily routine, stabilized occupations, and communal concern for the poor. The dominating feature of his utopia was the close religious supervision exercised by the bishop and parish priests, who tried hard to root out vice and to stimulate communal devotion in terms reminiscent of the decrees of the Council of Trent. At the same time the civil government used overseers and spies to supervise the crafts, solve family quarrels, check crime, and to direct the lives of the inhabitants in minute ways.[8] Agostini's imaginary republic suggests a Catholic version of Calvinist Geneva superimposed on the typical Renaissance utopia.

The Renaissance utopias had in common a rational, even geometrical, organization of the physical environment, and a highly regimented life for the inhabitants. The details varied from the slave society of Patrizi to equality of property in More and Guevara, but all were designed to present morally and socially reformed societies as examples for sixteenth-century rulers to follow. All the authors, with the partial exception of Filarete, were respected and highly placed members of society. The authoritarian governmental structure of all the utopias indicated a confidence that existing authority (although More entertained doubts about the nobility) would carry out reform. Similarly, the writers had enough optimism about the nature of most men to expect that they could be improved, morally and socially, through a better environment and authoritarian direction.

Primitivism

In their rejection of their times, the critics evoked societies of primitive simplicity. One of the themes to which they were drawn was antiquity's legend of the golden age, originating perhaps in Hesiod and given wide popularity by Ovid. According to this legend, the first age of man was one

---

[8] *La repubblica immaginaria,* ed. Luigi Firpo (Turin, 1957). See also Firpo, *Lo stato ideale della Controriforma. Ludovico Agnostini* (Bari, 1957).

of innocence in which men lived in perfect happiness. The earth provided all man's necessities without sowing or plowing. Men lived in perpetual peace without war or soldiers; since all were naturally good, there was no need for lawyers, judges, or courts. But the golden age passed into the silver, in which men were somewhat inferior in physical and mental ability and lived a less primitive life. Next came the bronze age, in which men became savage, warlike, and cruel. Finally came complete degradation—the age of iron, which was the present age of man. Force supplanted justice and evil passion superseded good. Suffering, toil, and war marked this age. Money and the concept of private property entered the world, and led men to do evil in order to possess. The earth became difficult to cultivate and men went hungry. Enmity replaced brotherly love in all mankind.[9]

Doni freely adapted the golden age myth to the current situation and his own viewpoint. The whole world had been at peace in the age of gold, he wrote. In the beginning of the world, all shared property equally, and everyone aided his neighbor. It was as if the king of France would help the king of England, and vice versa. In those happy days, men had passed their days thoughtlessly like children, had lived nakedly without shame, and slept unclothed because purity dwelt in the home. But then unidentified new peoples from beyond the seas had appeared. When the new peoples found that the best land was taken, they devised various inventions in order to usurp and dominate, using prohibitions against the use of this or that. The new peoples introduced inheritance, so that an unlettered ass of a signore might inherit his father's money. The arts and sciences were introduced in order to corrupt men.[10]

In a dialogue in *I Marmi*, Doni compared the idea of a progressive decadence in the world with two other views: the argument that every age was similar, and a Christian interpretation of man's wickedness. Not surprisingly, the first idea won. In the beginning, one speaker noted, all had lived in peace as each individual owned and worked a small piece of earth. Everyone "lived of their own just sweat and did not drink the blood of the poor." But then the world had declined. Simplicity became malice, men became warlike, good deeds were exchanged for evil thoughts, diabolic labor replaced repose, and the republic, which had been useful to men, now shed the blood of its citizens. A second speaker argued

---

[9] Arthur O. Lovejoy and George Boas, *Primitivism and Related Ideas in Antiquity* (Baltimore, 1935), 23–102.

[10] *I Mondi*, 1552 ed., 26–26ᵛ; *I Marmi*, 1928 ed., II, 141–43.

that no age was better or worse than another. But in the face of the forceful argument of the first speaker, he soon capitulated, and together they lamented the unhappy state of the contemporary world. Why should a rich man possess thousands of fields while another had only a tiny piece of land? In the end, three yards of earth were enough for rich and poor. The third participant, a priest, presented the Christian interpretation of man's misery, beginning with Adam's fall. He offered St. Augustine's dictum that man's heart would find rest only in God, and concluded with a call to return to God. When the priest finished and departed, the others agreed that they had liked the spirit of his Christian discourse, but doubted that his words were of any use, for the world went on as it willed.[11]

Erasmus possibly suggested a second concept which the critics modified in order to describe the ideal life. In the *Praise of Folly,* Erasmus had used several meanings of the word "folly" to impale corrupt clerics, while looking with a benign eye on the human folly involved in love, birth, and old age. He concluded by recommending the foolishness of Christ as preferable to the wisdom of Pharisees, i.e., the sin and hypocrisy of the world. Although not acknowledging Erasmus as a source, the critics used *pazzia* ("folly" or "madness") to characterize an ideal existence, simple, thoughtless, and uncommitted, which was in sharp contrast to the contemporary world. For example, a narrator named Pazzo might criticize the vices of the signori, or the life of men in the golden age be described as a *pazza vita.*

In every age, wrote Lando, existed free pazzi who were liberated from cares. The pazzo was not concerned to possess states, to build towns, to be Guelph or Ghibelline, or to take a wife. Indifferent toward food and dress, he despised greatness and honors, and was not avid to acquire a prelacy. He did not recognize points of honor that provoked duels, sell himself as a soldier to the high for a few coins, or pay tribute to signori. Subject to no one, he lived in every way "freely and openly." Since he lived a healthy, robust life untroubled by quarrels, he neither needed nor was threatened by the rich. The pazzo was innocent of fraud and astuteness; he was always happy and thoughtless.[12]

The anonymous *La Pazzia* (Venice, c. 1541) amplified the ideal of the pazza vita and almost gave it formal stature as a utopian state.[13] *La*

[11] *I Marmi,* 1928 ed., I, 267–73.

[12] *Paradossi,* 1545 ed., 21–22ᵛ.

[13] For a discussion of the authorship of *La Pazzia* and editions of the work, see Appendix V.

Pazzia borrowed material from Erasmus' *Praise of Folly* but attempted to erect its own ideal of pazzia, distinguishing between good and bad kinds. The latter was a kind of crazed, destructive anger exemplified by the villanous Turks and the impious Lutherans. Good pazzia was a sweet, joyous liberation from cares. These pazzi did not hate, nor did they know shame, need, fear, hope, ambition, envy, avarice, or remorse. Esteemed by all, they spent their days singing, joking, and dancing. They feared neither death nor hell; because they lived without feeling or thought they could not sin, and at death went directly to paradise.[14] In contrast to the blessed pazzi, *savi* (wise men) gave their attention to studies, sciences, to governing states, ruling republics, and dealing with the affairs of great signori. Such *arcisavi* (arch wise men) who presumed to rule and to reform the world were deservedly hated by all peoples. The author used as examples of arcisavi the Spanish, whom he disliked. If a pazzo relinquished his happy life to be a ruler, he betrayed his existence and brought evil upon himself and the city that he ruled.[15]

To explain how happy men could be without savi, the author of *La Pazzia* briefly evoked a utopia based on the age of gold, Plato's *Republic,* and his concept of native life in the newly discovered West Indies. These blessed natives lived without letters and savi. Since they did not prize gold or jewels, they were neither avaricious nor ambitious. They did not know any craft; they lived on the fruits produced by the earth. Comparing the natives to Plato's *Republic,* the author noted that they held everything, even women, in common. The children were nursed and brought up communally. Hence they recognized everyone as fathers. All lived together happily, in perpetual love, as in the times of the "fortunate century of gold." But the Spanish who mastered the West Indies brought in too much knowledge and too many laws, and destroyed the happy native life. Like the opening of Pandora's box, they unleashed legions of worries and evils that now filled the land.[16]

[14] *La Pazzia,* 1546 ed., ff. 15ᵛ, 16, 17ᵛ.

[15] *Ibid.,* ff. 3, 12, 11, 5ᵛ.

[16] "Ma quanto fussero felici i popoli senza questi Savii, si puo facilmente guidicar la vita e i costumi de i popoli novamente ritrovati nelle indie occidentali, i quali beati senza legge, senza lettere, e senza savii, non apprezzavano ne oro, ne gioie, non cognoscevano ne avaritia, ne ambitione, ne arte veruna si nutrivano dei frutti che la terra senza arte producevano haveva si come nella Republica di Platone, ogni cosa commune insino alle donne, è i fanciulli che nascevano, come proprij comunamente nutrivano, & allevavano, e quelli riconoscendo tutti come padri, senza odio, ne passion alcuna viveano in perpetuo amor, e carita, si come nel secolo fortunato, e veramente d'oro dal vecchio Saturno, il qual giocondo, e riposato vivere

The dream of the age of gold and the use of pazzia were methods by which these writers, and the author of *La Pazzia,* indicated their preference for a simpler society. Primitive simplicity was for them an attractive alternative in society just as it was in religion and learning.

Doni's New World

Doni brought together the themes of pazzia and the golden age by writing a utopia, a "New World," which summarized much of the rejection of the age in which he lived. His New World was cast on the model of the Renaissance utopia, but with differences. A critical and satirical attitude was apparent from the beginning. The utopia constituted the major part of the sixth of the seven worlds of *I Mondi*—the *Mondo de' Pazzi* (world of the madmen), narrated by two speakers, Savio and Pazzo. In the introductory discourse,[17] Savio, playing on the meanings of "pazzia" and "saviezza" in a way reminiscent of Erasmus' *Praise of Folly,* commented that he was not certain whether his words ought to be called crazy or wise, because the world had little certainty on the subject. Thus, his readers could call "this New World" he was about to describe either

---

del tutto gli hanno sturbato, & interrotto gli ambitiosi, e avari Spagnoli, li quali capitando in quelle regioni col lor troppo sapere, e con leggi durissime, non altramente che se, el bossolo di Pandora portato v'havessero, di mille squadre di noie, e di mali gli hanno riempiti." *La Pazzia,* 1546 ed., ff. 10ᵛ-11.

[17] All the modern editions of Doni's New World omit the introductory discourse with the tale of the astrologers, missing the self-mockery and cynicism with which Doni began his utopia. The New World dialogue is available in the following modern editions: *Le più belle pagine di Anton Francesco Doni,* ed. Mario Puccini (Milan, Rome, 1932), 78–85; *Utopisti e riformatori,* ed. Curcio, 3–15; *Scritti scelti di Pietro Aretino e di Anton Francesco Doni,* ed. Giuseppe Guido Ferrero (Turin, 1951), 478–90. Luigi Firpo has edited the utopias of Guevara and Doni in his "Il pensiero politico del Rinascimento e della Controriforma," in *Grande Antologia Filosofica,* ed. M. F. Sciacca, X, *Il pensiero della Rinascenza e della Riforma (Protestantesimo e Riforma Cattolica)* (Milan, 1964), 561–81. Secondary accounts of Doni's New World have been brief. See Santoro, *Il concetto dell'uomo nella letteratura del Cinquecento,* 194–206; Luigi Firpo, *Lo stato ideale della Controriforma,* 254–55, and his "L'utopia politica nella Controriforma," in *Contributi alla storia del Concilio di Trento e della Controriforma,* I (Florence, 1948), 84. Also see Curcio, *Dal Rinascimento alla Controriforma,* 120–29, and *Utopisti e riformatori,* viii–xii. References in the text are to the first edition (1552) of *I Mondi.*

pazzo or savio as they pleased; neither did Savio mind if they called it a "hermaphroditic world" (90).

To illustrate his point, Savio narrated a satirical tale freely based on the biblical flood. A great deluge covered the earth. After the waters receded, a powerful stench which maddened men remained. Seeing the madness, which affected the whole world, astrologers gathered together in a small, closed room to pool their wisdom. After long study, they emerged with the aim of leading men from madness to wisdom. But the people of the world continued in their crazy ways. The wise astrologers attempted unsuccessfully to regulate and halt the madness; but because the pazzi were more numerous they soon overcame the savi, and forced them to act, against their will, like the pazzi, so that soon all were pazzi. The narrator, Savio, clearly speaking for Doni, concluded that although one could construct a "wise" world, he suspected that it would soon become a "crazy" world. That is, if there was such a thing as wisdom in the world, it could not prevail (90–92).

In this satirical, self-mocking vein, Doni began his dialogue on the perfect city. By way of contrast, Thomas More began his *Utopia* with a meeting between two gentlemen on a mission to Antwerp and a stranger, who narrated his visit to an exotic land. The other utopias had similarly sober introductions. Doni manifested a different spirit with an introduction that mocked his own "wise" new world.

Savio and Pazzo began to narrate a vision shown them by Jove and Momus. For the most part, Savio explained the structure of the New World while Pazzo added interpretative comments or prodded Savio with questions. In the vision, the two gods led Savio and Pazzo to a great city, the only city in a province the size of Lombardy, Tuscany, or the Romagna. The city's walls were built in the form of a star, like the Sforzinda of Filarete. In its center was a very high temple, "higher than the cupola [of the cathedral] of Florence by four or six times."[18] The temple had a hundred doors from which, "like the rays of a star," a hundred streets radiated out to the hundred gates of the city.

A high degree of uniformity characterized the life of the city. On every street were two related crafts; for example, on one side were all the tailors and on the other were cloth shops. The pharmacists worked on one side of a street, with the hospitals and doctors on the other. Shoemakers cobbled across the way from tanners, bakers labored across the street from

---

[18] ". . . quì nel mezzo dove io fo questo punto, sia un tempio alto, grande come è la cupola di Fiorenza quattro o sei volte." *I Mondi*, 1552 ed., 94ᵛ.

FIG. 8. Doni's star city in the New World, from *Les Mondes Celestes*, 1578 ed., p. 197

the mills, and women spun thread on one side of a street while the weavers toiled on the other side. The hundred streets held two hundred different crafts (although Doni did not enumerate all of them), with each artisan specializing in his own craft and no other. The craftsmen did not sell their products, but produced them for the people of the city. If anyone had need of something, he went to the appropriate street, as to the street of the tailors for a coat, and the article was made for him (95).

The same kind of specialization marked the lives of the peasants who lived outside the city, and produced food to feed it. Each part of the earth was "fruitful by its nature," so that the peasants planted only the crop (wheat, hay, vines, etc.) suitable to a particular patch of ground. The peasants too specialized, each group cultivating only one crop so that in a few years they could know "the nature of the plant." With this experience they produced miraculous harvests (94^v-95).

The utopian uniformity of the star city continued in every aspect of the lives of the inhabitants, to a degree more marked than in the other Renaissance utopias. At mealtimes, the people went to the streets of the inns, where they all ate the same few, simple dishes in equal, moderate quantity. All lived in homes furnished exactly alike in extreme simplicity. All wore uniform clothing in colors which corresponded to their ages. Children up to ten years wore white, young adults aged eleven to twenty wore green, those between twenty-one and thirty dressed in peacock blue, those from thirty-one to forty years of age wore red, and after forty black was worn. Moreover, these were the only colors used in the city (95-95^v). When one of the inhabitants was ill, he went to the street of the hospitals where knowledgeable physicians had medicines to cure any disease within an hour. All the aged and infirm were cared for, without favor or discrimination, in the hospitals (95^v), but children born deformed were thrown into a well in order that no deformities would exist in the New World. All would be "beautiful, good, healthy, and fresh" (96). In Doni's words, everything from birth to death went according to one line and rule in the star city (95^v). Doni, who described man's life in the Cinquecento as restless and unhappy, proposed in his new world a uniform life of perfect equality.

As he continued to explain the complete equality of the star city, his social and moral criticism of his own time became more evident. The star city had one or two streets of women who were possessed in common. Doni explained through Savio that there were three good reasons for this. First, social distinctions would be wiped out. Since women were used in common, the inhabitants never knew who their parents were (95ᵛ). Honored families and noble houses would be extinguished.[19] Secondly, holding women in common eliminated moral evils and social disturbances. Since marriage did not exist, the social and moral problems surrounding it in the Cinquecento would be eliminated. There were no angry families, contested dowries, challenged honors, tumultuous marriages, adulteries, cuckoldries, and murders in the New World. Third, as Doni the moralist gave way to Doni the cynical wit, holding women in common eliminated the heartbreak of unrequited love and loveless matches. No such difficulties occurred in the New World. Because love was nothing more than the privation of the loved object, the longing that arose from the absence of the beloved was cancelled immediately (96ᵛ–97).

In his star city Doni eliminated the Cinquecento social and economic structure which he had criticized elsewhere. There was no noble class existing idly on the labor of others in the New World. Pazzo worried about possible laziness, but Savio brought him up short with the New World dictum that "He who does not work, does not eat."[20] There were no distinctions between rich and poor because there was no money. The inhabitants lived by barter. Weights and measures, which were nothing more than means to torture (*straziare*) the people, did not exist. Notaries, procurators, lawyers, and "other intriguing thieves" disappeared because there were no deceiving merchants. Because all the needs of the citizens were met, robbery did not exist. In short, "Everything was in common, and the peasants dressed like those in the city, because everyone carried away the reward of his labor and took what he needed."[21]

The other utopias also criticized Renaissance society, but their authors all constructed alternative societies. Doni, on the other hand, simply tore down the existing one. His star city lacked a governmental structure, means for defense, and a program of education. The New World had no way to enforce the simple, primitive way of life that he outlined. There were no police, laws, or courts in the city. He assumed that there would be no crime because all man's necessities were provided, and his desires

[19] ". . . si sono spente le famiglie honorate, & le case nobilissime." *Ibid.*, 97.

[20] "Chi non lavora non mangia adunque." *Ibid.*, 97.

[21] "Tutto era commune, et i contadini vestivano come quei della città, perche ciascuno portava giù il suo frutto della sua fatica, & pigliava cio che gli faceva bisogno." *Ibid.*, 1567 ed., 96.

either satisfied or blunted. Doni did indicate a minimal direction in the city—the great temple housed one hundred priests, with each priest having charge over one of the hundred streets of the city; the eldest priest was the "head of the land." But he did not elaborate what sort of direction the priests exercised, or in what way the eldest one was the head. Rather, in the same sentence he stressed equality; even the oldest priest had nothing more than the other inhabitants of the city (95).

What would the inhabitants of the star city do if they were attacked by another city, asked Pazzo. Savio replied that no other country or city should wish to attack it. The people of the star city lacked the "pomps, fashions, and tournaments" which moved others to anger and useless aggression (97-97ᵛ). Thus Doni turned the issue into another criticism of the Cinquecento mentality.

Neither did Doni, in contrast to More, provide an educational curriculum for the New World. As the children grew, they were taken from their mothers and raised in common. When they were old enough, they studied or learned a craft, according to the natural tendency of each child (95ᵛ). However, Doni wrote nothing more about education, and instead of developing an educational curriculum, he insisted upon a close tie between the arts and physical life. For example, poets in the star city performed other tasks, like fishing and hunting, in order that their writings should be close to nature. After working all day, the people came to the temple every evening to hear music. Painters and sculptors filled the land with their creations (98).

All the other Renaissance utopias placed heavy emphasis on religion, although the type of religion varied. Doni left the religious features of his New World vague. The people of the star city celebrated every seventh day as a feast day on which they all went to the temple and remained there "with great devotion" the entire day. But he did not indicate if the people prayed or practiced religious rites in the temple. Similarly, all visited the temple every morning before beginning work, and again before sunset in order to "make a feast of their work" (96). But again he did not elaborate how they did this. It is very unlikely that Doni, the renegade monk who criticized clerics, would lay any store by religion in the New World. Indeed, he came close to denying an afterlife in the star city. When one of the inhabitants died, the body was treated "as a piece of coarse meat (*carnaccia*), no more a man [but] a cadaver, and not a thing from something else. It was placed in earth in order to render to earth something which had consumed so much time from earth. It was treated as an ordinary thing, like a natural accident."[22] This also had beneficial social implications. Since funerals were eliminated, the financial expenses of death did not ruin the survivors. It made no difference if a widow remarried or if she did not.[23] A dead man who had no property did not leave a will and testament for his heirs to struggle over (98ᵛ). The statement quoted above was not overtly unorthodox because it mentioned only man's body. Moreover, at the end of the New World dialogue, Doni added a brief Christian coda. But the tone of his remarks concerning burial, taken in the context of a primitive, natural new world in which marriage was eliminated and deformed children dropped into a well, argued for materialism—a view openly suggested in Doni's later writings.

In their concluding discourses, Savio and Pazzo gave free rein to their enthusiasm for the New World. How wonderful was this city in which goods meant nothing! Goods were not possessed and hoarded, but could go where they might. Men could live and die without suffering the pangs and troubles of inheritances. Vices and vanities were gone. The people of the star city had nothing in their houses but beds for sleep. What sorrow could men experience at death when they left only this (98–98ᵛ)?

For all intents and purposes, these impassioned words completed the dialogue, except for the orthodox religious coda (99). Savio promised to speak again of the New World, but Doni never returned to the topic. In the following dialogue of *I Mondi,* Savio and Pazzo made brief inconsequential remarks on the possibility of the truth of dreams, and went on to other subjects (99ᵛ ff.).

Thus the New World dialogue completed the critics' rejection of their world. Doni resolved man's restlessness by devising a way of life in which all lived according to a rule. He eliminated distinctions of wealth and noble signori by eliminating possessions, money, and family life. In the star city, every man earned his bread by his own sweat. No princes ruled, but all worked together to provide for man's needs. By his running commentary in the New World dialogue, Doni pointed out how the

---

[22] ". . . mettilo là senza troppi *funus,* et senza menarlo atorno a procissione, a farlo vedere vestito d'oro o di seta, ma come un pezzo di carnaccia, (non piu huomo, cadavero, & non cosa da qualche cosa) si metteva la in terra a rendere alla terra quello che gli haveva consumato tanto tempo della terra: et come cosa ordinaria si stimava, come accidente naturale." *I Mondi,* 1552 ed., 98ᵛ.

[23] This was a slip on Doni's part, for a dead man could not leave a widow if women were held in common.

provisions of the star city checked social abuses and moral vices of men. He outlined the primitive natural society for which he longed.

Among the other utopias of the time, only the Garamanti of Guevara lived in an equality that approached Doni's. More, for example, had equality of property, but also a governing elite and slaves. Doni swept aside all but an extremely rudimentary structure of society, because he felt that organized governments were solely means to subjugate and cheat men. His extremely negative attitude toward the Cinquecento world came from his low opinion of man's nature. More, by way of contrast, held a more optimistic view of man. His prescriptions for reform in the *Utopia* were often based on ingenious appeals to man's reason; for instance, the binding of the slaves with chains of gold in order to educate the Utopians to reject gold. More also tried to foster a spirit of service to the city in a citizen militia, and retained the family.[24] For Doni, since man was susceptible, weak, and incapable of helping himself, the only way to improve him was to remove nearly all of Cinquecento civilization so that he might live in primitive simplicity. In the New World, men had no loyalty to spouse, family, city, or next world. The people of Doni's star city had all their wants satisfied and avoided vice, but it was a life without aspiration. As Savio put it, what sorrow could men have at death upon leaving this kind of world? The primary purpose of the other utopias was didactic; Doni's purpose was destructive. More, Guevara, and Agostini were counselors to kings who attempted through their books and civil careers to persuade rulers to follow a more humane Christian policy. Doni, the low-born literary adventurer, hated the signori. His New World was a total rejection of his time.

[24] *Utopia,* 75, 82, 86, 107-11, 118-29.

°§⟦ *Chapter VII* ⟧§°

MORALISTS OR *MALDICENTI?*

T HE books of the critics were widely
available in the sixteenth century and, despite difficulties with the *Index*
and Inquisition, reached a large number of readers. After their deaths,
their works continued to be printed, translated, and plagiarized in Italy,
France, Spain, and England through the first quarter of the seventeenth
century. Readers understood the critical message of Lando, Franco, and
Doni, and looked upon them as moralists with a bitter message concerning the ills of man and society.

The diffusion of their works

Each of these three writers averaged approximately one edition a year
from the time that he began publishing until about the end of the first
decade of the seventeenth century, when the rate of publication dropped
sharply. From 1534 through 1604, Lando had 70 editions, Franco from
1535 through 1617 had 31 editions, and Doni from 1543 through 1611 had
99 editions.[1] These totals count all their works, including translations
done by the critics, in Italian, Latin, French, Spanish, and English, but
exclude works that they edited or printed, and collections containing
small contributions from them. Nor do the figures take into account that
Doni's books, printed individually in the first edition, were often combined in later printings. For example, the 11 editions of *I Mondi* from
1562 through 1606 also included the *Inferni,* and the seven editions of *La
Zucca* from 1565 through 1607 also contained *Le Pitture.*

---

[1] For complete documentation, see the bibliographical appendices.

The heaviest concentration of editions in Italy appeared from 1535 to 1555, when the critics were most active. For Lando 32 editions were printed in Italy through 1555 and only three in the following decade. For Franco, 17 editions appeared through 1555 and but one in the next ten years. Doni was less affected by this pattern. From 1543 through 1555, there were 29 editions of his works, and from 1556 through 1564, 11 editions. The total number of editions that appeared in Italy between 1534 and 1555 was 78, about four per year.

The number of copies in a printing of the critics' works probably ranged from a few hundred to about 2,000. Information on the size of editions is, however, very sparse for sixteenth-century Italian presses.[2] In 1553 Giolito wrote that he had printed 1,800 copies of Ludovico Dolce's translation of Ovid's *Metamorphoses* in four months.[3] A concordance of Boccaccio by Francesco Alunno printed by the Aldine press in 1543 had a printing of more than 2,000.[4] In 1590 a little-known Venetian printer, Girolamo Polo, printed 1,125 copies of a new edition of the *Vitae pontificum* by the Quattrocento author, Bartolomeo Sacchi or il Platina (1421–81).[5] The author of a famed commentary on the *Materia medica* of Dioscorides, Pietro Andrea Mattioli, boasted in the second edition that more than 30,000 copies of the first edition of his work had been sold between 1557 and 1568.[6] At the other extreme, the 1536 edition of Lando's *Forcianae Quaestiones,* printed by a little-known Neapolitan printer, ran to only 300 copies.[7] In comparison, the ordinary printing of the well-known Plantin press of Antwerp in the second half of the sixteenth century was 1,250 to 1,500 copies, but the total could be as high as 2,500 and as low as 800.[8] From this evidence, one can infer that works of Lando, Franco, and Doni published by large, active printers such as Giolito and Marcolini possibly ran to about 2,000 copies while editions by small

---

[2] There is some information on the size of editions of Quattrocento Italian presses but nothing on the size of Cinquecento editions in Lucien Febvre and H. J. Martin, *L'apparition du livre* (Paris, 1958).

[3] *Le transformationi* . . . (Venice, 1553). "Ai Nobili e Sinceri Lettori. Gabriel Giolito," ff. x–xi.

[4] *Le Ricchezze della lingua Volgare* . . . (Venice, 1551), f. 2.

[5] ASV, Santo Uffizio, Processi, Bu. 66, Processo Girolamo Polo.

[6] *De i discorsi* . . . *Nelli sei Libri di Pedacio Dioscoride Anazarbeo, della materia medicinale* . . . (Venice, 1585), dedication letter, dated 1568, sig. *7. The first edition appeared in 1557.

[7] Letter of Antonio Lovinto in *Forcianae Quaestiones,* 1857 ed., 54.

[8] Febvre and Martin, *L'apparition du livre,* 331.

Venetian and non-Venetian printers were probably smaller, running from a few hundred to a little over a thousand.

Scattered comments indicate that the books of the critics were widely available in Italy. In a dialogue of Domenichi printed in 1562, one of the speakers lamented that infamous and dishonest books were printed and sold in Venice. He listed Franco's *Priapea*, Aretino's *La cortigiana*, and Doni's *I Marmi, I Mondi, Inferni*, and *La Zucca*. According to Domenichi's speaker, it was impossible to pass by the bookstores of the city without seeing these dirty invectives against good people on the shelves, "soiled by the flies." He regretted that these books gave bad example to the simple people who read them. But mindful of Domenichi's own dependence on printers such as Giolito, his speakers decided that the authors, not the printers, were at fault for these bad works.[9]

Prohibitions of the Tridentine *Index* slowed the Italian publication of Lando's works, but affected only a few works by Franco and Doni.[10] All Lando's works under his own name and his aliases were prohibited from 1564 on. The introduction of expurgation in place of outright condemnation in the 1590 *Index* did not lighten this prohibition. Nevertheless, an edition of the *Commentario* appeared in Venice in 1569, and expurgated

[9] "Non vi pare egli cosa infame, & vituperosa, che si leggano a stampa tante dishonestà, come noi veggiamo? non havete voi letto, o veduto almeno la Priapea del Franco, le Cortigiana con le figure, & mille altre opere lascive. . . . Non havete voi udito ragionare . . . de' Marmi, Mondi, Inferni, zucche senza sale, fiori, foglie, mescolanze d'ogni lordura. . . . È impossibile, che voi passando dalle librarie di questa città, non habbiate veduto su per li banchi, a esser lordate dalle mosche, le librerie, le invettive sporche contro la fama, & l'honor de' virtuosi & buoni, & vivi, & morti, con pessimo, & dannoso essempio di quelle persone semplici, chi a leggerle vi perdono quel tempo." *Dialoghi* . . . (Venice, 1562), 389–90.

[10] In this discussion the Parma *Index* of 1580 is omitted. It was extremely severe but unofficial, although it may have served as a guide for the 1590 *Index* of Sixtus V. It added new prohibitions for all three authors to the condemnations of the Tridentine *Index*, and forbade all Doni's works because of their geomancy. It also specifically prohibited his *Rime del Burchiello*. It forbade the *opera omnia* of Franco, naming his *Dialogi Piacevoli* and *Philena*. The *opera omnia* of Lando had already been condemned; the Parma *Index* added specific condemnations of the *Sferza de' Scrittori, Dubbi*, and a Venice, 1568, edition of the *Paradossi* (which has not been located and may be a mistaken reference). See Reusch, *Die Indices librorum prohibitorum*, 582–83, 588–90. The Parma *Index* did not halt the publication of Doni's works in the decade 1580–90, nor did it have any noticeable effect on Lando and Franco, who were infrequently printed in Italy from 1564 until 1590 in any case.

versions of the *Paradossi* in Bergamo, 1594, and Vicenza, 1602. A purged edition of the *Dubbi* was printed in Piacenza in 1597, and two early seventeenth-century editions of the *Sermoni Funebri* in Venice.

Doni had little difficulty with the *Indices*. Before the Tridentine *Index* of 1564, 40 editions of his works appeared in Italy and from 1564 through 1606, another 32 editions were issued. Doni's *Lettere* were prohibited by the Tridentine *Index,* by that of Sixtus V in 1590, and again by the 1596 *Index* of Clement VII, and were not printed after 1552. The reasons were not given, but all the editions of the *Lettere* contained substantial anticlericalism, and the 1547 *Lettere* included the weaver's confession. The rest of Doni's works, however, did not suffer prohibition, and were steadily printed throughout the sixteenth century, with a moderate increase in number after 1590. The *Index* of that year ordered the expurgation of his works,[11] perhaps thereby encouraging printers to publish amended versions. Beginning with an edition of *La Zucca* in 1589, *I Mondi, Inferni, I Marmi, La Zucca,* and *Le Pitture* were printed in purged editions. Anticlerical statements were omitted, but other changes were generally minor. The only important expurgation in *La Zucca* was the omission of the pessimistic "Pittura della Riforma." In *I Mondi* and *Inferni,* the censors took seriously Doni's mocking discourses on demonology and either altered or omitted them.[12]

In the new atmosphere of post-Tridentine Italy, however, even unprohibited books by the critics could provoke difficulty for their owners. In 1574 a Venetian accused of heresy was asked by the Inquisition to account for several prohibited books in his library, as well as for a copy of Doni's *Mondi celesti, terrestri, et infernali,* which was not prohibited. He responded that he had purchased the book (an edition of either 1562, 1567, or 1568) from a bookseller in Venice two or three years previously.[13] The Inquisitors may have been mistaken or overzealous.

Only Franco's poems against Aretino were prohibited by the *Indices,* and these were not printed after 1548. However, despite this failure to

[11] The *Index* of 1590 carried the notation "Antonii Francisci Doni opera omnia," with the directive "donec juxta regulas hujus indicis revideantur et approbentur." Reusch, *Die Indices librorum prohibitorum,* 463.

[12] For example, the section entitled "Discorso sopra gli spiriti che entrano et escono ne corpi" in *Inferni,* 1553 ed., 88–95, was omitted in *Mondi Celesti,* 1606 ed., after Doni's introductory statement on II, 51. For examples of the way censors softened passages, compare *I Mondi,* 1552 ed., 100, with the 1606 ed., I, 119; and *I Mondi,* 1552 ed., 102, with the 1606 ed., I, 122.

[13] ASV, Santo Uffizio, Processi, Bu. 37, Processo Giovanni Battista Sanudo.

prohibit, none of his works appeared in Italy between 1559 and 1590. Thereafter his two major works, the *Dialogi Piacevoli* and *Pistole Vulgari,* enjoyed a new, expurgated, popularity. The *Dialogi Piacevoli* were published by Giolito in 1539, 1541, 1542, 1545, 1554, and 1559, but never again by him, although he continued to print until 1578. Expurgated versions appeared in 1590, 1593, 1596, 1598, 1599, 1606, and 1609, from five different Venetian printers. Giolito may have been hesitant to print Franco in the stricter moral climate of the 1560's, or he may have reasoned that his books would no longer sell. After 1590, however, Franco again became popular.

The *Index* and Inquisition hindered the appearance of the prohibited works of Lando, Franco, and Doni but did not eliminate them from the shelves of private libraries and bookshops, where they continued to appear many years after the establishment of the Tridentine *Index*. For example, a number of prohibited books including the *Rime contro Aretino et la Priapea* (last printed edition 1548) were discovered in the library of a priest at the church of San Salvatore in Venice.[14] In 1574, an investigating priest from the Inquisition purchased a copy of Franco's *Rime* from a Venetian bookseller.[15] In 1587 one or more copies of Doni's *Lettere* (edition unspecified) were found by the Inquisition in the shop of a Venetian printer and bookseller.[16] Prohibited books could appear quite far from Venice, years after the date of publication. In 1569 the bishop of Crete wrote to the Venetian Inquisition asking for advice concerning a number of books of "damned authors" found in Crete. In the list was a 1545 Venetian edition of Lando's *Paradossi*.[17]

Despite the blanket prohibition of Lando's books, they continued to be available in bookshops and to appear in the libraries of Venetians through the first half of the seventeenth century. In 1584, a Venetian bookseller had a copy of the *Ragionamenti Familiari* in his inventory.[18] In 1604 another Venetian bookseller had the *Vari Componimenti, Paradossi,* and the *Forcianae Quaestiones* (Naples edition of either 1535 or 1536) for

---

[14] ASV, Santo Uffizio, Processi, Bu. 38, Processo Fra Leonardo (1574).

[15] The bookseller was arrested. ASV, Santo Uffizio, Processi, Bu. 37, Processo Bartolomeo de Sabio.

[16] ASV, Santo Uffizio, Processi, Bu. 59, Processo Gioachino Brugnoli.

[17] The Inquisitors' response, if any, is not included. ASV, Santo Uffizio, Processi, Bu. 27, Processi Emmanuele Mara, Francesco Cassimati, e Francesco Gentile.

[18] ASV, Giudici di Petizion, Inventari, Bu. 338, no. 44 Auzollo Bonfadini, f. 17.

sale.[19] Lando's *Commentario* (1548 ed.), *Paradossi* (1602), and the Italian translation of the *Forcianae Quaestiones* by Marco Bandarino (1556), appeared in the library of a Venetian who died in 1640.[20] In 1657, an edition of the *Paradossi* (date not given) appeared in another Venetian death inventory.[21]

Prohibited books of Lando and Doni were still available in southern Italy as well. In early January 1565, an informer reported to the Neapolitan Inquisition that six copies of a "Dialogo del Lando" (probably the *Dialogo della Sacra Scrittura*, 1552) and four copies of Doni's *Lettere* (for which the last edition was 1552) were on the shelves of a Neapolitan bookstore owned by Giolito but operated by a representative. An investigation two and a half weeks later failed to uncover these books. Either the informer had been mistaken, or they were surreptitiously removed.[22] If the informer was correct, the books of Lando and Doni were available in a number of copies far from Venice and years after their publication.

Some of the prohibited books printed in Italy may have circulated beyond the peninsula. A copy of Lando's *Commentario* (Venice, 1548) inscribed by Lando to Johann Jacob Fugger has been found in Munich.[23] Johann Albrecht von Widmanstetter had a copy of Lando's *Cicero relegatus et Cicero revocatus* and mentioned his *Forcianae Quaestiones* as well.[24]

In addition to works printed in France, in the original or in translation, Italian printings of these authors were available there. The printer of a 1576 translation of Lando's *Sermoni Funebri* explained the procedure by which he brought Italian books to the French. Periodically he received a shipment of books from Venice; from these he selected those which pleased him and arranged to have them translated. Such was the procedure followed with the *Sermoni Funebri,* which he warmly recommended. He also endorsed Lando's *Commentario* and *Vari Componi-*

---

[19] "Inventario della libreria di Giovanni Vincenzo Pinelli ereditata da Francesco Pinelli," Venice, Biblioteca Marciana, Mss. Italiani, Classe X, Cod. LXI (6601), ff., 20, 70, 76.

[20] ASV, Giudici di Petizion, Inventari, Bu. 356, no. 67 Marco Antonio Felette, ff. 60ᵛ, 67.

[21] ASV, Giudici di Petizion, Inventari, Bu. 364, no. 90 Gasparo Chechel, f. 22.

[22] Bongi, *Annali di Giolito,* I, lxxxv–ci.

[23] P. Lehmann, *Eine Geschichte der alten Fuggerbibliotheken,* I Teil, (Tübingen, 1956), 48, as cited in Conor Fahy, "Un'opera sconosciuta di Lando," 263, n. 1.

[24] See n. 9 of Ch. II.

menti, which he did not have translated.[25] Presumably he had Venetian copies to sell.

It is clear that some books were still available in bookshops years after the date of publication. A Venetian bookseller in 1584 had for sale Doni's *La Zucca* (either in the first edition of 1551 or the second edition of 1565), his *Rime del Burchiello* (either in the first edition of 1553 or the second edition of 1566), and Lando's *Ragionamenti Familiari* (1550). He also had two copies of the *Lettere facete* collection (1575), which contained Doni's *L'Asinesca* and some letters, and Giulio Landi's *Lode dell'ignoranza.*[26] Another Venetian bookseller had in his inventory in 1604 the *Libraria* of Doni (the last edition was in 1580), Lando's *Vari Componimenti, Paradossi,* and *Forcianae Quaestiones,* and the *Lettere facete* collection (edition of either 1575 or 1601).[27] In 1649, the Venetian printer Giovanni Giacomo Herz advertised that he had one or more copies of the *Lettere di Nicolò Franco* (edition of 1604 or 1615) for sale.[28]

An inventory of the library of a Venetian at his death in 1640 included, within a magnificent library of about 3,500 volumes, seven titles of works by Doni, Franco, and Lando. They were Doni's *La Zucca* (editions of 1551 and 1565), his translation of the *Epistole* of Seneca (1549), Franco's *Lettere* (1604), the *Dialogi maritimi* (1547) which contained some of Franco's *rime,* Lando's *Commentario* (1548), *Paradossi* (1602), and Bandarino's 1556 Italian translation of the *Forcianae Quaestiones.* In addition, the library included the ubiquitous *Lettere facete* (1601 ed.),[29] which also appeared in another private library inventoried at the death of its Venetian owner in 1602.[30] At death in 1657, a wealthy Venetian with a library of over 600 books had eight titles of works by Doni and one by Lando. They were *I Mondi* (first edition of 1552), *Inferni* (first edition of 1553), *Le Pitture* (1564), two copies of *La Moral Filosophia* (no date given), *Le Rime del Burchiello* (no edition given),

---

[25] *Regrets facetieux, et plaisantes harengues funebres sur la mort de divers animaux . . .* (Paris, 1576), sig. Aiiij^v, p. 98.

[26] ASV, Giudici di Petizion, Inventari, Bu. 338, no. 44, ff. 7^v, 13^v, 16^v, 17.

[27] "Inventario della libreria di Pinelli," Venice, Biblioteca Marciana, Mss. Italiani, Classe X, Cod. LXI (6601), ff. 16, 20, 70, 76, 107^v.

[28] "Libri stampati da Gio: Giacomo Herz in Venetia," 9, appended to [Francesco Sansovino], *Le cose notabili, Et maravigliose della citta di Venetia. Riformate . . . da Leonico Goldioni . . .* (Venice, 1649).

[29] ASV, Giudici di Petizion, Inventari, Bu. 356, no. 67, ff. 19, 22^v, 23, 59, 60, 60^v, 63^v, 67.

[30] ASV, Giudici di Petizion, Inventari, Bu. 342, no. 26 Lodovico Usper, f. 15.

La Fortuna di Cesare (1550), *Disegno* (1549), *La Zucca* (no edition given), and Lando's *Paradossi* (no date). In addition, the library included the *Lettere facete,* and an undated edition of *L'argute et facete lettere,* an extensive plagiarization of Doni by Cesare Rao.[31]

A few manuscript copies of the works of the critics were available. Sometimes Doni made autograph copies of his works for presentation to expected patrons.[32] After the Inquisition and *Index* made it more difficult to print some titles, manuscript copies were made of the prohibited printed editions.[33] This was an active enterprise: in 1630 the Venetian Inquisition apprehended a Venetian scribe who was found to be copying and selling prohibited works of Aretino. He received a five-year prison sentence.[34]

The large number of reprinted editions, the availability of copies in bookstores, and their existence in private libraries indicate that despite difficulties with the *Index* and Inquisition the books of the critics were in demand and widely available.[35]

[31] On Rao, see below. ASV, Giudici di Petizion, Inventari, Bu. 364, no. 90, ff. 19ᵛ, 21, 22, 28ᵛ, 29ᵛ, 30, 30ᵛ, 31.

[32] For example, there is an autograph ms. of *Lo Stufaiolo* in Florence, Biblioteca Riccardiana, Ms. 1184, dedicated to Jacopo Piccolomini. An autograph copy of the "Discorsi del Doni" dedicated to Luigi d'Este (1538–86) is in Florence, Biblioteca Nazionale Centrale, Fondo Landau Finaly, no. 257. His autograph ms. of the "Ornamento della lingua toscana" dedicated to Baccio Tolomei is in *ibid.,* Fondo Nuovi Acquisti, no. 268. An autograph copy of "Una nuova opinione del Doni circa all'imprese amorose militari" dedicated to David Otto is in *ibid.,* Fondo Nuovi Acquisti, no. 267. Doni dedicated an incomplete undated autograph copy of *Le Pitture* to Luigi d'Este. The ms. is in the Biblioteca Vaticana, Fondo Patetta (no shelf mark). Kristeller, *Iter Italicum,* II, 606, notes the ms.

[33] A seventeenth-century ms. of Franco's *Rime contro Aretino* and *Priapea,* which is a copy of the 1548 printed edition, exists in the Columbia University Library. "Franco M. Niccolò. Rime contro Pietro Aretino." A ms., dated 1751, of the 1548 printed *Rime,* copied from a previous ms. in Florence, exists in Venice, Biblioteca Marciana, Mss. Italiani, Classe IX, Cod. CDL (6497).

[34] ASV, Santo Uffizio, Processi, Bu. 87, Processo Girolamo Chiaramonte.

[35] Not enough copies have been located to make any generalization about the groups in society, outside the literary circles and the academies, that were most likely to read these writers. The copies found in private libraries came from the collections of a priest and of wealthy, but not patrician, Venetians. One can surmise that interest was not limited to one group in society, for the critics made no exclusive appeal to a particular group comparable to, for example, that made by "middle-class literature" in Elizabethan England. (Louis B. Wright in *Middle-Class Culture in Elizabethan England* [Ithaca, New York, 1958], has identified a body of literature,

The contemporary judgment

Contemporaries viewed the critics as angry iconoclasts attacking society. In 1548 the editor of Lando's *Commentario* warned readers that the author was "biting, angry, and slanderous" because he was desperate. If he could, Lando would like to "demolish the whole world" as if it were a fragile pane of glass.[36] In 1545 another editor advised readers that they would find an infinite number of moral precepts in the *Paradossi*. To be sure, the author was a capricious and bizarre person who would praise in one paradox and condemn in another. But readers who were displeased by the lack of respect shown to Aristotle, Cicero, and Boccaccio still ought to pay attention to Lando's message, he advised.[37]

These comments probably represented a conscious attempt to build up the image of the critics as iconoclasts, just as Aretino boasted that he wrote in order to dirty the white walls of respectability. Obviously, the editors also wished to stimulate the sales of their books. But what they said indicates that they understood, and expected readers to understand, the critical message of Lando beneath the wit, anecdote, and travelogue.

Contemporary readers did indeed understand. A copy of Lando's

---

utilitarian and self-improving in content, which he considers to be specifically directed to the ambitious merchant seeking to rise in society.) The critics indeed advertised that they were writing for a variety of men and hoped that their books would please a diversified audience. This was probably true. Most commentators acknowledged that their books were well-written, pleasing, and witty, therefore likely to gather an audience even among those who did not agree with the critical message often underlying the witty dialogues. There was an obvious appeal, in the complaints against the signori, to the literate urban population below the nobility— merchants, tradesmen, and artisans. The professional classes, for instance, lawyers, doctors, and the clergy, were traditionally inclined to read although the heavy criticism of their professions might upset them. The subject matter was of lesser appeal to the nobility, but a sophisticated Italian aristocrat might nonetheless read them for their wit.

[36] "Nicolo Morra alli lettori. . . . Se in qualche cosa ti parerà mordace, & furioso, & maldicente: habbili compassione, perche egli era allhora in croce quando queste cose scriveva, & era pieno di desperatione: havrebbe egli voluto poter rovinare tutto il mondo, & certo s'egli fusse stato di vetro lo havrebbe piu d'una volta spezzato." *Commentario,* 1550 ed., 47ᵛ.

[37] "Paulo Mascranico alli Cortesi Lettori," *Paradossi,* 1545 ed., [86–86ᵛ].

Sferza de' Scrittori (1550) contained a sonnet, addressed to him, which praised him for uncovering the falseness of learning. The owner of the book, one Pier Maria Dal Pozzo, a Venetian contemporary of Lando, may have written this complex poem. Its first quatrain declared the present age to be the age of gold in which every deceit and lie of those authors whom the world esteemed great scholars and masters was revealed, an obvious reference to the content of the book. In the second quatrain, the sonneteer attacked the age for its false learning; it was, he said, the century of iron in which ignorance was covered over, and worthwhile poetry and eloquence called error. In the first tercet the sonnet addressed the author of *La Sferza:* "Oh fortunate spirit in whom such lively intelligence shows, your light shines clearly in the ancient darkness." In the second tercet, it attacked an unnamed personification of the ignorance of the present: "Oh curse of our days, in the midst of abundance you have become head and leader of those who censure the cleansed writings"—presumably, the writings of Lando.[38]

Aretino was also impressed by Lando's *Sferza de' Scrittori,* and in a letter of August 1550 praised him for seeing the defects of so many

[38] "Al compositore di questo libro.

> Questa è l'età de l'oro in cui si scuopre
> Ogn'inganno e bugia di quei scrittori
> Che fur stimati al mondo gran dottori
> Et maestri eccellenti di bell'opre.

> Quest'è 'l secol di ferro in cui si cuopre
> L'ignorantia; chiamando espressi errori
> Le poesie pregiate, e d'oratori
> L'arte, che par tra noi tanto s'adopre.

> O fortunato spirto, in cui riluce
> Si vivo ingegno, che palese mostri
> Ne le tenebre antiche la tua luce:

> O vituperio delli giorni nostri:
> Nuotar tra i pomi, e farsi capo e duce
> Di quei che biasman gli purgati inchiostri."

As quoted in Sforza, "Ortensio Lando," 62, n. 3. The phrase "Nuotar tra i pomi" (to swim among the apples) is obscure. Because of the mention of fruit and the context of the golden age, I believe that it is a reference to abundance. The "curse of our days" may signify a literary or scholarly dictator like Bembo or Speroni.

The copy was owned by Sforza; I have been unable to locate it. It was inscribed "Petri Marie Puthei et amicorum," who was identified by Sforza. From a comparison of the handwriting, he concluded that the sonnet may have been written by Dal Pozzo.

ancient and modern authors. Knowledgeable men all agreed, said Aretino, that Lando's penetrating and shrewd, subtle and elegant books enriched the world.[39] Earlier, tongue in cheek, he had praised Lando as the "lamp of the most learned schools."[40] Domenichi, on the other hand, acknowledged Lando's ability and praised his "ready intelligence," but disliked him when he was "invidious and malicious." He would, he said, honor him when he was "virtuous and literate."[41] Alberto Lollio of Ferrara (1508–c. 1568), orator and dramatist, judged Lando to be a man of sharp mind who possessed uncommon literary ability.[42]

Francesco Sansovino in 1575 summed up the view of Doni as a witty, inventive moralist. Including him in a group of capsule notices of famous authors of his age, Sansovino wrote that he was famous for his new inventions. Initially readers found in Doni a pleasing wit which lured them to his philosophy, the purpose of which was to win back evil men from their deeds. Thus with his witty humour Doni led readers to taste the saving precepts of his writing.[43]

An admirer from Rimini wrote Doni in 1552 with high praise for his books, remarking that no less a personage than Giovanni Della Casa had recommended the *Inferni* to him. Upon reading it, the Rimini admirer

[39] "Al Lando. Signore Hortensio, anchora che in tutte l'opre date in luce dalla cortesia vostra prestate: si vegga felicità d'ingegno, grandezza di studio, & eccellenza di Dottrina; . . . vengono tenuti cotanti antichi scrittori, & moderni i cui difetti toccate si adentro nel vivo . . . si penetra con la menta, che giudica tutte le cose, che uscir' della penna altrui; senza giuditio in le carte . . . onde giurano i saputi; che in esse [Lando's works] consistano le sottilità dialetiche, le sententie philosophiche, le elegantie delle poesie, le memorie de i legisti, le voci de i tragici & i gesti de gli academici. & pero arricchitene il mondo, & il secolo; . . . hor, penetrativo, & arguto, & hor pieno di efficatia, & di forza. Di Agosto in Vinetia. M.D.L." *Lettere*, 1609 ed., V, 307–7^v.

[40] In 1548. *Lettere*, 1609 ed., V, 60^v–61.

[41] "Potrebbe forse sentirne dispiacere quel bellissimo & prontissimo ingegno, & da me ricordato & riverito con ogni sorte d'honore, dico M. Hortensio Lando, quando egli non virtuoso & letterato, ma invidioso fosse & maligno:" *La nobiltà delle donne*, 1549 ed., preface, [5].

[42] Fontanini, *Biblioteca dell'eloquenza italiana*, I, 125. On Lollio, see Pompeati, *Dall'umanesimo al Tasso*, 709, 854.

[43] "Anton Francesco Doni, fu parimente famoso [as Bernardo Tasso] per le sue nuove inventioni, percioche trovando con piacevole ingegno nuove cose che allettavano i lettori, con una certa filosofia fatta a suo modo: riprendendo gli huomini cattivi delle loro operationi, tirava il lettore con le sue argutie a ridere, & parimente a gustar i precetti salutiferi delle sue scritture." *Sopplimento delle croniche universali* . . . (Venice, 1575), 596.

claimed, he was so impressed by Doni's books that he threw all his own books into the fire. He went on to praise other books of Doni. In *I Marmi* one found mirrored the clergy, women, artisans, letterati, poets, and every other sort of man. By the acuteness of his penetration, Doni had surpassed those whom the world called learned. This reader praised *La Zucca* and *I Mondi,* and claimed to have read all of Doni's printed letters. He stated that in the bookstores one found nothing but the books of Doni.[44]

The same view was expressed in 1544 by two Venetian patricians, who signed the permission granting Doni a license to have his *Lettere* and *Dialogo della Musica* printed. The officials, Nicolò Priuli and Tommaso Contarini, commented that Doni's work was "penetrating and ingenious" (*arguta et ingeniosa*).[45] Aretino, whose judgment was keen when not dulled by feuds or adulation, commented as early as 1545 on the sharpness of Doni's writings, and in September 1550 he praised his works, advising him to ignore those who hated him for what he wrote. Aretino boasted that he had never cared what others said of him; he urged Doni to persevere although some gnashed their teeth on their pens at his name. Their dislike masked fear; continue to write even if you suffer malice and poverty, he wrote.[46]

In 1545 Luca Contile, businessman and amateur author, evaluated Doni as rabid and vengeful, but a virtuoso of great ability.[47] In 1552, Andrea Calmo (1510–71), Venetian author of comedies and burlesque discourses, praised Doni as a "modern prophet," and a "penetrating humorist." Calmo was also grateful to Doni for including him in the latter's *Libraria.*[48] In 1565 Tommaso Porcacchi described Doni, "whose

[44] Letter to Doni from Pietro Maria Buoni da Rimini, December 31, 1552, from Ravenna, in *I Mondi,* 1583 ed., 279–82.

[45] This was one of the very few times that the examiners commented on a book. Consiglio di Dieci Not. Reg., April 21, 1544, signed by Nicolo di Prioli [Priuli], C. di X., and Thomaso Contarini, C. C. X., as copied in "Privilegi veneziani," Cod. 2500 (12077), f. 142.

[46] Aretino, *Lettere,* 1609 ed., III, 280–80ᵛ; V, 315–15ᵛ.

[47] Contile, *Il primo volume delle lettere,* 95–97ᵛ.

[48] Letter to Doni, "A l'astutissimo banchier de la bizarie sciential. . . . Hora ben mo per tornar a quel che voio dir, dignissimo profeta moderno e argutissimo humorista vulgar e suficientissimo indivinaor temporal e honorandissimo fabuloso penetrativo. . . ." Andrea Calmo, *Le Lettere,* ed. Vittorio Rossi (Turin, 1888), 210–11. This was first published in Calmo's *Supplimento delle piacevoli, ingeniose, et argutissime lettere . . .* (Venice, 1552), 42ᵛ–43ᵛ.

fame by now all know," as "most acute of wit, and of subtle and wide-awake intellect," and related a facezia about him to illustrate the point.[49] Over twenty years later a Florentine Servite monk and literary historian found Doni to be "erudite and eloquent," "acute and witty," in spite of the condemnation of his *Lettere* by the *Index* and his desertion of the Servite Annunziata monastery in Florence.[50]

Franco received only epithets from Aretino and his friends after 1538. In a dialogue by Giuseppe Betussi printed in 1543, there was mentioned a certain "N. F." of Aretino's household who had attempted to revenge himself by writing poems against the Scourge of Princes. A second speaker added that this was the one who had "spoken through Lucerna" —a reference to Franco's critical letter from Lucerna in the *Pistole Vulgari*. Betussi condemned Franco's bad nature and pedantry, and stated that by publishing his writing he had proclaimed to the world his own dishonor.[51]

Others took a less hostile view, and urged Franco to continue his criticism. Domenichi in 1541 praised his clear intelligence, valor, and frankness, punning on *franco*, i.e., "frank" or "blunt."[52] In or about 1560, a Palermo acquaintance of Franco urged him to continue to "speak ill" (*dir male*) of kings and princes.[53] Even Sperone Speroni, who was part of the literary orthodoxy to which the critics objected, wrote a sonnet that praised him as courteous, good, and modest, after Franco, during his flight from Venice in 1540, had visited Speroni in Padua.[54] Few others agreed with this evaluation of Franco.

[49] "Messer Anton Francesco Doni, il quale è di quel grido e fama ch'ormai si sa per tutto, come acutissimo d'ingegno e d'intelletto sottile e svegliato. . . ." *Facetie, Motti, et Burle di diversi signori & persone private* (Venice, 1565), 489–90. The Doni anecdote is in the section of *motti* attributed to Porcacchi.

[50] Poccianti, *Catalogus scriptorum florentinorum,* 19.

[51] ". . . come ha fatto un certo non so chi N. F. gia suo Famiglio, che gli ha fatto certe rimaccie contra per vendicarsi di un fregio . . . il poveraccio, che ha publicato a molti gli suoi dishonori, che erano noti a pochi. . . . Questo è quel, che ha fatto parlare alla lucerna & che con l'intitolar mille baiaccie al divinissimo & Ill. Monsignore Leone Orsino Vescovo di Fregius . . . perche tosto, che il nobilissimo Signore conobbe la pessima natura sua, & quelle pedantesche sforzate sue virtuti non lo volse piu vedere." *Dialogo Amoroso di Messer Giuseppe Betussi* (Venice, 1543), 22–22ᵛ.

[52] Letters of April 18, 1541 and September 10, 1541 to Franco in Vaticanus Latinus 5642, ff. 5–5ᵛ, 18–19.

[53] Giovanni Campo of Palermo was the author of this advice. See Carlo Simiani, "Due componimenti inediti di Nicolò Franco," *GSLI,* 30 (1897), 270.

[54] Sperone Speroni, *Opere* (Venice, 1740), IV, 381.

In addition to the above evaluations, there were other, adulatory references to the critics in their own books and in the books of others.[55] An exchange of letters and sonnets sometimes served the purpose of spreading the fame of the mutual admirers. Excluding these references, the contemporary response to Lando, Doni, and Franco was to view them as iconoclasts.

The reaction from 1570 to 1650

From about 1570 to the middle of the seventeenth century, the critics were viewed in two ways, but in each case linked to the corruption and decadence of the times. On one hand the critics were seen as part of the decadence, as propagators of false and destructive ideas. They were viewed as enemies of reputable men, ideas, and institutions. They were especially condemned for their slander (*maldicenza*)[56] against respectable society and signori. On the other hand, they were praised for uncovering man's evils. For these sympathetic observers, Lando, Franco and Doni became moralists—a view implying that the writer to a certain extent agreed that society was morally or socially ill.

The monk Tommaso Garzoni of Bagnacavallo (1549–89), a popular and prolific author, whose books were a storehouse of the social history of his time, denounced the critics several times in his writings, and found much that was objectionable in their works.[57] He saw a great deal of decadence and corruption in his century and did not hesitate to condemn it in the censorious tones of the Counter-Reformation.

In his *Teatro de vari, e diversi cervelli mondani* (1583) Garzoni attempted to describe every kind of brain. In a section entitled "Concern-

[55] For example, see Doni, *Lettere*, 1547 ed., 12ᵛ–13, 19, 60ᵛ, 63. Also see Pietro Lauro's letter to Lando. *De le lettere di M. Pietro Lauro Modonese. Il primo libro* . . . (Venice, 1552), 179–81.

[56] The meaning of "maldicenza" depended on one's viewpoint. For the critics' enemies, maldicenza meant not only slander, but connoted vulgarity, cursing, or foul speech not tolerated in polite society. On the other hand, the critics prided themselves on their maldicenza, by which they meant a kind of tough and frank speech unheedful of consequences. A *maldicente,* of course, was a slanderer.

[57] On Garzoni, see Benedetto Croce, "Pagine di Tommaso Garzoni," in *Poeti e scrittori*, II, 208–20; and Giuseppe Cocchiara, *Popolo e letteratura in Italia* (Turin, 1959), 54–56. By 1620 Garzoni's books had gone through more than 30 editions in Italian, French, Spanish, and English. No comprehensive study of him nor bibliography of his works exists.

ing malignant, perverse, divisive, perjured, perfidious, cursed, and invidious brains," he wrote that in his age maldicenza had passed the limits of taste and honesty in the works of Aretino, Franco, Lando, and the "new Momuses"—possibly a reference to Doni, because Momus (Momo) was his spokesman in *I Mondi* and *Inferni.*[58] In *La Piazza Universale* (1585) Garzoni condemned the "filthy and dishonest" books of Aretino, and denounced "Hortensio Lando who writes in his *Paradossi* with overly subtle reasons against wealth, liberty, and other things." He also disliked the "extremely satirical" writings of Nicolò Franco, and the impious inventor of the *Sferza de' Scrittori,* i.e., Lando again. The works of these authors were as bad as the works of heretics, the *Koran* of Mohammed, and Agrippa's *De vanitate.* Aretino, Franco, and Doni had sinned greatly by searching for the applause of the mob and honor from the vulgar.[59]

Garzoni disliked the critics for attacking the sixteenth-century world, especially its learning. He noted that Franco and Doni in his *Inferni* wrote against scholars, and that Lando in the *Sferza* attacked philosophers.[60] In another book he vilified the praise of ignorance by the "sacrilegious" Lando, Doni, and Rao. Writing in 1589, he suggested that one should deposit their praises, "made in their own imitation," into the nearest urinal.[61] Garzoni lamented that today in "our depraved century,"

---

[58] "De' Cervellazzi Maligni, & perversi; & divisi in perfidi, spergiuri, Maldicenti, & Invidi. Discorso XLVI. . . . E questa petulante maldicenza ha passato si i termini del giusto, e dell'honesto all'età nostra, che si sono visti novi Theoni da denti rabbiosi, novi Zoili, e novi Momi, nell'Aretino, nel Franco, nel Lando, & in moltri altri. . . ." *Il Theatro de vari, e diversi cervelli mondani. Nuovamente formato, & posto in luce* . . . (Venice, 1595), 76-76ᵛ. The statement is the same in 1585 and 1598 editions that I have seen.

[59] ". . . altre volte troppo sporco, & dishonesto, come son l'opere communemente dell'Aretino: . . . è Hortensio Lando, che fece quei Paradossi con troppo sottil ragioni contra la ricchezza, la libertà, & altre cose naturalmente al contrario desiate: alle volte troppo satirico, come Nicolo Franco insieme col suo maestro. & l'inventore della sfera de' scrittori: . . . Nel fine peccano molti, cercando solamente applauso dalla plebe, honor dal vulgo; utile da stampatori, premio da Mecenati, guadagno da Signori, gratia dalle Madonne, cortesie da tutte le bande." *La Piazza Universale* . . . (Venice, 1587), Discorso xxxii, 288.

[60] *La Piazza Universale* . . . (Venice, 1585), 743, 236. This work had great success, with Italian editions in 1585, 1586, 1587, 1589, 1592, 1595, 1599, 1601, 1610, 1617, 1638, 1651, and 1665, as well as several German and Latin editions.

[61] ". . . i scritti del Sacrilego Hortensio Lando, da Cesar Rao, & dal Doni: i quali han tolto un carico a un bel spirito dell'eta nostra, che, havendo pensato di acquistarsi una collana presso a un Prencipe, con un suo Encomio della ignoranza,

ignorance was honored in many places.[62] In a discourse entitled "De pazzi sfrenati come un Cavallo" in a fourth book (1586), Garzoni called Aretino, Franco, Burchiello, and Berni unbridled fools. By "pazzi sfrenati" he meant insolent writers who rashly and licentiously usurped a freedom to offend others. They felt that the whole world was theirs, and that they could freely insult anyone. These authors deserved to be hanged so that they could no longer vomit forth the bitterness in their breasts.[63] In short, Garzoni saw the critics as symptomatic of Cinquecento corruption and condemned them for their maldicenza. He also consistently viewed the critics as a group and linked them with Aretino, Burchiello, Francesco Berni, and Rao.

Another member of respectable society who disliked Franco was Remigio Nannini (Fiorentino) (1521–81), Dominican monk and author. Early in his own career Remigio had been more concerned with poetry than piety, but he had only scorn for Franco in his report of the latter's execution. In his lifetime, wrote Remigio, Franco had practiced the professions of "blasphemer, liar, insulter, and impudent." According to him, a sign was hung around Franco's neck at the gallows stating that the sentence was punishment for writing evil "of princes and of his betters" —a sentence thoroughly deserved, in Remigio's opinion.[64]

On the other hand, the historian of Florence, Scipione Ammirato

---

fatto a imitatione loro, per consiglio d'un mio amico, ha posto i scritti nell'orinale a macerarsi. . . ." *La Sinagoga de gl'Ignoranti* . . . (Venice, 1589), 197. Another reference to Doni on ignorance is on 193–94.

[62] "Et l'ignoranza oggidì (essendo il secolo nostro depravato) viene honorata in moliti luoghi con un profluvio di vivande a punto." *La Sinagoga de gl'Ignoranti*, 195.

[63] One must allow for Garzoni's rhetoric: these four authors were already deceased. *L'Hospidale de' Pazzi incurabili* . . . (Venice, 1586), Discorso xxviii, ff. 63–64. See also the English edition, *The Hospitall of incurable fooles* (London, 1600), discourse 28.

[64] "Ne gl'ultimi anni poi del medesimo Pontefice gli venne nelle mani Nicolo Franco, che in vita sua non haveva fatto mai altro professione, che di maledico, dishonesto, maligno, e sfacciato . . . fu gastigato in su le forche della sua maldicenza, accennata dal breve ch'ei portava al collo, le cui parole dicevano. Per haver detto male e scrittor male de Principi, & de suoi maggiori, & certo che la sua mala lingua non meritava altre morte che quella." *Considerationi civili sopra l'historie di M. Francesco Guicciardini, e d'altri Historici* . . . (Venice, 1582), 117. This work was translated into French by Gabriel Chappuys, and from the French into English, with the same notice concerning Franco. See *Civill Considerations upon many and sundrie Histories* . . . (London, 1601), 224.

(1531–1601), was more sympathetic. In reporting Franco's death, Ammirato implied that heinous deeds went unpunished in Rome while Franco was condemned for "slight faults of language." He commented that Franco had written ten pleasing dialogues (the *Dialogi Piacevoli*), the *Priapea,* and pasquinades against Paul IV.[65]

Giovanni Battista Marino (1569–1625) wrote a poem to Franco praising his "biting language" against *i Grandi* ("the great"), while lamenting that he had become a "martyr to Pasquino."[66] The poem was reprinted by a seventeenth-century historian of literature, Lorenzo Crasso, who remarked that Franco had been famous in the Cinquecento for his maldicenza against princes; in Crasso's judgment, Franco had surpassed Aretino in composing such satires.[67]

In the first half of the seventeenth century, Franco's reputation as well as the memory of his unfortunate death lived on. Cornelio Tollio, writing in 1647 on the unhappiness of men of letters, noted that Franco had been a poet of lively wit, but satirical. He listed the *Pistole Vulgari, Philena,* and a satire against the pope for which he had been hanged.[68] Alessandro Zilioli (d. 1650), Venetian political and literary historian, wrote that Franco had a "ready wit" (he praised especially *La Philena*) and had succeeded in making himself "famous with his slander" (*famoso col dir male*) all over Italy. He also noted that Franco was an example of the unhappy end that awaited those of such temerity.[69] In similar fashion, he judged Doni as a man who was impatient with the habits of others, bizarre, unstable, and extravagant, but who could write unceasingly, quickly, and well.[70]

In the late sixteenth and early seventeenth centuries, when their books were no longer topical, Italian and French presses continued to publish these authors' works as moral commentaries. Editors and translators praised them for their colorful description of the evils of man's

[65] *Opuscoli del Sig. Scipione Ammirato . . .* (Florence, 1637), II, 249–50.

[66] *La Galeria del Cavalier Marino Distinta in pitture & Sculture.* n. pl., n. d. [Dedication letter by the printer, Francesco Manolesso, is dated March 25, 1620, Ancona], pp. 227–28. In Ciotti's edition (Venice, 1623), the poem is on pp. 224–25; and in Gio. Pietro Brigonci's edition (Venice, 1667), on pp. 195–96.

[67] *Elogii d'huomini letterati scritti da Lorenzo Crasso* (Venice, 1666), I, 41–45.

[68] *La infelicità dei letterati di Pierio Valeriano ed Appendice di Cornelio Tollio* (Milan, 1829), 224–25.

[69] Venice, Biblioteca Marciana, Mss. Italiani, Classe X, Cod. I (6394), "Istoria delle vite de' poeti italiani di Alessandro Zilioli veneziano," pp. 106–7.

[70] *Ibid.,* p. 119.

condition. In 1590 a Bolognese friar, Girolamo Gioannini da Capugnano, offered an expurgated edition of Franco's *Dialogi Piacevoli* that appeared seven times through 1609, and added a sonnet praising Franco for showing man the cruel abyss of his evils. Again punning on the author's name, Gioannini credited Franco with discerning "frankly" man's state. For this, his fame resounded and temples should be built in his honor. Noble thought, art, judgment, and style marked his book.[71] Similarly, in his introduction to the 1597 expurgated edition of Doni's *I Mondi* and *Inferni,* Bernardo Macchietta praised the sparkle and extravagant fantasies of Doni's style. He then advised his readers that with his inventions and fables, Doni had uncovered the evils of diverse states and persons.[72]

The reaction was the same in France, where in 1578 Gabriel Chappuys of Lyons (1546–1611) translated Doni's *I Mondi* and *Inferni* as *Les Mondes Celestes*. Although he modified details, for instance substituting French place names for Italian, his translation was accurate and included a woodcut with an unknown artist's vision of the New World.[73] In his introduction, Chappuys lauded Doni as the most subtle of many inventive

[71] "Scelti pensieri, arguti motti, e sali.
　Arte, giudicio, stile, ingegno franco,
　Spiegansi qui, mostrandosi dal Franco,
　La voragin crudel de i nostri mali.

Molti veraci son a Mopso uguali,
　Ma quanto cela il Cielo, Ibero, e Franco
　Non scorgo a lui simile invitto, e franco,
　Ne l'aditar lo stato de' mortali.

L'alta fama ribombo hormai, e suona
　Fin dove il ciel, de due zone prescrisse,
　Facendo 'l glorioso ogni altro pari,

Ergansi dunque a lui templi, ed altari,
　V' quegli fu, che le colonne fisse,
　Da chiunque cole Febo, & Elicona."
Dialogi Piacevoli, 1609 ed., [8]. The praise did not prevent Gioannini from censoring anticlerical passages. Gioannini also expurgated Doni's *La Zucca* in the editions of 1589, 1591, 1592, 1595, and 1607 (twice).

[72] "il Doni fu uno dei primi che cominciò a far del capriccioso, a dar alle stampe scritti d'ogni parte che brillavano di ghiribizzi, e di fantasie stravaganti . . . sotto inventioni, favole, fittioni, e trovate scuopre i mali di diversi state, e persone." Bernardo Macchietta, "Burattata sopra li Mondi del Doni," in *Mondi Celesti,* 1597 ed., [1–2].

[73] For example, Paris rather than Venice became the city of peace, love, and charity. *Les Mondes Celestes* . . . (Lyons, 1580), 8. The woodcut is on 204, and on 197 in the Lyons, 1578 ed.

Italian authors. After commenting favorably on the *Libraria,* he appraised *Les Mondes Celestes.* Under the pleasant fantasies, readers would find a rich treasure of secrets. Doni, according to Chappuys, used these inventions deliberately in order to hide the sharpness of his message, or, as he elsewhere phrased it, as a sweet syrup to coat the bitterness of his medicine. After thus whetting his readers' curiosity, the translator did not indicate the nature of Doni's medicine, but opined that his words would touch the hearts of his readers.[74] The following year, the indefatigable Chappuys published a French translation of Franco's *Dialogi Piacevoli.* In the dedicatory letter, he explained that he had translated these dialogues because the author had painted human vices so realistically that one could touch them, and expressed the hope that with this aid the French could correct vices in themselves.[75]

In 1634 the *Inferni* of Doni were published in another French edition under the title *Les visions italiennes.* The unsigned introduction, possibly written by the anonymous translator, praised Doni as one of the *plus beaux esprits de l'Italie.* His *Inferni* made "powerful impressions on the spirit of men," as it demonstrated maladies of the soul.[76]

Italian influence, 1570–1650

As might be expected, restless spirits like Tommaso Campanella were attracted to the writings of Doni, Franco, and Lando.

In 1570, for a younger admirer, Doni was an audacious writer who pointed to new directions in thought. The *Lettere facete,* Book II, published in 1575, included a letter to Doni dated April 1570, Venice, from "A. Persio," praising his audacity, and calling him a "new philosopher" who by his profound science would provoke tumults. The letter did not elaborate on Doni's new science, but praised his *Rime del Burchiello* and *La Moral Filosophia,* and referred to *La Zucca,* in a bizarre style reminis-

---

[74] *Ibid.,* [1–7].

[75] "J'ay voulu traduire ces dialogues pour les faire voir à nos Françoys qui pourront corriger en eux-mesmes quelques vices qu'ils y verront naïffvment depaints et tant bien descrits qu'ils les pourront toucher du doigt." Dedicatory letter to Vincent Lodovici de Lucques, in *Dix plaisans dialogues du S. Nicolo Franco . . .* (Lyons, 1579), as quoted in Louis Berthé de Besaucèle, *J. B. Giraldi, 1504–1573* (Paris, 1920), 278.

[76] *Les visions italiennes tirees du sieur de Doni . . .* (Paris, 1634), [3–5].

cent of Doni's own. After mentioning a previous visit to Monselice to see Doni, Persio offered a gift of seven sonnets.[77]

"A. Persio" could be either the philosopher Antonio Persio (1542–1612) or his younger brother Ascanio (1554–c. 1605). The younger Persio was a philologist and professor of Greek at Bologna from about 1586 until his death, but little else is known of his life. Antonio Persio became a disciple of Bernardino Telesio and Campanella. Arriving in Venice about 1572, he devoted the following twenty years to editing and publishing Telesio's works. In 1592 he met the youthful Tommaso Campanella (1568–1639), also a devoted disciple of Telesio, and remained a friend and advocate of Campanella until his death.[78]

If the "A. Persio" who admired Doni in 1570 was Antonio he may have provided a personal link between Doni and Campanella. If not, Campanella may have read one of the eight Italian editions of *I Mondi* between 1552 and 1606—years during which there appeared in Italy more editions of Doni's *I Mondi* than of More's *Utopia*.[79] In any case, Campanella knew of Doni's New World and was inspired by Doni's suggestion in the introduction to the New World, that the pazzi would prevail over the savi, to write a sonnet on the subject. In prison in 1601, the year before the composition of the *Città del Sole,* he wrote a sonnet, *Senno senza forza de' savi delle genti antiche esser soggetto alla forza de' pazzi* (Good judgment without force of the wise men of ancient peoples is to be subject to the force of madmen).

> The astrologers, having foreseen in a land a constellation that maddened men, took counsel to flee; then, having remained healthy, to rule the injured people. Returning afterward to do their royal deeds, they advised these madmen with well-chosen words to live the old way, with good food and dress. But everyone attacked them with

[77] *Delle lettere facete, et piacevoli, di diversi grandi huomini,* ed. Turchi (Venice, 1575). The letter is on 389–93, and the attribution to A. Persio on [12].

[78] On Persio, see Luigi Firpo, "Appunti campanelliani," *Giornale critico della filosofia italiana,* 21 (1940), 435–44. If the author of the letter is Antonio Persio, it places him in Venice two years earlier than Firpo believes he arrived there. Ricottini, *A.F.D. scrittore e stampatore,* 238, makes a probable attribution to Bartolomeo Arnigio da Brescia, but presents no evidence for her attribution.

[79] More's *Utopia* was printed in Latin at Florence in 1519, translated into Italian by Lando in 1548, and printed in Latin again in Milan in 1620. Lando's Italian translation was reprinted in Francesco Sansovino's *Del governo de i regni et delle repubbliche* in 1561, 1567, 1578, and 1607. The 1548 and 1561 Italian translations are difficult to find, indicating that they were probably not large printings. See R. W. Gibson, *St. Thomas More: A Preliminary Bibliography,* 3–4. For More's influence in Italy, see Luigi Firpo, "Tommaso Moro e la sua fortuna in Italia."

kicks and blows. So that the wise men were compelled to live as fools, in order to avoid death, because the greatest madman carried the royal burden. They lived with good sense only behind closed doors, in public applauding in deed and name the insane and wrong desires of others.[80']

It is generally agreed that the sonnet refers to Doni's dialogue of the star city.[81]

In the following year Campanella wrote the *Città del Sole,* published in 1623. Because of the common features of the Renaissance utopia form, one cannot ascribe to Doni a definite influence on Campanella. Nevertheless, there were similar features in Doni's New World and the city of the sun. Everything was held in common, including women. Campanella explained that if men had their own homes and families, self-love and concern for their sons outweighed the good of the city. Because the Solarians held all things in common, no one went in need, and the desire for goods was eradicated. The city (*la communità*) cared for all. Campanella emphasized social equality and condemned poverty, as had Doni.[82]

The Solarians lived regulated lives similar to those of the inhabitants of the New World. After weaning, the children were raised in common by the city. The Solarians ate together and wore uniform clothing—white

[80] "Gli astrologi, antevista in un paese
costellazion che gli uomini impazzire
far dovea, consigliarsi di fuggire,
per regger sani poi le genti offese.
Tornando poscia a far le regie imprese,
consigliavan que' pazzi con bel dire
il viver prisco, il buon cibo e vestire.
Ma ognun con calci e pugni a lor contese.
Talché, sforzati i savi a viver come
gli stolti usavan, per schifar la morte,
chè 'l piú gran pazzo avea le regie some,
vissero sol col senno a chiuse porte,
in pubblico applaudendo in fatti e nome
all'altrui voglie forsennate e torte."

Tommaso Campanella, *La Città del Sole e Poesie* (Milan, 1962), 76. Luigi Firpo, *Ricerche campanelliane* (Florence, 1947), 255, dates the sonnet in the second half of 1601.

[81] The lone dissenter is Romano Amerio, who affirms that the sonnet was autobiographical, that Campanella referred to the madness he feigned in order to live. The two interpretations are not mutually exclusive, as the sonnet could refer to Doni's dialogue as well as contain a reflection on Campanella's own lot. See *Opere di Giordano Bruno e di Tommaso Campanella* (Milan, Naples, 1956), 799, n.

[82] *La Città del Sole,* 8–9, 19–21.

during the day and red at night or upon leaving the city. They suffered few infirmities and diseases because they ate healthy, natural foods; when disease struck, their great knowledge provided cures. Doni had eliminated money, and Campanella found it useful only for trade with other peoples who used it.[83]

The physical organization of the two utopian cities was similar, but also fitted within the Renaissance utopian genre. The city of the sun was situated on a high hill within a fertile plain in a land called Taprobane. The city was constructed in the form of a circle with four streets and four gates that looked to the four directions. In the city, a series of walls, fortifications, and palaces in concentric circles led to the very summit of the hill which was crowned with a circular temple. Doni's central temple, also circular, was crowned with a high cupola, while Campanella's had a large dome and a vault. The temple of the city of the sun was the center of worship of the Solarians and the residence of the high priest, Hoh, who ruled the city, just as the oldest priest was the ruler of Doni's New World.[84]

But the city of the sun differed from the negativism of the New World by its positive program for a new life. Campanella described a complex relationship between learning and the life of the city of the sun. Hoh, the high priest, was also named Metaphysic. Three princes called Power, Wisdom, and Love combined government and learning derived from many sources to assist Hoh in ruling the Solarians. The city of the sun had a complex hierarchy of laws, courts, and magistrates who punished transgressors. It also possessed a military organization to defend the city from attack, and Campanella's syncretic religious system. Campanella wished to foster in the Solarians a positive spirit of unity and love for all, and so emphasized the role of the city in the lives of the citizens more than Doni had. Rather than leave the generation of children to chance, city officials guided procreation toward the public good by means of elaborate regulations.[85] The city of the sun revived much of the structure of society which Doni had swept away. Doni's dialogue was a brief, brilliant summary of his criticism of the Cinquecento. Campanella wrote the *Città del Sole* during a period of enforced reflection in Neapolitan prisons after years of intense study and his ill-fated Calabrian conspiracy. It was a synthesis of the thought of one of the most complex figures of this period of Italian history.

[83] *Ibid.*, 10, 13, 20, 32–33, 28.
[84] *Ibid.*, 5–6.
[85] *Ibid.*, 15–19.

In *Lo spaccio de la bestia trionfante* (1584) Giordano Bruno (1548–1600) argued in terms reminiscent of the critics that learning was irrelevant. The purpose of *Lo spaccio* was to guide man away from the ignorance, superstition, prejudice, and vice (all personified by the "triumphant beast") which distorted his reason. In one passage Bruno mocked contemporary learning. Grammarians disputed over the parts of speech and attributions of obscure classical works, he wrote. Dialecticians busied themselves with syllogisms and captious sophistries while metaphysicians argued about the principle of individuation, being and essence, substance and accident. Physicists argued whether knowledge of natural things was possible, and in effect spent their time on useless investigations of the obvious. Vain versifiers passed themselves off as poets while pseudo-historians repeated the same old shopworn stories.[86] However, there is no direct proof of influence—Bruno made no mention of Franco, Lando, or Doni.

There are other possible areas of influence. To convey his tradition-shattering ideas, Bruno sought a new language and broke the old rules. His deformed syntax, lexicological experimentation, and reliance on popular idiom opposed the ordered, logical prose of Bembo and Speroni. Possibly he found some stimulating antecedents in Doni and Franco. From Doni, he may have derived his technique of breaking down the traditional narrative that proceeded according to a consistent structure of introduction, exposition, and conclusion. Doni avoided this obvious structural organization to give the appearance of an abandonment of order. He elongated his periods in order to break down traditional coherence, and, in many dialogues, preferred to a narrative development a technique of theme and variation, with the theme sometimes implied by the tone of the discourse. Franco tended to multiply internal variations on a situation, as did Bruno in *Lo spaccio,* and his use of mythological structure for satirical purposes in the *Dialogi Piacevoli* was extended by Bruno in such works as the *Spaccio.* One literary historian, indeed, argues that Bruno completed the experimental destruction of the ordered Renaissance prose of Boccaccio, Bembo, and Speroni which was initiated by Doni, Franco, Aretino, Berni, and Folengo.[87]

[86] Giordano Bruno, *The Expulsion of the Triumphant Beast,* trans. Arthur D. Imerti (New Brunswick, N. J., 1964), third dialogue, pt. 1, pp. 211–13.

[87] See Giorgio Barberi Squarotti, "L'esperienza stilistica del Bruno fra Rinascimento e Barocco," in *La critica stilistica e il barocco letterario* (Florence, 1958), 154–69.

A satirist who noted Doni's work was Adriano Banchieri of Bologna (c.1567–1634), a monk and musician who wrote humorous, involved discourses in order to satirize customs. His most popular work, *La nobiltà dell'asino* (1592), was another contribution to the genre which praised the ass and condemned man. In his introduction Banchieri named authors who had dealt with the same theme, including *un certo Academico Peregrino,* i.e., Doni, whose two works praising the ass had appeared under that pseudonym.[88] Banchieri's book included many of the standard arguments proving the worth of the ass as against evil man, but lacked much of Doni's social criticism.

In 1623, Secondo Lancellotti (1583–1643), an often-published monk from Perugia who lived a restless, unhappy life and expressed iconoclastic opinions reminiscent of the critics, quoted at length a letter from Doni's *La Zucca.*[89] Thirteen years later, he paraphrased three pages of Lando's material on the diverse natures of Italians and foreigners from the *Forcianae Quaestiones.* Lancellotti knew Lando only under the pseudonym of "Philalethes Polytopiensis."[90] His references did not note important material by Doni and Lando, but they did demonstrate that their works continued to be read by restless spirits.

Plagiarizations

In the years between 1560 and 1620, the critics' description of man's restlessness, their rejection of learning, and longing for a simple life of

[88] "Et se bene dei moderni Giulio Camillo, Pietro Messia, & un certo Academico Peregrino, il Rao in un sua lettera, & un'altro, che ne fece una digressione n'hanno scritto alcuna cosa raccontando qual che considerabili qualita di detto ASINESCA. . . ." *La Nobiltà dell'Asino di Attabalippa dal Perù Provincia del Mondo novo* . . . (Venice, 1592), a' lettori.

[89] *L'hoggidì overo il mondo non peggiore ne più calamitoso del passato* . . . (Venice, 1623), 118–20. Compare with *La Zucca,* 1565 ed., 94ᵛ–95, 96–98ᵛ. Lancellotti's work was reprinted in 1627, 1630, 1637, and 1680. On Lancellotti, see Giovanni Battista Vermiglioli, *Biografia degli scrittori perugini e notizie delle opere loro* (Perugia, 1829), II, 51–60; also Carmine Jannaco and Martino Capucci, *Il Seicento* (Milan, 1963), 645–46, 657–58, and biography therein.

[90] *Hoggidì overo gl'ingegni non inferiori a' passati* . . . *Parte Seconda* . . . (Venice, 1681), 12–13. Compare with *Forcianae Quaestiones,* 1536 ed., 15–17. This work was printed in 1636 and 1637 as well.

uncommitted ignorance also reached Italian readers through the extensive plagiarization of Doni by Cesare Rao (1532/33–c.1587). Born in the small town of Alessano in the southern province of Apulia, Rao's life was as restless as the critics'. He left home at eighteen, lived a short time in Naples, and then traveled north. He studied at Pisa under Simone Porzio, a Neo-Aristotelian follower of Pomponazzi, and possibly acquired a degree at Pavia, where he began to write. About 1553 he returned to Alessano and presumably remained there through 1560. From 1561 to 1563 he visited Rome, Florence, Lucca, Genoa, Milan, Brescia, Pavia, Mantua, Ferrara, and Venice. The first edition of his *L'argute et facete lettere* was published in Brescia in 1562. No more is known until April 1573, when he appeared in Pavia. After 1573 he returned to the south, where he published two scientific works in Naples in 1577, and another at Venice in 1582. After the publication of his *Invettive, orationi et discorsi* (dated November 1, 1586) at Venice in 1587, nothing more is known of him.[91]

Rao's most successful work, *L'argute et facete lettere,* was similar to the critics' books, and at several points plagiarized Doni, particularly in the way it echoed his sarcastic, critical, and bizarre tone. Like Doni, Rao was concerned with man's restless nature and foolish deeds. He used much of Doni's vocabulary and Doni's device of piling phrases one on another in order to give the impression of incoherence. Rao set the mood of the book in the first letter in which he attempted to show that all those who pretended to be wise were really crazy. Students, professors, lawyers, judges, physicians, astrologers, logicians, philosophers, grammarians, orators, magicians, geomancers, and many others were mad, not wise. Where did the emperor of the pazzi find more subjects than in the palaces of princes? The world was a cage of pazzi.[92]

In the second letter, Rao plagiarized Doni's semi-autobiographical discourse of Inquieto and Doni's idea of the constant motion of the world. Rao's narrator, Instabile ("the unstable one"), described the mutability of all things. Then, like Doni's Inquieto, he was stricken by restless melan-

---

[91] On Rao, see Nicola Vacca, "Cesare Rao da Alessano detto 'Valocerca,'" *Archivio Storico Pugliese,* I, fasc. 1 (1948), 1–28. Vacca does not note the plagiarizations.

[92] *L'argute, et facete lettere di M. Cesare Rao . . .* (Venice, 1622), 1–6ᵛ (quote 6–6ᵛ). Among terms common to both Doni and Rao are the following: pazzi, *girelle* ("circles"), *farnetici* ("lunatics"), *buggiardi* ("liars"), *incostante* ("inconstant"), *girare* ("to whirl"), *balordo* ("slow-witted"), *cervello balzano* ("dancing brain").

choly. Instabile changed his table a hundred times, and his bed a thousand times. Like Inquieto, he tried several monastic orders. The words were Doni's with a few alterations.[93] Instabile continued for two pages to describe how everything whirled. Here Rao borrowed and expanded Doni's words.[94] He concluded this letter like the first; men were fantastic, capricious, and inconstant, and the world a cage of pazzi.[95]

Elsewhere in *L'argute et facete lettere* Rao plagiarized Doni's discourse on "ignoranza da bene" and Giulio Landi's *Lode dell'ignoranza*. Referring to a "new division" between types of ignorance "made by Doni," he then copied his discussion for two pages, omitting only references to religion.[96] His "Oratione in lode dell'ignoranza" was closely modeled on Landi's,[97] and in the *Invettive* (1587), he copied verbatim the introductory sentence of each section of the *Lode dell'ignoranza* and then greatly amplified Landi's remarks.[98]

A letter on the nobility of the ass in *L'argute et facete lettere* was similar to Doni's *L'Asinesca* or *Il valore de gli Asini*. The ass was described as strong, humble, patient, and useful, in contrast to sinful and aggressive man.[99] Rao's letter, however, was only half as long as Doni's work, and lacked much of its caustic social criticism. In a further plagiarization, Rao used Doni's device of letters by members of an Accademia

---

[93] Compare Doni: "Cento volte l'anno fo mutar la tavola per casa dove io mangio. . . ." in *I Marmi,* 1928 ed., II, 207–8, with Rao: "Cento volte in un dì feci mutar la tavola, dove io mangio. . . ." *L'argute, et facete lettere,* 1622 ed., 7–7ᵛ.

[94] Compare Rao, *L'argute, et facete lettere,* 1622 ed., 8–9, with *I Mondi,* 1552 ed., 78–79; *I Marmi,* 1928 ed., II, 178–79; and *La Seconda Libraria,* 1551 ed., 5–7.

[95] " . . . o pazzissimi voi, che chiamiate me pazzo; o instabilissimi voi, che chiamate me instabile, o canaglia, o canaglia, o povera volgare, e cieca gente, o poveri d'argomento, e di consiglio, egri del tutto, e miseri mortali, non siamo tutti una gabbiata de pazzi?" *L'argute, et facete lettere,* 1622 ed., 11ᵛ. Doni also used the expression "a cage of madmen" in the discourse of Inquieto in *I Marmi,* 1928 ed., II, 209.

[96] Compare Doni: "Ignoranza per non haver cognitione; quella che chiamò l'Agrippa vita felicissima. Ignorante per non sapere; ignorantone per dapoco & cattivo; & ignorantaccio per astuto e tristo. . . ." in *La Zucca,* 1565 ed., 65ᵛ–66, with Rao: "Ignoranza per non haver cognitione, quella che chiamò l'Agrippa vita felicissima. Ignorante per non sapere; Ignorantone per da poco e cattivo. Et ignorantaccio per astuto e tristo. . . ." *L'argute, et facete lettere,* 1622 ed., 59ᵛ–60ᵛ.

[97] *Ibid.,* 35ᵛ–46ᵛ.

[98] *Invettive, orationi, et discorsi di Cesare Rao* (Venice, 1587), 157–83ᵛ.

[99] *L'argute, et facete lettere,* 1622 ed., 99–109.

Peregrina, calling himself at one point "lo Svegliato Accademico Pere-grino," a name that Doni used.[100]

Despite Rao's use of Doni's words and ideas, he did not exhibit Doni's depth of pessimism. His social criticism was sparse and lacked Doni's sharpness, while he was more conscious of correct grammar, syntax, and orthography, in effect often harnessing Doni's free style. But since he wrote in the same spirit and on the same subjects, Rao was both Doni's and the other critics' literary heir. He knew Doni's *I Marmi, La Zucca, Pistolotti Amorosi, L'Asinesca* and/or *Il valore de gli Asini* and Landi's *Lode dell'ignoranza*. Possibly he knew *I Mondi* and *La Seconda Libraria* as well. He referred to Doni by name three times in *L'argute et facete lettere*.[101] By the number of editions of his works, Rao aided the spread of the critics' ideas. *L'argute et facete lettere* was printed in 15 Italian editions from 1562 through 1622. Gabriel Chappuys translated the work into French in 1584, and this was reprinted in 1609. The *Invettive* were printed in Italian editions of 1587, 1592, and 1622.[102]

Lando and Franco were also plagiarized. A seventeenth-century au-thor, Eugenio Raimondi of Brescia, borrowed freely from Lando. Rai-mondi's *Della sferza delle scienze, et de' scrittori* (Venice, 1640) borrowed the name, general outline, and some statements from Lando's *Sferza de' Scrittori*, criticizing physicians, legists, historians, philosophers, and theo-logians in some of Lando's words. He expanded his discussion, however, to include new material, for instance, listing Jean Bodin's *Methodus* of 1566 in the section condemning history. As part of another work, *Il dottissimo passatempo* (Venice, 1627), Raimondi plagiarized without changes Lando's *Oracoli de moderni ingegni*. He retained the title, the sayings, and the names of the people to whom they were attributed with the exception of those credited to Aretino—which he claimed as his own. Raimondi showed no signs of grasping the shrewdness of Aretino or the import of Lando's words. For him knowledge was a collection of curious

[100] *Ibid.*, 46ᵛ–48ᵛ, 111–13. For Doni's use of Svegliato, see *I Marmi*, 1928 ed., I, 5, 20–21, 45; and *I Mondi*, 1567 ed., 59–78. Doni used members of the Accademici Peregrini (or Pellegrini) often in *I Marmi* and *I Mondi* as narrators.

[101] The reference to Doni on p. 75 of *L'argute, et facete lettere*, 1622 ed., concerns his *Pistolotti Amorosi*. Other references to Doni by name are on 16, 59ᵛ.

[102] The Italian editions of *L'argute, et facete lettere* are Brescia 1562, Pavia 1567 and 1573, Trent 1575, Pavia 1580 and 1584, Trent 1585, Vicenza 1585, Trent 1590, Fano 1591, Vicenza 1596, Venice 1598, 1601, 1616, and 1622. The French editions were Lyons 1584 and Rouen 1609 or 1610. All three editions of the *Invettive* were printed in Venice. See Vacca, "Cesare Rao da Alessano," bibliography.

facts and ideas to while away the time, as the title of his work indicated.[103]

A seventeenth-century Spanish author found Franco's *Dialogi Piacevoli* worth borrowing from. The *Diálogos satyricos* (1616) of Francisco de Cáceres were a plagiarization of dialogues one, two, six (with the lament to Jove concerning the lack of justice on earth), and seven of Franco. Cáceres, of whom little is known, admitted that his work was *una versión de italiano,* but did not reveal the name of the author. The translation was faithful to Gioannini's expurgated version rather than to earlier editions of Franco's work. It is also probable that the *Dialogi Piacevoli* influenced a 1585 manuscript of Juan de la Cueva (1550–1609), a Spanish author and poet of more importance.[104]

French and English influence: wit and language

Outside Italy, these authors were appreciated for the intellectual adroitness often attributed to Italian writers. Perhaps for this reason Lando's *Paradossi* enjoyed great popularity in France. Italian editions were printed in Lyons in 1543 and 1550, and Charles Estienne made a French translation which was printed, completely or in part, at least 14 times between 1553 and 1603 at Lyons, Paris, Caen, Rouen, and Poitiers, with another edition appearing in 1638. Estienne introduced a few changes, such as French places for Italian but, on the whole, remained faithful to the original. As the title page of his translation indicated, the paradoxes were "forensic declamations" designed to exercise "young spirits in difficult cases."[105] He hoped that the paradoxes would prove stimulating and witty to young lawyers.

From France, Lando's *Paradossi* passed over the channel to England. In 1593 Anthony Mundy published the *Defence of Contraries,* which contained the first twelve paradoxes of Lando translated from the French of Charles Estienne. Mundy intended to translate all of them but did not

---

[103] The *Oracoli* of Lando are in *Il Dottissimo Passatempo di Eugenio Raimondi* . . . (Venice, 1627), 197–320. On the title page of the Newberry Library's copy, a seventeenth-century critic added under the author's name "destruttor del Metodo, e Autor della Confusione." His name is scratched out but the date, December 9, 1644, remains. See Appendix II for the citation of Raimondi's *Della sferza delle scienze.*

[104] See Robert H. Williams, "Francisco de Cáceres, Niccolò Franco, and Juan de la Cueva," *Hispanic Review,* XXVII (1959), 194–99.

[105] See Appendix II.

finish. This work was printed again in 1602 under a new title.[106] In 1613 seven of Lando's paradoxes appeared in the large miscellaneous compilation of materials from Italian sources entitled *The Treasurie of Auncient and Moderne Times* edited by the anonymous "T. Milles."[107] The paradoxes had altered titles and were prefaced with a short, new introductory paragraph before Lando's material. The translations were free, at times adding new material and omitting some of Lando's words. In 1634 a collection of three discourses on health and temperate living included Lando's paradox 24 (credited to a "famous Italian") under the title that a frugal life was better than a sumptuous one.[108]

John Hall published a collection of paradoxes in 1653 which included one by Lando. Hall's own paradoxes were in the spirit of Lando; he argued, for instance, that absolute tyranny was the best form of government.[109] John Dunton's collection of two thousand paradoxes, *Athenian Sport* (1707) contained six of Lando's paradoxes, including a close translation of the third one, that it was better to be ignorant than learned. Dunton's collection included paradoxes from the first half of the *Paradossi* as well as the more frequently printed paradoxes from the second half of Lando taken from the *Treasurie*.[110] In addition to the paradoxes, English authors published some of the questions and answers in Lando's *Dubbi*, again by way of the French translations.[111] Since the English versions of

---

[106] The 1602 title was *Paradoxes against common opinion Debated in form of declamations in place of publique censure: Onelie to exercise young wittes in difficult matters.* See Rice, "The *Paradossi* of Ortensio Lando," 67–70.

[107] *The Treasurie of Auncient and Moderne Times* . . . (London, 1613), II, ch. 22, 176–80 (paradox 23); III, ch. 23, 291–93 (paradox 14); IV, ch. 38, 390–92 (paradox 16); V, ch. 30, 485–86 (paradox 17); VI, ch. 28, 612–14 (paradox 19); VII, ch. 43, 723–25 (paradox 18); VIII, ch. 38, 834–37 (paradox 20).

[108] *The Temperate Man, or the Right Way of Preserving Life and Health* . . . (London, 1678), 157–68.

[109] John Hall, *Paradoxes by J. De la Salle* (London, 1653), 135–65 (Lando's paradox 10).

[110] [John Dunton], *Athenian Sport: or Two Thousand Paradoxes Merrily Argued, To Amuse and Divert the Age* (London, 1707), 30–36 (Lando's paradox 24); 241–45 (paradox 14), 245–48 (paradox 10), 357–65 (paradox 3), 406–8 (paradox 2), 435–38 (paradox 13).

[111] Thompson, *The Seventeenth-Century English Essay*, 99–100, states that some of Lando's *dubbi* are contained in [John Dunton], *The Athenian Gazette: or Casuistical Mercury, Resolving all the most Nice and Curious Questions proposed by the ingenious* . . . (London, 1691, 1693); and in Dunton's *The Athenian Oracle* . . . , three vols. and supplement (London, 1706, 1708, 1710, 1716). I have not

the *Paradossi* were free renderings of a French edition that at times omitted Italian references, it is often difficult to determine when a free translation became an adaptation. Noticeably missing from the English paradoxes were Lando's wealth of contemporary Italian references which added pungency. Shorn of these, the paradoxes became displays of intellectual adroitness rather than essays in moral and social criticism.

Doni's writings were known in Elizabethan England. The noted Anglo-Italian propagator of Italian Renaissance attitudes and teacher of Italian, John Florio (c.1553–1625), borrowed two passages from *I Marmi* for his *First Fruits* (1578), a series of dialogues, of increasing complexity, in both Italian and English on a variety of subjects. The purpose of the work was to give linguistic practice and examples of cultural discussions. The stolid Florio somewhat toned down Doni's sprightly Italian, but the fact that he was aware of Doni's natural, racy language (in contrast to the Italian of Bembo and the archaic purists) indicated that he found it of some literary value.[112]

Florio, in his well-known Italian-English dictionary, *A Worlde of Wordes* (first edition 1598), listed, among the 75 Italian works which were his sources, four of Doni's works—*La Zucca, I Marmi, I Mondi,* and the *Pistolotti Amorosi;* he added the comment that Doni was "fantasticall and so strange."[113] Doni's *La Moral Filosophia* was also known to the Elizabethans through the English translation of Sir Thomas North in editions of 1570 and 1601.[114]

From this survey of the diffusion and influence of the writings of the critics it is clear that contemporary Italians understood their rebellion against society and its values. In particular, Doni's descriptions of man's restlessness and Lando's rejection of learning in the *Sferza de' Scrittori* struck responsive chords, as the hostility of observers like Garzoni

---

attempted to locate Lando's *dubbi* among the thousands of questions and answers contained in these works.

[112] Compare *I Marmi*, 1928 ed., I, 161, with *First Fruits,* facsimile reprod., ed. Arundell del Re (Taihoku, Formosa, 1936), 129–30; and *I Marmi*, 1928 ed., I, 150, with *First Fruits,* 140–41. For further details and the quoted passages, see D. G. Rees, "John Florio and Anton Francesco Doni," *Comparative Literature,* XV (1963), 33–38. On Florio, see Frances Yates, *John Florio: The Life of an Italian in Shakespeare's England* (Cambridge, 1934).

[113] See Maria Grazia Bellorini, "Thomas North traduttore di Anton Francesco Doni," *Aevum,* XXXVIII (1964), 91.

[114] For a discussion of North's translation of *La Moral Filosophia,* see *ibid.,* 84–103.

PARADOSSI

CIOE, SENTENTIE FVORI
Del comun parere, Nouella/
mente uenute in luce.

OPRA NON MEN DOTTA CHE
piaceuole, & in due parti separata.

IN VINEGIA. MD XLIIII.

Fig. 9. Title page of Lando's *Paradossi,* 1544

showed. Reprinting and the plagiarization of their works enabled them to reach many readers despite partial prohibition by the *Index*. Later in the Cinquecento, when the immediate relevance of their words had passed, they were viewed as moralists with a vivacious literary style. Outside Italy, they continued to be translated and adapted through much of the seventeenth century for their wit and intellectual adroitness.

Conclusion

Doni, Franco, and Lando were in a unique position to learn and to reflect ideas from many groups and regions in Italy. They had in common their lowly origins and the fact that their publishing careers centered on Venice. They did not write for one social group only—for example, for noble or courtly circles—but expressed ideas drawn from a broad spectrum of Italian society, excluding the very great, the popes and princes. To these they had no close ties, leaving aside Franco's short period at the papal court, and they had little opportunity to acquire intimate knowledge of affairs of state.

The critics' strength lay in their knowledge of the rest of Italy, from Naples to the Alps, from the artisans to the lower nobility, from the orthodox in the cloister to the heretics outside. Furthermore, the printers' shops in Venice were good listening posts, offering excellent opportunities to hear and sense public opinion, as well as to report observations and judgments to the reading public. Thus the critics voiced a kind of public commentary on what was being said and done in the peninsula. Although no small group of authors could portray all of Cinquecento Italy, Lando, Franco, and Doni depicted much of it.

Attempts have been made to discuss an "end of the Renaissance," a "Counter-Renaissance," an "anti-Renaissance," a "crisis of Renaissance thought," and an "end of humanism" in the sixteenth century.[115] In so far as the humanists of the Italian Renaissance maintained belief in a political

---

[115] Such are the views advanced by the following authors, respectively: Eric Cochrane, "The End of the Renaissance in Florence," *Bibliothèque d'Humanisme et Renaissance,* XXVII (1965), 7–29; Hiram Haydn, *The Counter-Renaissance* (New York, 1950); Eugenio Battisti, *L'antirinascimento* (Milan, 1962), esp. 19–45; Nauert, *Agrippa and the Crisis of Renaissance Thought,* 3–5, 333–34, and Arnold Hauser, *Mannerism: The Crisis of the Renaissance and the Origin of Modern Art* (London, 1965), I, 3–114; Toffanin, *La fine dell'umanesimo,* 1–14.

system of republican city-states and princes, allegiance to the Catholic Church despite much anticlericalism, and adherence to the studia human- itatis as a path to civic virtue and the active life, then Doni, Franco, and Lando repudiated their central values. (One must hasten to add that the Quattrocento Renaissance involved other values as well, however.)

In all areas of thought—political, social, religious, educational—Doni, Franco, and Lando desired a simpler alternative. They preferred a primi- tive social structure based on an equitable division of labor. They wanted a simple religion of faith and Scripture. They preferred ignorant with- drawal to education for the vita civile, and they composed utopias which solved man's problems by severely limiting his choices. In each case they receded from the attempt to control man's destiny on earth and rejected the committed life of active participation.

Beyond this negative statement, it is hard to go. Franco, Lando, and Doni occupied themselves with fundamental problems of their times but they were not major thinkers or literary figures, and generally did not explore these problems in depth. Nor did they provide any positive directions—merely a few hints. Their thought was often superficial, but weightier speculation would have been inappropriate to their literary genre.

The Italian situation after 1559 was less turbulent. Peace descended and political writers reserved their highest praises for those rulers who preserved peace and prosperity in their dominions. Politically, Italy settled down to local affairs. The spiritual vitality of revived Catholicism ab- sorbed the energies of some. The more militant could rally to a Christian crusade against the Turks and justly take credit for Italian prowess in arms at Lepanto. New intellectual concerns and a new mood were in evidence.

The lives and thought of Lando, Franco, and Doni should be seen in the context of the differences between the Italy of 1500 and that of 1600. By this time Telesio and Galileo had rethought Aristotelianism, Campa- nella and Bruno reformulated a philosophy of man, and Botero and others, while using Machiavelli, constructed a different science of politics. Italians thought of the vita civile in terms of the rules which guided them to serve princes in a hierarchical society. The Counter-Reformation brought a different religious spirit, more intense and militant if less free than that of 1500. In their limited way, Doni, Franco, and Lando helped to prepare for these changes. After they had mocked the idols, it was easier for later and intellectually better equipped men to substitute new ones.

Appendices

Note on Appendices I–III

The following bibliographies of the printed works of Franco and Lando with some locations are offered with the knowledge that they may be incomplete. Nevertheless, the effort seems worthwhile, in the hope that they are more complete than their predecessors (Simiani on Franco in 1894 and Bongi on Lando in 1851). Moreover, they will give the reader an idea of the frequency of publication of the works of Franco and Lando. Since Doni has received an excellent bibliographical study by Ricottini, I am including only a brief checklist of his works, and citing in full only in Appendix III works used in this study. The books located in Florence, at the Biblioteca Nazionale Centrale, were examined before the flood of November 4, 1966.

ABBREVIATIONS

BM   British Museum, London
BNF   Biblioteca Nazionale Centrale, Florence
BNP   Bibliothèque Nationale, Paris
FM   Florence, Marucelliana
MB   Milan, Braidense
MC   University of Manchester, Christie Collection. Entries from *Catalogue of the Christie Collection, comprising the printed books and manuscripts bequeathed to the library of the University of Manchester by the late Richard Copley Christie, LL. D.* Compiled under direction of Charles W. E. Leigh. Manchester, 1915.
C   Columbia University, New York
Ch   University of Chicago
F   Folger Shakespeare Library, Washington, D.C.
H   Harvard University, Cambridge, Mass.
Hu   Henry E. Huntington Library, San Marino, Cal.
LC   Library of Congress, Washington, D.C.

N   Newberry Library, Chicago
NYP   New York Public Library
Pn   University of Pennsylvania
Pr   Princeton University
T   University of Toronto
VM   Venice, Marciana
Y   Yale University

Baudrier   Baudrier, H. L., and Baudrier, J. *Bibliographie Lyon-naise: Recherches sur les imprimeurs, libraires, relieurs et fondeurs de lettres de Lyon au XVIe siècle.* 12 vols. Lyons, Paris, 1895–1921.

Bongi, "Catalogo"   Bongi, Salvatore. "Catalogo delle opere del Lando," in *Novelle di M. Ortensio Lando* (Lucca, 1851), xxxi–lxv.

Bongi, *Giolito*   Bongi, Salvatore. *Annali di Gabriel Giolito de' Ferrari da Trino di Monferrato, stampatore in Venezia.* 2 vols. Rome, 1890–97.

Brunet   Brunet, Jacques C. *Manuel du libraire et de l'amateur de livres* . . . 6 vols. Paris, 1860–65.

Sanesi   Sanesi, Ireneo. *Il cinquecentista Ortensio Lando.* Pistoia, 1893.

Sforza, "Lando"   Sforza, Giovanni. "Ortensio Lando e gli usi ed i costumi d'Italia nella prima metà del Cinquecento," *Memorie della R. Accademia delle Scienze di Torino,* ser. II, 64, no. 4 (1914), 1–68.

Simiani   Simiani, Carlo. "Edizioni delle Opere di N. F.," *La vita e le opere di Nicolò Franco* (Turin, Rome, 1894), 157–67.

NICOLÒ FRANCO:
PRINTED WORKS

1535

1. Nicolai Franci Beneventani Hisabella. In fine: Neapoli, typis Johannis Sussebachii germani et Matthaei Cansii brixiani. MDXXXV.

    BM   Simiani

[1535?]

2. Tempio d'Amore di M. Nicolo Franco. [No date, place, or printer.] The text and pages are identical but the type is different from the 1536 edition.

    BM (Venice? 1535?)   BNF   VM   Casali, *Annali di Marcolini,* 28 Simiani

1536

3. Tempio d'Amore, di M. Nicolo Franco. In fine: In Vinegia per Francesco Marcolini da Forlì, Nel MDXXXVI. del mese di Agosto.

    BM   VM   Simiani

1539

4. Le Pistole Vulgari di M. Nicolo Franco. In fine: In Vinetia ne le stampe d'Antonio Gardane, a li xx d'Aprile, nel' anno del Signore MDXXXIX. Con gratia et privilegio.

    BM   BNF   H   Hu   N   T   VM   Simiani

5. Il Petrarchista, Dialogo di M. Nicolo Franco, Nel quale si scuoprono nuovi Secreti sopra il Petrarca. E si danno a leggere molte lettere, che il medemo Petrarca, In lingua Toschana scrisse a diverse persone. Cose rare, ne mai piu date a luce. Con gratia et Privilegio. Venetiis apud Iohannem Giolitum de Ferrariis. MDXXXIX. In fine: del Mese d'Ottobre.

    F   H   Pn   VM   Bongi, *Giolito,* I, 22   Simiani

6. Dialogi Piacevoli di M. Nicolo Franco. Con Privilegio del Senato Veneto per anni x. Apud Joannem Giolitum, de Ferrariis. Venetiis, MDXXXIX.
BM BNF BNP VM Bongi, *Giolito,* I, 19 Simiani

1541

7. Il Petrarchista, Dialogo di M. Nicolo Franco, Nel quale si scuoprono nuovi Secreti sopra il Petrarca. E si danno a leggere molte lettere, Che il medemo Petrarca, In lingua Thoscana scrisse a diverse persone. Cose rare, ne mai piu date a luce. Con gratia et privilegio. In Vinegia per Gabriel Iolito de Ferrarii. MDXLI. In fine: del Mese di Livio.
BM H Hu T Bongi, *Giolito*

8. Dialogi Piacevoli di M. Nicolo Franco. Con Privilegio, Del Senato Veneto per Anni X. In Venetia per Gabriel Giolito de Ferrarii. MDXLI. In fine: Del Mese d'Agosto.
Bongi, *Giolito,* I, 30, indicates that some copies of 1541 carry 1542 in front.
BM (1542; 1541 in fine) BNF (1541) FM (1542) C (1542) H (1542; 1541 in fine) Hu (1542) NYP (1542; 1541 in fine) T (1541) VM (1542) Simiani (1541)

1542

9. Dialogo di M. Nicolo Franco. Dove si ragiona delle Bellezze. Alla Eccellentissima Marchesana Del Vasto. In fine: in Casale di Monferrato, nelle Stampe di Gioanantonio Guidone. Del mese d'Aprile. Del MDXLII.
F N NYP Pn Pr VM Simiani

10. Dialogo di M. Nicolo Franco. Dove si ragiona della Bellezze. Alla eccellentissima Marchesana del Vasto. Venetiis Apud Antonium Gardane. MDXXXXII.
BM BNF H VM Simiani

11. Le Pistole Vulgari di M. Nicolo Franco. Venetiis apud Antonium Gardane. MDXXXXII.
BM BNF Ch LC Pn VM Y Simiani
Brunet, II, 1377, lists an edition of 1562 without place or printer. I have not located this.

1543

12. Il Petrarchista dialogo di Messer Nicolo Franco, Nel quale si scuoprono nuovi Secreti sopra il Petrarca. E si danno a leggere molte lettere, che il medemo Petrarca scrisse a diverse persone. Cose rare, ne mai piu date a luce. Con Gratia et Privilegio. In Venetia Appresso Gabriel Gioli di Ferrarij. MDXLIII. In fine: il Maggio.
BM H VM Y Bongi, *Giolito,* I, 53 Simiani

1545

13. Dialogi piacevoli di M. Nicolo Franco, con la tavola di tutto quello, che ne l'opera si contiene. Con gratia & Privilegio. In Vinegia Appresso Gabriel Giolito de Ferrari. MDXLV.

BM   H   LC   VM   Bongi, *Giolito,* I, 97   Simiani

1547

14. Dialogi maritimi di M. Gioan Iacopo Botazzo. Et alcune rime maritime di M. Nicolo Franco, et d'altrui diversi spiriti, dell'Accademia de gli Argonauti. All'Eccellenza del Marchese di Soncino, il S. Conte Massimiano Stampa. In Mantova per Iacopo Ruffinelli, nell'anno MDXLVII.

BM   C   Ch   H   Hu   LC   N   NYP   Pr   VM   Y   Simiani
Franco's *rime* are on pp. 128–42, 143^v, 146, 147^v, 148^v.

15. La Philena di M. Nicolo Franco. Historia amorosa ultimamente composta. Al suo nobil signore il Conte di Popoli. In fine: In Mantova per Iacomo Ruffinelli venetiano. nell'Anno MDXLVII.

BM   BNF   F   H   Hu   NYP   Pr   T   VM   Y   Simiani

16. De le lettere di diversi autori, raccolte da Venturin Ruffinelli. Libro primo. Con una Oratione a gli Amanti, per M. Gianfrancesco Arrivabene. In Mantova del XLVII.

Simiani, "Due componimenti inediti di Nicolò Franco," 265, refers to a letter of Franco in the above. I have not located the work.

1548

17. Delle Rime di M. Nicolo Franco contro Pietro Aretino, et de la Priapea Del medesimo, terza editione, colla Giunta di molti Sonetti nuovi. Oltre la vera & ultima correttione, ch'a tutta l'opera intera ha data l'Autore istesso, per non haverne piu cura, come colui c'ha gia rivolti tutti li studi ad imprese di lui piu degne. Con Gratia & Privilegio Pasquillico. MDXLVIII.

BNF   [Basilea, Michel Grineo al Falcone]   Bongi, *Giolito,* I, 458
[Messer Michele Grineo impressore in Basilea, al Falcone]   Simiani
[il Grineo, Basel]

Simiani lists two earlier editions, although he was not able to see them. I have not located them either. They are: (1) Del le Rime di M. Nicolo Franco, contro Pietro Aretino, et de la Priapea del Medesimo. Torino, Guidone, 1541.

(2) Delle Rime di M. Nicolo Franco, contro Pietro Aretino, et de la Priapea del Medesimo. [No place, date, or printer.]

References to the *Rime* in Franco's letters and in Betussi, *Dialogo Amoroso,* (Venice, 1543), 22^v, indicate that they were written by 1541 and existed at least in manuscript form.

1554

18. Dialogi Piacevoli di M. Nicolo Franco, con la tavola di tutto quello che nell'opera si contiene. Con Privilegio. In Vinegia appresso Gabriel Giolito de Ferrari, et fratelli. MDLIIII.

    BM   VM   Bongi, *Giolito*, I, 458   Simiani

1559

19. Dialogi Piacevoli di M. Nicolo Franco, con nuova tavola di tutto quello che ne l'opera si contiene. Con Privilegio. In Vinegia appresso Gabriel Giolito de' Ferrari. MDLIX.

    VM   Bongi, *Giolito*, II, 80   Simiani

1579

20. Dix plaisans dialogues du S. Nicolo Franco, Contenans, Le Debat de Sannio & des Dieux . . . Traduits d'Italien en François. [by Gabriel Chappuys] A Lyon, Par Iean Beraud. 1579. Avec privilege du Roy.

    BM   L. Berthé de Besaucèle, *J. B. Giraldi, 1504–1573*, 292   Baudrier, V, 36–37

1590

21. Dialoghi piacevolissimi di Nicolò Franco da Benevento; Con permissione de' Superiori; Espurgati da Girolamo Gioannini da Capugnano Bolognese. In Vinegia, Presso Altobello Salicato. MDXC. Alla Libraria della Fortezza.

    BNF   H   Pr   T   Y   Simiani

1593

22. Dialoghi piacevolissimi di Nicolò Franco da Benevento; Con permissione de' Superiori; Espurgati da Girolamo Gioannini da Capugnano Bolognese. In Venetia, MDXCIII. Appresso Francesco Zuliani et Giovanni Cerutto.

    BNF   N   H   LC   VM   Simiani

1596

23. Dialoghi Piacevolissimi di Nicolò Franco da Benevento; Con permissione de' Superiori; Espurgati da Girolamo Gioannini da Capugnano Bolognese. In Vinegia, MDXCVI. Presso Altobello Salicato.

    Pn   VM

1598

24. Dialoghi Piacevolissimi di Nicolò Franco da Benevento. Con permissione de' Superiori Espurgati da Girolamo Giovannini da Capugnano Bolognese. In Vinegia, MDXCVIII. Presso Altobello Salicato.
   Cited by Sborselli, ed., *Dialoghi piacevolissimi,* 1925 ed., 165.

1599

25. Dialoghi Piacevolissimi di Nicolò Franco da Benevento; Con permissione de' Superiori. Espurgati da Girolamo Gioannini da Capugnano Bolognese. In Venetia, MDXCIX. Presso Gio. Battista Bonfadino.
   BNF BNP F VM Y

1604

26. De le lettere di Nicolò Franco, scritte a Prencipi, Signori, & ad altri Personaggi, e suoi Amici, Libri tre; Ne le si scuopre l'arte del polito, e del terso scrivere. Di nuovo ristampate, & a candida lezzione ridotte. In Vicenza, Presso Gio. Pietro Gioannini, & Francesco Grossi. MDCIV. Con licenza de' Superiori.
   BNF F H N VM Simiani
   This is an expurgated edition of the *Pistole Vulgari.*

1606

27. Dialoghi Piacevolissimi di Nicolò Franco da Benevento; Espurgati da Girolamo Gioannini da Capugnano Bolognese. In Venetia, 1606, Appresso Lucio Spineda.
   BM BNF F NYP

1609

28. Dialoghi piacevolissimi di Nicolò Franco da Benevento, Espurgati da Girolamo Gioannini da Capugnano Bolognese. In Venetia, MDCIX. Appresso Pietro Farri.
   Author's copy; I have found no other copies or references to this edition.

1615

29. De le lettere di Nicolò Franco, Scritte à Prencipi, Signori, & ad altri Personaggi, e suoi Amici, Libri tre; Ne le quali si scuopre l'arte del polito, e del terso scrivere. Di nuovo ristampate, & à candida lezzione ridotte. In Venetia, MDCXV. Appresso Giorgio Valentino.
   VM Simiani
   An expurgated edition of the *Pistole Vulgari.*

1616

30. Francisco de Cáceres. Dialogos satyricos. Francaforte, 1616.
Spanish translation of the first, second, sixth, and seventh dialogues of the *Dialogi Piacevoli*. See Robert H. Williams, "Francesco de Cáceres, Niccolò Franco and Juan de la Cueva," 194–99.

1617

31. Francisco de Cáceres. Dialogos satyricos. Amsterdam, 1616. Dedicated to D. Juan Zamet, en Paris.
Same text as 1616 ed., issued a month later. See Williams.

1623

32. Li due Petrarchisti dialoghi di Nicolò Franco, & di Ercole Giovannini: Ne'quali con vaga dispositione si scuoprono bellissime Fantasie, nuovi, & ingegnosi Secretti sopra il Petrarca; E si danno à leggere molte Lettere Missive, e Responsive, che lo stesso Petrarca in lingua Toscana scrisse al Re Roberto di Napoli . . . Et ad altri molti, & eglino à lui. Cose pregiatissime, e rare, & la maggior parte mai più date in luce. Con Licenza de' Superiori, & Privilegio. In Venetia, MDCXXIII. Appresso Barezzo Barezzi.
BNF FM Ch F H LC N Pn Pr VM Y Bongi, *Giolito,* I, 23 Simiani

1731

33. Rime de' piu illustri poeti italiani scelte dall'Abbate Antonioni, Parte prima. In Parigi, MDCCXXXI.
VM. Two sonnets of Franco are on pp. 164–65.

[1784?]

34. La Priapea, Sonetti Lussuriosi satirici. Peking regnante Kien-Long, nel xviii secolo.
BNF [London? 1784?]

1786

35. Baldi. Rota. Franco. De Vasto Fidentio. Maritimi e Pedanteschi del Secolo XVI [Andrea Rubbi, ed.]. Venezia, MDCCLXXXVI. Presso Antonio Zatta e figli. Con Licenza de' Superiori et Privilegio.
T VM (1787) Y (1787) Simiani. Eight *rime* by Franco on pp. 200–7.

[1 7 9 0 ?]

36. Il vendemmiatore, poemetto in ottava rima di Luigi Tansillo; e La priapea, sonetti lussuriosi-satirici di Niccolò Franco. A Pe-king, regnante Kien-long, nel XVIII secolo.
    BNF [Paris? 1790?] VM Y Simiani

1 8 5 0

37. Sonetti Lussuriosi e satirici con la priapea. Alvisopoli, 1850.
    N

1 8 8 7

38. Delle Rime di M. Nicolo Franco . . . Terza ed., MDXLVIII. Edizione Facsimilata, fatta a Londra nel 1887, per cura di un bibliofilo, in 60 esemplari per gli amici dell'editore.
    N

1 9 1 6

39. Rime di Nicolo Franco contro Pietro Aretino. Scrittori italiani e stranieri. Lanciano, 1916.
    Ch N Pn

40. La Priapea, Lanciano, [1916].
    C Ch

1 9 2 5

41. Dialoghi piacevolissimi di Nicolò Franco. Introd. Gaetano Sborselli, 2 vols. Lanciano, 1925.
    Ch
    This edition is based on the expurgated editions and is not reliable.

⁍ *Appendix II* ⁌

ORTENSIO LANDO:
PRINTED WORKS

1534

1. Cicero relegatus et Cicero revocatus Dialogi festivissimi. Impressum Venetiis per Melchiorum Sessan: Anno domini MDXXXIIII.
   BM BNF MB MC N VM

2. Cicero relegatus et Cicero revocatus. Dialogi festivissimi. Apud Seb. Gryphium. Lugduni, 1534.
   BM BNF BNP MB MC F Baudrier, VIII, 74–75 Sanesi
   For comments on this edition and other locations, see Conor Fahy, "Press and Pen Corrections in a 1534 edition by Sebastianus Gryphius," 406–9.
   Brunet, III, 812, also cites editions of Lipsiae, apud Mich. Blum, 1534, and Venetiis, Melchiorum Sessa, 1539. I have not located these.

1535

3. Forcianae quaestiones, in quibus varia Italorum ingenia explicantur, multaque alia scitu non indigna. Autore Philalethe Polytopiensi Cive. Neapoli, Excudebat Martinus de Ragusia. Anno MDXXXV.
   BNF BNP MB MC Bongi, "Catalogo" Sanesi

1536

4. Forcianae quaestiones, in quibus varia Italorum ingenia explicantur, multaque alia scitu non indigna. Autore Philalethe Polytopiensi Cive. Neapoli excudebat Martinus de Ragusia. Anno MDXXXVI.
   BM BNP MC C F H Pn VM Y Bongi, "Catalogo"

1540

5. In Des. Erasmi Roterodami Funus, Dialogus lepidissimus, Nunc primum in lucem editus. Basileae, MDXL. In fine: Basileae. Mense Augusto, MDXL
   MC H Bongi, "Catalogo"

1541

6. Forcianae quaestiones, in quibus varia Italorum ingenia explicantur, multaque alia scitu non indigna. Autore Philalethe Polytopiensi Cive. In:
[Johann Gast]. Convivalium sermonum liber, meris iocis, ac salibus non
impudicis, neque lascivis, sed utilibus et serijs refertus. nonnunquam etiam
admixtae sunt iucundae, & verae narrationes, eaque omnia ex varijs cum
veterum, tum recentium monumentis decerpta. per Ioannẽm Peregrinum
Petroselanum. Libellum de varijs moribus Urbium, Virorum & Mulierum
sane perquam elegantem & frugiferum adiecimus. Basileae. MDXLI.
   BNP   MC   H   Pn   Bongi, "Catalogo"

1542

7. Forcianae quaestiones, in quibus varia Italorum ingenia explicantur, mul-
taque alia scitu non indigna. Autore Philalete Politopiensi cive. In [Johann
Gast] Convivalium sermonum liber . . . Basileae. In fine: Basileae apud
Barptolomaeum Westhemerum, Anno salutis MDXLII Mense Aug.
   BNP   MC   Ch   N   Bongi, "Catalogo"

1543

8. Paradossi cioè, sententie fuori del comun parere, novellamente venute in
luce, opra non men dotta, che piacevole, & in due parti separata. Lione,
Gioanni Pullon da Trino. 1543.
   BM   BNF   BNP   MB   MC   Bongi, "Catalogo"

1544

9. Paradossi cioe, sententie fuori Del comun parere, Novellamente venute in
luce. Opra non men dotta che piacevole, & in due parti separata. In
Vinegia. MDXLIIII.
   BNF   MC   Ch   H   NYP   Pn   T   VM   Y
   There seem to have been two 1544 editions. The VM has two copies
   which vary slightly in type spacing. MC notes that there were two
   editions which differed slightly. See also the comments on the 1545
   Paradossi.

[1544 or 1545]

10. Confutazione del libro de paradossi nuovamente composta, et in tre
orationi distinta. [No place, date, or printer]
   BNF   MC   VM   Sanesi   Bongi, "Catalogo"
   The date was probably 1545 because Lando spoke of Otto von Truchsess
   as a cardinal (p. 8), an event which occurred on December 19, 1544.
   See Conor Fahy, "Un'opera sconosciuta di Lando," 263, n. 1.

1545

11. Un brieve trattato dell'Eccellentia delle Donne. Composto dal prestantissimo Philosopho (il Maggio) & di latina lingua in Italiana tradotto. Vi si e poi aggiunto un'essortatione a gli huomini perche non si lascino superar dalle Donne, mostrandogli in gran danno che lor e per sopravenire. In fine: Stampato in Brescia per maestro Damiano de Turlini Nel Anno 1545.
BM
Lando was the author of the *essortatione a gli huomini*. . . . See Conor Fahy, "Un'opera sconosciuta di Lando," 260–66.

12. Paradossi cioe, sententie fuori del comun Parere: Novellamente venute in luce. Opera non men dotta Che piacevole: & in due parti separata. In Venetia. MDXLV.
BM BNF MC C F Hu LC N T VM
The printer was probably Andrea Arrivabene. The T copy differs slightly from the others. It has one title page insert instead of the usual two, and the text is printed in italic type instead of the more common roman type. The text is the same and the contents of individual pages in the T copy do not vary from other copies. Walter L. Bullock, "The 'Lost' *Miscellaneae Quaestiones* of Ortensio Lando," 50, n. 7, notes that there were at least four Venetian editions of the Paradossi in 1544 and 1545, three of them by Andrea Arrivabene, but provides no additional information.

1548

13. Commentario della piu notabili, et mostruose cose d'Italia, & altri luoghi, di lingua Aramea in Italiana tradotto, nel qual s'impara, & prendesi istremo piacere. Vi si e Poi aggionto un breve Catalogo delli inventori delle cose, che si mangiano, & se beveno, novamente ritrovate, & da M. Anonymo di Utopia, composto. MDXLVIII.
BM BNF BNP MB MC H NYP Pr VM Bongi, "Catalogo"
The place of publication was Venice as it carries the privilege of the Venetian Senate.

14. Lettere di molte valorose donne, nelle quali chiaramente appare non esser ne di eloquentia ne di dottrina alli huomini inferiori. Con Privilegio. In Vinegia appresso Gabriel Giolito de Ferrari. MDXLVIII.
BM (colophon dated 1549) BNF MB MC (colophon 1549) H (colophon 1549) NYP (colophon 1549) Pn (colophon 1549) VM Bongi, *Giolito*, I, 213

15. Sermoni funebri de vari authori nella morte de diversi animali. Con Privilegio. In Vinegia appresso Gabriel Giolito de Ferrari. MDXLVIII.
BM BNF BNP MB MC C NYP VM Y Sanesi Bongi, *Giolito*, I, 231.

There were two 1548 editions, both by Giolito. The pagination was the same, but there were different dedicatory letters, one to Johann Jacob Fugger, the other to Nicolò delli Alberti da Bormo. Some examples of both have colophons dated 1549.

16. La Republica nuovamente ritrovato, del governo dell'isola Eutopia, nella qual si vede nuovi modi di governare Stati, reggier Popoli, dar Leggi à i senatori, con molta profondità di sapienza, storia non meno utile che necessaria. Opera di Thomaso Moro Cittadino di Londra. In Vinegia, MDXLVIII.

BM BNF MB MC F Ricottini, *Doni,* no. 17 Bongi, "Catalogo"
In 1561 Francesco Sansovino attributed the translation to Lando. See his *Del governo de i regni et delle republiche* (Venice, 1561), sig. *3ᵛ.
Bongi believed the printer to be Aurelio Pincio.

1549

17. Lettere di molte valorose donne nelle quali chiaramente appare. Non esser ne di eloquentia ne di dottrina alli huomini inferiori. Di nuovo stampate & con sommo studio reviste; & in molti luoghi corrette. Con Privilegio. In Vinegia Appresso Gabriel Giolito de Ferrari. MDXLIX.

BM BNF MC C F Hu N Bongi, *Giolito,* I, 239

1550

18. Commentario de le piu notabili, & mostruose cose d'Italia, & altri luoghi, di lingua Aramea in Italia tradotto, nel quale s'impara, & prendesi estremo piacere. Vi si è poi aggiunto un breve Catalogo de gli inventori de le cose che si mangiano, & si bevano, novamente ritrovato, & da Messer Anonymo di Utopia composto. In Vinetia, Al Segno del Pozzo. MDL. In fine: SUISNETROH SUDNAL, ROTUA TSE.

BNF MC VM Sanesi Bongi, "Catalogo"
"Segno del Pozzo" was the printer Andrea Arrivabene.

19. Consolatorie de diversi autori Novamente raccolte, & da chi le raccolse; devotamente consecrate al S. Galeoto Picco Conte della Mirandola & Cavallier di S. Michele. Con Privilegio. In Vinegia al segno del pozzo. MDL.

BNF MB MC C F H N VM Sanesi Bongi, "Catalogo"

20. Miscellaneae quaestiones nunc primum in lucem emissae. Cum Privilegio. Venetiis Apud Gabrielem Iolitum et Fratres de Ferrariis. MDL.

BNF MB Sanesi Bullock, "The 'Lost' *Miscellaneae Quaestiones* of Ortensio Lando"

21. Oracoli de' moderni ingegni si d'huomini come di donne, ne quali, unita si vede tutta la philosophia morale, che fra molti Scrittori sparsa si leggeva. Con Privilegio. In Vinetia appresso Gabriel Giolito di Ferrarii e fratelli, 1550.

BM BNF MB MC Ch F Hu N VM Sanesi Bongi, *Giolito*, I, 298

22. Ragionamenti familiari di diversi Autori, non meno dotti, che faceti, et dedicati alla rara cortesia del molto Reverendo & Illust. Signore il Sig. Andrea Mattheo d'Acqua Viva. Con Privilegio. In Vinegia al segno del Pozzo. MDL. In fine: In Vinegia per Pietro, & Zuanmaria fratelli di Nicolini da Sabbio ne l'anno del Giubileo. MDL.

    BM BNF MB MC C F Hu Pn VM Bongi, "Catalogo"

23. La sferza de scrittori antichi et moderni di M. Anonimo di Utopia alla quale, è dal medesimo aggiunta una essortatione allo studio delle lettere. Con privilegio. In Vinegia, MDL.

    BM BNF MB MC C F H Pn VM Sanesi Bongi, "Catalogo"

    The title page carries the mark of *Segno del Pozzo,* i.e., Arrivabene.

24. Paradossi, per Jaccobo de Millis, 1550. In fine: Stampato in Lione, per Giovanni Pullone da Trino.

    BNP MC Baudrier, IV, 196 Brunet, IV, 361

    Brunet, IV, 362, lists a Spanish ed. of the *Paradossi* which I have not located: Paradoxas o sentencias, traduzidas de ytaliano en castellano. Medina del Campo, 1552.

25. Forcianae quaestiones, In quibus varia Italorum ingenia explicantur, multaque alia scitu non indigna. Autore Philalethe Polytopiensi Cive. Lovanii, Excudebat Iacobus Thenius, Anno 1550. Prostant apud Martinum Rotarium.

    BNP MC Bongi, "Catalogo"

26. Vita del Beato Ermodoro Alessandrino da Theodoro Cipriano scritta, & nella nostra volgar lingua tradotta. Vinegia, al segno del Pozzo. MDL.

    BNF Bongi, "Catalogo" Sforza, "Lando," 9, n. 4 Sanesi

    This is a translation by Lando.

1552

27. Dialogo di M. Hortensio Lando, nel quale si ragiona della consolatione, et utilità, che si gusta leggendo la Sacra Scrittura. Trattasi etiandio dell'ordine, che tener si dee nel leggerle, & mostrarsi essere le Sacre lettere di vera eloquenza, e di varia dottrina alle Pagane lettere superiori. In Vinetia al Segno del Pozzo. MDLII. In fine: In Vinegia per Comin da Trino di Monferrato, L'anno MDLII.

    BNF MB MC F Hu VM Sanesi Bongi, "Catalogo"

28. Due panegirici nuovamente composti, de quali l'uno è in lode della S. Marchesiana della Padulla & l'altro in commendatione della S. Donna Lucretia Gonzaga da Gazuolo. Con Privilegio. In Vinegia, appresso Gabriel Giolito de Ferrari et Fratelli. MDLII.

    BNF MB MC Ch VM Sanesi Bongi, *Giolito,* I, 367

29. Quattro libri de dubbi con le solutioni a ciascun dubbio accommodate. La materia del primo è naturale, del secondo è mista (benche per lo piu sia Morale) del Terzo è Amorosa, & del Quarto è Religiosa. Con Privilegio. In Vinegia Appresso Gabriel Giolito de Ferrari, et Fratelli. MDLII.

> BNF MB MC F H Pn VM Sanesi Bongi, *Giolito,* I, 368
> In fine: "Gabriel Giolito a Lettori: Io promissi di darvi quattro libri de Dubbi, hor non havendo fin hora potuto impetrare la licentia dei Dubbi amorosi, sono sforzato a darvene solamente tre." The *dubbi amorosi* were included in the 1556 ed.

30. Vari Componimenti di M. Hort. Lando nuovamente venuti in luce. Quesiti amorosi colle risposte. Dialogo intitolato Ulisse. Ragionamento occorso tra un cavalliere, & un huomo soletario. Alcune novelle. Alcune favole. Alcuni scroppoli, che sogliono occorrere nella cottidiana nostra lingua. Con Privilegio. Vinegia appresso Gabriel Giolito de Ferrari et fratelli. MDLII.

> BNF FM MB MC H Pn Pr Sanesi Bongi, *Giolito,* I, 370

31. Lettere della Molto illustre Sig. la Sʳᵃ˙Donna Lucretia Gonzaga da Gazuolo con gran diligentia raccolte, & a gloria del sesso Feminile nuovamente in luce poste. Con Privilegi In Vinegia, MDLII. In fine: Appresso Gualtero Scotto

> BNF MB MC H N Pn Bongi, "Catalogo"

32. Una Breve pratica di medicina per sanare le passioni dell' animo. Al magnifico signor David Otho. Appresso Gratioso Perchacino.

> MC Bullock, "The 'Lost' *Miscellaneae Questiones* of Ortensio Lando," p. 50 Sanesi Bongi, "Catalogo" ("in Padova")

1552/1553

33. Sette libri de cathaloghi a varie cose appartenenti, non solo antiche, ma anche moderne: opera utile molto alla historia, & da cui prender si po materia da favellare d'ogni proposito che ci occorra. Con Privilegio. In Vinegia appresso Gabriel Giolito de' Ferrari, e fratelli. MDLII. In fine: MDLIII.

> BNF BNP MC Ch F H LC N NYP Pn VM Sanesi Bongi, *Giolito,* I, 371

1553

34. Commentario delle più notabili, & mostruose cose d'Italia, & altri luoghi: di lingua Aramea in Italiana tradotto. Con un breve Catalogo de gli inventori delle cose che si mangiano & beveno, novamente ritrovato. In Vinetia per Bartholomeo Cesano. MDLIII.

> BM BNF MC N VM Sanesi Bongi, "Catalogo"

35. Predica del Reverendo Monsi. Cornelio Vescovo di Bitonto fatta in Trento il giorno di San Donato l'anno MDXLV. Per l'allegrezze che si fecero

venuta la nuova, ch'era nato il primogenito del Principe de Spagna figliuolo di Carlo Quinto Imperatore. Nella quale si tratta delle Gratie & delli doni d'Iddio, & della nobiltà & dignità dell'Huomo. Con Privilegio. In Vinegia appresso Gabriel Giolito de Ferrari e fratelli. MDLIII.

> BNF   VM   Bongi, *Giolito*, I, 390
> Sermon of Cornelio Musso (1511–74) edited by Lando.

36. Paradoxes, ce sont propos contre la commune opinion: debatus, en forme de declamations forēses pour exerciter les ieunes advocats, en causes difficiles. A Paris, Par Charles Estienne, imprimeur du Roy, 1553

> BNP   MC   Y   Sanesi   Bongi, "Catalogo"
> Charles Estienne (c. 1505–64) translated 25 of Lando's paradoxes, omitting nos. 11 and 27–30.

37. Paradoxes, ce sont propos contre la commune opinion: debatuz, en forme de Declamations forēses: pour exerciter les ieunes esprits, en causes difficiles. Reveuz & corrigez pour la seconde fois. A Paris, Par Charles Estienne, Imprimeur du Roy. MDLIII. Avec privilege dudict Seigneur.

> MC   H   F   N   Pn

38. Paradoxes, ce sont propos contre la commune opinion: debatus, en forme de Declamations forenses: pour exerciter les jeunes advocats, en causes difficiles. Ian de Marnes: Poitiers, 1553.

> BM   Brunet, IV, 362
> Estienne's translation of 25 of Lando's paradoxes as well as the anonymous paradox (probably written by Estienne) "Que le plaider est chose tres utile, & necessaire a la vie des hommes." This paradox was not based on Lando, but was included several times with the French editions of Lando's paradoxes.

Bongi, *Giolito*, I, 389, attributes the following work of 1553 on diseases to Lando. I have not seen it.

Incerti authoris brevis elocubratio nuper inventa, de his morbis, à quibus humana corpora infestari corrumpique solita sunt. Cum Privilegio. Venetiis apud Gabrielem Iolitum de Ferrariis et fratres MDLIII.

1554

39. Commentario delle piu notabili & mostruose cose d'Italia, & altri luoghi: di lingua Aramea in Italiana tradotto. Con un breve catalogo de gli inventori delle cose che si mangiano, & beveno, novamente ritrovato. MDLIIII.

> BM[B. Cesano for Heirs of G. Padovano: Venice]   MC   LC [Venezia?]   VM   Y [Venezia?]   Brunet, III, 812   Bongi, "Catalogo"

40. Paradoxe Qu'il vaut mieux estre pauure que riche. Traicté non moins plein de doctrine, que de recreation pour toutes gens. A Caen, De l'imprimerie de Martin & Pierre Philippe. 1554.

> BM
> Contains Estienne's translation of Lando paradoxes nos. 1, 2, 3, 4, 5, and

6. It also contains the anonymous paradox "Que le plaider est chose tres utile. . . ."

41. XXV Paradoxes ou sentences, débattues et élégamment déduites contre la commune opinion, traité non moins plein de doctrine que de récréation pour toutes gens. Lyon, par Jean Temporal, 1554. In fine: Impr. à Lyon, chez Barthelemy Frein.

Brunet, IV, 361, reports that this is a reprint of one of the editions of 1553. Renouard, *Annales des Estienne,* 206, confirms an edition of Lyons, 1554.

42. XXV. paradoxes . . . Plus adjousté de nouveau le paradoxe que le plaider est chose tres utile, & necessaire à la vie des hommes. Paris, 1554.

MC Renouard, *Annales des Estienne,* 206.

Brunet, IV, 362, mentions another 1554 edition at Rouen, citing an old catalogue. I have not located this.

1554/1555

43. Varii Componimenti di M. Hort. Lando. Nuovamente venuti in luce. Dialogo intitolato Ulisse. Ragionamento occorso tra un Cavalliere, & un'huomo soletario. Alcune novelle. Alcune favole. Alcuni scroppoli, che sogliono occorrere nella cottidiana nostra lingua. Con Privilegio. In Venetia Appresso Gabriel Giolito de Ferrari, et Fratelli. MDLIIII.

BNF MB MC (colophon 1555) F (1555) H (1555) N (1555) Y (1555) Bongi, *Giolito,* I, 439, gives 1554 but notes that some copies are 1555.

1555

44. Paradoxes, ou Sentences, debates, & elegamment deduites contre la commune opinion. Traité non moins plein de doctrine, que de recreation pour toutes gens. Reueu, & augmenté. A Lyon, par Thibauld Payan, 1555.

Brunet, IV, 361: Thibauld Payen   Baudrier, IV, 266, notes that this and the following edition are identical except for the printers' marks.

45. Paradoxes, ou sentences debatues et elegamment deduites contre la commune opinion . . . A Lyon, par Jean Temporal, 1555.

Baudrier, IV, 266   MC notes a Lyons, 1555, edition but does not list the printer.

1556

46. Quattro libri de dubbi con le solutioni a ciascun dubbio accomodate. La materia del primo è amorosa, del Secondo è Naturale, del Terzo è Mista, ben che per lo più sia Morale, e del Quarto è Religiosa. Con Privilegio. In Vinegia appresso Gabriel Giolito de' Ferrari. MDLVI.

BNF MC C Sanesi Bongi, *Giolito,* I, 499

47. Le due giornate del poeta Bandarino dove si tratta de tutti i costumi, che in le città de Italia a loco per loco usar si sogliono. 1556.
BM VM Sanesi Sforza, "Lando," 35, n. 1 Bongi, "Catalogo"
Italian translation of the *Forcianae Quaestiones* by Marco Bandarino.

1557

48. Paradoxes, ou Sentences debatues, &, elegammēt deduites contre le commune opinion. Traicté non moins plein de doctrine, que de recreatiō pour toutes gens. Plus adiousie de nouueau le Paradoxe que la plaider est chose tres utile, & necessaire à la vie des hommes. A Paris. Par Magdaleine Boursetre, en la Rue sainct Iacques à l'enseigne de l'Elephant devant les Machurins. 1557. In fine: Imprimé à Paris par Marin Massellin, Pour la vefue Françoys Regnault.
Pr Brunet, IV, 362

1558

49. Questions diverses, et responses d'icelles, Divisées en troys livres: Assavoir, Questions d'Amour. Questions Naturelles. Questions Morales & Politiques. Nouuellement traduites de Tuscan en Françoys. A Lyon. A l'Escude Milan, Par Gabriel Cotier. 1558. Avec Privilege. In fine: Imprimé à Lyon, par Iean d'Ogerolles. 1558.
BM BNF BNP H Sanesi Brunet, IV, 1015 Baudrier, IV, 69
This is a translation of the *Dubbi* omitting the *dubbi religiosi*.

1559

50. Sermoni funebri de vari authori nella morte de diversi animali. In Genova. MDLVIIII.
BM BNF MC F Bongi, "Catalogo"
Bongi, "Catalogo," also lists a Genoa, 1558, edition of the above.

1559/1561

51. Paradoxes ou sentences debatues, & elegamment deduites contre la commune opinion. Traité non moins plein de doctrine que de recreation pour toutes gens. Reueu, & augmente. A Lyon, Par Iean Temporal. MDLIX. In fine: A Lyon, Par Nicholas Perrineau, 1561.
Baudrier, IV, 392, gives 1561 as the correct date. Brunet, IV, 361–62, notes the two dates, gives "Nicolas Parrineau" as printer, and notes that it contains 26 paradoxes.

1561

52. XXV. Paradoxes, ou sentences debatues, & elegamment deduites contre la commune opinion. Traicté non moins plein de doctrine, que de recreation pour toutes gens. Plus adiousté de nouueau le Paradoxe que le plaider est

chose tres vtile, & necessaire à la vie des hommes. A Paris, De l'Imprimerie de Maurice Menier, demourant aux faulxbourgs S. Victor, Rue neufue, à enseigne S. Pierre. 1561.

BNP   Brunet, IV, 362

1563

53. Paradossi cioè sententie fuori del comun parere novellamente venute in luce. Opera non men dotta, che piacevole, & in due parti separata. Con l'indice delle cose degne di memoria, di nuovo aiunto. In Venetia, appresso Andrea Arrivabene. MDLXIII.

> This edition is sometimes bound with the *Confutazione de Paradossi.*
> BM (with *Confutazione*) BNF BNP MB (with *Confutazione*) MC VM (with *Confutazione*)   Bongi, "Catalogo"

1569

54. Commentario delle piu notabili & mostruose cose d'Italia, & altri luoghi: di lingua Aramea in Italiana tradotto. Con un breve catalogo de gli inventori delle cose che si mangiano & beveno, novamente ritrovato. In Venetia, Appresso Giovanni Bariletto. MDLXIX.

> BM BNF BNP MC F H   Brunet, III, 812   Bongi, "Catalogo"
> This edition was not expurgated.

55. Harangues lamentables sur la mort de divers animaux, extraictes du Tuscan, rendues et augmentées en nostre vulgaire . . . A Lyon, par Benoist Rigaud, 1569.

> Sanesi, p. 140   Brunet, V, 310
> Brunet notes that this is a translation by Claude de Pontoux of eight of the eleven *Sermoni Funebri.*
> Baudrier, III, 267, adds an edition of Lyons, Rigaud, 1570.

1570

56. Questions diverses, et responses d'icelles, Divisees en trois Livres: Assavoir, Questions d'Amour. Questions Naturelles. Questions Morales & Polytiques. Nouuellement traduites de Tuscan en Françoys. A Lyon, A l'Escu de Milan, Par la veufue Gabriel Cotier. 1570. Avec Privilege du Roy. In fine: Imprimé à Lyon par Iean Marcorelle. 1570.

> BM   Brunet, IV, 1015
> A translation of three parts of the *Dubbi* omitting the dubbi religiosi.

1572

57. Questions diverses et responses d'icelles. Divisées en trois livres. A sçavoir: questions d'amour, questions naturelles, questions morales & polytiques. Nouvellement traduites . . . en françoys. Paris, 1572.

> MC

Brunet, IV, 1015, also cites the following editions: Lyons, Benoit Rigaud, 1583; Lyons, Benoit Rigaud, 1596; Rouen, Claude le Villain, 1610 or 1617; no place or printer, 1635; and an early seventeenth-century edition by Jacq. Caillové.

A Spanish translation of the *Dubbi* has been noted: Girolamo Campas, Sylva de varias questiones naturales y morales con sus respuestas y soluciones, sacadas de muchas autores griegos y latinos. Anvers, 1575.

Brunet, I, 1527   Sanesi

1576

58. Paradoxes, ou sentences debatues en forme de Declamations forenses, Pour exerciter les practiciens en causes difficiles. Traité non moins plein de doctrine que de recreation pour toutes gens. Reueu & augmenté de nouveau A Lyon Par Benoist Rigaud. 1576.
   Baudrier, III, 331–32   Brunet, IV, 362

59. Regrets facetieux, et plaisantes harengues funebres sur la mort de divers animaux, pour passer le temps et resveiller les esprits melancholiques: non moins r'emplies d'éloquence que d'utilité et gaillardise. Traduictes de Toscan en Françoys, par Thierri de Timofille, Gentil-homme Picard. La table d'icelles se void en la page suivante. A Paris, Chez Nicolas Chesneau, & Iean Poupy, rue Sainct Iacques, au Chesne verd. MDLXXVI. Avec Privilege du Roy.
   H   Brunet V, 310   Sanesi   Bongi, "Catalogo"
   French translation of the *Sermoni Funebri;* Brunet and Bongi indicate that François d'Amboise was the translator.

1583

60. Regrets facetieux et plaisantes harengues funebres sur la mort de divers animaux, pour passer le temps & resueiller les esprits melencoliques: non moins r'emplis d'eloquence que d'vtilité & gaillardise. Traduictes de Toscan en Françoys, par Thierri de Timofille, Gentil-homme picard. La table d'icelles se void en la page suyuantes. A Paris, Par Nicolas Bonfons, rue neuue nostre Dame, à l'enseigne Sainct Nicolas. 1583.
   BNP   Brunet, V, 310
   Translation of the *Sermoni Funebri.*

61. Paradoxes, autrement Propos contraires à l'opinion de la plupart des hommes: livre non moins profitable que facetieux. Rouen, Nic. Lescuyer, 1583
   BNP   MC   Brunet, IV, 362

1590

62. Orationes funebres in obitus aliquot animalium, olim ex Italicis Gallicae per Claud. Pontosum, Postea è Gallicis Latinae factae per Gulielmum

Canterum, & nunc primum editae. Quarum Indicem vide pagina sequenti. Lugduni Batavorum, Ex officina Plantiniana, Apud Franciscum Raphelengium. CIƆ IƆ XC. Issued with: I. Dousae Filii rerum caelestium liber primus in laudem umbrae declamatio et carmen. . . . Quibus additae sunt orationes funebres In obitus aliquot animalium, Interprete Gulielmo Cantero. . . . Lugduni Batavorum, Ex officina Plantiniana, Apud Franciscum Raphelengium. CIƆ IƆ XCI.

BNP Ch Hu Y

A   Latin translation of the *Sermoni Funebri*.

1591

63. Forcianae quaestiones, in quibus varia italorum ingenia explicantur, multaque alia scitu non indigna. Authore Philalethe Polytopiensi Cive. In: De arte peregrinandi libri II. Variis exemplis: in primis vero agri Neapolitani descriptione illustrati. . . . Quibus accesserunt in fine Quaestiones forcianae. . . . MDXCI. In fine: Noribergae, In officina typographica Catharina Gerlachie.

H

The *Forcianae Quaestiones* are on pp. 181–228.

1593

64. The Defence of Contraries. Paradoxes against common opinion, debated in forme of declamations in place of publike censure: only to exercise yong wittes in difficult matters. Wherein is no offence to Gods honour, the estate of Princes, or private mens honest actions: but pleasant recreation to beguile the iniquity of time. Translated out of French by A. M. one of the Messengers of her Maiesties Chamber. Imprinted at London by Iohn Windet for Simon Waterson. 1593.

F

These are the first 12 paradoxes translated from Estienne's French translation by Anthony Mundy. See Rice, "The *Paradossi* of Ortensio Lando," 68; and Celeste Turner, *Anthony Mundy,* 90–92, 209.

1594

65. Paradossi cioe sentenze fuori del comun parere, Ristaurate, et purgate con la presente nova impressione. Opera non men dotta, che piacevole. Con l'auttorità de' Superiori. In Bergamo, CIƆ IƆ XCIIII. Per Comin Ventura.

BM BNF MB MC VM Bongi, "Catalogo" Brunet, IV, 361

This is part one of the *Paradossi* (the first 17 paradoxes), expurgated.

1597

66. Selva di bellissimi dubbi con dotte solutioni a ciascun dubbio accommodate, Divisa in due parti. Delle quali nella prima i Naturali, nell'altra i Morali

si contengono: Di nuovo rivista & d'utili annotationi arricchita da Annibale Novelli Piacentino, come à questo segno* vedere si potrà. In Piacenza, Appresso Giovanni Bazachi. 1597. Con licenza de' Superiori.

 BNF MC Bongi, "Catalogo" Bongi, *Giolito,* I, 369

 The first two parts of the *Dubbi,* annotated.

1602

67. Paradossi, cioè sentenze fuori del commun parere. Ristaurate, & purgate con la presente nuova impressione. Opera non men dotta, che piacevole. In Vicenza, Per Pietro Bertelli Libraro in Padova. 1602. Con licenza de' Superiori.

 BM MC

 This edition contains twenty-five paradoxes omitting the last five.

68. Paradoxes against common opinion: debated in form of declamations in place of publique censure: onelie to exercise young wittes in difficult matters. 1602.

 A reissue of the first 12 paradoxes of Mundy's 1593 translation from Estienne's French edition. See Rice, "The *Paradossi* of Ortensio Lando," 68, 70, who states that the "unique copy of this issue is imperfect, consisting of only the first thirty-four pages of the original text."

1603

69. Les déclamations paradoxes. Où sont contenuës plusieurs Questions debat- tuës contre l'opinion du vulgaire. Traitté vtile et recreatif, propre à esveiller la subtilité des esprits de ce temps. Reueu et enrichi d'annotations fort sommaires, par Jean du Val Aucerrois. Au faux-bourg S. Germain les Paris, Par Flevry Bourriquant, en la ruë Neufue, au coing de la ruë du petit Lyon. MDCIII.

 BNP MC

 Brunet, IV, 362, cites another edition of 1603/1604 with the same title, but printed in Paris, Jean Micard, ou du Breuil.

1604

70. Dilettevoli orationi nella morte di diversi animali, in: Consigli degli Animali, cioè ragionamenti civili, di Agnolo Firenzuola fiorentino. Dis- corso di F. Jeronimo Capugnano domenichino, ove prova che gli animali ragionano insieme. Venetia, appresso Barezzo Barezzi, 1604.

 Bongi, *Giolito,* I, 232 Brunet, VI, 310

 The *Sermoni Funebri:* see the 1622 edition for complete citation.

1613

71. The Treasurie of Auncient and Moderne Times . . . translated out of that Worthy Spanish Gentleman, Pedro Mexio And M. Francesco Sansovino.

. . . London, Printed by W. Iaggard, 1613.
N
Edited [T. Milles]; it includes seven of Lando's paradoxes. See II, ch.
22, 176–80 (paradox 23); III, ch. 23, 291–93 (paradox 14); IV, ch. 38,
390–92 (paradox 16); V, ch. 30, 485–86 (paradox 17); VI, ch. 28,
612–14 (paradox 19); VII, ch. 43, 723–25 (paradox 18); VIII, ch. 38,
834–37 (paradox 20).

1616

72. Forcianae quaestiones. . . . Francofurti, 1616.
MC

1618

73. Harangues facetieuses, remplies de doctrines et sentences, sur la mort de
divers animaux, composées par divers autheurs. Traduit . . . par P. R. L.
Lyon, Pierre Roussin, 1618.
MC   Brunet, V, 310
Translation of *Sermoni Funebri.*

1622

74. Undeci Orationi in lode di varij Animali, in: Consigli de gli animali, Cioe
ragionamenti civili, Di Agnolo Firenzuola Fiorentino, Ne'quali con mara-
viglioso, e vago arteficio trà loro parlando, raccontano Simboli, Averti-
menti, Istorie, Proverbi, e Motti, che insegnano il viver Civile, & a
governare altri con prudenza. Aggiuntovi un Discorso di F. Ieronimo
Capugnano Domenichino, ove prova, che gli Animali ragionano insieme.
Et con tal occasione si tratta di tutti i Parlari, & come si favelli in Cielo, nel
Mondo, & nel Centro della Terra. Et di più undeci Orationi in lode di varij
Animali. In Venetia, Presso il Barezzi. 1622. Con licenza de' Superiori, &
Privilegio.
MB   N   VM   Bongi, *Giolito,* I, 232   Bongi, "Catalogo"
The *Undeci Orationi* are the *Sermoni Funebri.*

1627

75. Il Dottissimo passatempo di Eugenio Raimondi Bresciano, dove si leggono
curiosi Oracoli, Sentenze gravi, con precetti, et ammaestramenti Politici, e
Christiani, Publicati da antichi, e moderni Scrittori. Ne quale unita si vede
tutta la Dottrina Morale, Politica, et Istorica, Opera non men utile, che
curiosa, e dilettevole. Venetia, G. Anesi, 1627.
N
The *Oracoli de' moderni ingegni* are reprinted on 197–320.

1630

76. Il Dottissimo passatempo di Eugenio Raimondi Bresciano, dove si leggono curiosi Oracoli, Sentenze gravi, con precetti, et ammaestramenti Politici, e Christiani Publicati da antichi, e moderni Scrittori. Ne quale unita si vede tutta la Dottrina Morale, Politica, et Istorica, Opera non men utile, che curiosa, e dilettevole. In Vinetia, MDCXXX, Appresso Gervasio Anesi.
   Sanesi, p. 120.
   The same plagiarization of the *Oracoli de' moderni ingegni* as in the 1627 edition.

1632

77. Regrets facetieux et plaisantes harangues funebres du sieur Thomassin, sur la mort de divers animaux, oeuvre tres utile pour passer le temps, et resveiller les esprits melancoliques. avec plusieurs chansons joviales et comiques. Le tout dedié au sieur Gautier Garguille. Rouen, David Ferrand, 1632.
   BNP   Brunet, V, 833–34
   French ed. of the *Sermoni Funebri.*

1634

78. Hygiasticon, Cambridge, 1634.
   The third part is Lando's paradox 24. See Thompson, *The Seventeenth-Century English Essay,* 99.

1638

79. Paradoxes ou les opinions renversées de la plus part des hommes: livre non moins profitable que facetieux; par le Doctor incognu. Paris, Jacques Caillové, 1638.
   MC   Brunet, IV, 362

1640

80. Delle Sferza delle scienze, et de' scrittori. Discorsi satirici di Eugenio Raimondi Bresciano. Fondati nella vanitá Delle cose, appogiati alla frenetica & malinconica natura de' viventi, & alla giusta lode de'Immortali. . . . Con Licenza de' Superiori, e Privilegi. In Venetia, MDCXL. Presso Gervasio Annisi.
   N   Bongi, "Catalogo"   Sanesi
   A free plagiarization of the *Sferza de' Scrittori,* integrating new material.

1 6 5 1

81. Harangues burlesques sur la vie et sur la mort de divers animaux, dédiées
à la Samaritaine du Pont-Neuf, par M. Raisonnable. Paris, Ant. de
Sommaville, 1651.
   BM   MC   Brunet, III, 39
   French ed. of *Sermoni Funebri.*

1 6 5 3

82. [John Hall]. Paradoxes by J. De la Salle, London, printed for Francis
Eaglesfield, at the Marygold in Paul's Church-yard. 1653.
   N
   Lando's paradox 10 is on 135–65.

1 6 7 8

83. The Temperate Man, or the Right Way of Preserving Life and Health
. . . in Three Treatises. The first written by the Learned Leonardus
Lessius, the Second by Lodowick Cornaro . . . of Venice, The Third by a
Famous Italian. London, Printed by J. R. for John Starkey, at the Miter in
Fleetstreet, near Temple Bar, 1678.
   N   Pr
   Lando's paradox 24 (the frugal life), a reprint of the 1634 *Hygiasticon,*
   is on 157–68. Lando is the "Famous Italian."

1 6 9 1 & 1 6 9 3

84. [Dunton, John]. The Athenian Gazette: or Casuistical Mercury, Resolving
all the most Nice and Curious Questions proposed by the ingenious from
Tuesday, March 17th to Saturday, May 20, 1691. First volume. . . .
London, Printed for John Dunton, at the Raven in the Poultry, MDCXCI.
———. Tome II, from Tuesday, July 11 to Saturday, Oct. 21, 1693.
   N
   Thompson, *The Seventeenth-Century English Essay,* 99, writes that
   some questions and answers of the 1570 French *Dubbi* appeared in
   Dunton's work.

1 7 0 6 , 1 7 0 8 , 1 7 1 0 , 1 7 1 6

85. [John Dunton]. The Athenian Oracle. . . . London, 1706, 1708, 1710, 1716
(3 vols. & supplement)
   N
   According to Thompson, *The Seventeenth-Century English Essay,* 99,
   this contains some of Lando's dubbi.

1707

86. [John Dunton]. Athenian Sport: or Two Thousand Paradoxes Merrily Argued, To Amuse and Divert the Age. London. Printed for B. Bragg in Pater-noster Row, 1707.
   N
   Contains six of Lando's paradoxes: 30–36, paradox 24; 241–45, paradox 14; 245–48, paradox 10; 357–65, paradox 3; 406–8, paradox 2; 435–38, paradox 13.

1712

87. Dilettevoli orationi nella morte di diversi animali. . . . Venetia, 1712.
   MC

1738

88. Cicero relegatus et Cicero revocatus . . . in J. Vorstii . . . de Latinitate selecta. . . . Jena, 1738.
   MC

1754

89. Girolamo Zanetti, ed. Del Novelliero italiano. 4 vols. Venezia, 1754.
   T Y
   Vol. 3, 161–82, contains four *novelle* from *Vari Componimenti*.

1763

90. Forcianae Quaestiones, In quibus varia Italorum ingenia explicantur, multaquae alia scitu non indigna. Autore Philalethe Polytopiensi Cive. Lucae, MDCCLXIII. Ex Typographia Jacobi Justi. Superiorum Permissu.
   BNF BNP MC VM Bongi, "Catalogo"

1821

91. Utopia di Tommaso Moro Cancelliere d'Inghilterra. Milano, Per Vincenzo Ferrario, MDCCCXXI.
   BNF Ricottini, *Doni,* p. 173
   Reprint of the 1548 translation of the *Utopia*.

1825

92. Roscoe, Thomas. The Italian Novelists: selected from the most approved authors in that language; from the earliest period down to the close of the

eighteenth century: arranged in an historical and chronological series, translated from the original Italian. Accompanied with notes critical and biographical. 4 vols. London, 1825.

BM BNF FM N

Contains four novelle, nos. IV, V, VI, XIII, from the *Vari Componimenti,* in vol. II, 293–327. Another edition of the above appeared in 1836 (Y).

1851

93. Bongi, Salvatore, ed. Novelle di M. Ortensio Lando: con diligenza ristampate e corrette procedute dalla sua vita. In Lucca, Presso Giovanni Baccelli, 1851.

MC Ch T

1857

94. Le Forciane Questioni, Nelle quali i varii costumi degli Italiani e molte cose non indegne da sapersi si spiegano di Filalete Cittadino Politopiense (Ortensio Lando) tradotte da Giovanni Paoletti. Venezia, dalla tipografia di Sante Martinengo, 1857.

BNF MC VM

Italian translation of *Forcianae Quaestiones.*

1889

95. Axon, William E. A., ed. The frugal life: that a spare diet is better than a splendid and sumptuous diet. Manchester, 1889.

MC H

A reprint of the third part of the *Hygiasticon,* 1634 and 1678.

1916

96. Ortensio Lando Novelle. Lanciano, 1916.

CH H VM

ANTON FRANCESCO DONI:
PRINTED WORKS

The check-list gives, with brief citations, all Doni's published editions before the nineteenth century. It does not include works that he edited or printed, works in which he wrote only a letter or sonnet, unpublished manuscripts, or collections which contained less than a complete work of his. The list is based on Ricottini, *A.F.D., scrittore e stampatore*, which is a complete, annotated bibliography. It is followed by a selected bibliography of Doni's works used in this study, cited in full.

Check-list of editions from 1543 to 1637

1543

1. Lettera di Doni, con Sonetti d'alcuni Gentilhuomini Piacentini. Piacenza, Simoneta.

1544

2. Dialogo della Musica. Venice, Scotto.
3. Lettere. Venice, Scotto.

1545

4. Lettere. Venice, Scotto.

1546

5. Lettere. Florence, Doni.
6. Gli Spiriti Folletti. Florence, Doni.

1547

7. Lettere. Florence, Doni.
8. Prose Antiche di Dante, Petrarcha, et Boccaccio. Florence, Doni.

1549

9. Disegno del Doni. Venice, Giolito.
10. L'Epistole di Seneca. Venice, Pincio.

1550

11. La Libraria. Venice, Giolito.
12. La Libraria. Venice, Giolito.
13. La Fortuna di Cesare. Venice, Giolito.
14. La Prima Parte de le Medaglie. Venice, Giolito.
15. Sopra l'Effigie di Cesare. Venice, n. p.
16. Le Medaglie, Venice, [Giolito?].
17. Le Medaglie. Venice, [Giolito?].

[1550]

18. Stanze d'Amore alla villanesca. Bologna, Leonardo detto il **Furlano**.

1551

19. La Seconda Libraria. Venice, Marcolini.
20. La Zucca. Venice, Marcolini.
21. La Zucca. Venice, Marcolini (Spanish trans.).

1552

22. La Moral Filosophia. Venice, Marcolini.
23. Pistolotti Amorosi. Venice, Giolito.
24. Tre Libri di Lettere. Venice, Marcolini.

1552-53

25. I Marmi. Venice, Marcolini.
26. I Mondi. Venice, Marcolini.

1553

27. Inferni. Venice, Marcolini.
28. L'Asinesca Gloria. Venice, Marcolini.
29. Rime del Burchiello Comentate dal Doni. Venice, Marcolini.

1554

30. Pistolotti Amorosi. Venice, Marcolini.

1555

31. La Seconda Libraria. Venice, Marcolini.

1556

32. Teremoto. Venice, n. p.

1557

33. La Libraria & La Seconda Libraria. Venice, Giolito.

1558

34. La Libraria & La Seconda Libraria. Venice, Giolito.
35. Tre Libri di Pistolotti Amorosi. Venice, Giolito.
36. Il Valore de gli Asini. Venice, Marcolini.

1562

37. Il Cancellieri: Libro dell'Eloquenza. Venice, Giolito.
38. Il Cancellieri: Libro della Memoria. Venice, Giolito.
39. Dichiaratione sopra il XIII. Cap. dell'Apocalisse. Venice, Giolito.
40. Espositione sopra del XIII. Cap. dell'Apocalisse. Padua, Perchacino.
41. I Mondi & Inferni. Venice, Giolito.

1564

42. Le Pitture. Padua, Perchacino.

1565

43. La Zucca, including Le Pitture. Venice, Rampazetto.

1566

44. Le Rime del Burchiello. Venice, Rampazetto.
45. Le Ville. Bologna, Benacci.

1567

46. La Moral Filosophia. Venice, Heredi di Sessa.
47. I Mondi & Inferni. Venice, Farri.

1568

48. I Mondi & Inferni. Venice, Cavalli.

1570

49. The morall philosophie of Doni. London, H. Denham.

1575

50. I Mondi & Inferni. Venice, Farri.
51. Il Valore de gli Asini, and letters, in Lettere Facete, Raccolte per Francesco Turchi. Venice, n. p.

1577

52. La Seconda Libraria. Venice, n. p.

1578

53. Les Mondes Celestes & Infernaux. Lyons, Honorati.

1580

54. La Libraria. Venice, Salicato.
55. Les Mondes Celestes et Infernaux. Lyons, Honorati.
56. Les Mondes Celestes et Infernaux. Lyons, Michel.

1583

57. I Mondi & Inferni. Venice, Moretti.
58. Les Mondes Celestes et Infernaux. Lyons, Honorati.

1588

59. La Filosofia Morale. Trent, Gelmini.

1589

60. Il Cancellieri: Libro della Memoria. Venice, I Gioliti.
61. La Zucca, including Le Pitture. Venice, Polo.

1590

62. La Filosofia Morale. Ferrara, Mammorello.

1591

63. La Zucca, including Le Pitture. Venice, Farri.

1592

64. La Zucca, including Le Pitture. Venice, Farri.

1594

65. La Filosofia Morale. Trent, Sabbio.

1595

66. La Zucca, including Le Pitture. Venice, Matteo Zanetti, & Comino Presegni.

1597

67. La Filosofia Morale. Vicenza, Greco.
68. I Mondi & Inferni. Vicenza, Heredi di Perin.
69. Rime del Burchiello. Vicenza, Heredi di Perin.

1601

70. The morall Philosophie of Doni. London, S. Stafford.
71. Il Valore de gli Asini, and letters, in Lettere Facete, Raccolte per F. Turchi. Venice, Salicato.

1606

72. La Filosofia Morale. Venice, Bertoni.
73. I Mondi & Inferni. Venice, Bertoni.
74. La Sibilla. Recanati, Braida.

1607

75. La Zucca, including Le Pitture. Venice, Bissuccio.
76. La Zucca, including Le Pitture. Venice, Farri.

1609

77. I Marmi. Venice, Bertoni.

1611

78. L'Epistole di Seneca. Milan, Bidelli.
79. La Fortuna di Cesare. Milan, Melchion & Heredi di Tradate.

1634

80. Les visions italiennes. Paris, Villery (French trans. of Inferni).

1637

81. La Fortuna di Cesare. Rome, Totti.
   Doni was not published again until the nineteenth-century collections of his novelle.

A selected bibliography of Doni's works

Lettera di M. Antonfrancesco Doni Fiorentino, con Sonetti d'alcuni Gentil-huomini Piacentini in sua lode. MDXLIII. In fine: Stampata in Piacenza, ad instanzia del S. Barbassoro Principe dell'Academia per Gio. Maria Simoneta Cremonese.

Canto Dialogo della Musica di M. Antonfrancesco Doni Fiorentino. In Vinegia Appresso Girolamo Scotto. MDXLIIII

Lettere d'Antonfrancesco Doni. Con gratia et privilegio. In Vinegia Appresso Girolamo Scotto. MDXXXXIIII.

Lettere di M. Antonfrancesco Doni, Libro Primo. Con alcune altre lettere nouvamente alla fine aggiunte. Con gratia et privilegio. In Vinegia Appresso Girolamo Scotto. MDXXXXV.

Lettere del Doni Libro Primo. Stampato in Fiorenza. MDXLVI. In fine: In Fiorenza per il Doni

Lettere del Doni Libro Secondo. In Fiorenza MDXLVII. In fine: Stampata in Fiorenza Appresso il Doni Adi ix di Settembre MDXLVII.

Disegno del Doni, partito in piu ragionamenti, ne quali si tratta della scoltura et pittura; de colori, de getti, de modegli, con molte cose appartenenti a quest'arti: & si termina la nobiltà dell'una et dell'altra professione. Con historie, essempi, et sentenze. & nel fine alcune lettere che trattano della medesima materia. Con privilegio. In Vinetia Appresso Gabriel Giolito di Ferrarii MDXLIX.

L'Epistole di Seneca. Ridotte nella lingua toscana, per il Doni. All'Ill. S. Silvia di Somma Contessa di Bagno. In Vinegia MDXLIX. In fine: In Vinegia MDXLVIII. Per Aurelio Pincio.

La Libraria del Doni Fiorentino. Nella quale sono scritti tutti gl'Autori vulgari con cento discorsi sopra quelli. Tutte le tradutioni fatte all'altre lingue, nella nostra & una tavola generalmente come si costuma fra Librari. Con privilegio. In Vinegia Appresso Gabriel Giolito de Ferrari. MDL.

La Libraria del Doni Fiorentino. Nella quale sono scritti tutti gl'Autori vulgari con cento discorsi sopra quelli. Tutte le traduttioni fatte dall'altre lingue, nella nostra & una tavola generalmente come si costuma fra Librari. Di novo ristampata, corretta, & molte cose aggiunte che mancavano. Con privilegio. In Vinegia Appresso Gabriel Giolito de Ferrari et Fratelli. MDL.

La Fortuna di Cesare. Tratta da gl'autori latini. All'honorato Signor Giovanbattista Guardi. Con privilegio. In Vinegia Appresso Gabriel Giolito de Ferrari e Fratelli. MDL.

La Prima Parte de le Medaglie del Doni. Con alcune lettere, d'huomini illustri nel fine, et le risposte. In Vinegia Appresso Gabriel Giolito de Ferrari. MDL.

La Seconda Libraria del Doni. Al S. Ferrante Caraffa. In Vinegia MDLI. Con privilegii. In fine: In Venetia per Francesco Marcolini MDLI. Nel Mese di Zugno.

La Zucca del Doni. In fine: Jn Vinegia, per Francesco Marcolini. MDLI.

La Moral' Filosophia del Doni, Tratta da gli antichi scrittori; Allo Illustriss. S. Don Ferrante Caracciolo dedicata. Con Privilegio. Jn Vinegia per Francesco Marcolini MDLII.

Pistolotti Amorosi del Doni, con alcune altre lettere d'amore di diversi autori, ingegni mirabili et nobilissimi. Con privilegio. In Vinegia Appresso Gabriel Giolito de Ferrari e Fratelli MDLII.

Tre libri di Lettere del Doni. E i termini della lingua Toscana. Con privilegio. In fine: Jn Vinegia per Francesco Marcolini MDLII.

I Marmi del Doni, Academico Peregrino. Al Mag.ᶜᵒ et Eccellente S. Antonio da Feltro Dedicati. Con privilegio In Vinegia per Francesco Marcolini MDLII. In fine: In Vinegia per Francesco Marcolini MDLIII.

I Mondi del Doni, Libro Primo. Jn Vinegia Per Francesco Marcolini, Con privilegio MDLII.

Inferni del Doni Academico Pellegrino. Libro Secondo de Mondi. In Vinegia per Francesco Marcolini Nel MDLIII.

L'Asinesca Gloria dell'inasinito Academico Pellegrino. Jn Vinegia nell'Academia Pellegrina per Francesco Marcolini, MDLIII.

Rime del Burchiello Comentate dal Doni. Jn Vinegia per Francesco Marcolini. MDLIII.

Pistolotti Amorosi, De Magnifici Sig^{ri} Academici Pellegrini. Jn Vinegia nell'Academia Pellegrina, per Francesco Marcolini, MDLIIII.

Tre Libri di Pistolotti Amorosi del Doni, per ogni sorte generatione de Brigate: Con alcune altre lettere d'amore di diversi Autori, ingegni mirabili, & nobilissimi intelletti, poste nel fine; con una tavola in somma, quanto il suggetto delle lettere contiene. Con privilegio. In Vinegia Appresso Gabriel Giolito de' Ferrari. MDLVIII.

Il Valore de gli Asini. Dell'Inasinito Academico Pellegrino. In Vinegia, Per Francesco Marcolini, MDLVIII.

Pitture del Doni Academico Pellegrino. Nelle quali si mostra di nuova inventione: Amore, Fortuna, Tempo, Castità, Religione, Sdegno, Riforma, Morte, Sonno & Sogno, Huomo, Republica, & Magnanimità; Divise in due Trattati. Consacrati à gli Illustrissimi Signori, i Sig. Academici Eterei. Libro Primo. In Padova, Appresso Gratioso Perchacino 1564.

La Zucca del Doni Fiorentino. Divisa in Cinque Libri di gran valore, sotto titolo di poca consideratione. Il Ramo, di Chiacchiere, Baie, & Cicalamenti. I Fiori, di Passerotti, Grilli, & Farfalloni. Le Foglie, di Dicerie, Favolè, & Sogni. I Frutti, Acerbi, Marci, & Maturi. & Il Seme; di Chimere, & Castegli in aria. Con privilegio. In Venetia, Appresso Fran. Rampazetto, ad instantia di Gio. Battista, & Marchio Sessa fratelli. In fine: MDLXV.

Le Ville del Doni. Con licentia de i Superiori, In Bologna, Appresso Alessandro Benacci. MDLXVI.

La Filosofia Morale, del Doni, Tratta da molti degni Scrittori Antichi prudenti. Scritta per amaestramento universale de governi, & reggimento particolare de gli huomini; Con modi dotti, & piacevoli, Novelle, Motti, Argutie, & sententie. Con privilegio. In Venetia, Appresso li heredi di Marchiò Sessa. MDLXVII.

Mondi Celesti, Terrestri, et Infernali, de gli Academici Pellegrini. Composti dal Doni; Mondo Piccolo, Grande, Misto, Risibile, Imaginato, de Pazzi, & Massimo, Inferno, de gli Scolari, de Malmaritati, delle Puttane, & Ruffiani, Soldati & Capitani poltroni, Dottor cattivi, Legisti, Artisti, de gli Usurai, de Poeti & Compositori ignoranti. In Vinegia, appresso Domenico Farri. MDLXVII.

Mondi Celesti, Terrestri, et Infernali, de gli Accademici Pellegrini, composti dal Doni; Mondo Piccolo, Grande, Misto, Risibile, Imaginato, de Pazzi, et Massimo. Inferno de gli Scolari, da Malmaritati, delle Puttane, & Ruffiani, Soldati, & Capitani poltroni, Dottor cattivi, Legisti, Artisti, de gli Usurai, de Poeti & Compositori ignoranti. In Venetia, Appresso Domenico Farri. MDLXXV.

Il Valore de gli Asini, and two letters, in: Delle Lettere Facete, et Piacevoli, di Diversi Grandi Huomini, et Chiari Ingegni, Scritte sopra diverse materie, Raccolte per M. Francesco Turchi, Libro Secondo. In Venetia, MDLXXV. Col Privilegio.

Les Mondes, Celestes, Terrestres et Infernaux. Le Monde petit, Grand, Imaginé, Meslé, Risibile, des Sages & Fols, & le Tresgrand, L'enfer des Escoliers, des mal Mariez, des Putains & Ruffians, des Soldats & Capitaines poltrons, des pietres Docteurs, des Usuriers, des Poëtes & Compositeurs ignorans: Tirez des oeuvres de Doni Florentin, par Gabriel Chappuis Tourangeau. Depuis, reueuz, corrigez & augmentez du Monde des Cornuz, par F. C. T. A Lyon, Pour Barthelemy Honorati. 1580. Avec Privilege du Roy.

Mondi Celesti, Terrestri, & Infernali, de gli Academici Pellegrini Composti da M. Anton Francesco Doni Fiorentino, Espurgati con permissione de' Superiori, & da quel che in lor offender poteva il Lettore. E dedicati al Clariss. Signore Giorgio Giorgi. Jn Vicenza, Appresso gli Heredi di Perin Libraro. Con licentia de' Superiori. 1597.

Mondi Celesti, Terrestri, et Infernali, de gli Academici Pellegrini Composti da M. Anton Francesco Doni Fiorentino Espurgati con permissione de' Superiori, & da quel che in lor offender poteva il Lettore. Con licentia de' Superiori, & Privilegio. In Venetia, Appresso Gio. Battista Bertoni, Libraro, al segno del Pellegrino. MDCVI.

La Zucca del Doni Fiorentino, divisa in cinque libri di gran valore, sotto titolo di poca consideratione. Il Ramo, di Chiacchiere, Baie, & Cicalamenti. I Fiori, di Passerotti, Grilli, & Farfalloni. Le foglie di Dicerie, Favole, & Sogni. I Frutti, Acerbi, Marci, & Maturi. & Il Seme di Chimere, & Castegli in aria. Espurgata, corretta, riformata, con permissione de' Superiori. Da Ieronimo Gioannini da Capugnano Bolognese. In Venetia, MDCVII. Appresso Daniel Bissuccio.

Les visions italiennes tirees du sieur de Doni. Premiere Vision. Des Escoliers, & des Pedans. II. Des mal mariez & des Amoureux. III. Des Riches Avares, & des Pauvres liberaux. IV. Des Putains, & des Ruffiens. V. Des Docteurs ignorans. VI. Des Poëtes, & des Autheurs ignorans. VII. Des Soldats & Capitaines Poltrons. Sur l'Imprimé A Paris, Chez Iacques Villery, MDCXXXIV.

Nuova Opinione sopra le Imprese Amorose e Militari di Anton Francesco Doni. Venezia, MDCCCLVIII. Tipi della Gazzetta Uffiziale.

Humori di Messer Anton Francesco Doni Fiorentino 1550 (dall'Autografo Correriano di Venezia) Venezia, Tipografia di G. B. Merlo. MDCCCLX.

Lo Stufaiolo commedia in prosa di Antonfrancesco Doni. Lucca Presso B. Canovetti 1861.

Il Terremoto di M. Anton Francesco Doni contro M. Pietro Aretino Secondo la copia dell'anno M. D. LVI. Lucca Per Bartolomeo Canovetti 1861.

I Marmi di Antonfrancesco Doni ripubblicati per cura di Pietro Fanfani con la vita dell'autore scritta da Salvatore Bongi. Due Volumi. Firenze, G. Barbèra, Editore. 1863.

Dal Canto Quarto della Guerra di Cipro Poemetto di A. F. Doni, in: *Nozze Vianello-Maluta* [Padova—Stab. Prosperini, 1889].

Doni Scritti. Instituto Editoriale Italiano, Milano [1916?].

I Marmi, a cura di Ezio Chiorboli. 2 vols. Bari, Gius. Laterza & Figli, Tipografi-Editori-Librai, 1928.

Le più belle pagine di Anton Francesco Doni scelte da Mario Puccini.

Treves-Treccani-Tumminelli, Edizioni Fratelli Treves-Milano-Roma, 1932.

Scritti scelti di Pietro Aretino e di Anton Francesco Doni a cura di Giuseppe Guido Ferrero. Torino, U.T.E.T., 1951 ("Classici italiani," collez. diretta da Ferdinando Neri, vol. 37).

La Lumiera del Doni, in: Chiappelli, Fredi, "Un poema inedito e sconosciuto di Anton Francesco Doni," *La Rassegna della letteratura italiana,* a. 58, serie VII, n. 4 (ott.-dic. 1954), 561–68.

Dialogo della Musica, a cura di G. Francesco Malipiero. Vienna-Londra-Milano, 1965.

DONI'S "WEAVER'S CONFESSION"

From Doni, *Lettere*, 1547 ed., 50ʳ–52; it is not reprinted in any other edition of his works. Accents have been added and typographical errors corrected.

(50v)   A . M . B A S I L I O   G U E R R I E R I .

Non sono quindici giorni passati, che venne a morte un fedel christiano, il quale benchè fosse idiota, cioè senza lettere mondane sì come quello ch'era tessitor di drappi, & attendeva a governare la bottega, la moglie, e i figliuoli, nondimeno era tanto infiammato dello spirito di Dio, che le cose della Scrittura benissimo intendeva, & sapevane ragionarne meglio di molti, che theologi vogliono esser chiamati: & oltra ciò con sì buono essempio metteva in opera le sue ottime parole, che la sua innocentissima vita era tenuta a uno specchio & essemplare da tutte le persone di sincera mente. Et perchè troppo lungo sarei, se io vi volessi di ciò minutamente ragionare; senza che la cosa è tanto fresca, che tutti i suoi lodevoli costumi sono anchora in memoria d'ognun che lo conobbe, io lascierò di dirvi molte cose, ch'egli operò vivendo tutte degne di lode & d'honore; & solo verrò a quello ch'io gli ho udito favellare nell'estremo di sua vita, due hore inanzi che si morisse: le quali parole ho sì fisse nell'animo, che non sono per uscirsene così tosto. Et gioverammi ridirle a voi, che sete per farne fidissima conserva. Et questa fu la confessione & ragione che fece & rese di sua fede in propria persona di tal tenore.

Io confesso che non è più che un solo Dio, il quale è spirito, che opera & compie tutte le cose in tutte le cose: dal quale si dee sperare & aspettare ogni bene: perciò che esso è omnipotente, buono, sopra tutti pieghevole & pietoso. Miseri dunque coloro che adorano & chiamano in aiuto altro che lui: il che è non haver fede della bontà & benignità d'Iddio.

Io confesso che GIESU CHRISTO è il figliuolo & sembianza del padre; nel quale habita tutta la pienezza della divinità, per lo quale noi conosciamo il padre: il quale CHRISTO è nostro solo mezzano & avocato. Egli non fa dunque mistiero havere altri padroni appresso Iddio, (51) nè di forte correre hor qua hor là per dolcemente favellargli. Ma quantunque tu ti sia solo, & senza avocato, quando tu medesimo preghi in nome di CHRISTO certo tu sei essaudito per suo amore.

250

Io confesso che lo spirito santo è nostro consolatore; per l'aspiration del quale noi facciamo preghiere; & habbiamo conoscimento d'ogni verità: il quale senza noi opera ogni cosa buona in noi. Et è certo che noi non possiamo cosa alcuna senza la gratia dello spirito santo; perciochè la legge richiede lo spirito per adempirla spiritualmente, & noi siamo sottoposti al peccato: là onde noi non possiamo adempire per nostra virtù et libero arbitrio.

Io confesso che ciascuno deve adorare un solo Iddio in spirito & in verità; & non sotto figura o cosa visibile.

Io confesso la Predestinatione & la providenza di Dio, per la quale *ab eterno* sono chiamati & eletti tutti coloro che si salveranno.

Io confesso che la parola di Dio è per sè bastevole a salute, alla quale non fa di misterio aggiungere o scemare alcuna cosa, secondo la quale bisogna parimente reggersi & governarsi, lasciando da parte ogni altro ordinamento humano contrario a quella.

Io confesso una sola chiesa, la quale è la ragunanza di tutti gli eletti per predestination divina; i quali sono stati dal principio del mondo & saranno insino alla fine; della qual chiesa è capo GIESU CHRISTO.

Io confesso che i ministri della chiesa, come i vescovi & i preti, debbono esser tali, che a ragione non possano esser ripresi, così nella vita, come nella dottrina; altrimenti si debbono rimovere da cotali ufficij, & riporne altri migliori ne' luoghi loro.

Io confesso che i Re, i Principi, & i magistrati sono ordinati & fermati per ministri d'Iddio; ai quali si dee ubbidire: perciochè essi portano la spada per difesa de' buoni, & per gastigo de' malvagi.

Io confesso che la fede è dono d'Iddio, per lo quale sentiamo per prova, & habbiamo vera & certa esperienza della bontà & della promessa d'Iddio. Et certo noi siamo salvati per gratia per la fede, & non per nostro operare perciochè questo è dono d'Iddio non dato per opere; acciochè nessuno habbia di potersi laudare.

Io confesso che 'l battesmo dell'acqua è un visibile & esterno segno, il quale secondo la natura de' segni significa & rappresenta quello effetto invisibile, ch'è dentro di noi, cioè rinovamento di spirito & mortificamento del vecchio huomo, cioè delle nostre membra carnali in GIESU CHRISTO: per lo quale modo anchora noi siamo ricevuti nella santa brigata del popolo d'Iddio: venendo a manifestare per tale opra nel conspetto di detta santa brigata la nostra fede, & la nostra volontà di mutamento di vita.

Io confesso che la cena del Signore è una santa memoria & ringratiamen(51ᵛ)to della morte & della passione di GIESU CHRISTO, la quale noi facciamo insieme in fede e in charità; dalla quale si debbono mandar via tutti quegli che sono infedeli.

Io confesso che lo stato matrimoniale è buono, degno di riverenza, santo, & ordinato da Dio; dal quale non bisogna rimovere persona alcuna di qualunque conditione essa si sia; se per aventura non fosse impedito per il predicare la parola di Dio.

Io confesso che ciascuno huomo infin del suo nascimento è peccatore & trappassatore de' comandamenti di Dio in Adam. Et però l'huomo senza lo spirito di Dio, non è altro che carne, vanità, & hippocrisia; sì come colui che non conosce il bene, & non può, & non vuol farlo, & ciò per cagion della sua guasta natura per lo peccato del primo huomo. La qual cosa ottimamente pensata ha forza di molto abbassare, & quasi ridurre a niente il nostro orgoglio, & farne perdere & gettar via la speranza di noi medesimi; & ritrovare & abbracciare quella che ci è dalle scritture comandata della bontà di Dio verso i peccatori per GIESU CHRISTO: senza la quale noi non possiamo non solo fare alcune bene, ma nè pur pensare.

Io confesso liberamente, che i peccati sono perdonati per il mezzo di GIESU CHRISTO, il quale ha sodisfatto alla divina giustitia con la sua morte non meritata per li peccati di tutti gli eletti, non solo di quegli che sono stati inanzi la sua morte, ma anchora di noi altri che la seguitiamo: & alcuno altro non bastava a ciò fare. S'alcuno dunque vuole o cerca altro sodisfacimento che il sangue di CHRISTO sparso nella sua morte, costui gli fa ingiuria, negando l'efficacia & virtù di sua santa passione: & in vero è pur troppo prosontuoso & superbo volendo sodisfare con sue operationi; considerato ch'esso & esse non sono altro che imperfetto.

Io confesso che la vera principale & necessaria confessione è quella per la quale noi confessiamo i nostri peccati davanti da Dio, sperandon da lui solo il perdono.

Io confesso che il digiuno è afflittione & humiliatione del corpo fatta non solo per domare & amazzare la focosità della ribellante carne; ma anchora per più agevolmente potere intendere all'orationi; il ch'è molto necessario ad ogni persona, & sommamente comendato nelle scritture sante.

Io confesso che l'oratione è ragionamento spirituale, santo, infiammato, & affettuoso, che fa l'huomo con Dio per grandezza di fede, & con certa speranza d'essere essaudito; la quale ha maggior ragione dal core, che dalla bocca, senza risguardo di tempo o di loco.

Io confesso che già a Giudei furono vietati certi cibi; ma a Christiani tutto è lasciato libero per GIESU CHRISTO, il quale n'ha liberati da ogni servitù spirituale & temporale. (52)

Io confesso che il sabbato & certi altri giorni, i quali erano dati a festeggiare al popolo Hebreo per certe ombre & figure del riposo & della festa, che s'ha ora l'ultimo giorno in CHRISTO, del quale hora habbiamo l'anima in speranza, per quella libertà, che ci ha col suo sangue acquistata GIESU CHRISTO, ci son diventati tutti eguali et senza differenza alcuna.

Io confesso che la scomunicatione si è un partire & gettar fuori alcuni della brigata del nostro Signor GIESU CHRISTO, la quale non si può fare da altro che dalle chiese secondo i luoghi; & ciò contra i publici et ostinati peccatori.

Detto queste parole & alcune altre molto pie, domando che li fosse letto alcuna parte de' vangeli: perche venendo al evangelio di Giovanni, dove ragiona della passione di Christo. tutto si vedeva struggere & rapire in spirito: tanto che finito quello & alcuni salmi, quietissimamente & quasi che si fosse posto a dormire spirò con grandissima consolatione di noi che v'eravamo presenti. La quale allegrezza ho voluto participare con esso voi, come frutto della nostra novella amicitia: & voi sarete contento comunicarla agli altri fratelli. State sano. Alli xxviij di Novembre. MDXLVI. Di Fiorenza.

LA PAZZIA

The identity of the author of *La Pazzia* eludes scholars. Brunet attributed the work to Ascanio Persio, despite the fact that he was not born until 1554, and Melzi to Vianesio Albergati of Bologna (c. 1490/1500–1532/33). (G. Melzi, *Dizionario di opere anonime e pseudonime* . . . [Milan, 1852], II, 323.) This attribution is doubted by Alberigo, Albergati's recent biographer. Albergati was a prelate and Roman curial official all his life—an unimaginative and competent but dull diplomatic secretary and nuncio who showed no signs of the critical opinions expressed in the book. (G. Alberigo, "Vianesio Albergati," *Dizionario biografico degli italiani* I, 621–24.)

An eighteenth-century bibliographer attributed the work to Lando. (See Bongi, "Catalogo," lxiv.) There are similarities in content between *La Pazzia* and Lando's works—the rejection of learning, criticism of Italian cities, and the dream of the thoughtless life of the pazzo—but Lando's paradox that it was better to be a pazzo than a savio employed different words, arguments, and images. (*Paradossi,* 1545 ed., 20–24.) The only autobiographical reference in *La Pazzia* seems to preclude Lando. The author spoke of studying in Rome in 1527 and losing two brothers and friends in the sack. (*La Pazzia,* 1546 ed., fol. 14ᵛ.) There is no evidence that Lando ever studied in Rome nor that he suffered through the sack of the city.

Despite borrowing from Erasmus' *Praise of Folly* (ff. 1ᵛ–2, 8ᵛ–10, 12ᵛ, 19ᵛ), the work is more than "a bad translation without originality" (Alberigo, "Vianesio Albergati," 623) or a "very mediocre rehash" of the *Praise of Folly*. (Benedetto Croce, "Sulle traduzioni e imitazioni italiane dell' 'Elogio' e dei 'Colloqui' di Erasmo," in *Aneddoti di varia letteratura* [2nd ed., Bari, 1953], I, 414.) The prose is clumsy but the criticism of learning, emphasis on Italian liberty, espousal of the life of the *pazzo,* utopian eulogy, and lack of anticlericalism mark its differences from the *Praise of Folly* and establish it as a typical book of protest of the 1540's.

La Pazzia had at least six Italian and two French editions. I have seen three identical Italian editions:

(1) *La Pazzia.* Stampata in Vinegia per Giovanni Andrea Vavassore detto

Guadagnino, & Florio fratello. Nelli anni del Signore. MDXXXXIII A di XI Zugno;

(2) *La Pazzia* (no place or printer), MDXLVI;

(3) *La Pazzia* (no place or printer), MDLX.

In addition, Bongi cites editions of 1541 (no place or printer); an edition in Venice, Vavassore, 1547; and an edition marked only "In India pastinaca." (Bongi, "Catalogo," lxiv, n. 2.) The British Museum lists an edition without place or printer and attributes it to Venice, 1550. (*Short-Title Catalogue of Books Printed in Italy,* 496.) French translations which I have seen are: *Louanges de la folie, traicté fort plaisant en forme de paradoxe, traduict d'italien en françois, par feu messire Jehan du Thier,* Paris 1566; and *Les Louanges de la folie, Traicté fort plaisant en forme de Paradoxe, traduict d'Italien en François par feu messire Iean du Thier, Chevalier, Conseiller du Roy & Secretaire d'Estat & des Finances du dict Seigneur. A Lyon, Par Benoist Rigaud.* 1567. Avec permission. Brunet, IV, 459, cites a third French edition which I have not seen: *Louanges de la folie. . . .* Poictiers, chez les de Narnef et Bouchets frères, 1566.

Bibliography
&
Index

BIBLIOGRAPHY

Archival

Venice: Archivio di Stato
Giudici di Petizion, Inventari. Buste 337–67 (1580–1659).
Santo Uffizio, Processi. Buste 7–88 (1547–1631).

Manuscripts

Florence: Biblioteca Nazionale Centrale
Fondo Landau Finaly, no. 257, "Discorsi del Doni."
Fondo Nuovi Acquisti, no. 267, "Una nuova opinione del Doni circa all'imprese amorose militari."
Fondo Nuovi Acquisti, no. 268, "Ornamento della lingua toscana del Doni Fiorentino."
Florence: Biblioteca Riccardiana
Ms. 1184, "Lo Stufaiolo commedia in prosa di Antonfrancesco Doni."
New York: Columbia University Library
Ms. "Franco, M. Niccolò. Rime contro Pietro Aretino."
Rome: Biblioteca Apostolica Vaticana
Fondo Patetta, "Le Nuove Pitture del Doni Fiorentino."
Vaticanus Latinus 5642, "Nicolò Franco Lettere."
Venice: Biblioteca Marciana
Mss. Italiani, Class VII, Cod. 2500–2 (12077–79), "Privilegi veneziani per la stampa concessi dal 1527 al 1597, copiati da Horatio Brown."
Mss. Italiani, Classe IX, Cod. CDL (6497), "La Priapea di Niccolò Franco Beneventano."
Mss. Italiani, Classe X, Cod. I (6394), "Istoria delle vite de' poeti italiani di Alessandro Zilioli veneziano."
Mss. Italiani, Classe X, Cod. LXI (6601), "Inventario della libreria di Giovanni Vincenzo Pinelli ereditata da Francesco Pinelli."

Other primary sources

Agostini, Lodovico. *La repubblica immaginaria,* a cura di Luigi Firpo. Turin, 1957.

Agrippa, Heinrich Cornelius. *L'Agrippa Arrigo, Cornelio Agrippa della vanita delle scienze tradotto per M. Lodovico Domenichi.* In Venetia, MDXLVII.

———. *The Vanity of Arts and Sciences.* London, 1676.

Alberti, Leon Battista. *Momus o del principe.* Testo critico, trad., introd. e note a cura di Giuseppe Martini. Bologna, 1942.

Alunno, Francesco. *Le Ricchezze della lingua Volgare . . . di sopra il Boccaccio novamente ristampate. . . .* In Vinegia nell'anno MDLI. In Casa de' Figliuoli di Aldo.

Ammirato, Scipione. *Opuscoli del Sig. Scipione Ammirato. . . .* 3 vols. Florence, 1637–42.

Anonymous. *La Pazzia,* Stampata in Vinegia per Giovanni Andrea Vavassore detto Guadagnino, & Florio fratello. . . . MDXXXXIII A di XI Zugno.

———. *La Pazzia.* n. pl. MDXLVI.

———. *La Pazzia.* n. pl. MDLX.

———. *Louanges de la folie, traicté fort plaisant en forme de paradoxe,* traduict d'Italien en françois, par feu messire Johan du Thier, Paris, 1566.

———. *Les Louanges de la folie, Traicté fort plaisant en forme de Paradoxe,* traduict d'Italien en François par feu messire Jean du Thier, Chevalier Conseiller du Roy & Secretaire d'Estat & des Finances du dict Seigneur. A Lyon, Par Benoist Rigaud. 1567.

Aretino, Pietro. *Lettere di M. Pietro Aretino.* In Parigi, Appresso Matteo il Maestro, 1609.

———. *Lettere,* a cura di Fausto Nicolini. 2 vols. in 3. Bari, 1913–16.

———. *Lettere: il primo e il secondo libro,* a cura di Francesco Flora. Verona, 1960.

———. *Piacevoli e capricciosi ragionamenti,* a cura di Antonio Piccone Stella. 2nd ed. Milan, 1944.

———. *Scritti scelti di Pietro Aretino e di Anton Francesco Doni.* See Appendix III.

———. *The Works of Aretino,* trans. Samuel Putnam. 2 vols. New York, 1933.

———. *See also* Landoni, Teodorico.

Banchieri, Adriano. *La Nobiltà dell'Asino di Attabalippa dal Perù Provincia del Mondo novo,* Tradotta in lingua Italiana. Con Privilegio. In Venetia, Appresso Barezzo Barezzi, MDXCII.

Bandello, Matteo. *Tutte le opere,* a cura di Francesco Flora. Terza edizione. 2 vols. Verona, 1952.

Berni, Francesco. *Poesie e prose,* a cura di Ezio Chiorboli. Florence, 1934.

Betussi, Giuseppe. *Dialogo Amoroso di Messer Giuseppe Betussi.* In Venetia al segno del pozzo, MDXLIII.

———. *Il Raverta, dialogo di messer G. B. nel quale si ragiona d'amore, e degli effetti suoi,* In Venetia, Appresso Gabriel Giolito di Ferrarii, MDXLIIII.

Bruno, Giordano. *The Expulsion of the Triumphant Beast,* trans. Arthur D. Imerti. New Brunswick, N.J., 1964.

———— and Tommaso Campanella. *Opere di Giordano Bruno e di Tommaso Campanella,* a cura di Augusto Guzzo e di Romano Amerio. La letteratura italiana, vol. 33. Milan, Naples, 1956.

Bullinger, Heinrich. *Bullingers Korrespondenz mit den Graubündnern,* herausgegeben von Traugott Schiess. 3 vols. Basel, 1904–6.

Calmo, Andrea. *Le Lettere,* a cura di Vittorio Rossi. Turin, 1888.

————. *Supplimento delle piacevoli, ingeniose, et argutissime lettere.* . . . In Vinegia, appresso Stefano de Alessi, alla Libraria del Cavalletto, in Calle della Bissa, 1552.

Campanella, Tommaso. *La Città del Sole e Poesie,* a cura di Adriano Seroni. Milan, 1962.

————. *See also* Bruno, Giordano.

Caracciolo, Tristano. *De varietate fortunae.* Rerum Italicarum Scriptores, N. S., tomo XXII, parte I. Bologna, 1934–35.

Castiglione, Baldesar. *The Book of the Courtier,* trans. Charles S. Singleton. Garden City, N.Y., 1959.

Contile, Luca. *Il primo [secondo] volume delle lettere di Luca Contile Diviso in due Libri.* . . . In Venetia, MDLXIIII.

Della Casa, Giovanni. *A Renaissance Courtesy-Book, Galateo of Manners and Behaviours by Giovanni della Casa,* introd. J. E. Spingarn. Boston, 1914.

Del Tempio alla divina signora Donna Giovanna d'Aragona, fabricato da tutti i più gentili Spiriti, & in tutte le lingue principali del mondo. . . . In Venetia, per Plinio Pietrasanta, MDLV.

Dolce, Lodovico. *Dialogo della Pittura . . . intitolato l'Aretino.* . . . In Vinegia appresso Gabriel Giolito de' Ferrari. MDLVII.

————. *Dialogo . . . nel quale si ragiona delle qualità, diversità, e proprietà de i colori.* . . . In Venetia Appresso Gio. Battista, Marchio Sessa, et Fratelli. [1565].

————. *Giornale delle historie del mondo.* . . . Riveduto, corretto, & ampliato da Guglielmo Rinaldi. . . . In Venetia, Al Segno della Salamandra. 1572.

————. *Tragedie . . . cioè, Giocasta, Didone, Thieste, Medea, Ifigenia, Hecuba.* . . . In Vinegia appresso Gabriel Giolito de' Ferrari. MDLX.

————. *Le transformationi.* . . . In Venetia Appresso Gabriel Giolito de' Ferrari e Fratelli. MDLIII.

————. *Vita dell'invittiss. e gloriosiss. imperador Carlo Quinto.* . . . In Vinegia Appresso Gabriel Giolito de' Ferrari, MDLXI.

————. *Vita di Ferdinando primo Imperadore di questo nome . . .* In Vinegia appresso Gabriel Giolito de' Ferrari. MDLXVI.

Domenichi, Lodovico. *Dialoghi di M. L. D.; cioè, D'Amore, Della vera Nobiltà, de' Rimedi d'Amore.* . . . In Vinegia, appresso Gabriel Giolito de' Ferrari, MDLXII.

————. *Facetie, Motti, et Burle di diversi signori & persone private,* raccolta per M. Lodovico Domenichi . . . con una nuova aggiunta di Motti:

raccolti da Thomaso Porcacchi. . . . In Vinetia, Presso Giorgio de' Cavalli, MDLXV.

——. *Facezie,* a cura di Giovanni Fabris. Rome, 1923.

——. *Historia Varia . . . nella quale si contengono molte cose argute, nobili, e degne di memoria.* . . . In Vinegia Appresso Gabriel Giolito de' Ferrari. MDLXIIII.

——. *La nobiltà delle Donne di M. Lodovico Domenichi.* In Vinetia Appresso Gabriel Giolito di Ferrarii. MDXLIX.

[Dunton, John]. *The Athenian Gazette: or Casuistical Mercury, Resolving all the most Nice and Curious Questions proposed by the ingenious.* . . . Vols. 1, 2. London, 1691, 1693.

[Dunton, John]. *The Athenian Oracle.* . . . 3 vols. & supplement. London, 1706, 1708, 1710, 1716.

Erasmus, Desiderius. *Desiderii Erasmi Roterodami Opera Omnia.* . . . 10 vols. in 11. Leiden, 1703–6.

——. *Opus epistolarum Des. Erasmi Roterodami,* ed. P. S. Allen, H. M. Allen, and H. M. Garrod. 12 vols. Oxford, 1906–58.

Florio, John. *First Fruits.* Facsimile reprod., ed. Arundell del Re. Memoires of the Faculty of Literature and Politics, Taihoku Imperial University, vol. 3, no. 1. Taihoku, Formosa, 1936.

Folengo, Teofilo ("Cocai, Merlin"). *Il Baldo.* Testo maccheronico con trad. italiana di Giuseppe Tonna. 2 vols. Milan, 1958.

——. *Opere italiane,* a cura di Umberto Renda. 3 vols. Bari, 1911–14.

Garimberto, Girolamo. *De regimenti publici de la città.* . . . In Vinegia. Appresso Girolamo Scotto, MDXLIIII.

Garzoni, Tommaso. *L'Hospidale de' Pazzi incurabili Nuovamente formato.* . . . In Venetia, Appresso Gio. Battista Somascho. MDLXXXVI.

——. *The Hospitall of incurable fooles.* London, 1600.

——. *La Piazza Universale di tutte le professioni del mondo.* . . . In Venetia, Appresso Gio. Battista Somascho, 1585.

——. *La Piazza Universale di tutte le professioni del mondo.* . . . In Venetia, Appresso Gio. Battista Somasco, 1587.

——. *La Sinagoga de gl'Ignoranti.* Nuovamente formata. . . . In Venetia, Appresso Gio. Battista Somasco. MDLXXXIX.

——. *Il Theatro de' vari, e diversi cervelli mondani.* . . . In Venetia, Appresso Fabio, & Agostin Zoppini, fratelli, 1585.

——. *Il Teatro de vari, e diversi cervelli mondani.* . . . In Venetia, Appresso Giacomo Antonio Somascho. 1595.

——. *Il Theatro de vari, e diversi cervelli mondani.* . . . In Venetia, Appresso gli Zoppini. 1598.

Gelli, Giambattista. *La Circe e I Capricci del Bottaio,* ed. Severino Ferrari, new ed. G. G. Ferrero. Florence, 1957.

Gilio, Giovanni Andrea. *Due Dialogi di M. Giovanni Andrea Gilio da Fabriano . . . Con un discorso sopra la parola Urbe, Città.* . . . In Camerino per Antonio Gioioso. MDLXIIII.

Giovio, Paolo. *Le Vite del Gran Capitano e del Marchese di Pescara,* volgarizzate da Ludovico Domenichi, a cura di Costantino Panigada. Bari, 1931.

Guevara, Antonio de. *Comiença el primero libro del famosissimo emperador Marco Aurelio con el Relox de principes nuevamente annadido: compuesto por el muy reverendo y magnifico señor don Antonio de Guevara* . . . Barcelona, 1532.

———. *Institutione del prencipe christiano, di Mambrino Roseo.* In Roma nella Contrada del Pellegrino per Madonna Girolama Moglie che fu del sig. Baldassare de Cartolari. MDXLIII.

———. *Institutione del prencipe christiano,* tradotto di Spagnuolo in lingua Toscana per Mambriano Roseo da Fabriano. . . . In Venetia per Bernardin De Bindoni Mediolanensis Anno Domini, MDXLV.

Guicciardini, Francesco. *History of Italy,* trans. Cecil Grayson. New York, 1964.

———. *Storia d'Italia,* a cura di Costantino Panigada. 5 vols. Bari, 1929.

Lancellotti, Secondo. *Hoggidì overo gl'ingegni non inferiori a' passati . . . Parte Seconda.* . . . In Venetia, MDCLXXXI, Per Gio: Francesco Valvasense.

———. *L'hoggidì overo il mondo non peggiore ne più calamitoso del passato.* . . . In Venetia Appresso Gio. Guerigli, MDCXXIII.

Landi, Giulio. *La Vita di Cleopatra Reina d'Egitto . . . Con una oratione nel fine recitata nell'Academia dell'Ignoranti; in lode dell'Ignoranza.* . . . In Vinegia. MDLI.

Landoni, Teodorico, ed. *Lettere scritte a Pietro Aretino.* 2 vols. Bologna, 1873–75.

Lauro, Pietro. *De le lettere di M. Pietro Lauro Modonese. Il primo libro.* . . . In Venetia, Nel MDLII.

Marino, Giovanni Battista. *La Galeria del Cavalier Marino Distinta in pitture & Sculture.* [Ancona: Francesco Manolesso, 1520.]

———. *La Galeria.* . . . In Venetia, MDCLXVII. Presso Gio: Pietro Brigonci.

Mattioli, Pietro Andrea. *De i discorsi . . . Nelli sei Libri di Pedacio Dioscoride Anazarbeo, della materia medicinale.* . . . MDLXXXV. In Venetia, Appresso Felice Valgrisio.

Mexía, Pedro. *Dialoghi di Pietro Messia tradotti nuovamente di Spagnuolo in Volgare da Alfonso d'Ulloa.* . . . In Venetia, per Plinio Pietrasanta. MDLVII.

———. *De la Selva di varia lettione.* In Venetia per Michele Tramezzino, Nel MDL.

Montaigne, Michel de. *The Essays of Montaigne,* trans. E. J. Trechmann, introd. J. M. Robertson. 2 vols. London, 1927.

More, St. Thomas. *Utopia,* ed. Edward Surtz. Yale Edition of the Works of St. Thomas More. New Haven and London, 1964.

Muzio, Girolamo. *Avvertimenti Morali Del Mutio Iustinopolitano.* . . . In Venetia, appresso Gio. Andrea Valvassori, detto Guadagnino. MDLXXII.

———. *Lettere del Mutio Iustinopolitano.* . . . In Vinegia Appresso Gabriel Giolito de Ferrari e Fratelli. MDLI.

Nannini, Remigio. *Considerationi civili sopra l'historie di M. Francesco Guic-*

ciardini, e d'altri Historici. . . . In Venetia, Appresso Damiano Zenaro. MDLXXXII.

——. *Civill Considerations upon many and sundrie Histories.* . . . At London . . . 1601.

Palmieri, Matteo. *Della Vita Civile. De Optimo Cive di Bartolomeo Sacchi detto il Platina,* a cura di Felice Battaglia. Scrittori politici italiani, 14. Bologna, 1944.

Parabosco, Girolamo. *Lettere Amorose.* . . . Vinegia, Appresso Gabriel Giolito. MDXLV.

Piccolomini, Alessandro. *De la institutione di tutta la vita de l'huomo nato nobile e in citta libera.* . . . Venetiis apud Hieronymon Scotum, 1542.

Pico della Mirandola, Gianfrancesco. *Examen vanitatis doctrinae gentium et veritatis Christianae disciplinae.* . . . Impressit Mirandulae Ioannes Maciochus, 1520.

Rao, Cesare. *L'argute, et facete lettere di M. Cesare Rao di Alessano Città della Leucadia.* . . . In Venetia, Appresso Giovanni Alberti, MDCXXII.

——. *Invettive, orationi, et discorsi di Cesare Rao di Alessano, Città di Terra d'Otranto.* . . . In Vinegia, Appresso Damiano Zenaro, MDLXXXVII.

Sansovino, Francesco. *L'avvocato e il segretario,* a cura di Piero Calamandrei. Florence, 1942.

——. *Le cose notabili, Et maravigliose della citta di Venetia.* Riformate . . . da Leonico Goldioni. . . . In Venetia, MDCXLIX. Appresso Gio: Giacomo Herz.

——. *Cronologia del mondo.* . . . In Venetia. Nella Stamperia della Luna. MDLXXX.

——. *Del governo de i regni et delle repubbliche.* . . . In Venetia, Appresso Francesco Sansovino. MDLXI.

——. *L'historia di Casa Orsina.* . . . In Venetia, Appresso Bernardino, & Filippo Stagnini, fratelli. MDLXV.

——. *Delle orationi volgarmente scritte da diversi huomini illustri de tempi nostri, Libro Primo* . . . Raccolte . . . Francesco Sansovino. . . . In Vinegia, Presso Altobello Salicato, 1584. Alla Libraria della Fortezza.

——. *Della origine, et de' fatti delle famiglie illustri d'Italia.* . . . In Vinegia, Presso Altobello Salicato. MDLXXXII.

——. *Il simolacro di Carlo Quinto Imperadore.* . . . In Venetia, Appresso Francesco Franceschini, MDLXVII.

——. *Sopplimento delle croniche universali del Mondo di F. Iacopo Filippo da Bergamo.* . . . In Venetia, MDLXXV.

——. *Venetia città nobilissima et singolare, Descritta in XIII libri.* . . . In Venetia, Appresso Iacomo Sansovino. MDLXXXI.

Seneca, Lucius Annaeus. *Ad Lucilium Epistulae Morales.* Loeb Classical Library. 3 vols. Cambridge, Mass., 1961–62.

Speroni, Sperone. *Opere.* 5 vols. Venice, 1740.

Suetonius. *The Twelve Caesars,* trans. Robert Graves. Baltimore, 1957.

Tomitano, Bernardino. *Quattro libri della lingua Thoscana.* . . . In Padova. Appresso Marcantonio Olmo. MDLXX.

Turchi, Francesco, ed. *Delle lettere facete, et piacevoli, di diversi grandi huomini, et chiari ingegni. . . .* Raccolte per M. Francesco Turchi, Libro Secondo. In Venetia, MDLXXV.

Utopisti e riformatori sociali del Cinquecento: A. F. Doni—U. Foglietta—F. Patrizi da Cherso—L. Agostini. Ed. Carlo Curcio. Scrittori politici italiani, 19. Bologna, 1941.

Valeriano, Pierio. *La infelicità dei letterati di Pierio Valeriano ed Appendice di Cornelio Tollio.* Traduzione dal Latino. Milan, 1829.

Varchi, Benedetto. *Lezioni sul Dante e prose varie di Benedetto Varchi la maggior parte inedite,* a cura di Giuseppe Aiazzi e Lelio Arbib. 2 vols. Florence, 1841.

Watt, Joachim von. *Die Vadianische Briefsammlung der Stadtbibliothek St. Gallen,* herausgegeben von Emil Arbenz und Hermann Wartmann. (Mitteilungen zur Vaterländischen Geschichte, Herausgegeben vom Historischen Verein in St. Gallen, XXV–XXXa.) 7 vols. St. Gall, 1894–1913.

Secondary sources

Albertini, Rudolf von. *Das Florentinische Staatsbewusstsein im Übergang von der Republik zum Prinzipat.* Bern, 1955.

Ascarelli, Fernanda. *La tipografia cinquecentina italiana.* Florence, 1953.

Badaloni, Nicola. "Natura e società in Nicolò Franco," *Società,* XVI (1960), 735–77.

Barberi Squarotti, Giorgio. "L'esperienza stilistica del Bruno fra Rinascimento e Barocco," in *La critica stilistica e il barocco letterario,* Atti del secondo congresso internazionale di studi italiani, Venezia, 26 settembre–30 settembre 1956 (Florence, 1958), 154–69.

Baron, Hans. *The Crisis of the Early Italian Renaissance: Civic Humanism and Republican Liberty in an Age of Classicism and Tyranny.* 2 vols. Princeton, N. J., 1955 (Revised ed. 1966).

———. "Franciscan Poverty and Civic Wealth as Factors in the Rise of Humanistic Thought," *Speculum,* XIII (1938), 1–37.

———. "Secularization of Wisdom and Political Humanism in the Renaissance," *Journal of the History of Ideas,* XXI, no. 1 (1960), 131–50.

Battisti, Eugenio. *L'antirinascimento.* Milan, 1962.

Baudrier, H. L., and Baudrier, J. *Bibliographie Lyonnaise: Recherches sur les imprimeurs, libraires, relieurs et fondeurs de lettres de Lyon au XVI* siècle.* 12 vols. Lyons, Paris, 1895–1921.

Bellorini, Maria Grazia, "Thomas North traduttore di Anton Francesco Doni," *Aevum,* XXXVIII (1964), 84–103.

Benetti Brunelli, Valeria. *Il rinnovamento della politica nel pensiero del secolo xv in Italia.* Turin, Milan, 1927.

Berengo, Marino. *Nobili e mercanti nella Lucca del Cinquecento.* Turin, 1965.

Bersano Begey, Marina. *Le Cinquecentine Piemontesi: Torino.* Turin, 1961.

Berthé de Besaucèle, L. *J. B. Giraldi, 1504–1573. Etude sur l'Evolution des*

Théories Littéraires en Italie au XVI° siècle, Suivie d'une Notice sur G. Chappuys, Traducteur français de Giraldi. Paris, 1920.

Bongi, Salvatore. *Annali di Gabriel Giolito de' Ferrari da Trino di Monferrato, stampatore in Venezia.* 2 vols. Rome, 1890–97.

Born, Lester K. "Erasmus on Political Ethics: The 'Institutio Principis Christiani,'" *Political Science Quarterly,* 43 (1928), 520–43.

Brown, Horatio. *The Venetian Printing Press.* London, 1891.

Brunet, Jacques C. *Manuel du libraire et de l'amateur de livres.* . . . 6 vols. Paris, 1860–65.

Bullock, Walter L. "The 'Lost' *Miscellaneae Quaestiones* of Ortensio Lando," *Italian Studies,* II (1938), 49–64.

Burney, Charles. *A General History of Music from the Earliest Ages to the Present Period.* Vol. 3. London, 1789.

Campana, Augusto. "The Origin of the Word Humanist," *Journal of the Warburg and Courtauld Institutes,* 9 (1946), 60–73.

Cantagalli, Roberto. *La guerra di Siena (1552–1559).* Siena, 1962.

Cantimori, Delio. *Eretici italiani del Cinquecento: ricerche storiche.* Florence, 1967 (reprint of 1939 ed.).

———. "Nicodemismo e speranze conciliari nel Cinquecento italiano," in *Contributi alla Storia del Concilio di Trento e della Controriforma,* Quaderni di *Belfagor,* I (Florence, 1948), 12–23.

———. "Note su Erasmo e la vita morale e religiosa italiana nel secolo XVI," in Saitta, Armando, ed., *Antologia di critica storica,* II, *Problemi della civiltà moderna* (2nd ed., Bari, 1958), 473–93.

———. *Prospettive di storia ereticale italiana del Cinquecento.* Bari, 1960.

———. "La riforma in Italia," in E. Rota, ed., *Problemi storici e orientamenti storiografici* (Como, 1942), 557–84.

Cantù, Cesare. *Les hérétiques d'Italie,* French trans. Anicet Digard and Edmond Martin. 5 vols. Paris, 1869–70.

———. *La letteratura esposta alla gioventù per via d'esempj.* Milan, 1851.

Carcereri, L. "Cristoforo Dossena, Francesco Linguardo e un Giordano, librai processati per eresia a Bologna (1548)," *L'Archiginnasio,* V, no. 5 (1910), 177–92.

Casali, Scipione. *Annali della tipografia veneziana di Francesco Marcolini da Forlì.* Forlì, 1861.

Catalano, Franco. "La crisi italiana alla fine del secolo xv," *Belfagor,* XI (1956), 393–414, 505–27.

———. "Il problema dell'equilibrio e la crisi della libertà italiana," in *Nuove questioni di storia medioevale,* Vol. I (Milan, 1964), 357–98.

Cecchi, Emilio, and Sapegno, Natalino, eds. *Storia della letteratura italiana.* Vol. 4, *Il Cinquecento.* Milan: Garzanti, 1966.

Ceretta, Florindo. *Alessandro Piccolomini: letterato e filosofo senese del Cinquecento.* Siena, 1960.

Chabod, Federico. *Per la storia religiosa dello stato di Milano durante il dominio di Carlo V.* Note e documenti. Seconda edizione a cura di Ernesto Sestan. Rome, 1962.

Chiappelli, Fredi. "Sull'espressività della lingua nei 'Marmi' del Doni," *Lingua nostra*, VII, fasc. 2 (1946), 33–38.

Christie, Richard Copley. *Etienne Dolet, the Martyr of the Renaissance*. London, 1880.

Chubb, Thomas Caldecot. *Aretino, Scourge of Princes*. New York, 1940.

Church, Frederic C. *The Italian Reformers, 1534–1564*. New York, 1932.

Cicogna, Emmanuele A. *Delle iscrizioni veneziane*. 6 vols. Venice, 1824–53.

———. "Memoria intorno la vita e gli scritti di Messer Lodovico Dolce letterato veneziano del secolo xvi," *Memorie dell'I. R. Istituto Veneto di scienze, lettere e arti*, X (1862), 93–200.

Cocchiara, Giuseppe. *Popolo e letteratura in Italia*. Turin, 1959.

Cochrane, Eric. "The End of the Renaissance in Florence," *Bibliothèque d'Humanisme et Renaissance*, XXVII (1965), 7–29.

Colie, Rosalie L. *Paradoxia Epidemica: The Renaissance Tradition of Paradox*. Princeton, N.J., 1966.

Crasso, Lorenzo. *Elogii d'huomini letterati scritti da Lorenzo Crasso*. 2 vols. Venezia, 1666.

Croce, Benedetto. *Aneddoti di varia letteratura*. 2nd ed. 4 vols. Bari, 1953–54.

———. *Poeti e scrittori del pieno e del tardo Rinascimento*. 3 vols. Bari, 1945–52.

———. *La Spagna nella vita italiana durante la rinascenza*. Bari, 1917.

———. *Storia del Regno di Napoli*. Bari, 1925.

Curcio, Carlo. *La politica italiana del '400: contributo alla storia delle origini del pensiero borghese*. Florence, 1932.

———. *Dal Rinascimento alla Controriforma: contributo alla storia del pensiero politico italiano da Guicciardini a Botero*. Rome, 1934.

De Caprariis, Vittorio. "Qualche precisazione sulla morte di Erasmo," *Rivista Storica Italiana*, XLIII (1951), 100–8.

De Gaetano, Armand L. "G. B. Gelli and the Rebellion Against Latin," *Studies in the Renaissance*, XIV (1967), 131–58.

———. "Giambattista Gelli: A Moralist of the Renaissance." Unpubl. Ph. D. diss., Columbia University, 1954.

———. "Tre lettere inedite di G. B. Gelli e la purgazione de I capricci del bottaio," *GSLI*, CXXXIV (1957), 297–313.

De Michele, Giuseppe. "La 'Filena' di N. Franco," *Rassegna critica della letteratura italiana*, 30 (1925), 8–28.

———. "Nicolò Franco. Biografia con documenti inediti," in *Studi di letteratura italiana*, diretta da Erasmo Percopo, XI (Rome, 1915), 61–154.

De Sanctis, Francesco. *History of Italian Literature*, trans. Joan Redfern, introd. Benedetto Croce. 2 vols. New York, 1931.

Del Vita, Alessandro. *L'Aretino: "Uomo libero per grazia di Dio."* Arezzo, 1953.

Di Tocco, Vittorio. *Ideali d'indipendenza in Italia durante la preponderanza Spagnuola*. Messina, 1926.

Dictionnaire historique & biographique de la Suisse. 7 vols. Neuchâtel, 1920–33.

Dionisotti, Carlo. "La letteratura italiana nell'età del Concilio," in *Il Concilio di Trento e la Riforma Tridentina,* Atti del Convegno Storico internazionale, Trento 2–6 settembre 1963 (2 vols, Rome, Freiburg, 1965), I, 315–43.

Dizionario biografico degli Italiani. Rome, 1960—.

Drei, Giovanni. *I Farnese. Grandezza e decadenza di una dinastia italiana,* a cura di G. A. Tassoni, pref. Roberto Andreotti. Rome, 1954.

Einstein, Alfred. "Il 'Dialogo della musica' di Messer Anton Francesco Doni," *La Rassegna Musicale,* VII, no. 6 (nov.-dic. 1934), 405–14.

Ercole, Francesco. *Da Carlo VIII a Carlo V: La crisi della libertà italiana.* Florence, 1932.

Fahy, Conor. "Per la vita di Ortensio Lando," *GSLI,* 142 (1965), 243–58.

————. "Press and Pen Corrections in a 1534 edition by Sebastianus Gryphius," *Bibliothèque d'Humanisme et Renaissance,* XXVIII (1966), 406–9.

————. "Un trattato di Vincenzo Maggi sulle donne e un' opera sconosciuta di Ortensio Lando," *GSLI,* 138 (1961), 254–72.

Febvre, Lucien, and Martin, H. J. *L'apparition du livre.* Paris, 1958.

Ferrari, Luigi. *Onomasticon. Repertorio bio-bibliografico degli scrittori italiani dal 1501 al 1850.* Milan, 1947.

Ferrero, Giuseppe Guido. "Politica e vita morale del '500 nelle Lettere di Paolo Giovio," *Memorie della R. Accademia delle Scienze di Torino,* serie II, 70–71 (1940), parte seconda, 57–102.

Firpo, Luigi. "Appunti campanelliani," *Giornale critico della filosofia italiana,* 21 (1940), 431–51.

————. "La città ideale del Filarete," in *Studi in memoria di Gioele Solari* (Turin, 1954), 11–59.

————. "Tommaso Moro e la sua fortuna in Italia," *Occidente, rivista di studi politici,* VIII, nos. 3–4 (1952), 225–41.

————. *Ricerche campanelliane.* Florence, 1947.

————. *Lo stato ideale della Controriforma. Ludovico Agostini.* Bari, 1957.

————. "L'Utopia politica nella Controriforma," in *Contributi alla Storia del Concilio di Trento e della Controriforma,* Quaderni di *Belfagor,* I (Florence, 1948), 78–108.

Flamini, Francesco. *Il Cinquecento.* Milan, 1901.

Flora, Francesco. *Storia della letteratura italiana.* 5 vols. Verona, 1952.

Fontanini, Giusto. *Biblioteca dell'eloquenza italiana . . . con le annotazioni del Signor Apostolo Zeno. . . .* 2 vols. Venice, 1753.

Friedlaender, Walter. *Mannerism and Anti-Mannerism in Italian Painting.* New York, 1957.

Gagliardo, D. "Il ciceronismo nel Cinquecento e Ortensio Lando," *Le parole e le idee,* III, nos. 1–2 (1961), 15–21.

Garin, Eugenio. *La cultura filosofica del Rinascimento. Ricerche e documenti.* Florence, 1961.

————. *L'educazione in Europa (1400–1600). Problemi e programmi.* Bari, 1957.

————, ed. *L'educazione umanistica in Italia.* 3rd ed. Bari, 1959.

——. *Italian Humanism: Philosophy and Civic Life in the Renaissance,* trans. Peter Munz. Oxford, 1965.

——. *Medioevo e Rinascimento, studi e ricerche.* Bari, 1954.

——. *L'umanesimo italiano: filosofia e vita civile nel Rinascimento.* Bari. 1952.

Gesner, Conrad. *Bibliotheca [universalis] instituta et collecta primum a Conrado Gesnero . . . Josephum Simlerum . . . Joannem Jacobum Frisium.* Zurich, 1583.

Getto, Giovanni. *Storia delle storie letterarie.* Milan, 1942.

Ghilini, Girolamo. *Teatro d'huomini letterati aperto dall'abate G. G., accademico incognito.* In Venetia, Per li Guerigli, MDCXLVII.

Gibson, R. W. *St. Thomas More: a Preliminary Bibliography of His Works and of Moreana to the year 1750. . . .* With a Bibliography of Utopiana compiled by R. W. Gibson and J. Max Patrick. New Haven, 1961.

Gilbert, Allan H. *Machiavelli's Prince and Its Forerunners. The Prince as a Typical Book de Regimine Principum.* Durham, N.C., 1938.

Gilbert, Felix. *Machiavelli and Guicciardini: Politics and History in Sixteenth-Century Florence.* Princeton, N.J., 1965.

Grendler, Paul. "Five Italian Occurrences of *Umanista,* 1540–1574," *Renaissance Quarterly,* XX (1967), 317–25.

——. "Francesco Sansovino and Italian Popular History," *Studies in the Renaissance,* XVI (1969). To be published.

——. "The Rejection of Learning in Mid-*Cinquecento* Italy," *Studies in the Renaissance,* XIII (1966), 230–49.

——. "Religious Restlessness in Sixteenth-Century Italy," *Study Sessions 1966.* Canadian Catholic Historical Association, vol. 33 (Ottawa, 1966), 25–38.

——. "Utopia in Renaissance Italy: Doni's 'New World,' " *Journal of the History of Ideas,* XXVI, (1965), 479–94.

Griffith, T. Gwynfor. *Bandello's Fiction: An Examination of the Novelle.* Oxford, 1955.

Haar, James. "Notes on the *Dialogo della Musica* of Antonfrancesco Doni," *Music & Letters,* 47 (1966), 198–224.

Hale, J. R., Highfield, J. R. L., Smalley, B., eds. *Europe in the Late Middle Ages.* London, 1965.

Hall, Robert A. *The Italian Questione della lingua. An interpretative essay.* Studies in the Romance Languages and Literatures, no. 4. Chapel Hill, N.C., 1942.

Hauser, Arnold. *Mannerism: The Crisis of the Renaissance and the Origin of Modern Art.* 2 vols. London, 1965.

Haydn, Hiram. *The Counter-Renaissance.* New York, 1950.

Haym, Nicola F. *Biblioteca italiana; o sia, notizia de' libri rari italiani.* 2 vols. in 1. Milan, 1771–73.

Hexter, J. H. *More's Utopia: The Biography of an Idea.* Princeton, N.J., 1952.

Hoogewerff, Goffredo. "L'editore del Vasari: Lorenzo Torrentino," in *Studi vasariani,* Atti del convegno internazionale per il IV centenario della prima edizione delle "Vite" del Vasari, Firenze 16–19 sett. 1950 (Florence, 1952), 93–104.

Huizinga, Johan. *Erasmus and the Age of Reformation,* trans. F. Hopman. New York, 1957.

Jannaco, Carmine, con la collaborazione di Capucci, Martino. *Il Seicento.* Milan, 1963.

Jedin, Hubert. *A History of the Council of Trent,* trans. Dom Ernest Graf O.S.B. 2 vols. London, 1957–61.

———. *Papal Legate at the Council of Trent: Cardinal Seripando,* trans. F. C. Eckhoff. St. Louis, London, 1947.

Jung, Eva-Maria. "On the Nature of Evangelism in 16th-Century Italy," *Journal of the History of Ideas,* XIV (1953), 511–27.

Kristeller, Paul O. *Iter Italicum: A Finding List of Uncatalogued or Incompletely Catalogued Humanistic Manuscripts of the Renaissance in Italian and Other Libraries.* 2 vols. London, Leiden, 1965–67.

———. *Renaissance Thought: The Classic, Scholastic, and Humanistic Strains.* New York, 1961.

La Cute, Pietro. *Ortensio Lando e Napoli nella prima metà del '500.* Lucera, 1925.

Lievsay, John L. *Stefano Guazzo and the English Renaissance, 1575–1675.* Chapel Hill, N.C., 1961.

Lovejoy, Arthur O., and Boas, George. *Primitivism and Related Ideas in Antiquity.* Baltimore, 1935.

Luzio, Alessandro. "L'Aretino e il Franco, appunti e documenti," *GSLI,* 29 (1897), 229–83.

Malipiero, Gianfrancesco. *Antonfrancesco Doni musico.* Venice, 1946.

Mancini, Augusto. *Storia di Lucca.* Florence, 1950.

Marini, Lino. *La Spagna in Italia nell'età di Carlo V.* Bologna, 1961.

Martines, Lauro. *The Social World of the Florentine Humanists, 1390–1460.* Princeton, N.J., 1963.

Maylender, Michele. *Storia delle accademie d'Italia.* 5 vols. Bologna, 1926–30.

McConica, James K. *English Humanists and Reformation Politics under Henry VIII and Edward VI.* Oxford, 1965.

McNair, Philip. *Peter Martyr in Italy. An Anatomy of Apostasy.* Oxford, 1967.

Melzi, Gaetano. *Dizionario di opere anonime e pseudonime di scrittori italiani, o come che sia aventi relazione all'Italia.* 3 vols. Milan, 1848–59.

Mercati, Angelo. *I costituti di Niccolò Franco (1568–1570) dinanzi l'Inquisizione di Roma esistenti nell'Archivio Segreto Vaticano.* Studi e Testi, 178. Vatican City, 1955.

Müller, Max. *Johann Albrecht v. Widmanstetter, 1506–1557: Sein Leben und Wirken.* Bamberg, 1908.

Näf, Werner, *Vadian und seine Stadt St. Gallen.* 2 vols. St. Gall, 1944–57.

Nauert, Charles G. Jr. *Agrippa and the Crisis of Renaissance Thought.* Urbana, Ill., 1965.

Negri, Giulio. *Istoria degli scrittori fiorentini la quale abbraccia intorno à due mila Autori. . . .* Ferrara, 1722.

Nelson, John Charles. *Renaissance Theory of Love. The Context of Giordano Bruno's Eroici Furori.* New York, 1958.

The New Cambridge Modern History. Vol. II, *The Reformation 1520–1559.* Cambridge, 1958.

Nissim, Lea. *Gli "scapigliati" nella letteratura italiana del Cinquecento.* Prato, 1922.

Parrella, P. P. "Le 'Pistole Vulgari' di Nicolò Franco e il I libro delle 'Lettere' dell'Aretino," *Rassegna critica della letteratura italiana,* V (1900), 97–122.

Paschini, Pio. *Venezia e l'inquisizione romana da Giulio III a Pio IV.* Padua, 1959.

Pepe, Mario. "Di alcune lettere di Anton Francesco Doni e di una sua opera perduta," *Accademie e biblioteche d'Italia,* XXXIV (1966), 136–40.

Pesenti, Giuliano. "Libri censurati a Venezia nei secoli XVI–XVII," *La Bibliofilia,* XVIII (1956), 15–30.

Petrocchi, Giorgio. *Pietro Aretino tra Rinascimento e Controriforma.* Milan, 1948.

Poccianti, Michele. *Catalogus scriptorum florentinorum omnis generis.* . . . Florentiae, apud Phillippum Iunctam, MDLXXXIX.

Poggiali, Cristoforo. *Memorie per la storia letteraria di Piacenza.* 2 vols. in 1. Piacenza, 1789.

Pompeati, Arturo. *Storia della letteratura italiana.* 4 vols. Turin, 1958.

Primo catalogo collettivo delle biblioteche italiane. Rome, 1962—.

Pusinich, Guido. "Un poligrafo veneziano del Cinquecento," *Pagine istriane,* VIII (1910), 121–30, 145–51.

Rees, D. G. "John Florio and Anton Francesco Doni," *Comparative Literature,* XV (1963), 33–38.

Renouard, Ant. Aug. *Annales de l'Imprimerie des Estienne ou Histoire de la famille des Estienne et de ses éditions.* 2nd ed. Paris, 1843.

Reusch, Franz H., ed. *Die Indices librorum prohibitorum des sechzehnten Jahrhunderts.* Stuttgart, 1886.

Rice, Warner C. "The *Paradossi* of Ortensio Lando," *Essays and Studies in English and Comparative Literature by Members of the English Dept. of the University of Michigan* (Ann Arbor, Michigan, 1932), 59–74.

Ricottini Marsili-Libelli, Cecilia. *Anton Francesco Doni, scrittore e stampatore.* Florence, 1960.

Saitta, Giuseppe. *Il pensiero italiano nell'umanesimo e nel Rinascimento.* Seconda edizione corretta e accresciuta. 3 vols. Florence, 1961.

Salza, A. *Delle commedie di Lodovico Dolce.* Melfi, 1899.

———. "Intorno a Lodovico Domenichi," *Rassegna bibliografica della letteratura italiana,* VII (1899), 204–9.

Sanesi, Ireneo. *Il cinquecentista Ortensio Lando.* Pistoia, 1893.

Santoro, Mario. *Il concetto dell'uomo nella letteratura del Cinquecento.* Naples, 1967.

———. *Fortuna, ragione e prudenza nella civiltà letteraria del Cinquecento.* Naples, 1966.

Sbaragli, Luigi. *Claudio Tolomei: umanista senese del Cinquecento. La vita e le opere.* Siena, 1939.

Schaff, Philip. *Creeds of Christendom.* 3 vols. New York and London, 1905.

Schmitt, Charles B. *Gianfrancesco Pico della Mirandola (1469–1533) and His Critique of Aristotle.* Archives Internationales d'Histoire des Idées, 23. The Hague, 1967.

——. "Who Read Gianfrancesco Pico della Mirandola?" *Studies in the Renaissance,* XI (1964), 105–32.

Schullion, Dorothy M. "Nicolò Franco, Vilifier of Medicine," *Bulletin of the History of Medicine,* 24 (1950), 26–37.

Sciacca, M. F., ed. *Grande Antologia Filosofica.* Vol. X, *Il pensiero della Rinascenza e della Riforma (Protestantesimo e Riforma Cattolica).* Milan, 1964.

Scott, Izora. *Controversies over the Imitation of Cicero as a Model for Style and Some Phases of their Influence on the Schools of the Renaissance.* New York, 1910.

Scrivano, Riccardo. *Il Manierismo nella letteratura del Cinquecento.* Padua, 1959.

Sforza, Giovanni. "Francesco Sansovino e le sue opere storiche," *Memorie della R. Accademia delle Scienze di Torino,* serie II, vol. 47 (1897), 27–66.

——. "Ortensio Lando e gli usi ed i costumi d'Italia nella prima metà del Cinquecento," *Memorie della R. Accademia delle Scienze di Torino,* serie II, vol. 64, no. 4 (1914), 1–68.

——. "Riflessi della Controriforma nella Repubblica di Venezia," *Archivio Storico Italiano,* XCIII (1935); pt. 1, 5–34, 189–216; pt. 2, 25–52, 173–86.

Short-Title Catalogue of Books Printed in Italy and of Italian Books Printed in Other Countries from 1465 to 1600 Now in the British Museum. London, 1958.

Sicardi, Enrico. "L'anno della nascita di Nicolò Franco," *GSLI,* 24 (1894), 399–404.

——. "Ancora dell'anno della nascita di N. Franco," *GSLI,* 25 (1895), 170–72.

Simeoni, Luigi. *Le Signorie.* 2 vols. Milan, 1950.

Simiani, Carlo. "Due componimenti inediti di Nicolò Franco," *GSLI,* 30 (1897), 264–70.

——. *La vita e le opere di Nicolò Franco.* Turin, Rome, 1894.

——. "Un plagio di Nicolò Franco," *Rassegna critica della letteratura italiana,* V (1900), 19–26.

Sisto da Siena, Fra. *Bibliotheca Sancta a F. Sixto Senensi, ordinis praedicatorum, ex praecipuis catholicae ecclesiae autoribus collecta . . . et in octo libros digesta. . . .* Lugduni, apud Carolum Pesnot, MDLXXV.

Spini, Giorgio. *Tra Rinascimento e Riforma: Antonio Brucioli.* Florence, 1940.

Stella, Aldo. "Utopie e velleità insurrezionali dei filoprotestanti italiani (1545–1547)," *Bibliothèque d'Humanisme et Renaissance,* XXVII (1965), 133–82.

Stevanin, Silvio. *Ricerche ed appunti sulle opere di Anton Francesco Doni con appendice di spigolature autobiografiche.* Florence, 1903.

Storia di Milano. Vol. IX, *L'epoca di Carlo V (1535–1559).* Milan: Fondazione Trecanni, 1961.

Suttina, Luigi. "Anton Francesco Doni e il Duca di Ferrara," *GSLI*, 99 (1932), 276–78.

Tedeschi, John, ed. *Italian Reformation Studies in Honor of Laelius Socinus*. Università di Siena, Facoltà di Giurisprudenza. Collana di Studi "Pietro Rossi," nuova serie, vol. IV. Florence, 1965.

Tenenti, Alberto. *Il senso della morte e l'amore della vita nel Rinascimento*. Turin, 1957.

———. "L'utopia nel Rinascimento (1450–1550)," *Studi Storici*, VII (1966), 689–707.

Thompson, Elbert N. S. *The Seventeenth-Century English Essay*. University of Iowa Studies: Humanistic Studies, III, 3. Iowa City, Iowa, 1926.

Tiraboschi, Girolamo. *Storia della letteratura italiana*. 9 vols. in 11. Florence, 1805–13.

Toffanin, Giuseppe. *Il Cinquecento*. 6th ed. Milan, 1960.

———. *La fine dell'umanesimo*. Milan, Turin, Rome, 1920.

Tognetti, Giampaolo. "Sul 'romito' e profeta Brandano da Petroio," *Rivista Storica Italiana*, 72 (1960), 20–44.

Trinkaus, Charles E. *Adversity's Noblemen: The Italian Humanists on Happiness*. New York, 1940.

———. "Humanist Treatises on the Status of the Religious: Petrarch, Salutati, Valla," *Studies in the Renaissance*, XI (1964), 7–45.

Turner, Celeste. *Anthony Mundy: an Elizabethan Man of Letters*. Berkeley, Cal., 1928.

Les Utopies à la Renaissance, colloque international (avril 1961). Avant-propos par Jean Lameere. Brussels, Paris, 1963.

Vacca, Nicola, "Cesare Rao da Alessano detto 'Valocerca,'" *Archivio Storico Pugliese*, I, fasc. 1 (1948), 1–28.

Vaganay, Hugues. "Antonio de Guevara et son oeuvre dans la littérature italienne. Essai de bibliographie," *La Bibliofilia,* XVII (1916), 335–58.

Valeri, Nino. *L'Italia nell'età dei principati, dal 1343 al 1516*. Vol. V of *Storia d'Italia*. Milan: Mondadori, 1949.

———, ed. *Storia d'Italia*. 5 vols. Turin, 1959–60.

Vecchietti, Filippo. *Biblioteca Picena o sia notizie istoriche delle opere e degli scrittori Piceni*. Vol. V. Osimo, 1796.

Ventura, Angelo. *Nobiltà e popolo nella società veneta del '400 e '500*. Bari, 1964.

Vermiglioli, Giovanni Battista. *Biografia degli scrittori perugini e notizie delle opere loro*. Vol. II. Perugia, 1829.

Vinay, Valdo. "Die Schrift 'Il Beneficio di Giesu Christo' und ihre Verbreitung in Europa nach der neueren Forschung," *Archiv für Reformationsgeschichte*, 58 (1967), 29–72.

Visconti, Alessandro. *L'Italia nell'epoca della Controriforma dal 1516 al 1713*. Vol. VI of *Storia d'Italia*. Milan: Mondadori, 1958.

Volpicelli, Luigi, ed. *Il pensiero pedagogico della Controriforma*. Florence, 1960.

Weinberg, Bernard. *A History of Literary Criticism in the Italian Renaissance.* 2 vols. Chicago, 1961.

Williams, Robert H. "Francisco de Cáceres, Niccolò Franco, and Juan de la Cueva," *Hispanic Review,* XXVII (1959), 194–99.

Woodward, William H. *Vittorino da Feltre and Other Humanist Educators.* New York, 1963.

Wright, Louis B. *Middle-Class Culture in Elizabethan England.* Ithaca, N.Y., 1958.

Yates, Frances. *John Florio: The Life of an Italian in Shakespeare's England.* Cambridge, 1934.

∘⟦ INDEX ⟧∘